Praise for

REPORTING
ALWAYS

"[This] volume is a rich pleasure and an encounter with pioneering vision. . . . One of Ross's greatest talents lies in the cool clarity of her gaze: somehow she sees things and people simultaneously unsentimentally and with great warmth. . . . And we like them not because she has told us to, but because she has shown us, with candor and respect, who they are."

—*Boston Review*

"Lillian Ross largely invented the modern entertainment profile."
—*The New York Times*

"Ross's pieces paint vivid and insightful portraits of her subjects without resorting to criticism, hyperbole, or sensationalism. . . . Aspiring journalists will benefit from studying Ross's narrative pieces, which offer a master class in journalism. Fans of will also enjoy reading articles that are as fresh today as when they were originally printed."
—*Library Journal*

"Readable and rewarding . . . full of exemplary reporting."
—*Kirkus Reviews*

"[Lillian Ross] grew up to become not just one of the most important female reporters in history but a singular if underappreciated influence on generations of journalists."
—*Columbia Journalism Review*

"While Ross is dedicated to reporting—to teasing out the truth of a character, a setting, or situation—also on full display here are the stunning, if quieter, literary and storytelling techniques that inform her

—*The Christian Science Monitor*

"By the journalist who essentially invented the celebrity profile, this sparkling collection showcases the delicacy with which the much-imitated Ross has covered a wide range of personalities in her seventy years at *The New Yorker*."

—*O, The Oprah Magazine*

"Readers are invested in Ross's work because she's invested. She has the ability to dive deep into the minds and hearts of interviewees, and readers are lucky that through her writing, they are able to come along for the ride."

—*Minneapolis Star Tribune*

"Ross's capacity to observe and make the reader a part of the moment is quite remarkable."

—*New York Journal of Books*

"Her reportage transports us as well as any grainy documentary footage could. *Reporting Always* offers scintillating historical snapshots as well as a master class in prose."

—*The Independent* (UK)

"*Reporting Always* is a superb book. . . . A career omnibus of work by Lillian Ross, the ultimate *New Yorker* long-form reporter."

—*The Buffalo News*

"Ross tells all in this remarkable collection."

—*The Dallas Morning News*

"This collection, like the author, seems ageless. It's also priceless, restoring long forgotten pleasures to those of us who recall the thrill of finding a Lillian Ross piece in the magazine, and introducing those pleasures to those who, being younger, don't know yet what they've been missing."

—Faboverfifty.com

"*Reporting Always* contains . . . such remarkable examples of the art of the interview."

—*The Providence Journal*

"Lillian Ross is a consummate reporter, and therefore remains on the fringes of these unforgettable pieces of writing. But there is no doubt about her place in the pantheon of radical and dogged female storytellers. Millennials would do well to study Ross and to study her closely: her style, her technique, and her legend."

—Lena Dunham

"For anyone interested in movies from the fifties on, Lillian Ross's profiles were essential. They still are. And that was my way into her irreplaceable body of writing."

—Martin Scorsese

"There is only one Lillian Ross: spirited, funny, factual, and unforgettable. Her fabulous writing never goes out of style."

—Gay Talese

"Lillian Ross is the model for all narrative journalists. Open-eyed, sharp-witted, and fundamentally kindhearted, she has diamond-hard reporting skills and an effortlessly graceful way with words. Each story here shows her at her best, as keen storyteller and social observer, whether she is peering into the world of Hollywood swells or bumbling school kids or wherever else her curiosity takes her. This is a glorious collection by a master of the form."

—Susan Orlean

"Exceptionally curious, exceedingly brave, with a perfect ear: through Lillian Ross and her classic reporting, we've gotten the chance to sneak into the private worlds of the great and the fascinating (Chaplin, Hemingway, Truffaut, Huston). One of the most important and influential journalists alive."

—Wes Anderson

"Lillian Ross has elevated journalism—storytelling—to an art but it is her art, singular and brilliant. Her innate sense of form and eye for the telling, often humorous detail are part of what makes her work so indelible and influential—that and her understanding of how the family of man becomes just that."

—Hilton Als

ALSO BY LILLIAN ROSS

Lillian reporting on the set of John Huston's
The Red Badge of Courage, outside Los Angeles, 1950.

REPORTING ALWAYS

Writings from

THE NEW YORKER

LILLIAN ROSS

SCRIBNER

New York   London   Toronto   Sydney   New Delhi

SCRIBNER
An Imprint of Simon & Schuster, Inc.
1230 Avenue of the Americas
New York, NY 10020

First Scribner trade paperback edition November 2016

SCRIBNER and design are registered trademarks of The Gale Group, Inc., used under license by Simon & Schuster, Inc., the publisher of this work.

For information about special discounts for bulk purchases, please contact Simon & Schuster Special Sales at 1-866-506-1949 or business@simonandschuster.com.

The Simon & Schuster Speakers Bureau can bring authors to your live event. For more information or to book an event, contact the Simon & Schuster Speakers Bureau at 1-866-248-3049 or visit our website at www.simonspeakers.com.

Interior design by Kyle Kabel

Manufactured in the United States of America

1 3 5 7 9 10 8 6 4 2

The Library of Congress has cataloged the hardcover edition as follows:

Ross, Lillian, 1927–
[Essays. Selections]
Reporting always : writing for The New Yorker / Lillian Ross ;
foreword by David Remnick.
pages cm
I. New Yorker (New York, N.Y. : 1925) II. Title.
PN4874.R62A25 2015
070.4'4—dc23
2015013297

ISBN 978-1-5011-1600-1
ISBN 978-1-5011-1601-8 (pbk)
ISBN 978-1-5011-1602-5 (ebook)

To the talented pack of
selfless *New Yorker* editors 1945–2015

Contents

Foreword

DAVID REMNICK

"Come on over, kid, and I'll tell you all about the hassle."

This was John Huston summoning Lillian Ross by telephone, in 1950, to come to his suite at the Waldorf-Astoria so that he could fill her in on the alternately maddening and hilarious story of his attempt to make a film based on Stephen Crane's war novel, *The Red Badge of Courage*. Lillian Ross, a young staff writer for *The New Yorker*, was more than interested. She hustled over to the Waldorf and then she stayed on the story for months, "from beginning to end," as she put it, from the initial creative battles and financial negotiations to opening night and beyond. *Picture* was published, in 1952, in five parts in *The New Yorker* and later that year as a book. It is one of the few lasting works about the making of a motion picture—a stunningly honest portrait of a failed project and a distinctly American community—and it was also responsible, in the eyes of Norman Mailer and many others, for the invention of the nonfiction novel, a forerunner to *Armies of the Night* and *In Cold Blood*.

Lillian Ross has always preferred to think of her work in simpler terms. Not as the "nonfiction novel" or "reportage" or "creative nonfiction." She prefers to think of it as reporting. And she is just that—a hell of a reporter.

Labels aside, Lillian Ross was a pioneer and remains an enormous influence on other writers. Her hallmarks are her keen eyes and ears and an austere, straightforward style. (This is harder to achieve than words like *straightforward* make it seem.) As a storyteller, she has an abiding faith in the magical properties of facts. She has an antipathy to analysis, flourishes, and showing off. With an almost cinematic use of scenes, she makes her dramatic points by showing what she sees and hears, relying on the cumulative power of what happens. Her influences, she has said, are scattered across time and include Ernest Hemingway, Henry Mayhew, J. D. Salinger, and Laura Lee Hope. She loves works of nonfiction by novelists, including Turgenev's "The Execution of Tropmann" and Defoe's *A Journal of the Plague Year.*

In November 1944, Peggy Wright Weidman, an editor at a short-lived, no-advertising, left-wing daily called *PM*, wrote to William Shawn, then the number-two man at *The New Yorker*, recommending a young reporter named Lillian Ross who had been working at the paper for a year and a half.

"We have sent her on stories ranging in subject matter from politics to uplift brassieres and she's done splendidly by both," Weidman wrote to Shawn. "Another baffler is that she likes to work and does so, at any hour of the day, night, or weekend, with concentration and no nonsense."

With Weidman and Shawn's endorsement, Harold Ross, the founder and editor of the magazine, hired her. The truth was, he had chairs to fill. So many writers and editors had gone off to fight in Europe and Asia that Ross had a hard time filling the columns of the magazine. Harold Ross, who was not anyone's idea of a feminist crusader, found himself hiring women who eventually proved to be the heart of the place. Lillian began, as many young writers do, by working as a reporter for The Talk of the Town. She also started to stretch out. In 1948, she published "Come In, Lassie!," a glorious depiction of Hollywood's cowering reaction to the Red Scare in Washington. "Katharine Hepburn goes out and makes a speech for Henry Wallace. Bang! We're in trouble," a Hollywood executive told her. "Lassie doesn't make speeches. Not Lassie, thank God."

In May 1950, Ross published "How Do You Like It Now, Gentlemen?," her Hemingway Profile. She followed the writer on a brief sojourn in New York as he clowned around in his hotel room, enjoying caviar and drink, looked at pictures at the Met, shopped at Abercrombie & Fitch, and met with his old friend, "the Kraut," Marlene Dietrich. To her astonishment and Hemingway's, some readers thought the piece was a hatchet job, a work of aggression that besmirched the reputation of a great literary artist. Which seemed ridiculous to both writer and subject. Hemingway and Ross had become close, and he went to great lengths to reassure her of their enduring friendship: "All are very astonished because I don't hold anything against you who made an effort to destroy me and nearly did, they say," he told her. "I can always tell them, how can I be destroyed by a woman when she is a friend of mine and we have never even been to bed and no money has changed hands?" His advice to her was clear: "Just call them the way you see them and the hell with it."

Reading Ross's pieces about Hemingway, Chaplin, Otto Preminger, and so many others in public life, it is hard not to think she worked in blessed circumstances. Unhindered by public relations specialists, with their overweening demands and deals, she could do her work, reporting at length and in depth. "Somewhere along the line, a critic used the phrase 'fly on the wall' to describe my journalistic 'technique,'" she has said. Yet, Lillian rejects that. "What craziness! A reporter doing a story can't pretend to be invisible, let alone a fly; he or she is seen and heard and responded to by the people he or she is writing about. A reporter is always chemically involved in a story." I like that word: *chemically*. *Picture* includes extraordinarily three-dimensional portraits of its protagonists—John Huston, the producer Gottfried Reinhardt, the M-G-M chief Louis B. Mayer, and others—but it also brilliantly depicts the Hollywood studio system, the attempt to translate the internal voice of Crane's novel into a film, the interplay of egos, the role of money. There is so much information, so much reporting, and yet the plot gallops along, a well-plotted novel-in-fact. *Picture* is Ross's masterpiece.

Lillian Ross did not write only about the famous. Far from it. Some of her most charming and affecting work is about children. In 1964, J. D. Salinger wrote to Lillian about a delightful story she'd written about a young teacher preparing for a folk-dancing festival for her fifth and sixth graders at P.S. 31 on Sheep Meadow in Central Park. "I think 'Dancers in May' is one of the most beautiful pieces that you or anybody else has ever done," he said. "I came away from it, of course, wanting to know how everybody is, these days. How is Willy? How is Magdelena? The first and last thing you've done is redeem everything, not just make everything bearable." He went on to praise the way Ross gives some of the characters "their true and everlasting unimportance.

I'd better not try to pick out things from the piece or this will turn out to be a book. It's just one of the pieces of literature that I will always love and never forget." There was a postscript at the bottom of the page: "Miss White! My God."

Lucky for us, Lillian has had a long career. In more recent decades, besides a memoir about her long relationship with William Shawn, she has written countless Talk pieces. Each one she sends us is a gift, a reminder of how cunning that form can be. "I often think of making the story as a little film, with a beginning, a middle, and an end," she once told Susan Morrison, the editor of so many of Lillian's Talk pieces. One of the joys of this wonderful volume is that it shows a writer who has never ceased being curious. Curiosity: it's the first requirement of a reporter, and Lillian Ross is a master reporter.

Introduction

LILLIAN ROSS

What makes the writing emerge from a writer is mostly a mystery. A related mystery is the way a writer's inspirations are not revealed, boldfaced, in what the writer gives us. Behind the work often lurks an elusive spirit. For my part, I am keenly aware of the permeating influence in my writing of William Shawn, *The New Yorker*'s editor for thirty-five years. It is unshakably present in the stories here, many of them reprinted for the first time. They were written over seven decades, but all reveal the same spirit. As far as I can tell, I seem to have absorbed—and tried to bring alive in these stories—Shawn's hunger for the innocence and good in people. Finding it is actual joy.

Innocence is an often ridiculed and abused word. To me it is a reliable one. And it naturally translates into humor. It is what has always led me to my subjects.

Jerry Salinger, our colleague at *The New Yorker*, had his own unyielding kind of innocence. The trouble with all of us, he would say, is that when we were young nobody told us about the penalties of making it in the world on the usual terms. In a letter to me in the 1960s, he wrote, "I don't mean just the pretty obvious penalties, I mean the ones that are just about unnoticeable and that do really lasting damage, the kind the world doesn't even think of as damage." He talked about how easily writers could become vain, complaining that they got puffed up by the same "authorities" who approved putting monosodium glutamate in baby food. I wished that I had his inimitable strength and bravery to live the way he did.

Salinger loved children, but never with the sentimental fakery of admiring their "purity." When I adopted my son, Erik, Jerry was almost as exuberant as I was. "Unbelievable, stupendous," he said of one picture I sent: "He's roaring with laughter. Oh, if he can only hold on to it."

I have tried to gravitate toward subjects who *have* been able to hold on to it—people who are open to the possibilities of life, people who aren't constantly working an angle. Salinger didn't like worldliness, but he wanted to live, on his own terms, in the world. He liked what Ralph Waldo Emerson said. He quoted Emerson in a letter to me: "A man must have aunts and cousins, must buy carrots and turnips, must have barn and woodshed, must go to market and to the blacksmith's shop, must saunter and sleep and be inferior and silly." Writers, Salinger said, sometimes had trouble abiding by that, and he referred to Flaubert and Kafka as "two other born non-buyers of carrots and turnips."

I have been interested in journalistic writing for almost as long as I can remember. When I was a junior high school student, in Syracuse, a teacher asked me to write a story for the school paper about our new library. To my amazement, what I wrote was published. It was in black type. Two inches long. Here's my lede:

Fat books, thin books, new books, old books . . .

My words. It was an unforgettable rapture. I had discovered that I could do something with words that I could do with no other medium. That year, I read Byron's *Don Juan* in school and was haunted by this passage:

But words are things, and a small drop of ink,
Falling like dew, upon a thought, produces
That which makes thousands, perhaps millions, think.

That school paper incident showed me what I was going to do for the rest of the century. But most important was that the experience—both the reporting and the writing—gave me immediate pleasure.

In the early 1940s, I landed my first reporting job at a brash little newspaper called *PM*, where I experienced, for the first time, the help of an editor. Peggy Wright was in charge of Local Items, an imitation of *The New Yorker*'s Talk of the Town section. I loved the work, focusing on a range of subjects, from the sensational carryings-on of the asbestos heir and playboy Tommy Manville to the victims of the famous Hartford Circus Fire. One day Peggy asked me to do a story about General Charles de Gaulle's visit to New York City. It was July 1944, about a month after D-Day. I met up with Mayor Fiorello La Guardia, who led the general and his entourage up to the Rockefeller Center Observation Deck. I stood behind the very tall general. La Guardia pointed here and there. I heard de Gaulle ask "Où est le Coney Island?" I used that quote in my story. About a week later, I came across a photo in another publication, showing me standing, taking notes, behind the general, along with a story about my reporting that he asked "Où est Coney Island?" It is now engraved for all time on Google. I like seeing it there, a reminder of when and how I found my own way of reporting.

Around that time, William Shawn, the managing editor of *The New Yorker* under Harold Ross, asked Peggy Wright to come work for him. She didn't take the job, but she wrote him a letter, urging him to hire me. He did what she suggested.

When I started as a reporter at the magazine that year, I had to write my stories using the Talk of the Town's famous *we*, a device that masked the fact that I was a woman. Ross had resisted hiring female staff reporters until World War II, when many of his male employees were drafted. He reluctantly hired three young women (actually, he left the task to Shawn). The idea was that we women would report the "facts" for Talk stories, and then these would be handed off to the remaining men on staff, who would "rewrite" them. In a story I did about the fashion designer Coco Chanel, my pretend masculinity even extended to lighting Mlle. Chanel's cigarette. ("We lighted a cigarette for Mlle. Chanel and asked her how she had happened to be in retirement so long.")

Although Ross was impatient with the idea of having women on his staff (and he paid us less than the men), he was a good mentor. He said to me: "Follow your own bent." He didn't like to talk to writers much, but he wrote us what he called "notes," questioning various details and leading us to pin down the facts in our stories. It was marvelous training. When Shawn took over as editor in chief, in 1952, he not only abandoned Ross's practice of having the men "rewrite" the women's Talk stories, he also eventually paid us the same rates he paid the men.

When I was in high school, I was strongly influenced by a book called *City Editor* by Stanley Walker, of the then *New York Herald Tribune*. Walker wrote that women reporters were generally unwelcome at a newspaper, because if their stories were rejected, "they burst into tears." So I was determined from that moment on never to cry.

I always liked Talk's *we* form. I was comfortable with it. We indeed created the magazine. I began to abandon *we* when I felt like creating my pieces without exposition, in brief scenes. Like others in my generation, I grew up going to the movies, often several times a week. So it felt natural to me to start writing stories entirely in little scenes. I enjoyed showing everything using dialogue and action, with no authorial intrusions and no presumptions about what was going on inside the subject's head. Only one person, the subject, knows what he thinks and feels. This model—writing a piece as if it were a miniature movie—ended up informing all the longer pieces that I would go on to do.

In 1947, I went to Mexico to report a long fact story about Sidney Franklin, a bullfighter from Brooklyn. I drove with him from Mexico City to Acapulco in his new Cadillac. It was a wild ride down a mountainous road. I was able to do a good deal of reporting in the Cadillac. For the Franklin story, I wanted to talk to Ernest Hemingway, who was a friend of Franklin's and had a load of knowledge about bullfighting. I was not only ignorant about bullfighting, I was repelled by it. However, the idea of a young man from Brooklyn, the son of a policeman (a "bull" in the vernacular), tempted my curiosity.

On my way back from Mexico, I stopped in Hollywood. I found that single-industry town in a peculiar state of fear and near paralysis. World War II had ended, raising the spectre of Communism taking over the burgeoning movie industry. The House Un-American Activities Committee had been investigating possibly "dangerous" propaganda hidden in the creative content of films. So I wrote about what I saw and heard, in an unusual satiric piece called "Come In, Lassie!" Both Harold Ross and Bill Shawn were enthusiastic about the storytelling form I found for the piece. It's like a movie—showing everything from the outside, with lots of talking.

To lighten things up after all that bullfighting, I decided to take a look at what the Miss America contest was all about. So in 1949 I attended the pageant with Miss New York State, Wanda Nalepa, a twenty-two-year-old registered nurse from the Bronx. She lost. Miss Arizona, an eighteen-year-old student, won. My story, "Symbol of All We Possess," began with the words:

There are thirteen million women in the United States between the ages of eighteen and twenty-eight. All of them were eligible to compete for the title of Miss America in the annual contest staged in Atlantic City last month if they were high-school graduates, were not and had never been married, and were not Negroes.

Ross, who was still the magazine's editor, objected to the way I had so pointedly inserted my view of the pageant's racism. Shawn, then managing editor, gave me a copy of Ross's notes criticizing my opening. I insisted on keeping that opening. Shawn, who was my editor, published the lede as I had written it.

After I went out to Ketchum, Idaho, to interview Hemingway about Sidney Franklin, I told Bill Shawn about Hemingway's wonderful way of talking. A couple of years later, when Hemingway wrote to me about his plan to stop in New York en route to Europe, it was Shawn's idea that I write a piece about the author and limit it to his few days in New York, which I did. When it was published, I was shocked to find that a number of readers considered it highly critical. These people felt that in describing Hemingway accurately I was ridiculing or attacking him. But I liked Hemingway exactly as he was, and I'm happy that my profile caught him exactly as he was.

I have thought often, since the Profile was published, about Hemingway's generosity as a writer. He was positively encouraging toward the young Salinger. Jerry gave me a copy of a letter that Hemingway wrote to him during World War II, responding to three early stories he'd sent him. Hemingway wrote that all three stories were "excellent." "You are a damn good writer," he said. "And I will look forward to reading everything you write. You have a marvelous ear and you write tenderly and lovingly without writing wet. Your stuff is straight and good and fine."

Salinger later sent me a note about the Hemingway Profile:

I was riding in a car with someone who thought your Hemingway Profile merciless. I had the pleasure of arguing him down. It was a true and properly sad Profile, and the only thing merciless about it was reality itself.

Working in Hollywood, I developed friendships, cursory for the most part. But my experience with the director John Huston was different. It lasted. In 1950, Huston invited me to come and watch him work on his movie adaptation of Stephen Crane's *The Red Badge of Courage*. I started the reporting, and I realized that Huston and three other men closely involved in the making of the film were amazingly like fictional characters. I then wrote to Shawn (my letter is in the *New Yorker* archives in the New York Public Library) and asked, Why couldn't I write about the making of the movie in the form of a novel? He consulted with Ross, and they gave me a quick go-ahead. The resulting pieces were published consecutively over six weeks. When the stories appeared in book form as *Picture* (1952, and still in print), Hemingway wrote a blurb calling it "much better than most novels."

Over the decades, I've often kept in touch with my subjects, some of whom became genuine friends. So it has been easy to go back to them, years later, and write new stories about what they were currently working on. Robin Williams, Tommy Lee Jones, Al Pacino, Norman Mailer, Edward Albee, Harold Pinter, François Truffaut are all people whom I've revisited in print. Sometimes I write stories about various members of an extended family: in addition to writing about John Huston several times, I've reported on his daughter Anjelica and his son Tony. Michael Redgrave was the first of three generations of Redgraves I've written about. I went on to write about Tony Richardson, Vanessa Redgrave, Rachel Kempson, and Natasha Richardson. I have written about both Henry and Jane Fonda.

It's always uplifting to get responses from the people I write about. Perhaps the most unexpected reaction came from someone on the Beatles management team, in a telephone call from London, in 1967. I had written a Talk story about their album *Sgt. Pepper's Lonely Hearts Club Band*. The album represented a new concept in rock-and-roll music, and my piece was a kind of instructive essay. One of the people quoted at length is a "Mr. LeFevre"—a pseudonym for William Shawn, who was an enthusiastic fan of the Beatles. The person who called on the phone said it was so exciting for all of them to read, for the first time, words indicating a true understanding of the record's musical significance.

As an editor, Bill Shawn was in tune with every one of his writers and artists. He would say to us, "Do what you and only you can do." He always gave specifics. He had a way of making every writer and artist feel that he or she was the most precious one of the lot. He was also an exceptional writer, and he was driven to give his all to others. He actually wrote sections, long and short, for pieces he edited.

The New Yorker, I found, was replete with generous, selfless editors, who, like Shawn, rarely sought public recognition. When Tina Brown took over the *New Yorker*'s editorship in 1992, she brought a fresh spirit of fun to the magazine, without abandoning its traditional aims. She was not afraid to enter untried areas in both art and writing. Talk of the Town pieces were now signed with the writer's byline, rather than anonymous. And suddenly the magazine's vocabulary was freed from Harold Ross's restrictions, which had been faithfully maintained by Shawn.

David Remnick, the current editor, has steered the magazine on a reliable course, managing to maintain its charm, wit, grit, and success in an ever-changing technological, commercial, and political landscape. Remnick has opened the magazine to a dazzling array of new writers who defy (as well as encompass) all the new electronic challenges to the will to write. I strongly believe that words, good writing, can never be replaced by any kind of mechanics no matter how brilliant or innovative. There simply is no substitute for the written word of a human being.

I have always been grateful for the complete freedom I've enjoyed to have my little say about what I have found going on in our time. It is a privilege to write about whatever I choose and to get to know anybody I am interested in. I choose my subjects carefully. I am not interested in sensational revelations. I always want to find the special nature of each human being.

Recently, a young employee at *The New Yorker* asked me what I would do if someone I was reporting about denied me access or necessary information. My answer was easy to give. I have never wanted to write about anybody who did not want to be written about. And I never wished to go where I wasn't wanted. It doesn't matter how little or how much has been written about a person before. I always find what I want to say. Besides writing only about those who want to be written about, I have a few other basic rules: Write only what can be observed, what I see and hear and never what the subject might be "thinking." My point of view is always implicit in how I write the story. What interests me in the people I choose to write about is their talent. I always look for their individual ways of revealing it; those elements are what make for a "story." The challenge to me is to find it.

Another of my rules: Do not use a tape recorder. I have found that literal gabble often misleads and obscures truth. I prefer to take notes and to trust my own ear for dialogue in revealing character and humor, and I use it whenever possible in creating my little scenes. Bill Shawn immediately understood the way I wanted to write about living characters: Use what you see to present truth, and do it scrupulously. Now, years later—especially with all the "reality" this and "reality" that out there—I can say that this approach has never failed me. The compliment I always most enjoy hearing from readers is "You make me feel that I am right there." Words transcribed from a tape recorder or things you see on so-called reality television may be some version of reality, but they can also be a distortion of the truth.

I love reporting. I especially love writing Talk of the Town stories, what Bill Shawn called his "little gems." I find delight in those written by my colleagues, especially the new young writers. I am most appreciative of praise from my colleagues. In my experience, the better and more talented the writer or editor, the more generous and helpful he or she is with others. As a new employee at *The New Yorker* during World War II, I was privileged to have had help and positive feedback from Joe Mitchell, Wolcott Gibbs, James Thurber, Joe Liebling, Geoffrey Hellman, Brendan Gill, Philip Hamburger, and John McCarten. And when the battalions of fresh young writers come along, I am always grateful to hear from them. There are so many young super talents now at the magazine, it is impossible to name them all. I began to notice the profusion of them with the arrival, in the 1960s, of Ian Frazier, Mark Singer, Hendrik Hertzberg, and Calvin Trillin; and then, when Tina Brown became editor, in 1992, with the arrival of the special Anthony Lane and John Lahr, and the remarkable Rebecca Mead (I still carry around in my head a Talk piece she wrote about the actor Kenneth Branagh in a Village bookstore). I am steadily amazed to find in the magazine a constant flow of impressive writing by fresh people—Evan Osnos, Jon Lee Anderson, Ryan Lizza, Richard Brody, Dexter Filkins—and reassured when the name Roger Angell turns up. And the phenomenal Jill Lepore boggles the mind so regularly that we almost take her for granted. Lately I am haunted by the work of Emma Allen, Elizabeth Widdicombe, Nick Paumgarten, Lauren Collins, Ben McGrath, and Dana Goodyear, all of them scribbling in *The New Yorker*'s happy tradition for Susan Morrison. Reading what they give is for me sheer fun.

Hemingway and Salinger will always be heroes to me, because both had the strength to hold on to themselves. As a fiction writer, Salinger created people he could love. "That little boy," he would say about Holden Caulfield. "I owe so much to him. He made it possible for me to have my freedom to do what I love." I owe so much to those two writers, who taught me, by example, how to hold on to myself. More than ever, I respect them for their courage to have been like no one else on earth. And what they had in common was deepest innocence.

REPORTING
ALWAYS

I

PLAYERS

Lillian and Robin Williams, shortly after the release of
Good Morning, Vietnam, 1987.

Young and Happy
(Julie Andrews)

One of the great moments in the theatre is supposed to be when a shining-eyed young actress first sees her name on a marquee. That great moment actually arrives every now and then, and we're glad to say that we were on hand when it arrived last week. The girl was Julie Andrews, the nineteen-year-old English ingénue who plays the lead in *The Boy Friend*, and she is the only member of either the local company or the company in London, where the original version of the musical comedy is still running, to be so honored. We met the pretty creature at her hotel in midtown, where she shares a two-room apartment with Miss Dilys Lay, also of *The Boy Friend*, and three stuffed poodles. Miss Andrews is a tallish girl with a gentle voice, large blue-gray eyes, and brown hair, which she parts in the middle. On the occasion of our visit, she was wearing a red cardigan, a blue skirt, and high-heeled blue sandals. "Do sit down!" she exclaimed, sweeping a box of Chinese checkers from a couch. "I was just mailing some photographs of myself in the show to Mother. She hasn't seen me in it and wants to know how I look. There's a chance she may come over after the first of the year and I'll be so happy if she does. I do hope I've put enough stamps on the envelope. I'm terribly homesick. Not that I don't love New York, but one does get homesick. Would you like a cup of tea?"

We were aware that JULIE ANDREWS had just that day been affixed to the marquee outside the Royale Theatre, and we asked the owner of the name if, since it was getting on toward time for the evening performance, we might skip tea and escort her to the theatre, to which she replied that we might indeed. "Still, it is a comfort to have this little flat to drink tea in, isn't it?" she said. "And to sit in on Sundays and watch the television? Dilys and I share a dressing room at the theatre, too. We share almost everything. Each of us has a dog at home, whom we miss dreadfully. Mine is a Welsh corgi, the sort the Queen has. No tails, you know, and sweet little faces and tiny little bodies. Such lovely dogs! I was thinking of getting one here, but then I realized how stupid it would be to try and keep a dog in a flat in New York. Dilys gave me that stuffed white poodle over there, instead—as a present on my birthday, which was the day after the show opened. It was a marvelous birthday; except for the fact that I wasn't home, I think it was the best I've ever had or am ever likely to have."

Home to Miss Andrews is Walton-on-Thames, a small town eighteen miles south of London. "My pop used to be in show business with Mummy," she said. "His name is Ted Andrews and he has such a lovely voice. He used to sing ballads like 'Love, Could I Only Tell Thee How Dear Thou Art to Me.' It's a beautiful number, and I'd rather listen to it than anything. Mummy always wanted to be just Mummy, so Pop gave up show business. Now he has a nine-to-five job, and a very good one it is. I have three brothers, John, Donald, and Christopher, all younger than I am. If you've seen the show, you've heard me whistle. I say that if you can't whistle in a house that has three boys in it, you're simply no good. Perhaps we'd better be off." Miss Andrews sang a few bars of "Love, Could I Only Tell Thee" in a melting soprano as she put on her coat, then announced proudly that she had been practicing scales for a solid hour. "My voice really needed it," she said. "It was so stale. I had such a good practice. I feel very righteous."

En route to the theatre, Miss Andrews told us that her father started giving her voice lessons when she was seven. At the same time, she began attending a ballet school. When she was twelve, she embarked on a career in the music halls. "This is my first musical comedy," she said. "I'm more of a singer than an actress. I had to learn a wholly new way of acting for this show. My own style is rather quiet. I'm the only girl in the show who wears a wig, and nobody recognizes me without it when I leave the theatre. We're having a terribly good time, *The Boy Friend* company. We're all so young and happy. I didn't need to be especially thrilled when they told me the other day that they were going to give me featured billing. I think it would be being a bit of a big shot, don't you, to actually look at my name up there? Not that anyone would recognize me without my wig, but—" Our taxi pulled up just short of the theatre, and we got out. For a moment, Miss Andrews kept her face turned away from the theatre, then we heard her whisper, "Ah, there it is!" Over her head the marquee proclaimed:

THE
BOY FRIEND
SMASH HIT MUSICAL COMEDY
WITH JULIE ANDREWS

And, sure enough, her eyes were shining.

(NOVEMBER 11, 1954)

Come In, Lassie!

Hollywood is baffled by the question of what the Committee on Un-American Activities wants from it. People here are wondering, with some dismay and anxiety, what kind of strange, brooding alienism the Committee is trying to eliminate from their midst and, in fact, whether it was ever here. They are waiting hopefully for Chairman J. Parnell Thomas, or Congress, or God, to tell them. They have been waiting in vain ever since last November, when eight writers, a producer, and a director—often collectively referred to these days as "the ten writers"—were blacklisted by the studios because they had been charged with contempt of Congress for refusing to tell the Thomas Committee what political party, if any, they belong to. In the meantime, business, bad as it is, goes on. The place is more nervous than usual, but it is doing the same old simple things in the same old simple ways.

The simplicities of life in Hollywood are not, of course, like those anywhere else. This is still a special area where all the lakes in the countryside are labeled either For Sale or Not for Sale, and where guests at parties are chosen from lists based on their weekly income brackets—low ($200–$500), middle ($500–$1,250), and upper ($1,250–$20,000). During the last few months, party guests have tended to be politically self-conscious, whatever their brackets, but this is not especially embarrassing in Hollywood, where it is possible to take an impregnable position on both sides of any controversy.

The political self-consciousness at parties is, on the whole, rather cheerful. "I never cut anybody before this," one actress remarked happily to me. "Now I don't go anywhere without cutting at least half a dozen former friends." At some parties, the bracketed guests break up into subgroups, each eyeing the others with rather friendly suspicion and discussing who was or was not a guest at the White House when Roosevelt was president—one of the few criteria people in the film industry have set up for judging whether a person is or is not a Communist—and how to avoid becoming a Communist. Some of the stars were investigated several years ago, when the Un-American Activities Committee was headed by Martin Dies, and the advice and point of view of these veterans are greatly sought after. One actor who is especially in demand at social gatherings is Fredric March, who suddenly discovered, when called to account by Mr. Dies, that he was a Communist because he had given an ambulance to Loyalist Spain. Dies rebuked him, and it then turned out that Mr. March had also given an ambulance to Finland when she was at war with Russia. "I was just a big ambulance-giver," Mr. March said to his subgroup at a recent party, loudly enough for other subgroups to hear. "That's what I told Dies. 'I just like to give ambulances,' I told him, and he said, 'Well, then, Mr. March, before you give any more ambulances away, you go out and consult your local Chamber of Commerce or the American Legion, and they'll tell you whether it's all right.'"

Some groups play it safe at parties by refusing to engage in any conversation at all. They just sit on the floor and listen to anyone who goes by with a late rumor. There are all sorts of rumors in Hollywood right now. One late rumor is that the newest black-market commodity in town is the labor of the ten writers, who are reported to be secretly turning out scripts for all the major studios. Another is that one producer is founding a film company and will have all ten of the blacklisted men on his staff. Rumors that the FBI is going to take over casting operations at the studios are discounted by those who have lived in Hollywood for more than fifteen years. The casting director at Metro-Goldwyn-Mayer, a fidgety, cynical, sharply dressed, red-cheeked man named Billy Grady, Sr., who has worked in Hollywood for nearly twenty years, thinks that it would serve J. Edgar Hoover right if the casting of actors were handed over to the FBI. "Hoover thinks he's got worries!" Grady shouted at me in a Hollywood restaurant. "What does a G-man do? A G-man sends guys to Alcatraz! Ha! I'd like to see a G-man find a script about Abraham Lincoln's doctor in which we could work in a part for Lassie. What do you find inside of Alcatraz? Picture stars? Directors? Cameramen? No! The goddamn place is full of doctors, lawyers, and politicians. This is the fourth-biggest industry in the country, and only three men in this industry ever went to jail. There are fifty thousand people in this industry, and all they want is the right to take up hobbies. Spencer Tracy takes up painting. Clark Gable takes up Idaho. Dalton Trumbo, who got the sack, takes up deep thinking. Take away their hobbies and they're unhappy. When they're unhappy, I'm unhappy. For God's sake, Tracy doesn't paint when he's acting. Gable doesn't shoot ducks. Trumbo doesn't think when he's writing for pictures. I say let them keep their goddamn hobbies. They're all a bunch of capitalists anyway."

Almost the only motion-picture star who is taking conditions in his stride is Lassie, a reddish-haired male collie, who is probably too mixed up emotionally over being called by a girl's name to worry about the box office. Lassie is working more steadily, not only in films but on the radio, than anyone else in Hollywood. He is a star at M-G-M, the leading studio in Hollywood, which is fondly referred to out here as the Rock of Gibraltar. Visitors there are politely and desperately requested not to discuss politics or any other controversial matters with anyone on the lot. Louis B. Mayer, production chief of M-G-M, recently took personal command of the making of all pictures, of the purchase of all scripts, and of the writing of all scripts and commissary menus. The luncheon menu starts off with the announcement that meat will not be served on Tuesdays. "President Truman has appealed to Americans to conserve food, an appeal all of us will gladly heed, of course," it says. Patrons are politely and desperately encouraged to eat apple pancakes or broiled sweetbreads for lunch. Lassie eats apple pancakes for lunch. Visitors are politely and desperately introduced to Lassie, who ignores them. "We'd be in a hole if we didn't have Lassie," I heard an M-G-M man say. "We like Lassie. We're sure of Lassie. Lassie can't go out and embarrass the studio. Katharine Hepburn goes out and makes a speech for Henry Wallace. Bang! We're in trouble. Lassie doesn't make speeches. Not Lassie, thank God." At the moment, Lassie is making a picture with Edmund Gwenn about a country doctor in Scotland. Originally, the script called for a country doctor in Scotland who hated dogs, but a part has been written in for Lassie, the plot has been changed, and the picture is to be called *Master of Lassie*. "It will help at the box office," Lassie's director says. Only three other pictures are in production at M-G-M, the biggest of them being a musical comedy called *Easter Parade*, starring Fred Astaire and having to do with Easter on Fifth Avenue at the beginning of the century. One of Lassie's many champions at M-G-M told me that he had favored writing in a part for Lassie in *Easter Parade* but that he had dropped the idea. "I couldn't find a good Lassie angle," he explained.

An exceedingly active Hollywood agent, a woman, claims that since the start of the Congressional investigation the studios have been calling for light domestic comedies and have been turning down scripts with serious themes. "You might say the popular phrase out here now is 'Nothing on the downbeat,'" she said. "Up until a few months ago, it was 'Nothing sordid.'" The difference between "Nothing sordid" and "Nothing on the downbeat," she explained, is like the difference between light domestic comedy and lighter domestic comedy. After the investigation got under way, the industry called in Dr. George Gallup to take a public poll for the studios. Dr. Gallup has now submitted figures showing that seventy-one percent of the nation's moviegoers have heard of the Congressional investigation, and that of this number fifty-one percent think that it was a good idea, twenty-seven percent think not, and twenty-two percent have no opinion. Three percent of the fifty-one percent approving of the investigation feel that Hollywood is overrun with Communism. The studio executives are now preparing a campaign to convince this splinter three percent, and the almost-as-bothersome ninety-seven percent of the fifty-one percent, that there is not Communism in the industry. There is some disagreement about whether the industry should tackle the unopinionated twenty-two percent or leave it alone.

In the midst of the current preoccupation with public opinion, many stars are afraid that the public may have got a very wrong impression about them because of having seen them portray, say, a legendary hero who stole from the rich to give to the poor, or an honest, crusading district attorney, or a lonely, poetic, antisocial gangster. "We've got to resolve any conflicts between what we are and what the public has been led to believe we are," one actor told me. "We can't afford to have people think we're a bunch of strong men or crusaders." At the Warner Brothers studio, some time ago, I accepted a publicity representative's invitation to watch the shooting of a scene in *Don Juan*, a Technicolor reworking of the *Don Juan* made in 1926 with John Barrymore. Filming of the production has since been called off, owing to the illness of the star, Errol Flynn, but he was still in good health the day I was there. "I want you to meet Errol," said the publicity representative. "Just don't discuss anything serious with him—politics, I mean." Being a publicity man out here seems to have taken on some of the aspects of a lawyer's and an intelligence agent's duties and responsibilities. Studio visitors who are suspected of having ways of communicating with the public are always accompanied by a publicity man, or even two publicity men. The present-day importance of the publicity man is indicated by the fact that a member of the trade at M-G-M now occupies the office of the late Irving Thalberg, Thalberg still being to Hollywood what Peter the Great still is to Russia. I asked Flynn, who stood glittering in royal-blue tights and jerkin, golden boots, and a golden sword, how his version of *Don Juan* compared with Barrymore's. "That's like comparing two grades of cheese," he said moodily. "The older is probably the better. But I'm trying to make my Don Juan as human as possible. Jack's was a tough Don Juan. Mine is human. The script calls for one of the Spanish nobles to tell me that Spain is going to war. 'You're not afraid?' he asks me. 'Yes, I am afraid!' I reply. I added that line to the script myself. I don't want to be heroic. This picture is definitely nonsubversive."

Some producers express the interesting point of view that there are no Communistic pictures, that there are only good pictures and bad pictures, and that most bad pictures are bad because writers write bad stories. "Writers don't apply themselves," I was informed by Jerry Wald, a thirty-six-year-old Warner Brothers producer, customarily described as a dynamo, who boasts that he makes twelve times as many pictures as the average producer in Hollywood. "Anatole France never sat down and said, 'Now, what did a guy write last year that I can copy this year?'" Wald assured me. "The trouble with pictures is they're cold. Pictures got to have emotion. You get emotion by doing stories on the temper of the times." The Congressional investigation, he said, would have no effect on his plans for this year's pictures on the temper of the times. These will include one on good government (with Ronald Reagan), another about underpaid schoolteachers (with Joan Crawford), and an adaptation and modernization of Maxwell Anderson's *Key Largo* (with Humphrey Bogart, Lauren Bacall, Edward G. Robinson, and Lionel Barrymore). "Bogart plays an ejected liberal," Wald said, "a disillusioned soldier who says nothing is worth fighting for, until he learns there's a point where every guy must fight against evil." Bogart, who two or three months before had announced that his trip to Washington to protest against the methods of the Thomas Committee hearings had been a mistake, was very eager, Wald said, to play the part of an ejected liberal.

At Wald's suggestion, I had lunch one day with several members of the *Key Largo* cast, its director, John Huston, and a publicity representative at the Lakeside Golf Club, a favorite buffet-style eating place of stars on the nearby Warner lot. The actors were in a gay mood. They had just finished rehearsing a scene (one of the new economics at Warner is to have a week of rehearsals before starting to film a picture) in which Bogart is taunted by Robinson, a gangster representing evil, for his cowardice, but is comforted by the gangster's moll, who tells Bogart, "Never mind. It's better to be a live coward than a dead hero." Bogart had not yet reached the point where a guy learns he must fight against evil. Huston was feeling particularly good, because he had just won a battle with the studio to keep in the film some lines from Franklin Roosevelt's message to the Seventy-Seventh Congress on January 6, 1942: "But we of the United Nations are not making all this sacrifice of human effort and human lives to return to the kind of world we had after the last world war."

"The big shots wanted Bogie to say this in his own words," Huston explained, "but I insisted that Roosevelt's words were better."

Bogart nodded. "Roosevelt was a good politician," he said. "He could handle those babies in Washington, but they're too smart for guys like me. Hell, I'm no politician. That's what I meant when I said our Washington trip was a mistake."

"Bogie has succeeded in not being a politician," said Huston, who went to Washington with him. "Bogie owns a fifty-four-foot yawl. When you own a fifty-four-foot yawl, you've got to provide for her upkeep."

"The Great Chief died and everybody's guts died with him," Robinson said, looking stern.

"How would you like to see your picture on the front page of the Communist paper of Italy?" asked Bogart.

"Nyah," Robinson said, sneering.

"The *Daily Worker* runs Bogie's picture and right away he's a dangerous Communist," said Miss Bacall. "What will happen if the American Legion and the Legion of Decency boycott all his pictures?"

"It's just that my picture in the *Daily Worker* offends me, Baby," said Bogart.

"Nyah," said Robinson.

"Let's eat," said Huston.

A few weeks ago, many people in Hollywood received through the mails a booklet called *Screen Guide for Americans*, published by the Motion Picture Alliance for the Preservation of American Ideals and containing a list of dos and don'ts. "This is the raw iron from which a new curtain around Hollywood will be fashioned," one man assured me solemnly. "This is the first step—not to fire people, not to get publicity, not to clean Communism out of motion pictures but to rigidly control all the contents of all pictures for right-wing political purposes." The Motion Picture Association of America has not yet publicly adopted the *Screen Guide for Americans* in place of its own *A Code to Govern the Making of Motion and Talking Pictures*, which advances such tenets as "The just rights, history, and feelings of any nation are entitled to consideration and respectful treatment" and "The treatment of bedrooms must be governed by good taste and delicacy." Although it is by no means certain that the industry has got around to following these old rules, either to the letter or in the spirit, there is a suspicion that it may have already begun at least to paraphrase some of the *Screen Guide*'s pronouncements, which appear under such headings as "Don't Smear the Free Enterprise System," "Don't Deify the 'Common Man,'" "Don't Glorify the Collective," "Don't Glorify Failure," "Don't Smear Success," and "Don't Smear Industrialists." "All too often, industrialists, bankers, and businessmen are presented on the screen as villains, crooks, chiselers, or exploiters," the *Guide* observes. "It is the moral (no, not just political but moral) duty of every decent man in the motion picture industry to throw into the ashcan, where it belongs, every story that smears industrialists as such." Another admonition reads, "Don't give to your characters—as a sign of villainy, as a damning characteristic—a desire to make money." And another, "Don't permit any disparagement or defamation of personal success. It is the Communists' intention to make people think that personal success is somehow achieved at the expense of others and that every successful man has hurt somebody by becoming successful." The booklet warns, "Don't tell people that man is a helpless, twisted, drooling, sniveling, neurotic weakling. Show the world an American kind of man, for a change." The *Guide* instructs people in the industry, "Don't let yourself be fooled when the Reds tell you what they want to destroy are men like Hitler and Mussolini. What they want to destroy are men like Shakespeare, Chopin, and Edison." Still another of the don'ts says, "Don't ever use any lines about 'the common man' or 'the little people.' It is not the

American idea to be either 'common' or 'little.'" This despite the fact that Eric Johnston [head of the MPAA and former president of the Chamber of Commerce], testifying before the Thomas Committee, said, "Most of us in America are just little people, and loose charges can hurt little people." And one powerful man here has said to me, "We're not going to pay any attention to the Motion Picture Alliance for the Preservation of American Ideals. We like to talk about 'the little people' in this business."

I was given a copy of *Screen Guide for Americans* by Mrs. Lela Rogers, one of the founders of the Motion Picture Alliance for the Preservation of American Ideals. Mrs. Rogers, the mother of Ginger, is a pretty, blond-haired lady with a vibrant, birdlike manner. Mrs. Rogers is also writing screenplays. I wanted to know if she was following the dos and don'ts of the *Screen Guide for Americans*. "You just bet I am," she said. "My friend Ayn Rand wrote it, and sticking to it is easy as pie. I've just finished a shooting script about a man who learns how to live after he is dead."

Other people in the industry admit that they are following the *Guide* in scripts about the living. One man who is doing that assured me that he nevertheless doesn't need it, that it offers him nothing he didn't already know. "This is new only to the youngsters out here," he said. "They haven't had their profound intentions knocked out of them yet, or else they're still earning under five hundred a week. As soon as you become adjusted in this business, you don't need the *Screen Guide* to tell you what to do." A studio executive in charge of reading scripts believes that Hollywood has a new kind of self-censorship. "It's automatic, like shifting gears," he explained. "I now read scripts through the eyes of the DAR, whereas formerly I read them through the eyes of my boss. Why, I suddenly find myself beating my breast and proclaiming my patriotism and exclaiming that I love my wife and kids, of which I have four, with a fifth on the way. I'm all loused up. I'm scared to death, and nobody can tell me it isn't because I'm afraid of being investigated."

William Wyler, who directed the Academy Award picture *The Best Years of Our Lives*, told me he is convinced that he could not make that picture today and that Hollywood will produce no more films like *The Grapes of Wrath* and *Crossfire*. "In a few months, we won't be able to have a heavy who is an American," he said. The scarcity of roles for villains has become a serious problem, particularly at studios specializing in

Western pictures, where writers are being harried for not thinking up any new ones. "Can I help it if we're running out of villains?" a writer at one of these studios asked me. "For years I've been writing scripts about a Boy Scout–type cowboy in love with a girl. Their fortune and happiness are threatened by a banker holding a mortgage over their heads, or by a big landowner, or by a crooked sheriff. Now they tell me that bankers are out. Anyone holding a mortgage is out. Crooked public officials are out. All I've got left is a cattle rustler. What the hell am I going to do with a cattle rustler?"

Hollywood's current hypersensitivity has created problems more subtle than the shortage of heavies. *The Treasure of the Sierra Madre*, a film about prospecting for gold, was to have begun and ended with the subtitle "Gold, Mister, is worth what it is because of the human labor that goes into the finding and getting of it." The line is spoken by Walter Huston in the course of the picture. John Huston, who directed it, says that he couldn't persuade the studio to let the line appear on the screen. "It was all on account of the word *labor*," he told me. "That word looks dangerous in print, I guess." He paused, then added thoughtfully, "You can sneak it onto the sound track now and then, though." At a preview, in Hartford, Connecticut, of *Arch of Triumph*, attended by its director, Lewis Milestone, and by Charles Einfield, president of Enterprise Productions, which brought it out, the manager of the theatre asked Einfield whether it was necessary to use the word *refugees* so often in the picture. "All the way back to New York," says Milestone, "Charlie kept muttering, 'Maybe we mention the word *refugees* too many times?' 'But the picture is about refugees,' I told him. 'What can we do now? Make a new picture?'"

Jack L. Warner, busiest of the Brothers, is genially inclined to bolster up the courage of those who are ready to throw in the towel. "Don't worry!" he roars, slapping the backs of the lesser men around him. "Congress can't last forever!"

Most producers stick firmly to the line that there is no Communism whatever in the industry and that there are no Communistic pictures. "We're going to make any kind of pictures we like, and nobody is going to tell us what to do," I was informed by Dore Schary, the RKO vice president and winner of the Golden Slipper Square Club's Humanitarian Award. In sixteen years, Schary pioneered from a $100-a-week job as a junior writer to his present position, which brings him around

$500,000 a year. When he testified before the Thomas Committee, he said that RKO would hire anyone it chose, solely on the basis of his talent, who had not been proved to be subversive. The RKO Board of Directors met soon afterward and voted not to hire any known Communists. Schary then voted, like the other producers, to blacklist the ten men because they had been cited for contempt. He is talked about a good deal in Hollywood. Many of his colleagues are frequently critical of the course he has taken, and yet they understand why he has done what he's done. "I was faced with the alternative of supporting the stand taken by my company or of quitting my job," Schary told me. "I don't believe you should quit under fire. Anyway, I like making pictures. I want to stay in the industry. I like it." Schary is one of the few Hollywood executives who will talk to visitors without having a publicity man sit in on the conversation. "The great issue would have been joined if the ten men had only stood up and said whether or not they were Communists," he continued. "That's all they had to do. As it is, ten men have been hurt and nobody can be happy. We haven't done any work in weeks. Now is the time for all of us to go back to the business of making pictures, good pictures, in favor of anything we please." I asked Schary what he was planning to make this year. "I will assemble a list," he said. He assembled the following out of his memory, and I wrote them down: *Honored Glory* (in favor of honoring nine unknown soldiers), *Weep No More* (in favor of law and order), *Evening in Modesto* (also in favor of law and order), *The Boy with Green Hair* (in favor of peace), *Education of a Heart* (in favor of professional football), *Mr. Blandings Builds His Dream House* (in favor of Cary Grant), *The Captain Was a Lady* (in favor of Yankee clipper ships), *Baltimore Escapade* (in favor of a Protestant minister and his family having fun).

"Committee or no Committee," Schary said, "we're going to make all these pictures exactly the way we made pictures before."

(FEBRUARY 21, 1948)

Sgt. Pepper

M eet the Beatles, the first (January 1964) record album in the United States of John, Paul, George, and Ringo, has sold five million three hundred thousand copies to date. Pictures of the faces of John, Paul, George, and Ringo appeared on its cover. The songs "I Want to Hold Your Hand," "I Saw Her Standing There," and "All My Loving," among others, were featured. *Sgt. Pepper's Lonely Hearts Club Band*, the thirteenth and latest (June 1967) album of John, Paul, George, and Ringo, came out the week before last and has sold twelve hundred thousand copies to date, with ninety-five thousand more in back orders. On the cover, John, Paul, George, and Ringo are pictured, wearing old-timey satin-and-braid brass-band costumes, in the company of the faces of—to name just a few—Shirley Temple, H. G. Wells, Marilyn Monroe, Karl Marx, Lenny Bruce, Edgar Allan Poe, Lawrence of Arabia, Marlene Dietrich, Johnny Weissmuller, Dion, Carl Jung, Mae West, Fred Astaire, Tom Mix, W. C. Fields, Laurel and Hardy, Karlheinz Stockhausen, Bob Dylan, Oscar Wilde, and Madame Tussaud's wax figures of John, Paul, George, and Ringo. On this record, the Beatles (with Paul singing most of the solos) create the effect of a live show, starting with a number about "Sgt. Pepper" and going on, with no more than momentary interruptions, to numbers called, among others, "A Little Help from My Friends," "Lucy in the Sky with Diamonds," "Fixing a Hole," "She's Leaving Home," "When I'm Sixty-Four," "Lovely Rita," and "A Day in the Life." (The other Beatles albums: No. 2, *The Beatles' Second Album*, was brought out in April 1964. No. 3, *Something New*, was brought out in July 1964. No. 4, *A Hard Day's Night*, September 1964. No. 5, *The Beatles' Story*, November 1964. No. 6, *Beatles '65*, December 1964. No. 7, *The Early Beatles*, March 1965. No. 8, *Beatles VI*, June 1965. No. 9, *Help!*, the sound track of the movie of that name, August 1965. No. 10, *Rubber Soul*, December 1965. No. 11, *Yesterday and Today*, June 1966. No. 12, *Revolver*, August 1966.)

About a year ago, the screams of the Beatles' teenage fans abated somewhat, and other voices began to be heard, saying that the Beatles were "going too far," or were "burned out," or were "getting too serious," or weren't "funny anymore." Now *Sgt. Pepper* is out, and it's a huge success, and we've been talking to some record people about it. "We were the first to play it on the air," a WMCA disc jockey named Joe O'Brien told us. "We played 'A Day in the Life' on April eighteenth, six weeks before the album came out. This to me is the first album that's ever been made by a popular group. All others, including all other Beatles albums, are a collection of singles. This one is a forty-minute-long single."

"How did the listeners react?" we asked.

"Not much," O'Brien said. "They're unprepared. Just as people were unprepared for Picasso. That's because this album is not a teenage album. It's a terribly intellectual album. My youngest son is a freshman at Yale. He tells me that the day the album was issued, the entire student body of Yale went out and bought it. Exactly the same thing happened at Harvard. The college students are now the hard-core Beatles fans. This album is really a cantata. Teenagers don't want that."

"Proof positive of their musical maturity," was Murray the K's pronouncement to us. "The Beatles had the guts to go ahead and do something different from anything they've ever done before. There are very few commercial songs in this one, but it's a giant step forward. I've been playing the whole album, nonstop, on my show. I don't have to worry. My listeners are in the eighteen-to-twenty-five age group."

We went over to Sam Goody's West Forty-Ninth Street record shop, and there we ran into a couple of young men who were picking up the album. "It's like a show!" a tieless, shoeless guitar carrier named Richard Mellerton told us. "It stones you." We elicited a more detailed response from a dark-suited young man wearing gold-rimmed spectacles, who told us he was an English lit major at CCNY and is now a summer busboy at the Hotel Penn Garden Coffee House. The student, John Van Aalst, told us, "I'm really more interested in classical music, but this Beatles record goes beyond the sound of the record. It's technically interesting and imaginative. This is no longer computerized rock 'n' roll. This may have grown out of the hoodlum rock 'n' roll of the fifties, but it's an attempt to create music with meaning. It goes beyond making you feel good, although it does do that. It has aesthetic appeal. It conforms more to my conception of art."

One of Goody's staff men watched the parade of Beatles buyers with a friendly eye. The record, he told us, was big, very big, at Goody's. "We've sold thousands," he said. "It's selling like the first Horowitz Carnegie Hall return concert."

Up at the Colony Record Center, on Broadway at Fifty-Second Street, we came across a spirited, professorial-looking man named Lawrence LeFevre [actually William Shawn, but we decided to make him anonymous], who was plucking the Beatles' new record from a bin that contained the works of the Jefferson Airplane, the Blues Project, the Mamas and the Papas, and the Lovin' Spoonful. Mr. LeFevre gave us a little lecture: "This is really a coming of age for the Beatles," he said. "In musical substance, *Sgt. Pepper* is a much bigger advance than *Revolver*, and *Revolver* was a tremendous advance, if you recall. There are many musical structures here that are both new and extremely interesting, as well as new combinations of rhythms, new chord progressions, new instrumentations, and a continuation of the great fresh flow of melody. The Beatles, as you know, have drawn upon everything musical that has been done in the past, including Romantic, baroque, liturgical, and all the popular genres of music, including blues, jazz, the English music hall, English folk, and, of course, rock 'n' roll. Many people have pointed out how eclectic the Beatles are. They've drawn on everything. But now this is Beatles music. Hundreds of people are imitating what they do, but no one even gets close. This record is a musical event, comparable to a notable new opera or symphonic work. However, there is more going on musically in this one record than has gone on lately almost anywhere else. 'A Day in the Life' is not only the most ambitious thing they ever wrote but possibly the best piece of music they've done up to now. One can't say just what it is—it fits into no category—but it's a complex and powerful number. Another number, 'When I'm Sixty-Four,' has so much charm and taste. It's a parody, but, like the best parody, it is written with affection, and it has an excellence in its own right, independent of its value as parody. And 'Fixing a Hole' is right up there with the Beatles' nicest. The Beatles write to please themselves. Unlike many artists now, who get their kicks out of offending the public, they're having a great time with the stuff itself. It has enormous cheerfulness, along with the sadness that keeps turning

up. It's buoyant. This album is a whole world created by the Beatles. It's
a musical comedy. It's a film. Only, it's a record. There's no individual
number that's as downright lovely as, say, 'Michelle' or 'Here, There,
and Everywhere,' but you have to look at this album as an entity, and
as such it has considerable beauty. Of course, you can't talk about the
Beatles without mentioning the transcendent Duke Ellington. Just as
he has never fit into the jazz scheme of things, the Beatles don't fit
into the rock-'n'-roll scheme. They are off by themselves, doing their
own thing, just as Ellington always has been. Like Ellington, they're
unclassifiable musicians. And, again like Ellington, they are working in
that special territory where entertainment slips over into art. I might
add that in this record there isn't anything that is manufactured or
contrived or synthetic. All of it is spontaneous, inspired music. There's
a wry kind of sweetness in several of the numbers, some of which has
to do with McCartney's—excuse me, I mean Paul's—way of singing.
You never feel that the Beatles are writing themselves out. They have
a lot in reserve. This is just a beginning for them. The high point of
the high point for me is the delicate way, in 'A Day in the Life,' Len-
non—John—sings the words 'oh boy.' Let me add one last thing. The
Beatles have done more to brighten up the world in recent years than
almost anything else in the arts."

(JUNE 24, 1967)

Workouts
(Robin Williams)

During the past decade, Robin Williams, the thirty-four-year-old comic actor, who seems to connect with his audiences on some wild, deep level and to make them laugh in a special way, at once loud, true, and happy, has been featured in two television programs (*Mork & Mindy* and the 1977 revival of *Laugh-In*), six movies (*Popeye*, *The World According to Garp*, *The Survivors*, *Moscow on the Hudson*, *The Best of Times*, and the forthcoming *Club Paradise*), two concert performances on videocassette, and two record albums (*Reality . . . What a Concept* and *Throbbing Python of Love*). One kind of performing, however, Williams has been doing nonstop—before, during, and since his television, movie, concert, and recording activities—and that is working out, in unannounced appearances, in small, late-night comedy clubs: in the Comedy Store, in Los Angeles; in Yuk-Yuk's, in Toronto; in the Second City, in Chicago; in the Holy City Zoo, in San Francisco; in Catch a Rising Star, in New York; and in others that have become established since the early nineteen seventies in dozens of cities in the United States. Well, before flying west to be an Oscar host extraordinaire, Williams was in New York, helping to organize last week's *Comic Relief* cable-television show—a benefit to raise money for the nation's homeless—and we tagged along with him for a while as he embarked on his midnight-and-after workouts.

When we met Williams, he had been sitting for four hours at the Public Theatre watching *Hamlet*, and he emerged looking wilted and done in. He is a stocky, mild-seeming man with a rubbery face and body, which we were accustomed to seeing, in performance, go in seconds from Barry Fitzgerald to William F. Buckley, Jr., and on to Jerry Falwell, to Jesse Jackson, to Nadia Comaneci, and to God knows who or what else—always, in his inimitable way, simultaneously sharp and gentle. Now, wearing baggy brown pants tight at the ankles, black hiking boots, and a yellow rain jacket, he was calm and subdued. He expressed admiration for Kevin Kline as Hamlet and for Harriet Harris as Ophelia, noting that both actors were, like him, alumni of the Juilliard Theatre Center. He said that Jeff Weiss, a first-timer in a legitimate production, who had taken the roles of the Ghost, the Player King, and Osric, the unctuous courtier, was impressive. Then, in the taxi heading for Catch a Rising Star (First Avenue near Seventy-Seventh), Williams suddenly, quietly, became, successively, a Yiddish-accented Hamlet lamenting Yorick "buried in treyf"; an insane Hamlet in a mental institution playing all the parts in the play; a *Hamlet* featuring George Jessel as the Ghost; a Woody Allen Hamlet, sounding exactly like Woody Allen saying "I don't know whether I should avenge him or honor him"; a Jack Nicholson Hamlet, sounding exactly like Jack Nicholson saying "To be or not to bleeping be . . ."

Then Williams retreated into his own calm, and we spent the rest of the taxi ride having him give us a quick refresher course in his history: born in Chicago, an only child; his father an automobile-company vice president ("He looks like a British Army officer"), who retired and moved the family to Marin County, outside San Francisco; and his mother a "very funny" prankster and cutup, originally from the South, who loves to tell jokes. "I was good in languages and thought I'd go into the Foreign Service, or something like that," Williams told us. "In high school, I was heavily into cross-country running, which I loved, and wrestling, which gave me a chance to do some damage. I went to one of the Claremont Colleges, where I took courses in political science and economics and failed them. After the first year, I left Claremont and went to the College of Marin, near home, which had an amazing drama department, with teachers who told me about Juilliard. I auditioned for Juilliard, got a full scholarship, and stayed three years, doing Shakespeare and Strindberg. Back home, I started going nightly to a coffeehouse called the Intersection, on Union Street in San Francisco. During the day, I worked in an ice-cream parlor. One night, at the coffeehouse, for no reason at all, I got up and imitated a quarterback high on LSD. It felt great. This was fun. No one was telling me what to do. I liked the freedom."

By the time we arrived at Catch a Rising Star, it was packed: standees three deep at the bar in front; an audience of about a hundred and fifty in the back room, seated at little tables, having drinks, facing a small platform with a standing mike. On the wall behind the platform were signs saying "Break a Leg" and "Monogram Pictures Corp. Entrance," and nearby was a montage painting of famous comedians—Eddie Cantor, Charlie Chaplin, Milton Berle, and Abbott and Costello. On the platform, a young emcee—short, chubby, with dark curly hair, and wearing a long-sleeved sports shirt over a T-shirt—was getting ready laughs with routine questions of and comments on the audience, which consisted mostly of young singles, young couples, foursomes of young women, threesomes of young men. The m.c. left after introducing his replacement, a tall, rangy man with thinning hair who wore jeans and a red sweater. The replacement worked for about fifteen minutes, getting dutiful laughs by telling "family" jokes: "My mother had four children. I was the only vertebrate one," and "We have a dog. He's half retriever, half vulture. He's been circling Grandma."

The chubby m.c. returned and announced that Robin Williams was there, and the place went bananas. Screams, yells, whistles, shrieks, cheers, and tremendous applause. Williams took the mike. He said, speaking as an Oscar recipient, "Thank you for making this possible. [As a snobbish theatregoer] As long as I have my glasses on, the world is mine. I just went to see *Hamlet*. I want to see Hamlet played by Sly Stallone. [As Stallone] 'To be or what?' [As himself] Maybe he and Schwarzenegger can do a movie together. [As Schwarzenegger] With subtitles in English."

Williams went, again in seconds, from being one human cell to being Central Park squirrels, New York City pigeons ("I could fly, but I like it here"), another Oscar recipient ("I'd like to thank anybody who didn't try to kill me"), himself as penitent ("I'm sorry, God, I'm sorry that I made fun of everybody"), a Japanese manufacturer ("Not my faut, Amelican-made").

People in the audience called out subjects they had heard him do before, and these set Williams off on an even more manic scale. He went from gangster to drunk and on to Gorbachev, Reagan, Charles Kuralt covering toxic waste in New Jersey. He went from Mrs. Marcos to Louis Farrakhan and on to a small child watching his father leave and crying at a window and then turning away from the window, tearless, and saying, "Let's put on that Fisher-Price music and get crazy." (Williams has a three-year-old son, Zachary.)

Williams stayed on for about half an hour and came off looking refreshed and ready for anything. The following evening, in a taxi heading for the Improvisation (Forty-Fourth near Eighth), he gave us a minicourse in comedy clubs. "That audience last night was made up of the bridge-and-tunnel people. They come in from New Jersey and Connecticut. They're a challenge. You can get a big reception, but if it's not working—one time, twice—then there's nothing. Some comics have a lot of pride. They'll do the material they set out to do, no matter what. I'm more chameleonlike. I find the basic level of the audience. Last night, I felt in the groove. I felt comfortable. I like going to the clubs, because it peels away all pretensions. About a week ago, I went to the Comedy Store, in Los Angeles. I was talking about bizarre things. I got going doing this whole thing about traveling at the speed of light, losing your luggage beforehand, doing Albert Einstein as Mr. Rogers, improvising. It was fun. It was like running in an open field."

At the Improvisation, there was even louder screaming and yelling at the mention of Robin Williams. Again, he started out as an Oscar winner, sanctimoniously: "Thank you for your kindness. Your words are so meaningful." Then he was South Africa's Botha, and after that he became the state of Michigan and the Statue of Liberty and Frank Sinatra and Jewish hunters ("Let's go out to the country and see if anything died") and Lee Iacocca and Henry Kissinger and El Al Airlines.

After a while, someone in the audience called out "Dr. Ruth!"

"Dr. Rufe?" Williams asked, having obviously misheard the name. Then he got it, and immediately used the error to take off as a black woman preacher giving sex advice in a scolding vein. "Get yoh act together, now," he said. "Yoh look lahk a Ken doll. Don't yoh look at me wid dose mascara eyes goin' flip-flap. Get on dat highway and make sure de bridge is open." He kept it going for a good fifteen minutes. The audience was beside itself. At the end, Williams came off looking exhilarated and told us that that one had been brand-new—a breakthrough. He looked as though he had been running in an open field.

(APRIL 7, 1986)

Mr. and Mrs. Williams

When people in, or interested in, the movie business are asked casually to identify some women in the United States today who are producers, one usually hears the same names: Sherry Lansing (*Indecent Proposal*), Debra Hill (*The Fisher King*), Linda Obst (*Sleepless in Seattle*), Dawn Steel (*Sister Act*), Lauren Shuler-Donner (*Free Willy*), Gale Ann Hurd (*The Terminator*), Midge Sanford and Sarah Pillsbury (*Desperately Seeking Susan*), Lili Fini Zanuck (*Driving Miss Daisy*), and Kathleen Kennedy (*Jurassic Park*). One hears that Goldie Hawn and Bette Midler and Barbra Streisand "also produce," and then, irrelevantly, "but they're actresses, they're stars." Now the name of Marsha Garces Williams is on the list. She is a different kind of producer, and she is reinventing the job for 1993. Mrs. Williams and her husband, Robin, have founded and are running their own film company, Blue Wolf Productions, with Mrs. Williams as the president. In San Francisco, where they live, they have made their first film, *Mrs. Doubtfire*, with Sally Field, Pierce Brosnan, Harvey Fierstein, Robert Prosky, and, as Mrs. Doubtfire, Robin Williams. The production, under the watch of Twentieth Century Fox, is scheduled for release sometime in December.

It seems to be a practice in the movie business to have a variety of producers listed in the credits. For *Mrs. Doubtfire*, the credits will read, "Produced by Marsha Garces Williams, Robin Williams, and Mark Radcliffe; Executive Producer, Matthew Rushton; Co-Producer/Unit Production Manager, Joan Bradshaw." The practice of multiple producer crediting may raise questions of redundancy in the minds of people sitting in the dark multiplex theatre waiting impatiently for the movie to get going. But there is absolute clarity in the minds of the other producers and the staff of *Mrs. Doubtfire* that the leader of the enterprise is Mrs. Williams.

It started with the acquisition of Anne Fine's *Madame Doubtfire*—a children's book published in Great Britain in 1987—by Matthew Rushton and the late Frank Levy, who were the makers of, among other things, *My Stepmother Is an Alien*. They submitted the book to Elizabeth Gabler, who was then vice president of production at United Artists and is now senior vice president of production at Twentieth Century Fox. Kirk Kerkorian, who controlled both United Artists and M-G-M in the late eighties, merged the former company into the latter, leaving people associated with UA unhappy. "My former boss at United Artists, Roger Birnbaum, believed in this movie and loved it, as did I," Mrs. Gabler says. "It was always Robin Williams in our minds and hearts for this movie. But UA put the property into turnaround. Then Roger Birnbaum went to Fox to become president of worldwide production, and he got Fox to write a check acquiring all rights to the book."

Elizabeth Gabler joined Birnbaum at Fox a month later. Together they assigned a writer, Randi Mayem Singer, to do a screenplay based on the book. Marsha Williams, who had read the book about four years earlier and had liked it, happened to be in the office of her husband's managers on the Fox lot early last year and mentioned her interest in the book. By coincidence, the Singer script had just arrived in the office. Mrs. Williams read the script and had reservations about it. "It was too broad and did not tell the story I felt it should tell," she explained to me last March in San Francisco, during the preproduction period of the movie. Fox asked Mrs. Williams if she and her husband were interested in producing it. Mrs. Williams said yes and proceeded to work with Singer on rewriting the screenplay. Then Fox informed Mrs. Williams that Chris Columbus (*Home Alone, Home Alone II: Lost in New York*) was available to direct the movie. Mr. and Mrs. Williams said they'd like to have Columbus rewrite the script, which he did. Mrs. Williams told Fox that Columbus had done a "brilliant" job and that Mr. Williams would now commit, in the parlance, to act in the movie. Joe Roth, the chairman of Fox, committed; he telephoned Mrs. Williams and said, "You've got a 'go' movie." Robin and Marsha Williams committed to producing the film. As for Elizabeth Gabler, she says, "I was proud to be associated with *Mrs. Doubtfire*. Even more so now that Marsha and Robin were involved."

In *Mrs. Doubtfire*, Robin Williams plays the part of Daniel Hillard, described in the script as "a good-looking, rumpled fellow in his mid-thirties," who keeps getting fired from small-time television acting jobs.

His wife, Miranda, played by Sally Field, divorces him and is awarded custody of their three children. In order to be with his kids, Daniel gets himself professionally disguised, with mask, wig, false bosom, false behind, spectacles, and dress, and, calling himself Mrs. Doubtfire, goes to work as Miranda's housekeeper. As Mrs. Doubtfire, Robin Williams is astonishing: his voice, his English accent and inflections, his walk, his gestures, his eyes, and his impromptu responses, bodily and verbal, are utterly convincing. He put on the costume and makeup for the first time last March, before the filming began. I was in the *Mrs. Doubtfire* production office on a Saturday afternoon when someone new walked in—a heavyset gray-haired woman wearing spectacles, a pleated plaid skirt, a white blouse with a Peter Pan collar pinned with a brooch, a wool cardigan sweater, stockings, and cornily sensible Oxfords. Graciously, and somewhat shyly, she wished me good afternoon in a charming, soft English accent. I had been expecting her to show up, but it took me some time to realize who she was. It was almost immediately apparent that Mr. Williams, the actor, was becoming enamored of her. In the nearly four months of filming that followed, his affection for her never let up, and it created a groundswell of positive feeling for the lady on the part of the entire movie crew. Mr. Williams would speak about her as though she had sprung full-blown to her place in front of the camera, without any help from him. "What a sweet lady, with that gentle, lovely quality," he said to me, in her accent, weeks after he had finished playing her.

Also astonishing are his sudden transformations from one character to the other. There is a scene, for example, in which Mrs. Sellner, the social worker, comes to the divorced and displaced Daniel's seedy, messy apartment to check up on his habits. It calls for Mrs. Doubtfire to greet her and to explain that she is Daniel's visiting "sister." In this scene, Williams must run back and forth between the living room and the bedroom, put on his latex mask, his bodysuit with the big bosom and big behind, and his stockings and tight shoes while simultaneously calling out to Mrs. Sellner, alternately, in Daniel's voice and in Mrs. Doubtfire's. I watched Williams, wringing with sweat in his bodysuit, do sixteen takes just on the single master shot, and I stopped counting when he had to do the close-ups, the reverse angles, and the rest.

Williams is funny as Daniel and as Mrs. Doubtfire, and, miraculously, as both he is able to switch quickly from being very funny to being very poignant. As Daniel, he manages to make believable, without sinking into sentimentality, the pathos of a parent who is forcibly separated from his children. In a scene that takes place in a court-room, for example, Daniel pleads with the judge to alter the decision that has awarded custody of his children to their mother, with his visitation rights limited to a few hours a week. With the cameras on him, and the lights, and the grips and the soundmen and the visitors to the set and all the supposedly disturbing paraphernalia crowding in on him, Williams seemed to me to be reaching a higher level of acting than I'd ever seen him reach before. In various recent pictures, he had played the parts of a surreal innocent (*Toys*, 1992), a Spielbergian modification of Peter Pan (*Hook*, 1991), a gentle academic driven into hallucinations and nightmares by his wife's sudden death (*The Fisher King*, 1991), an idealistic, shy research doctor finding a way to bring to life comatose patients (*Awakenings*, 1990), and a devoted English teacher at a boys' prep school trying to imbue his students with his own love of literature (*Dead Poets Society*, 1989). Now, in this scene, he was trying to convey the feelings of a distraught and frightened father who, deprived of satisfaction in his work, is confronted with the ter-rifying possibility of being deprived of the daily, all-encompassing joy of seeing his children. After the "Cut!" was heard, people on the set, including me, were sobbing.

Mrs. Williams's mettle as producer was tested early on when she and Mr. Williams and Chris Columbus were urged to change the film's ending. "Everybody—our managers, our agents, people at the studio—said that the audience would want Daniel and Miranda to get back together or, at least, to leave their situation up in the air," she said. She paused for a beat, then added quickly and with startling passion, "When two people are harmful and wrong for each other, they do not belong together."

"The Norman Rockwell family doesn't exist," Mr. Williams said, even more strongly. "It's a myth." And Chris Columbus elaborated: "Ninety percent of parents who separate don't get back together again. We don't want our audience to see a dishonest film. We didn't set out to make *The Parent Trap*. We're going to protect *Mrs. Doubtfire*. We're keeping it honest."

Matthew Rushton, a very likable and very agreeable fellow, who turned up on the San Francisco set from Los Angeles sporadically, told me that he, too, preferred the "honest" ending. Then, with a shrug, he said, "I'm surprised that Fox has been so cooperative about the ending." With another shrug, he added, "I don't know what the studio executives might do if the first test screening produces a negative reaction."

"Marketing executives want to test everything these days," Mr. Williams said. "Now they're in the theatres testing the trailers. Pretty soon, they'll test a letter before sending it. Tests tend to frighten people off from doing what they need to do."

"Test screenings don't matter," Columbus said. "We just won't change it. Marsha and I are not going to bend."

The theme of family and the meaning and feeling of family are locked into the fabric of this movie. "We want to show that a family forms in any number of combinations, and that, as long as there is love, there is a family," Columbus said. In a sort of counterpoint to the tribulations of the fictional Hillard family, the makers of the movie had their own families—mothers, fathers, small children, big children, grandparents, babies, and dogs—on the set, at the meal breaks, and in the screening rooms for the "dailies," the shots taken on the previous day. During meal breaks, or while waiting for the start of a take, Chris Columbus would be seen holding his year-old son, Brendan, in his arms. With the mysteriously accurate perception of infants, one-and-a-half-year-old Cody Williams would respond to Mrs. Doubtfire's accent and greet his father with a loud "Da-da" of recognition. Even the exhausted-looking Joan Bradshaw, whose co-producing credits range from *Going in Style* and *Indiana Jones and the Last Crusade* to *One Good Cop* and *Death Becomes Her*, and who on *Mrs. Doubtfire* is both co-producer and unit production manager (either one being a highly demanding and nerve-racking job), and who had developed and finely honed the knack of avoiding eye contact with anybody who might lay a last straw on her, was seen on the set cuddling and comforting a newborn baby, sibling of the youngest child actor in the film. Columbus sometimes recruited visiting family members and friends and put them—including Cody; his then three-and-a-half-year-old sister, Zelda; their ten-year-old half brother, Zachary; and Mrs. Williams's mother—in bit parts of a few seconds.

One of the first lessons a neophyte on a movie-production site learns is the supreme importance of remembering names (the more important the name, the more important the remembering) and then quickly addressing each person by his or her first name and looking and sounding extremely enthusiastic and cheerful while doing so. Even the caterers engaged for the movie seemed to know this rule. Last spring, during the first week of shooting, I was amazed when I heard my own first name uttered in greeting by one of the children hanging around the set. Another basic precept seems to be: Talk fast— very, very, very fast. No matter what anybody is talking about, in this most competitive of competitive industries, almost everybody speaks to everybody else in a shared rhythm that escalates in speed as it goes on. The participants sound as though they were engaged in a contest to see who can put out the most verbiage in the shortest time, like radio broadcasters trained to squeeze in more and more syllables between commercials. The children around the *Mrs. Doubtfire* set seemed to be absorbing the time-is-money-in-this-business pace quite naturally, and their baby talk weirdly repeated the rhythms of their elders. Other rituals were followed impressively by even the youngest of the children. One evening, I noticed three-and-a-half-year-old Eleanor Columbus in respectful attendance at the dailies. The child sat watching for almost an hour in concentrated, silent attention. When the lights went on, I asked her who had taught her that one must not talk or make any noise at the screenings. She pointed to Porscha and Brittany Radcliffe, eleven- and nine-year-old daughters of the Williamses' producing associate, and said, "They did."

Mrs. Williams is in her thirties and has dark-brown hair worn long and free (or, occasionally, in a ponytail or braid), enormous dark eyes, delicate features, and a dazzling smile. She speaks softly and patiently.

If looks stem, as is said, from parents, Mrs. Williams's may be attributed to her father, Leon Garces, a chef, who was born in Cebu, the oldest city in the Philippines, and finished two years of medical school at the University of the Philippines before coming to the United States; and to her mother, Ina, the youngest of seven children of Finnish immigrants who wound up on a farm in Owen, Wisconsin, two hundred miles northwest of Milwaukee. "I'd walk a couple of miles in temperatures reaching forty below zero to get to a one-room grade school," Ina Garces told me at a big family-plus-friends Easter party. "We had to fight to go to high school. But our farm was a nice place to grow up. We worked very hard and always had food on the table," she said. Marsha was born in Milwaukee, the youngest of four children: Victor, the eldest, died a couple of years ago; Selina, the wife of a lawyer, lives in Tucson; and Carmen, whose husband is in sports medicine, lives in Phoenix, not far from her parents. Marsha told me that, unlike her sisters and her brother, she was a loner. "I grew up in a German community, where all the other kids were blond, and we were dark, so I know what it feels like to be what is considered different," she said, and added, matter-of-factly, "I was different even from my brother and sisters. They were very social. I was always by myself." She taught herself to read at the age of four by studying the label on a shampoo bottle. By nine, she was reading Tolkien's *The Lord of the Rings*. She was a voracious reader throughout her childhood, reading at the table or under the table at meals, and reading in a closet when she was supposed to be asleep. She is still a reader. "I always have a mountain of reading material by my bed," she said. (Some of the books by her bed: *Immortality*, by Milan Kundera; *A Personal Anthology*, by Jorge Luis Borges; *The Encyclopedia of Sexual Trivia*, by Robin Smith; *Drawing with Children*, by Mona Brookes; *Tales of Mystery and Imagination*, by Edgar Allan Poe; *The Solar Electric House—A Design Manual for Home-Scale Photovoltaic Power Systems*, by Steven J. Strong.) She wanted to study art and took art classes while working nights as a waitress. She worked as a bank supervisor but returned to working as a waitress, because she liked the job. "I learned that I had an instinct for making people feel comfortable," she explained. To pursue her interest in art, she took art classes at the University of Wisconsin in Milwaukee. Then she headed west, where she continued taking art classes, at San Francisco State College, and working as a waitress at night. "I just didn't want to be in Milwaukee anymore," she said.

Marsha met Robin at a party in San Francisco about twelve years ago. Her marriage to him is her third. "My parents were very good about letting me make my own mistakes," she said, with one of her quick smiles. In 1984, she took a job caring for Zachary, Williams's then year-old son by his first wife, Valerie Velardi. "I'm proud of how well I cared for him," she said. "I loved Zak then, and I love him now." Marsha stayed in the job for about a year, and throughout that time she was involved in a serious relationship with another man—a relationship that continued after she left the job. That period was a tempestuous and troubled one for Robin in his marriage. He, too, was involved with another person. He had experienced great success as the star of the *Mork & Mindy* TV show during its four-year run (1978–82), and he had gone on to act in movies, starting with *Popeye*, directed by Robert Altman, which was not a financial success. Discord continued in his marriage to Valerie. In early 1986, Robin and Valerie separated. Marsha, who was still involved with another man, went to work for Robin as his assistant, organizing and arranging his tours, taking care of his fan mail, and so on. Among other things, Robin was then giving a good deal of attention to efforts to help the homeless, by holding *Comic Relief* benefits. He also started paying attention again to his health and fitness, and returned to one of his favorite disciplines, running.

After Robin and Valerie had been living apart for about a year, Robin and Marsha became involved with each other. Marsha continued working as Robin's assistant, and when he went to Thailand to film *Good Morning, Vietnam,* she went with him. With the movie's release, in December of 1987, Robin Williams became a highly visible celebrity, and he and Marsha, who was now regularly by his side, became the targets of a certain amount of highly visible, cavalier tabloid attention. "The crazy, sleazy stuff they printed!" one of the Williamses' friends remarked to me recently. "Marsha is an original and exceptional woman, a real match for Robin."

It took almost three years for the divorce terms to be settled. On April 30, 1989, at Lake Tahoe, Robin and Marsha got married, with about thirty friends in attendance, including Mr. and Mrs. Billy Crystal, Mr. and Mrs. Barry Levinson, Mr. and Mrs. Mark Johnson, and Mr. and Mrs. Bob Goldthwait. Valerie Velardi, busy with a life of her own, had another baby about a year ago, by which time she and Robin and Marsha had worked out an equal time-sharing plan that Zachary and everybody related to him are comfortable with.

Robin has two half brothers: Todd Williams, who lives in Santa Rosa, is a regional distributor for a wine company, and McLauren Smith, who lives in Memphis, Tennessee, is a high-school physics teacher. Robin's father, who was an automobile-company vice president, died a few years ago. His mother, Laurie Williams, a spirited, chicly dressed, tennis-playing, joke-telling, fun-hungry woman, lives in Tiburon, outside San Francisco, and regularly spends Sundays with Robin and Marsha and their children. She always seems to be looking for a laugh. Laughing to me, she recited one of the earliest rhymes she had taught Robin:

> Sammy was a spider
> Bright in every way
> Except he didn't like to spin.
> He liked to crochet.

"I say to Robin, 'I feel your mission on earth is to bring joy to the world,'" she told me.

Taking a look at some of what Marsha Williams has done as a producer involved a kind of mind-boggling course in micromanagement. "Actually, what I'm doing is, to a great extent, what I've been doing with Robin for several years," she said. "I've been reading scripts for him, looking into possible projects, and giving him my opinions about all of it when he asks me. He doesn't always agree with me, and there have been movies that he embarked on without paying any attention to what I thought, but I've supported him in whatever decisions he's made."

"She waded right into it," Robin Williams said to me with a kind of calm amazement. "She likes the challenge of producing. My name is on *Mrs. Doubtfire* as producer, and we talk to each other about everything, but she does most of the work, and all that talking with other people. She has the patience to discuss a problem for hours and hours. I have to be busy preparing for my part. Anyway, I tend to be direct. I'll just say, 'That sucks!'"

According to Mr. Williams, Mrs. Williams learned the ways of a producer by watching some of his past producers—"the ones who know how to get the job done the good way, people like Steve Haft, who produced *Dead Poets Society*, and Mark Johnson, who produced *Good Morning, Vietnam*. Everybody picks up on the way Marsha deals with them—decently, humanely, treating people the way she has wanted to be treated."

Mrs. Williams and her staff attended the preproduction money meetings with the people from Fox. Once the budget was set, she was doing everything: scouting locations with her director, cinematographer, and crew; deciding that the canvas folding chairs for the deserving participants would have the names in white script on black canvas; OK'ing a huge Chromatrans by Pacific Studios showing the street and the San Francisco skyline, which would serve as a view from the window of Daniel's apartment; telephoning Pierce Brosnan at his Los Angeles home to welcome him to the cast; and diplomatically but forcefully instructing the Fox product-placement people that placement of name-brand-labeled products was strictly forbidden with or near Robin Williams in the movie, no matter how much money for Fox was at stake, and pointing out that "Robin has been offered a lot of money to make commercials and we've turned them all down."

She was on her cellular telephone constantly, even while driving. She preferred to drive herself, often in her electric car. It is a smallish white station wagon, called an Electron One, a modified Ford Escort. It is supposed to go forty miles on one charge, but on the city's hills it gets risky after twenty-five. Whenever she could, upon arriving at her destination she would find an open window and plug in the car with a cord through the window.

While taking care of *Mrs. Doubtfire*, she showed no letup in her attention to Blue Wolf Productions, her business responsibilities, or her care of her husband and their children, along with a myriad of burdens and problems she had taken on in the lives of her entire family and a long list of friends. (Her friends are such that one of them, a young pregnant wife, recently declared that she didn't want any of her own friends anymore; she just wanted the Williamses' friends.) Getting along on two or three hours of sleep at night, Mrs. Williams somehow often managed to take Zelda to school, to ballet class, to a friend's house, to shop for an Easter dress; or to take Cody, in a canvas carrier on her back, to the marina, to the Exploratorium, to Marine World. When the family traveled, she would pack and arrange for the tickets and transport. She remembered who got what medication and when for the children, for the pets, and for herself. She also often managed to give the kids their baths, put them to bed, and—with Robin—read to them, and conduct a lot of unflaggingly patient, interminable discussions or debates with them. She conferred with Robin's two CAA agents at the time, Michael Marcus and Michael Menchel, known to the Williamses as Mike and Mike (Marcus has just become the president of M-G-M); she consulted the Williamses' lawyer, Gerald Margolis; she listened to Fox marketing representatives (it often costs twenty million dollars just to market a film effectively these days, for example); and she heard from three gentlemen named Larry Brezner, David Steinberg, and Steve Tenenbaum, who, somewhere along the line in Robin Williams's career, had become officially associated with him as managers. To Mr. and Mrs. Williams, they are known as "the boys."

One of the boys, David Steinberg, turned up on the set early in the filming. The filmmakers were working on an exterior scene at the house from which Daniel was about to be dislodged after giving a wild party to celebrate his son's twelfth birthday: lots of messy kids, a large assortment of petting animals (a pony, a pig, a goat, and many chickens, among them), along with the standard balloons, cake, and whatnot. The crew immediately took notice of Steinberg's up-to-the-moment Hollywood regalia: graying hair fashionably but not Rockerly long, black silk shirt, perfect black jeans, black alligator belt with silver buckle in a chic loop, black leather Cole Haan loafers worn with no socks, and a cigar (Monte Cristo).

"I came up just to be supportive," Steinberg told me. "The other stuff we do with Marsha." He watched and kibitzed and enjoyed himself. "This picture is gonna be a huge one," he advised me. "Kids, animals, and Robin in drag. This one jumped up and grabbed Robin."

The transformation of Robin Williams from the thirtyish Daniel into the sixtyish Mrs. Doubtfire was a work of magic. Of the seventy days scheduled for filming, forty-one called for that transformation. It took four and a half hours to achieve, beginning at 5 a.m., so that Williams would be ready at nine thirty for the first shot of the day. At my first glimpse of "her," on that preproduction Saturday, I didn't know, let alone believe, that it had actually happened until the actor greeted me, albeit in his housekeeper's voice, by name. Ten weeks later, I found myself still staring at him as "her" and trying to remember Robin Williams's face. He is my friend, and I know his face, but when I looked at "her" I could not visualize him. He didn't seem to have that sort of difficulty holding on to himself, however much he cared for "her." One day during the filming of a scene that had Mrs. Doubtfire shopping in a grocery store—a location at the corner of Columbus and Vallejo Streets, just between North Beach and Chinatown, and near the hungry i, one of the nightclubs in which Williams used to appear—he emerged in full costume between takes and headed on foot toward North Beach. People on the street paid no attention to "her." "I kind of like to wander around this way," he told me. "To see what it's like."

In the early weeks of filming, Mrs. Williams regularly got up at 4 a.m. to join her husband on the set for the 5 a.m. call. Once his makeup session was over, she would discuss with him points bearing on questions of characterization, or arrange for such things as a foot massage during the meal-break release from Mrs. Doubtfire's painful shoes and other appliances, or agree with him that Mark Radcliffe should be promoted in the movie's credits from "executive producer" to "producer," because of the heavier contribution to the picture he was turning out to make, or consult with him on some particular lighting ideas that the cinematographer, Donald McAlpine (*Breaker Morant, Moscow on the Hudson, Down and Out in Beverly Hills*), had come up with, or inform him that their first assistant director, Geoff Hansen, who had gone to film school with Chris Columbus, had the most resonant and most effective voice of any first AD in the history of film, or tell him about the dailies (he never goes to see them), or bring good tidings of the enthusiasm from the Fox executives over the dailies.

She kept me posted on pertinent revelations. "Chris Columbus has so much energy, and he's not afraid to listen," she told me at one point. "Chris is confident. The confident ones are open to the fresh and the new."

Columbus is thirty-four, a gum-chewing, small-cigar-smoking, friendly, outgoing, alert man who resembles Macaulay Culkin stretched tall and disguised with large eyeglasses on his boyish face. Columbus is noticeably quick to grasp what is said to him. He was born in Warren, Ohio, and named Chris, not Christopher. His favorite utterance, frequently bestowed on Williams and the other actors at whom the camera was aimed, was "Great!" With the word came an appreciative and unmistakably joyous laugh. But he kept the camera rolling until he got what he wanted. And there was no mistaking the certainty, accompanied by impressively consistent good humor, with which he went for what he wanted. He said that he couldn't get over how lucky he was to have such "great actors" to work with, and that included the children—Lisa Jakub, Matthew Lawrence, and Mara Wilson, who play Daniel's thirteen-, twelve-, and five-year-olds, respectively, in the film. "The two older kids are so good, and at that age it's astounding," he said. He would speak the lines for the youngest and then hear them echoed exactly as he wanted her to say them. "Aren't these kids wonderful?" he said. "I never had kids like this before." It went differently with Williams. They consulted together after each take. No matter how late the hour, or how many takes had already been shot, both men were inexhaustible in trying a shot this way and that until they were satisfied. "Robin gives two hundred and fifty percent," Chris Columbus said. "I've never met an actor so giving. He's concerned about every aspect of the performance. He's not at all a guy who rests on his laurels."

Williams's energy was phenomenal enough, but when a shot was taken and Columbus called "Cut!" Williams had seemingly endless energy left over for antics, all of it raising the spirits and energy level of everybody else. For the cast members acting with Williams, his layer upon layer of inventiveness set off still more layers of responsive invention in them. "With Robin, you just get hold of the comet and hang on," Robert Prosky said.

One of the most serious scenes in the film has Miranda telling Daniel that she wants a divorce. As with most other movies, this scene was filmed out of chronological sequence in the story—in this case, weeks after the scene in the courtroom in which Daniel pleads with the judge not to separate him from his children. He shows shock, fear, and pathos in response to Miranda's range of emotions—sympathy, anguish, frustration, and sadness, along with determination. Columbus explained to me that in rewriting the script he had had a definite "rhythm" in mind for this scene.

"I wanted the pacing to have the highs and the lows when she tells Daniel, 'It's over,'" he said. "And then I wanted it to take on a quiet. You film your peaks, and then you go into the editing room and find the perfect balance."

"Can you remember each shot?" I asked him.

"I can remember every shot," he said, with a grin. "I have such a connection with them, I can remember every one." Columbus took the shot repeatedly—until Miranda spoke the words "I want a divorce" in the way he wanted to hear them eventually in the editing room. Miranda said softly, "I want a divorce." And, again, "I want a divorce." As Williams heard the words, the expression on his face was one of simple frozen agony. "Cut!" Columbus called. Everybody watching was deeply affected, and drained, and distraught. There was a moment or so of complete silence.

Williams took a breath, and suddenly erupted into stand-up comedy. "You can have the upstairs!" he yelled in a heavy Jewish accent.

"I'll take the downstairs! You can't have the whole house! I'll bring witnesses!" And everybody started laughing.

The Williamses are living in a four-bedroom rented house while they wait for the completion, planned for October, of a new home—a large stucco house with a tiled roof, which resembles a Mediterranean villa. (They also have a six-hundred-acre ranch, thick with cows, in the Napa Valley.) In addition to *Mrs. Doubtfire*, Mrs. Williams has been producing the remodeling of the villa. She has designed and planned every room, every floor, every ceiling, every molding, every hinge, every glazed argon-filled window (most energy efficient, like the electric car), every cedar and part-cedar shelf, every tile, every piece of woodwork, every piece of metal, every computer location, every light-switch plate, every button, and—so it seems to me—every view. The view from the master bedroom stretches from the Golden Gate Bridge to the Pacific Ocean.

"It's amazing," Mr. Williams said of this domestic production. "It's wonderful. And it's going to have what she calls 'all of your stuff and all of my stuff right in it. It's a warm, interesting home," he added, looking sort of stunned at the prospect, as though a family living together were a unique adventure.

The production picture at home is filled out by the presence of half a dozen loyal aides, two iguanas, two guinea pigs, and an aging rabbit. A sickly chameleon, Norton, was present until recently. Rebecca Spencer, one of the loyal aides, took care of Norton, but to no avail: he died and was buried, with a simple service, in the garden behind the house. Spencer, a freckle-faced protector with a spectacular head of long, wild red hair, is addicted to colorful ensembles featuring such items as purple high-top sneakers with orange laces, baseball knickers, and a denim vest with multiple pockets holding cellular phone, walkie-talkie, notebook, pen, bottled water, and lipstick. Her friendship with Williams began in 1980, when she was managing the comedy club Holy City Zoo and he was doing his stand-up there. She and her husband, the comic actor Dan Spencer, are steady fixtures in the life of the Williamses. Cyndi Margolis, a tall, pretty young woman whose job title for *Mrs. Doubtfire* is "assistant to Marsha Williams," is another. (She is also married to Gerald Margolis, the Williamses' lawyer.) Margolis, upon learning one day that the pet rabbit and guinea pigs had eaten all their hard-to-find timothy hay, organized a search all over the city for it and found it. "Everybody who works for us is our friend" was Mrs. Williams's comment on the expedition.

The kitchen of the Williamses' present home is a kind of hub of their lives. In the early evening, the kids are at the table drawing or reading or stringing beads or doing puzzles or doing homework or singing. A favorite song is "Friend Like Me," from *Aladdin*, the top-grossing film of 1992 ($215 million so far) and the highest-grossing film in Disney's history—a pinnacle that, as is acknowledged generally among film-business pundits, was reached thanks to Robin Williams's creation of the character of the Genie. Crayon drawings by the kids are tacked to the wall, including Zelda's rendition of a spider, showing it equipped with the requisite eight legs. ("Maybe she'll be the artist I started out to be," her mother says.) While monitoring the activities, Mrs. Williams might be cooking dinner with one hand and, with the other, holding a telephone to her ear, conferring with Chris Columbus about their decision to have Howard Shore compose the music for the film, and then shifting gears to reassure Columbus about his baby son, Brendan, who had a temperature of a hundred and three the night before ("He's fine if he's lively; when they're sluggish, you worry"), and going on to discuss with him "the meal penalty" or "the overtime penalty" or "the turnaround rule," or reminding Rebecca Spencer, serving as Robin's assistant on the set, to give him his cup of black coffee before he goes into makeup, because he "drinks it by the ton."

When Mr. Williams isn't working, he, too, sits at the kitchen table, handing Cody pieces of pasta; Cody squeezes one piece after another, shoving them all into his mouth, while keeping an eye on everybody else in the room. Ten-year-old Zachary, a saintly-faced, soft-spoken boy, revels in his father's comic antics at the dinner table and often sets them off with well-timed input of his own. Recently, at a huge take-out Chinese dinner that arrived with an ample supply of chopsticks, Zak, with a gleam in his eye, requested a fork. Robin Williams immediately went into a maniacal diatribe, in a staccato Chinese accent, on the etymology and the many uses of the word *fork*, rising to a shrill pitch with "Fork you!"—at which point Mrs. Williams stepped in and quieted things down. There always seems to be room at the table for a friend who shows up, or for the pet of a friend—in one case, a huge greyhound, whose huge feeding dishes were accommodated under the table. The kids greet newcomers and old-comers matter-of-factly and, often, by first name. At home, Mr. Williams may swing, almost imperceptibly, into some singular comic invention. One day last Christmas week, while I was visiting the family in the kitchen, a closed door leading from the kitchen to the cellar, which has sleeping quarters, a television set, and computer games, opened, and Mrs. Williams's twenty-three-year-old niece, Jennifer, and her boyfriend, Rob Sweet, emerged, followed by a couple of other visitors, including a woman from New York, a troubled friend, whom Mrs. Williams had invited to spend the holidays with the family. As the group straggled in, Mr. Williams, in a deep southern accent, began, "Miz Marsha Tubman's underground railroad . . ."

When he isn't in the kitchen, Mr. Williams may be found entrenched in his study, where he keeps an enormous collection of tiny toy soldiers and figures of fantasy—spacemen, samurai, knights, and robots, some of them less than an inch high and wearing micro armor. Near his desk is a *Hook* pinball machine, a gift from Steven Spielberg. (Top scorer in the family on *Hook* is Mrs. Williams, with a 175 million points.) The study also contains Mr. Williams's new state-of-the-art computer, with pedals and Thrustmaster joystick, for playing complicated interactive games. On top of the computer sits a ribboned sailor cap bearing a gold hammer and sickle within a red star and Russian lettering spelling CCCP and the name of the cap's designated ship (a souvenir from *Moscow on the Hudson* filming). From time to time, Cody toddles in, curls up in his father's lap, and concentrates totally on his father's playing of such interactive computer games as *Red Baron* (World War I dogfighting action) or *Star Wars X-Wing* (space combat simulator). One corner of the study is reserved for Zachary and contains his computer and stack of computer games, including his particular favorite, *Lemming Island.* Zachary positions himself in the study regularly with his father and Cody. At such moments, with the three males in the study (forty-something, ten-something, and one-something) serenely lost in their computers, and Marsha and Zelda (thirty-something and four-something) in the kitchen, the Williams household can look perilously close to an updated Norman Rockwell vision.

Ever since the preproduction of *Mrs. Doubtfire,* Mrs. Williams had been warning her husband about how physically taxing the role would be. To keep him in shape, she eventually enlisted the help of a trainer and a yoga instructor, who took turns working out with him. The workouts—running, stretching, biking, roller-blading, and being walked on—provided some perks for the rest of the family and their friends. Everybody got into the act. On weekends, the Williamses and their mob could be seen running or roller-blading or biking in the city's parks or along the marina, often with a child on the back of each parent, and with the latest addition to the family, a three-year-old formerly unwanted white boxer, galumphing behind.

Anybody who has ever visited a movie set knows what it looks like: there's the hardworking crew in jeans and sneakers, with the walkie-talkies, beepers, and tools hanging from their belts, logos on their jackets identifying them with past films they've worked on; the loud-voiced, commanding assistant director, with his walkie-talkie stuck in the back of his belt; the lights, cameras, camera cranes, dollies, catering trucks, snack tables, canvas folding chairs, video monitors, and sound booms. And what it sounds like: "Cut!" "It's a cut." "Check the gate!" "Stand by, please!" "Rolling!" "Sound speed!" "Action!" "Background!" "Stand by to lock it up!" "OK, guys, give the set to grips and electric!" And "MOS!"—the famous "Mit out sound!" sometimes attributed to Erich von Stroheim when he was first starting out as a director in the 1920s. With all this going on, a visitor can feel the kind of concentration, and the energy for the concentration, that is required. Mr. Williams seems always to have energy left over for what is loosely known as "the human consideration." During a lunch break on one of the early filming days, before everybody had got to know everybody else well, Mr. and Mrs. Williams were sitting down to their food at a long table when Mr. Williams noticed that Sally Field was looking around shyly for a place to sit. Immediately, he started yelling, in one of his southern accents, "Get over heah, Norma Rae! You just get right over heah, you mind me now, Norma Rae!"

Mr. Williams has his own special way of retreating at necessary intervals into his private quiet. He might look oblivious of his surroundings, but being around him one learned that he was absorbing every move, every gesture, every expression, every incident that transpired in his presence. Anyone who was around him on or off the set continued to witness sudden, unexpected explosions of what his mother calls his "mission on earth."

To some visiting kids—staring wide-eyed at him in his Mrs. Doubtfire costume and whispering to each other, "That's him," "No, that's her"—in a heavy Jewish accent: "This is Tante Zayde."

To Chris Columbus, after conferring with him between takes: "When in doubt, I'll just do this," putting his hands to the sides of his face à la *Home Alone* Macaulay Culkin.

Out of the blue, as a money saver with a heavy Scottish accent: "I bought clothes. Not many. One loafer for each child."

Out of the blue, as a resentful parent: "We didn't even have air when we were growing up. We had to go out and get our own oxygen and hydrogen."

To the current chairman of the Fox Film Corporation, Peter Chernin, visiting the set one day: in a tone of heavy appreciation, looking over Chernin's dark business suit, "Armani surplus!"

Chernin laughed. He didn't make any mention during his visit of the question of "the honest ending" of *Mrs. Doubtfire*.

Late one night, during a break between shots, I sat with Mr. and Mrs. Williams in his trailer, which was parked near the stage. His *Mrs. Doubtfire* bodysuit and dress and shoes were off for a few minutes. His wig and his latex face were on. Wearing a sleeveless plaid flannel vest and plaid flannel shorts for a brief, cooling respite, he held a Powerbook computer on his lap and was engrossed in playing a game. A few minutes later, he went to the back of the trailer to get dressed again as Mrs. Doubtfire. He was halfway through the filming of the movie. Eighty miles of film were now waiting for editing. There had been a grueling stretch of fifteen- or eighteen-hour days, during which Mrs. Williams worked the same hours as her husband.

I asked her why they had wanted to form their own production company.

"To have the control over when and where we were going to shoot," she replied promptly. "More than anything else, in order to protect Robin."

(SEPTEMBER 20, 1993)

Auteur! Auteur!
(Al Pacino)

The other Friday afternoon, Al Pacino, the fifty-five-year-old super-star with the burning, deep-set eyes, was starting his first key meeting with the composer Howard Shore, whom he had just engaged to do the score for his new movie, tentatively titled *Looking for Richard*. Pacino had paid the film's entire cost, just as he did with his first production, the fifty-two-minute, still-unreleased film he made seven years ago, *The Local Stigmatic*, for which Shore had also composed the score. Pacino's new film is a unique combination of filmed scenes from Shakespeare's *Richard III* interspersed with documentary material about the way actors and directors, along with various people on the street, feel about Shakespeare, Richard III, Acting, and Life. With Pacino producing, directing, and playing the leading roles (Richard III and Al Pacino), eighty hours of film were shot over a three-year period and have now been edited down to two hours.

Pacino had enlisted a mind-boggling cast of big names both for the filmed play scenes and for the documentary. For the first, he had, among others, Kevin Spacey as Buckingham, Alec Baldwin as Clarence, Harris Yulin as King Edward, Estelle Parsons as Queen Margaret, Winona Ryder as Lady Anne, and Aidan Quinn as Richmond. For the second, in addition to random construction workers, truck drivers, tourists, etc., he had Kenneth Branagh, Kevin Kline, James Earl Jones, Rosemary Harris, Peter Brook, F. Murray Abraham, Derek Jacobi, John Gielgud, Vanessa Redgrave, and Emrys Jones and Barbara Everett, a couple of Oxford scholars.

Pacino, wearing an oversized, multicolored ski parka over black shirt and pants, met Shore in the production company's high-floor New York office compartment: glaringly bright picture windows, comfortable sofas, tubular-steel office chairs with dark-blue cushions, a television set, numerous pictures of Pacino's dark-eyed six-year-old daughter, lots of books including *A World History of Photographs, Les Theatres de Paris,* John Gielgud and John Miller's *Acting Shakespeare.* For Shore, a slender, mild-speaking, attentive man several years younger than Pacino, this would be the fortieth movie he'd composed music for. Pacino, practically dancing with enthusiasm and contained energy, popped a cassette into the video monitor. He seemed to merge immediately into what appeared of the movie's start on the screen: the camera panning down over lofty tree branches and cathedral-like spires, and a voice-over proclaiming in elegant English-actor accents:

> Our revels now are ended. These our actors
> (As I foretold you) were all spirits, and
> Are melted into air, into thin air.

Next, the screen revealed Pacino in close-up, unshaven, mustached, his long black hair under a black baseball cap turned backward, and the rest of him in black except for an orange print scarf. "Who's gonna say 'Action' around here? Am I gonna say it?" he asks onscreen. There are mumbles of "You say it," "No, you say it" around him. "You say it," Pacino says to whoever is behind the camera.

Pacino is shown in a Manhattan playground, running around under a basketball hoop playing ball with a city kid. He interviews an electrician on the street who tells him Shakespeare's people talk too much and too fast, and are boring besides. Pacino brings up the subject of Shakespeare's feelings in his plays to a panhandler, who says, unhappily, "If we think words are things, and we have no feelings in our words, then we say things to each other that don't mean anything. But if we felt what we said, we would say less and mean more."

In his office, Pacino, holding a small bottle of water, took a stance in front of Shore. "It's always been my dream to communicate how I feel about Shakespeare," Pacino said. "How we feel."

"I know," Shore said sweetly.

"Even though we're actors, this will have the feeling of an experiment," Pacino said. "We're doing Shakespeare in a traditional way. But we want it to be relevant to us today. It's our quest."

Shore made some notes and smiled. "We'll get the quest feeling by using Elizabethan-style music for the documentary part," he said.

"What's it called—contrapuntally?" Pacino asked.

"Contrapuntally," Shore repeated approvingly.

Pacino, sipping his water, suddenly pointed to the TV screen. "Here," he said. "Now. This is the first time you see that." The image was of Pacino, as Richard III, in a long black cloak, horribly bent over, laboring to drag his crippled self down a long flight of steps. Onscreen, as Richard, Pacino says:

> Now is the winter of our discontent
> Made glorious summer by this son of
> York. . . .

As Pacino continues crookedly making his way down, he goes on:

> But I, that am not shap'd for sportive tricks,
> Nor made to court an amorous looking-glass . . .
> Deform'd, unfinish'd, sent before my time
> Into this breathing world, scarce half made up,
> And that so lamely and unfashionable
> That dogs bark at me as I halt by them. . . .
> And therefore, since I cannot prove a lover
> To entertain these fair well-spoken days,
> I am determined to prove a villain
> And hate the idle pleasures of these days.
> Plots have I laid . . .

"Ha!" Pacino said to Shore. "He says what he's thinking. He's announcing right away what he plans to do—to set his brother Clarence and the King 'in deadly hate the one against the other.' I need help here, Howard. Something to give a hint of what's to come."

Shore gave a conspiratorial smile. "Here we're in the play," he said confidently. "The music will come out of the play."

The screen image again switches to the documentary. The Shakespearean director Peter Brook is saying that the key word should be *discontent.*

"This is a way of letting the audience know what we go through," Pacino said. "It makes them privy to what's going on on a deeper level."

Onscreen, Clarence, Richard's brother, is expressing his love and fidelity to Richard. But Richard is saying:

> Simple plain Clarence, I do love thee so
> That I will shortly send thy soul to heaven.

"That family!" Pacino said. "They're clawing at each other for the throne. How about this old Queen?" On the screen, old Queen Margaret is cursing Richard as "the troubler of the poor world's peace," calling him an "elvish-mark'd, abortive, rooting hog" and a "loathed issue of thy father's loins."

"That's mystical, spooky," Shore said. He gave a theatrical shudder.

"She really, really scares me," Pacino said. He moved up close to the screen. "Here. The scene is The Wooing of Lady Anne."

Onscreen, he is saying, "May I have her . . . Ha!" He pauses for three beats, then says, "But I will not keep her long!"

He looked maniacally satisfied, onscreen and off.

"That will be like a sex dance," Shore said.

"Ha!" Pacino said, and he took another sip of water.

(OCTOBER 9, 1995)

Two Dames
(Maggie Smith and Judi Dench)

Judi Dench and Maggie Smith, both holders of the title Dame Commander of the Most Excellent Order of the British Empire, flew in from London the other day to help promote the Tribeca Film Festival premiere of *Ladies in Lavender*, in which they play sisters. Their plane landed at 5:10 p.m.; by 7 p.m., they were seated in the restaurant of the Ritz-Carlton hotel in Battery Park, valiantly projecting good nature about their mission.

"I so wanted to have a bath in my room," Dame Judi said. "Mog, could you work that metal stopper thing in your tub?"

"No-o-o," Dame Maggie said. "No bath for me, either."

Dame Maggie looked at her wristwatch and said, "It's about midnight for us." She gave a restrained yawn. Dame Judi yawned, too. She said, "So little time. Mog, remember, we must shop."

"Oh, Jude, yes. That large store, Tiff-something. We laughed so much the last time we shopped."

"Yes, yes. Tiffany," Dame Judi said. "If they let us out, we must go back there."

Dame Judi, who has deep-set, almond-shaped blue eyes and salt-and-pepper hair cut very short, wore a cream-colored pants suit; Dame Maggie, her eyes a lighter blue, her hair strawberry blond, full, and thick, had on a black suit. The Dames, born a couple of weeks apart in 1934, met and became friends in 1958, when they were at the Old Vic. Both are Oscar winners. Both had husbands who died a few years ago. Both are a bit under five and a half feet tall.

They ordered and quickly demolished lobster salads and a bottle of white wine. Then a businesslike young PR man arrived and presented them with their schedules for the next two days.

"'Eight a.m. hair/makeup,'" Dame Maggie read, then said, "I might just not go to bed . . ."

The start of the next morning had Dame Maggie giving an interview to *Time*, while Dame Judi traveled to ABC to do Regis and Kelly. Forty-minute drive to ABC. Dame Judi went on last, after Lucy Liu, who had ten minutes in which to talk about working for Unicef, and several pairs of grade-school children ballroom dancing. During her nine minutes, Dame Judi sat, smiling and relaxed, and told Regis that she was cast as a snail at the age of five, but then wanted to be a stage designer, and changed her mind when she saw her older brother go in for acting. "No kidding!" Regis said exuberantly. Kelly asked, "Can you have anyone beheaded when you're a Dame?" The audience laughed and applauded. Regis then showed a clip from *Ladies in Lavender*. He called Dame Judi a "great actress." That was that. Forty-minute drive back to the Ritz.

Together again at the hotel, the Dames did a taped segment for the *Today* show (thirty minutes); a *Daily News* interview and photo session (forty-five minutes); lunch with a *Post* reporter (an hour); a *Los Angeles Times* photo shoot (fifteen minutes) and phone interview (forty-five minutes); and an AARP radio interview (fifteen minutes). At 4:30 p.m., the Dames got into a car again and drove (half an hour) to midtown for an interview on NPR's *Weekend Edition*. Thirty minutes later, they were back in the car. Upon arrival at the hotel, they did what the PR man called a meet and greet, in the lobby. By that point, they said, they were trying to figure out how they might vary their answers to repetitions of the same questions, most of which concerned their long friendship and whether it got in the way of their acting. They'd started out explaining that their relationship helped their acting.

"Then Jude went to just 'No,'" Dame Maggie said.

"We gave up," Dame Judi said. "Tomorrow, Mog, we shop."

The second morning was given over to "Japanese Distributor Interview Contacts," which meant talking, via an interpreter, to Japanese journalists.

"Their questions were very long and very detailed," Dame Judi said. "They got things all mixed up, but one of them was charming."

At 1:20 p.m., it was up to the Municipal Building, for *The Leonard Lopate Show*, on WNYC (forty minutes). At 4 p.m., back at the hotel, they were photographed, after a long wait, for the *Washington Post*, posing back to back, then face to face. By 5:30 p.m., at the Bloomberg Building on Park Avenue, they were being greeted by Charlie Rose. He started laughing as soon as he saw them. "Can I say, 'two Dames'?" he asked. He broke himself up, laughing. Later, he said, "I can tell this is a real friendship."

It was 7 p.m. En route in the car to CNN, on Columbus Circle, the Dames craned their necks to look for Tiffany's. The driver said it was further east. "Oh, down there's where Rumpelmayer's used to be. Rumpelmayer's is gone," Dame Maggie said sadly. "That lovely counter! It was so divine."

"Where is Barneys?" Dame Judi asked. "Oh, after CNN I suppose it will be too late to shop."

Dame Maggie slumped. "I'd like to turn into a cat right now!" she said. *"Yeeehphph!"* she spat, pretending to claw.

The PR man said that they would be on CNN's *Showbiz Tonight*, live, following an interview with Lassie. At 7:40 p.m., the Dames went into the studio.

"You guys were perfectly cast as sisters," the CNN correspondent said. "How long have you guys known each other?"

(MAY 9, 2005)

II

WRITERS

(From right) Lillian, Ernest Hemingway, and his sons
Gregory and Patrick, in Ketchum, Iowa, in 1947.

How Do You Like
It Now, Gentlemen?
(Ernest Hemingway)

Ernest Hemingway, who may well be the greatest living American novelist and short-story writer, rarely comes to New York. He spends most of his time on a farm, the Finca Vigia, nine miles outside Havana, with his wife, a domestic staff of nine, fifty-two cats, sixteen dogs, a couple of hundred pigeons, and three cows. When he does come to New York, it is only because he has to pass through it on his way somewhere else. Not long ago, on his way to Europe, he stopped in New York for a few days. I had written to him asking if I might see him when he came to town, and he had sent me a typewritten letter saying that would be fine and suggesting that I meet his plane at the airport. "I don't want to see anybody I don't like, nor have publicity, nor be tied up all the time," he went on. "Want to go to the Bronx Zoo, Metropolitan Museum, Museum of Modern Art, ditto of Natural History, and see a fight. Want to see the good Breugel at the Met, the one, no two, fine Goyas, and Mr. El Greco's *Toledo*. Don't want to go to Toots Shor's. Am going to try to get into town and out without having to shoot my mouth off. I want to give the joints a miss. Not seeing news people is not a pose. It is only to have time to see your friends." In pencil, he added, "Time is the least thing we have of."

Time did not seem to be pressing Hemingway the day he flew in from Havana. He was to arrive at Idlewild late in the afternoon, and I went out to meet him. His plane had landed by the time I got there, and I found him standing at a gate waiting for his luggage and for his wife, who had gone to attend to it. He had one arm around a scuffed, dilapidated briefcase pasted up with travel stickers. He had the other around a wiry little man whose forehead was covered with enormous beads of perspiration. Hemingway was wearing a red plaid wool shirt, a figured wool necktie, a tan wool sweater-vest, a brown tweed jacket tight across the back and with sleeves too short for his arms, gray flannel slacks, argyle socks, and loafers, and he looked bearish, cordial, and constricted. His hair, which was very long in back, was gray, except at the temples, where it was white; his mustache was white, and he had a ragged, half-inch full white beard. There was a bump about the size of a walnut over his left eye. He was wearing steel-rimmed spectacles, with a piece of paper under the nosepiece. He was in no hurry to get into Manhattan. He crooked the arm around the briefcase into a tight hug and said that it contained the unfinished manuscript of his new book, *Across the River and into the Trees.* He crooked the arm around the wiry little man into a tight hug and said he had been his seat companion on the flight. The man's name, as I got it in a mumbled introduction, was Myers, and he was returning from a business trip to Cuba. Myers made a slight attempt to dislodge himself from the embrace, but Hemingway held on to him affectionately.

"He read book all way up on plane," Hemingway said. He spoke with a perceptible midwestern accent, despite the Indian talk. "He like book, I think," he added, giving Myers a little shake and beaming down at him.

"Whew!" said Myers.

"Book too much for him," Hemingway said. "Book start slow, then increase in pace till it becomes impossible to stand. I bring emotion up to where you can't stand it, then we level off, so we won't have to provide oxygen tents for the readers. Book is like engine. We have to slack her off gradually."

"Whew!" said Myers.

Hemingway released him. "Not trying for no-hit game in book," he said. "Going to win maybe twelve to nothing or maybe twelve to eleven."

Myers looked puzzled.

"She's better book than *Farewell*," Hemingway said. "I think this is best one, but you are always prejudiced, I guess. Especially if you want to be champion." He shook Myers's hand. "Much thanks for reading book," he said.

"Pleasure," Myers said, and walked off unsteadily.

Hemingway watched him go, and then turned to me. "After you finish a book, you know, you're dead," he said moodily. "But no one knows you're dead. All they see is the irresponsibility that comes in after the terrible responsibility of writing." He said he felt tired but was in good shape physically; he had brought his weight down to two hundred and eight, and his blood pressure was down too. He had considerable rewriting to do on his book, and he was determined to keep at it until he was absolutely satisfied. "They can't yank novelist like they can pitcher," he said. "Novelist has to go the full nine, even if it kills him."

We were joined by Hemingway's wife, Mary, a small, energetic, cheerful woman with close-cropped blond hair, who was wearing a long, belted mink coat. A porter pushing a cart heaped with luggage followed her. "Papa, everything is here," she said to Hemingway. "Now we ought to get going, Papa." He assumed the air of a man who was not going to be rushed. Slowly, he counted the pieces of luggage. There were fourteen, half of them, Mrs. Hemingway told me, extra-large Val-paks designed by her husband and bearing his coat of arms, also de-signed by him—a geometric design. When Hemingway had finished counting, his wife suggested that he tell the porter where to put the luggage. Hemingway told the porter to stay right there and watch it; then he turned to his wife and said, "Let's not crowd, honey. Order of the day is to have a drink first."

We went into the airport cocktail lounge and stood at the bar. Hem-ingway put his briefcase down on a chromium stool and pulled it close to him. He ordered bourbon and water. Mrs. Hemingway said she would have the same, and I ordered a cup of coffee. Hemingway told the bartender to bring double bourbons. He waited for the drinks with impatience, holding on to the bar with both hands and humming an unrecognizable tune. Mrs. Hemingway said she hoped it wouldn't be dark by the time they got to New York. Hemingway said it wouldn't make any difference to him, because New York was a rough town, a phony town, a town that was the same in the dark as it was in the light, and he was not exactly overjoyed to be going there anyway. What he was looking forward to, he said, was Venice. "Where I like it is out west in Wyoming, Montana, and Idaho, and I like Cuba and Paris and around Venice," he said. "Westport gives me the horrors." Mrs. Hemingway lit a cigarette and handed me the pack. I passed it along to him, but he said he didn't smoke. Smoking ruins his sense of smell, a sense he finds completely indispensable for hunting. "Cigarettes smell so awful to you when you have a nose that can truly smell," he said, and laughed, hunching his shoulders and raising the back of his fist to his face, as though he expected somebody to hit him. Then he enumerated elk, deer, possum, and coon as some of the things he can truly smell.

The bartender brought the drinks. Hemingway took several large swallows and said he gets along fine with animals, sometimes better than with human beings. In Montana, once, he lived with a bear, and the bear slept with him, got drunk with him, and was a close friend. He asked me whether there were still bears at the Bronx Zoo, and I said I didn't know but I was pretty sure there were bears at the Central Park Zoo. "I always used to go to the Bronx Zoo with Granny Rice," he said. "I love to go to the zoo. But not on Sunday. I don't like to see the people making fun of the animals, when it should be the other way around." Mrs. Hemingway took a small notebook out of her purse and opened it; she told me she had made a list of chores she and her husband had to do before their boat sailed. They included buying a hot-water-bottle cover, an elementary Italian grammar, a short history of Italy, and, for Hemingway, four woolen undershirts, four cotton underpants, two woolen underpants, bedroom slippers, a belt, and a coat. "Papa has never had a coat," she said. "We've got to buy Papa a coat." Hemingway grunted and leaned against the bar. "A nice, rainproof coat," Mrs. Hemingway said. "And he's got to get his glasses fixed. He needs some good soft padding for the nosepiece. It cuts him up brutally. He's had that same piece of paper under the nosepiece for weeks. When he really wants to get cleaned up, he changes the paper." Hemingway grunted again.

The bartender came up, and Hemingway asked him to bring another round of drinks. Then he said, "First thing we do, Mary, as soon as we hit hotel, is call up the Kraut." "The Kraut," he told me, with that same fist-to-the-face laugh, is his affectionate term for Marlene Dietrich, an old friend, and is part of a large vocabulary of special code terms and speech mannerisms indigenous to the Finca Vigia. "We have a lot of fun talking a sort of joke language," he said.

"First we call Marlene, and then we order caviar and champagne, Papa," Mrs. Hemingway said. "I've been waiting months for that caviar and champagne."

"The Kraut, caviar, and champagne," Hemingway said slowly, as though he were memorizing a difficult set of military orders. He finished his drink and gave the bartender a repeat nod, and then he turned to me. "You want to go with me to buy coat?" he asked.

"Buy coat and get glasses fixed," Mrs. Hemingway said.

I said I would be happy to help him do both, and then I reminded him that he had said he wanted to see a fight. The only fight that week, I had learned from a friend who knows all about fights, was at the St. Nicholas Arena that night. I said that my friend had four tickets and would like to take all of us. Hemingway wanted to know who was fighting. When I told him, he said they were bums. Bums, Mrs. Hemingway repeated, and added that they had better fighters in Cuba. Hemingway gave me a long, reproachful look. "Daughter, you've got to learn that a bad fight is worse than no fight," he said. We would all go to a fight when he got back from Europe, he said, because it was absolutely necessary to go to several good fights a year. "If you quit going for too long a time, then you never go near them," he said. "That would be very dangerous." He was interrupted by a brief fit of coughing.

"Finally," he concluded, "you end up in one room and won't move."

After dallying at the bar a while longer, the Hemingways asked me to go along with them to their hotel. Hemingway ordered the luggage loaded into one taxi, and the three of us got into another. It was dark now. As we drove along the boulevard, Hemingway watched the road carefully. Mrs. Hemingway told me that he always watches the road, usually from the front seat. It is a habit he got into during the First World War. I asked them what they planned to do in Europe. They said they were going to stay a week or so in Paris, and then drive to Venice.

"I love to go back to Paris," Hemingway said, his eyes still fixed on the road. "Am going in the back door and have no interviews and no publicity and never get a haircut, like in the old days. Want to go to cafés where I know no one but one waiter and his replacement, see all the new pictures and the old ones, go to the bike races and the fights, and see the new riders and fighters. Find good, cheap restaurants where you can keep your own napkin. Walk over all the town and see where we made our mistakes and where we had our few bright ideas. And learn the form and try and pick winners in the blue, smoky afternoons, and then go out the next day to play them at Auteuil and Enghien."

"Papa is a good handicapper," Mrs. Hemingway said.

"When I know the form," he said.

We were crossing the Queensboro Bridge, and we had a good view of the Manhattan skyline. The lights were on in the tall office buildings. Hemingway did not seem to be impressed. "This ain't my town," he said. "It's a town you come to for a short time. It's murder." Paris is like another home to him, he said. "I am as lonesome and as happy as I can be in that town we lived in and worked and learned and grew up in, and then fought our way back into." Venice is another of his home towns. The last time he and his wife were in Italy, they lived for four months in Venice and the Cortina Valley, and he went hunting, and now he had put the locale and some of the people in the book he was writing. "Italy was so damned wonderful," he said. "It was sort of like having died and gone to Heaven, a place you'd figured never to see."

Mrs. Hemingway said that she had broken her right ankle skiing there but that she planned to go skiing there again. Hemingway was hospitalized in Padua with an eye infection, which developed into erysipelas, but he wanted to go back to Italy and wanted to see his many good friends there. He was looking forward to seeing the gondoliers on a windy day; the Gritti Palace hotel, where they stayed during their last visit; and the Locanda Cipriani, an old inn on Torcello, an island in the lagoon northeast of Venice on which some of the original Venetians lived before they built Venice. About seventy people live on Torcello, and the men are professional duck hunters. While there, Hemingway went duck-hunting a lot with the gardener of the old inn. "We'd go around through the canals and jump-shoot, and I'd walk the prairies at low tide for snipe," he said. "It was a big fly route for ducks that came all the way down from the Pripet Marshes. I shot good and thus became a respected local character. They have some sort of little bird that comes through, after eating grapes in the north, on his way to eat grapes in the south. The local characters sometimes shot them sitting, and I occasionally shot them flying. Once, I shot two high doubles, rights and lefts, in a row, and the gardener cried with emotion. Coming home, I shot a high duck against the rising moon and dropped him in the canal. That precipitated an emotional crisis I thought I would never get him out of but did, with about a pint of

Chianti. We each took a pint out with us. I drank mine to keep warm coming home. He drank his when overcome by emotion." We were silent for a while, and then Hemingway said, "Venice was lovely."

The Hemingways were stopping at the Sherry-Netherland. Hemingway registered and told the room clerk that he did not want any announcement made of his arrival and did not want any visitors, or any telephone calls either, except from Miss Dietrich. Then we went up to the suite—living room, bedroom, and serving pantry—that had been reserved for them. Hemingway paused at the entrance and scouted the living room. It was large, decorated in garish colors, and furnished with imitation Chippendale furniture and an imitation fireplace containing imitation coals.

"Joint looks OK," he said. "Guess they call this the Chinese Gothic Room." He moved in and took the room.

Mrs. Hemingway went over to a bookcase and held up a sample of its contents. "Look, Papa," she said. "They're phony. They're pasteboard backs, Papa. They're not real books."

Hemingway put his briefcase down on a bright-red couch and advanced on the bookcase, then slowly, with expression, read the titles aloud—*Elementary Economics, Government of the United States, Sweden, the Land and the People,* and *Sleep in Peace,* by Phyllis Bentley. "I think we are an outfit headed for extinction," he said, starting to take off his necktie.

After getting his necktie off, and then his jacket, Hemingway handed them to his wife, who went into the bedroom, saying she was going to unpack. He unbuttoned his collar and went over to the telephone. "Got to call the Kraut," he said. He telephoned the Plaza and asked for Miss Dietrich. She was out, and he left word for her to come over for supper. Then he called room service and ordered caviar and a couple of bottles of Perrier-Jouët, *brut*.

Hemingway went back to the bookcase and stood there stiffly, as though he could not decide what to do with himself. He looked at the pasteboard backs again and said, "Phony, just like the town." I said that there was a tremendous amount of talk about him these days in literary circles—that the critics seemed to be talking and writing definitively not only about the work he had done but about the work he was going to do. He said that of all the people he did not wish to see in New York, the people he wished least to see were the critics. "They are like those people who go to ball games and can't tell the players without a score card," he said. "I am not worried about what anybody I do not like might do. What the hell! If they can do you harm, let them do it. It is like being a third baseman and protesting because they hit line drives to you. Line drives are regrettable, but to be expected." The closest competitors of the critics among those he wished least to see, he said, were certain writers who wrote books about the war when they had not seen anything of war at first hand. "They are just like an outfielder who will drop a fly on you when you have pitched to have the batter hit a high fly to that outfielder, or when they're pitching they try to strike everybody out." When he pitched, he said, he never struck out anybody, except under extreme necessity. "I knew I had only so many fast balls in that arm," he said. "Would make them pop to short instead, or fly out, or hit it on the ground, bouncing."

A waiter arrived with the caviar and champagne, and Hemingway told him to open one of the bottles. Mrs. Hemingway came in from the bedroom and said she couldn't find his toothbrush. He said that he didn't know where it was but that he could easily buy another. Mrs. Hemingway said all right, and went back into the bedroom. Hemingway poured two glasses of champagne, gave one to me, and picked up the other one and took a sip. The waiter watched him anxiously. Hemingway hunched his shoulders and said something in Spanish to the waiter. They both laughed, and the waiter left. Hemingway took his glass over to the red couch and sat down, and I sat in a chair opposite him.

"I can remember feeling so awful about the first war that I couldn't write about it for ten years," he said, suddenly very angry. "The wound combat makes in you, as a writer, is a very slow-healing one. I wrote three stories about it in the old days—'In Another Country,' 'A Way You'll Never Be,' and 'Now I Lay Me.'" He mentioned a war writer who, he said, was apparently thinking of himself as Tolstoy, but who'd be able to play Tolstoy only on the Bryn Mawr field-hockey team. "He never hears a shot fired in anger, and he sets out to beat who? Tolstoy, an artillery officer who fought at Sevastopol, who knew his stuff, who was a hell of a man anywhere you put him—bed, bar, in an empty room where he had to think. I started out very quiet and I beat Mr. Turgenev.

Then I trained hard and I beat Mr. de Maupassant. I've fought two draws with Mr. Stendhal, and I think I had an edge in the last one. But nobody's going to get me in any ring with Mr. Tolstoy unless I'm crazy or I keep getting better."

He began his new book as a short story. "Then I couldn't stop it. It went straight on into a novel," he said. "That's the way all my novels got started. When I was twenty-five, I read novels by Somersault Maugham and Stephen St. Vixen Benét." He laughed hoarsely. "They had written novels, and I was ashamed because I had not written any novels. So I wrote *The Sun* when I was twenty-seven, and I wrote it in six weeks, starting on my birthday, July twenty-first, in Valencia, and finishing it September sixth, in Paris. But it was really lousy and the rewriting took nearly five months. Maybe that will encourage young writers so they won't have to go get advice from their psychoanalysts. Analyst once wrote me, What did I learn from psychoanalysts? I answered, Very little but hope they had learned as much as they were able to understand from my published works. You never saw a counterpuncher who was punchy. Never lead against a hitter unless you can outhit him. Crowd a boxer, and take everything he has, to get inside. Duck a swing. Block a hook. And counter a jab with everything you own. Papa's delivery of hard-learned facts of life."

Hemingway poured himself another glass of champagne. He always wrote in longhand, he said, but he recently bought a tape recorder and was trying to get up the courage to use it. "I'd like to learn talk machine," he said. "You just tell talk machine anything you want and get secretary to type it out." He writes without facility, except for dialogue. "When the people are talking, I can hardly write it fast enough or keep up with it, but with an almost unbearable high manifold pleasure. I put more inches on than she will take, and then fly her as near as I know to how she should be flown, only flying as crazy as really good pilots fly crazy sometimes. Most of the time flying conservatively but with an awfully fast airplane that makes up for the conservatism. That way, you live longer. I mean your writing lives longer. How do you like it now, gentlemen?" The question seemed to have some special significance for him, but he did not bother to explain it.

I wanted to know whether, in his opinion, the new book was different from his others, and he gave me another long, reproachful look. "What do you think?" he said after a moment. "You don't expect me to write *The Farewell to Arms Boys in Addis Ababa*, do you? Or *The Farewell to Arms Boys Take a Gunboat?*" The book is about the command level in the Second World War. "I am not interested in the GI who wasn't one," he said, suddenly angry again. "Or the injustices done to *me*, with a capital *M*. I am interested in the goddamn sad science of war." The new novel has a good deal of profanity in it. "That's because in war they talk profane, although I always try to talk gently," he said, sounding like a man who is trying to believe what he is saying. "I think I've got *Farewell* beat in this one," he went on. He touched his briefcase. "It hasn't got the youth and the ignorance." Then he asked wearily, "How do you like it now, gentlemen?"

There was a knock at the door, and Hemingway got up quickly and opened it. It was Miss Dietrich. Their reunion was a happy one. Mrs. Hemingway came out of the bedroom and greeted the guest enthusiastically. Miss Dietrich stood back from Hemingway and looked at him with approval. "Papa, you look wonderful," she said slowly.

"I sure missed you, daughter," said Hemingway. He raised his fist to his face, and his shoulders shook as he laughed silently.

Miss Dietrich was wearing a mink coat. She sighed loudly, took off the coat, and handed it to Mrs. Hemingway. Then she sighed again and sat down in an overstuffed chair. Hemingway poured a glass of champagne, brought it to her, and refilled the other glasses.

"The Kraut's the best that ever came into the ring," he said as he handed me my glass. Then he pulled a chair up beside Miss Dietrich's, and they compared notes on friends and on themselves. They talked about theatre and motion-picture people, one of whom, a man, Hemingway referred to as a "sea heel."

Miss Dietrich wanted to know what a "sea heel" was.

"The sea is bigger than the land," he told her.

Mrs. Hemingway went into the serving pantry and came out in a few minutes with caviar spread on toast.

"Mary, I am telling Papa how I have to behave because I am a grandmother," Miss Dietrich said, taking a piece of toast. "I have to think always of the children. You know, Papa?"

Hemingway gave a sympathetic grunt, and Miss Dietrich took from her purse some snapshots of her grandson and passed them around.

He was eighteen months old, she told us. Hemingway said he looked like a winner, and that he would be proud to own a piece of him if he ever got into the ring.

Miss Dietrich said that her daughter was going to have another child soon. "I'll be a grandmother *again*, Papa," she said.

Hemingway gave her a bleak look. "I'm going to be a grandfather in a few months," he said. "My son Bumby's wife."

Mrs. Hemingway told me that Bumby is the nickname of her husband's eldest son, John, an Army captain stationed in Berlin. His two other sons, she said, are Patrick, known as Mouse, who is a twenty-one-year-old sophomore at Harvard and is planning to get married in June, and Gregory, known as Gigi, who is eighteen and a freshman at St. John's, at Annapolis. In addition to the present Mrs. Hemingway, Patrick is going to invite to his wedding his and Gigi's mother, Pauline Pfeiffer, who was Hemingway's second wife. Bumby's mother and Hemingway's first wife was Hadley Richardson, who is now Mrs. Paul Scott Mowrer, and Hemingway's third wife was Martha Gellhorn.

"Everything you do, you do for the sake of the children," Miss Dietrich said.

"Everything for the children," Hemingway said. He refilled Miss Dietrich's glass.

"Thank you, Papa," she said, and sighed. She lives at the Plaza, she told him, but spends a good deal of her time at the apartment of her daughter, who lives on Third Avenue. "Papa, you should see me when they go out," she said, and took a sip of champagne. "I'm the babysitter. As soon as they leave the house, I go around and look in all the corners and straighten the drawers and clean up. I can't stand a house that isn't neat and clean. I go around in all the corners with towels I bring with me from the Plaza, and I clean up the whole house. Then they come home at one or two in the morning, and I take the dirty towels and some of the baby's things that need washing, and, with my bundle over my shoulder, I go out and get a taxi, and the driver, he thinks I am this old washerwoman from Third Avenue, and he takes me in the taxi and talks to me with sympathy, so I am afraid to let him take me to the Plaza. I get out a block away from the Plaza and I walk home with my bundle and I wash the baby's things, and then I go to sleep."

"Daughter, you're hitting them with the bases loaded," Hemingway said earnestly.

There was a ring at the door, and a bellboy brought in a florist's box. Mrs. Hemingway opened it and took out some green orchids and read the card: "Love from Adeline." "Who the hell is Adeline?" she asked. Nobody knew. Mrs. Hemingway put the flowers in a vase and said it was time to order supper.

As we ate, the Hemingways and Miss Dietrich talked about the war. All three had seen it at first hand. Mrs. Hemingway, who, as Mary Welsh, was a *Time* correspondent in London, met Hemingway there during the war, and both saw a good deal of Miss Dietrich there and, later on, in Paris. Miss Dietrich was a USO entertainer and performed on almost every front in the European theatre. She grew a little sad as she talked about the war. She had loved entertaining the troops, and the spirit overseas, she said, was the best she had ever found in people anywhere. "Everybody was the way people should be all the time," she continued. "Not mean and afraid but good to each other."

Hemingway raised his glass in a toast to her.

"I've finally figured out why Papa sometimes gets mean now that the war is over," Mrs. Hemingway said. "It's because there is no occasion for him to be valorous in peacetime."

"It was different in the war," Miss Dietrich said. "People were not so selfish and they helped each other."

Hemingway asked her about some recordings she had made, during the war, of popular American songs with lyrics translated into German, and said he'd like to have them. "I'll give you manuscript of new book for recordings if you want to trade even, daughter," he told her.

"Papa, I don't trade with you. I love you," said Miss Dietrich.

"You're the best that ever came into the ring," Hemingway said.

Mrs. Hemingway said, "Who the hell is Adeline?"

Late the next morning, I was awakened by a telephone call from Hemingway, who asked me to come right over to the hotel. He sounded urgent. I had a fast cup of coffee, and when I turned up at the suite, I found the door open and walked in. Hemingway was talking on the telephone. He was wearing an orange plaid bathrobe that looked too small for him and he had a glass of champagne in one hand. His beard looked more scraggly than it had the day before. "My boy Patrick is coming down from Harvard and I'd like to reserve a room for him," he was saying into the telephone. "*P*, as in *Patrick*." He paused and took a sip of champagne. "Much obliged. He'll be down from Harvard."

Hemingway hung up and from his bathrobe pocket took a box of pills. He shook two of them into the palm of his hand and downed them with a mouthful of champagne. He told me that he had been up since six, that his wife was still asleep, and that he had done enough work for that morning and wanted to talk, an activity he finds relaxing. He always wakes at daybreak, he explained, because his eyelids are especially thin and his eyes especially sensitive to light. "I have seen all the sunrises there have been in my life, and that's half a hundred years," he said. He had done considerable revision that morning on the manuscript. "I wake up in the morning and my mind starts making sentences, and I have to get rid of them fast—talk them or write them down," he said. "How did you like the Kraut?"

Very much, I said.

"I love the Kraut and I love Ingrid," he said. "If I weren't married to Miss Mary and didn't love Miss Mary, I would try to hook up with either of them. Each one has what the other hasn't. And what each has, I love very much." For a moment, he looked bewildered, and then he said quickly, "Would never marry an actress, on account they have their careers and they work bad hours."

I asked him whether he still wanted to buy a coat, and he said sure but he didn't want to be rushed or crowded and it was cold outside. He went over to the vase of green orchids and looked at the card, which was still attached to them. Adeline, he said, was the name of nobody he knew or ever would know, if he could help it. On a serving table near the couch were two champagne coolers, each containing ice and a bottle. He carried his glass over there and held up one of the bottles and squinted at it. It was empty. He put it back in the cooler, head down. Then he opened the other bottle, and as he poured some champagne into his glass, he sang, "'So feed me am-mu-nition, keep me in the Third Division, your dog-face soldier boy's OK.'" Breaking off, he said, "Song of the Third Infantry Division. I like this song when I need music inside myself to go on. I love all music, even opera. But I have no talent for it and cannot sing. I have a perfect goddamn ear for music, but I can't play any instrument by ear, not even the piano. My mother used to make me play the cello. She took me out of school one year to learn the cello, when I wanted to be out in the fresh air playing football. She wanted to have chamber music in the house."

His briefcase was lying open on a chair near the desk, and the manuscript pages were protruding from it; someone seemed to have stuffed them into the briefcase without much care. Hemingway told me that he had been cutting the manuscript. "The test of a book is how much good stuff you can throw away," he said. "When I'm writing it, I'm just as proud as a goddamn lion. I use the oldest words in the English language. People think I'm an ignorant bastard who doesn't know the ten-dollar words. I know the ten-dollar words. There are older and better words which if you arrange them in the proper combination you make it stick. Remember, anybody who pulls his erudition or education on you hasn't any. Also, daughter, remember that I never carried Teddy bears to bed with me since I was four. Now, with seventy-eight-year-old grandmothers taking advantage of loopholes in the GI Bill of Rights whereby a gold-star mother can receive her son's education, I thought of establishing a scholarship and sending myself to Harvard, because my aunt Arabelle has always felt very bad that I am the only Hemingway boy that never went to college. But I have been so busy I have not got around to it. I only went to high school and a couple of military cram courses, and never took French. I began to learn to read French by reading the AP story in the French paper after reading the American AP story, and finally learned to read it by reading accounts of things I had seen—*les événements sportifs*—and from that and *les crimes* it was only a jump to Dr. de Maupassant, who wrote about things I had seen or could understand. Dumas, Daudet, Stendhal, who when I read him I knew that was the way I wanted to be able to write. Mr. Flaubert, who always threw them perfectly straight, hard, high, and inside. Then Mr. Baudelaire, that I learned my knuckle ball from, and Mr. Rimbaud, who never threw a fast ball in his life. Mr. Gide and Mr. Valéry I couldn't learn from. I think Mr. Valéry was too smart for me. Like Jack Britton and Benny Leonard."

Jack Britton, he continued, was a fighter he admired very much. "Jack Britton kept on his toes and moved around and never let them hit him solid," he said. "I like to keep on my toes and never let them hit me solid. Never lead against a hitter unless you can outhit him. Crowd a boxer," he said, assuming a boxing stance and holding his right hand, which was grasping the champagne glass, close to his chest.

With his left hand, he punched at the air, saying, "Remember. Duck a swing. Block a hook. And counter a jab with everything you own." He straightened up and looked thoughtfully at his glass. Then he said, "One time, I asked Jack, speaking of a fight with Benny Leonard, 'How did you handle Benny so easy, Jack?' 'Ernie,' he said, 'Benny is an awfully smart boxer. All the time he's boxing, he's thinking. All the time he was thinking, I was hitting him.'" Hemingway gave a hoarse laugh, as though he had heard the story for the first time. "Jack moved very geometrically pure, never one-hundredth of an inch too much. No one ever got a solid shot at him. Wasn't anybody he couldn't hit any time he wanted to." He laughed again. "All the time he was thinking, I was hitting him." The anecdote, he told me, had been in the original version of his short story "Fifty Grand," but Scott Fitzgerald had persuaded him to take it out. "Scott thought everybody knew about it, when only Jack Britton and I knew about it, because Jack told it to me," he said. "So Scott told me to take it out. I didn't want to, but Scott was a successful writer and a writer I respected, so I listened to him and took it out."

Hemingway sat down on the couch and nodded his head up and down sharply a couple of times to get my attention. "As you get older, it is harder to have heroes, but it is sort of necessary," he said. "I have a cat named Boise, who wants to be a human being," he went on slowly, lowering his voice to a kind of grumble. "So Boise eats everything that human beings eat. He chews vitamin B complex capsules, which are as bitter as aloes. He thinks I am holding out on him because I won't give him blood-pressure tablets, and because I let him go to sleep without Seconal." He gave a short, rumbling laugh. "I am a strange old man," he said. "How do you like it now, gentlemen?"

Fifty, Hemingway said, on reconsideration, is not supposed to be old. "It is sort of fun to be fifty and feel you are going to defend the title again," he said. "I won it in the twenties and defended it in the thirties and the forties, and I don't mind at all defending it in the fifties."

After a while, Mrs. Hemingway came into the room. She was wearing gray flannel slacks and a white blouse, and she said she felt wonderful, because she had had her first hot bath in six months. She walked over to the green orchids and looked at the card. "Who *is* Adeline?" she asked. Then she abandoned the problem and said she was going out to do her errands and suggested that Hemingway get dressed and go out and do his. He said that it was lunchtime and that if they went out then, they would have to stop someplace for lunch, whereas if they had lunch sent up to the room, they might save time. Mrs. Hemingway said she would order lunch while he got dressed. Still holding his glass, he reluctantly got up from the couch. Then he finished his drink and went into the bedroom. By the time he came out—wearing the same outfit as the day before, except for a blue shirt with a button-down collar—a waiter had set the table for our lunch. We couldn't have lunch without a bottle of Tavel, Hemingway said, and we waited until the waiter had brought it before starting to eat.

Hemingway began with oysters, and he chewed each one very thoroughly. "Eat good and digest good," he told us.

"Papa, please get glasses fixed," Mrs. Hemingway said.

He nodded. Then he nodded a few times at me—a repetition of the sign for attention. "What I want to be when I am old is a wise old man who won't bore," he said, then paused while the waiter set a plate of asparagus and an artichoke before him and poured the Tavel. Hemingway tasted the wine and gave the waiter a nod. "I'd like to see all the new fighters, horses, ballets, bike riders, dames, bullfighters, painters, airplanes, sons of bitches, café characters, big international whores, restaurants, years of wine, newsreels, and never have to write a line about any of it," he said. "I'd like to write lots of letters to my friends and get back letters. Would like to be able to make love good until I was eighty-five, the way Clemenceau could. And what I would like to be is not Bernie Baruch. I wouldn't sit on park benches, although I might go around the park once in a while to feed the pigeons, and also I wouldn't have any long beard, so there could be an old man didn't look like Shaw." He stopped and ran the back of his hand along his beard, and looked around the room reflectively. "Have never met Mr. Shaw," he said. "Never been to Niagara Falls, either. Anyway, I would take up harness racing. You aren't up near the top at that until you're over seventy-five. Then I could get me a good young ball club, maybe, like Mr. Mack. Only I wouldn't signal with a program—so as to break the pattern. Haven't figured out yet what I would signal with. And when that's over, I'll make the prettiest corpse since Pretty Boy Floyd. Only suckers worry about saving their souls. Who the hell should care about saving his soul when it is a man's duty to lose it intelligently, the way you would sell a position you were defending, if you could not hold it, as expensively as possible, trying to make it the most expensive position that was ever sold. It isn't hard to die." He opened his mouth and laughed, at first soundlessly and then loudly. "No more worries," he said. With his fingers, he picked up a long spear of asparagus and looked at it without enthusiasm. "It takes a pretty good man to make any sense when he's dying," he said.

Mrs. Hemingway had finished eating, and she quickly finished her wine. Hemingway slowly finished his. I looked at my wristwatch and found that it was almost three. The waiter started clearing the table, and we all got up. Hemingway stood looking sadly at the bottle of champagne, which was not yet empty. Mrs. Hemingway put on her coat, and I put on mine.

"The half bottle of champagne is the enemy of man," Hemingway said. We all sat down again.

"If I have any money, I can't think of any better way of spending money than on champagne," Hemingway said, pouring some.

When the champagne was gone, we left the suite. Downstairs, Mrs. Hemingway told us to remember to get glasses fixed, and scooted away.

Hemingway balked for a moment in front of the hotel. It was a cool, cloudy day. This was not good weather for him to be out in, he said sulkily, adding that his throat felt kind of sore. I asked him if he wanted to see a doctor. He said no. "I never trust a doctor I have to pay," he said, and started across Fifth Avenue. A flock of pigeons flew by. He stopped, looked up, and aimed an imaginary rifle at them. He pulled the trigger, and then looked disappointed. "Very difficult shot," he said. He turned quickly and pretended to shoot again. "Easy shot," he said. "Look!" He pointed to a spot on the pavement. He seemed to be feeling better, but not much better.

I asked him if he wanted to stop first at his optician's. He said no. I mentioned the coat. He shrugged. Mrs. Hemingway had suggested that he look for a coat at Abercrombie & Fitch, so I mentioned Abercrombie & Fitch. He shrugged again and lumbered slowly over to a taxi, and we started down Fifth Avenue in the afternoon traffic. At the corner of Fifty-Fourth, we stopped on a signal from the traffic cop. Hemingway growled. "I love to see an Irish cop being cold," he said. "Give you eight to one he was an MP in the war. Very skillful cop. Feints and fakes good. Cops are not like they are in the Hellinger movies.

Only once in a while." We started up again, and he showed me where he once walked across Fifth Avenue with Scott Fitzgerald. "Scott wasn't at Princeton anymore, but he was still talking football," he said, without animation. "The ambition of Scott's life was to be on the football team. I said, 'Scott, why don't you cut out this football?' I said, 'Come on, boy.' He said, 'You're crazy.' That's the end of that story. If you can't get through traffic, how the hell are you gonna get through the line? But I am not Thomas Mann," he added. "Get another opinion."

By the time we reached Abercrombie's, Hemingway was moody again. He got out of the taxi reluctantly and reluctantly entered the store. I asked him whether he wanted to look at a coat first or something else.

"Coat," he said unhappily.

In the elevator, Hemingway looked even bigger and bulkier than he had before, and his face had the expression of a man who is being forcibly subjected to the worst kind of misery. A middle-aged woman standing next to him stared at his scraggly white beard with obvious alarm and disapproval. "Good Christ!" Hemingway said suddenly, in the silence of the elevator, and the middle-aged woman looked down at her feet.

The doors opened at our floor, and we got out and headed for a rack of topcoats. A tall, dapper clerk approached us, and Hemingway shoved his hands into his pants pockets and crouched forward. "I think I still have credit in this joint," he said to the clerk.

The clerk cleared his throat. "Yes, sir," he said.

"Want to see coat," Hemingway said menacingly.

"Yes, sir," said the clerk. "What kind of coat did you wish to see, sir?"

"That one." He pointed to a straight-hanging, beltless tan gabardine coat on the rack. The clerk helped him into it and gently drew him over to a full-length mirror. "Hangs like a shroud," Hemingway said, tearing the coat off. "I'm tall on top. Got any other coat?" he asked, as though he expected the answer to be no. He edged impatiently toward the elevators.

"How about this one, sir, with a removable lining, sir?" the clerk said. This one had a belt. Hemingway tried it on, studied himself in the mirror, and then raised his arms as though he were aiming a rifle. "You going to use it for *shooting*, sir?" the clerk asked. Hemingway grunted and said he would take the coat. He gave the clerk his name, and the clerk snapped his fingers. "Of course!" he said. "There was *something*—" Hemingway looked embarrassed and said to send the coat to him at the Sherry-Netherland, and then said he'd like to look at a belt.

"What kind of belt, Mr. Hemingway?" the clerk asked.

"Guess a brown one," Hemingway said.

We moved over to the belt counter, and another clerk appeared.

"Will you show Mr. Hemingway a belt?" the first clerk said, and stepped back and thoughtfully watched Hemingway.

The second clerk took a tape measure from his pocket, saying he thought Hemingway was a size 44 or 46.

"Wanta bet?" Hemingway asked. He took the clerk's hand and punched himself in the stomach with it.

"Gee, he's got a hard tummy," the belt clerk said. He measured Hemingway's waistline. "Thirty-eight!" he reported. "Small waist for your size. What do you do—a lot of exercise?"

Hemingway hunched his shoulders, feinted, laughed, and looked happy for the first time since we'd left the hotel. He punched himself in the stomach with his own fist.

"Where you going—to Spain again?" the belt clerk asked.

"To Italy," Hemingway said, and punched himself in the stomach again. After Hemingway had decided on a brown calf belt, the clerk asked him whether he wanted a money belt. He said no—he kept his money in a checkbook.

Our next stop was the shoe department, and there Hemingway asked a clerk for some folding bedroom slippers.

"Pullman slippers," the clerk said. "What size?"

"Levens," Hemingway said bashfully. The slippers were produced, and he told the clerk he would take them. "I'll put them in my pocket," he said. "Just mark them, so they won't think I'm a shoplifter."

"You'd be surprised what's taken from the store," said the clerk, who was very small and very old. "Why, the other morning, someone on the first floor went off with a big roulette wheel. Just picked it up and—"

Hemingway was not listening. "Wolfie!" he shouted at a man who seemed almost seven feet tall and whose back was to us.

The man turned around. He had a big, square red face, and at the sight of Hemingway it registered extreme joy. "Papa!" he shouted.

The big man and Hemingway embraced and pounded each other on the back for quite some time. It was Winston Guest. Mr. Guest told us he was going upstairs to pick up a gun and proposed that we come along. Hemingway asked what kind of gun, and Guest said a ten-gauge magnum.

"Beautiful gun," Hemingway said, taking his bedroom slippers from the clerk and stuffing them into his pocket.

In the elevator, Hemingway and Guest checked with each other on how much weight they had lost. Guest said he was now down to two hundred and thirty-five, after a good deal of galloping around on polo ponies. Hemingway said he was down to two hundred and eight, after shooting ducks in Cuba and working on his book.

"How's the book now, Papa?" Guest asked, as we got out of the elevator.

Hemingway gave his fist-to-the-face laugh and said he was going to defend his title once more. "Wolfie, all of a sudden I found I could write wonderful again, instead of just biting on the nail," he said slowly. "I think it took a while for my head to get rebuilt inside. You should not, ideally, break a writer's head open or give him seven concussions in two years or break six ribs on him when he is forty-seven or push a rearview mirror support through the front of his skull opposite the pituitary gland or, really, shoot at him too much. On the other hand, Wolfie, leave the sons of bitches alone and they are liable to start crawling back into the womb or somewhere if you drop a porkpie hat." He exploded into laughter.

Guest's huge frame shook with almost uncontrollable laughter. "God, Papa!" he said. "I still have your shooting clothes out at the island. When are you coming out to shoot, Papa?"

Hemingway laughed again and pounded him on the back. "Wolfie, you're so damn big!" he said.

Guest arranged to have his gun delivered, and then we all got into the elevator, the two of them talking about a man who caught a black marlin last year that weighed a thousand and six pounds.

"How do you like it now, gentlemen?" Hemingway asked.

"God, Papa!" said Guest.

On the ground floor, Guest pointed to a mounted elephant head on the wall. "Pygmy elephant, Papa," he said.

"Miserable elephant," said Hemingway.

Their arms around each other, they went out to the street. I said that I had to leave, and Hemingway told me to be sure to come over to the hotel early the next morning so that I could go with him and Patrick to the Metropolitan Museum. As I walked off, I heard Guest say, "God, Papa, I'm not ashamed of anything I've ever done."

"Nor, oddly enough, am I," said Hemingway.

I looked around. They were punching each other in the stomach and laughing raucously.

The following morning, the door of the Hemingway suite was opened for me by Patrick, a shy young man of medium height, with large eyes and a sensitive face. He was wearing gray flannel slacks, a white shirt open at the collar, argyle socks, and loafers. Mrs. Hemingway was writing a letter at the desk. As I came in, she looked up and said, "As soon as Papa has finished dressing, we're going to look at pictures." She went back to her letter.

Patrick told me that he'd just as soon spend the whole day looking at pictures, and that he had done a bit of painting himself. "Papa has to be back here for lunch with Mr. Scribner," he said, and added that he himself was going to stay in town until the next morning, when the Hemingways sailed. The telephone rang and he answered it. "Papa, I think it's Gigi calling you!" he shouted to the bedroom.

Hemingway emerged, in shirtsleeves, and went to the phone. "How are you, kid?" he said into it, then asked Gigi to come down to the Finca for his next vacation. "You're welcome down there, Gigi," he said. "You know that cat you liked? The one you named Smelly? We renamed him Ecstasy. Every one of our cats knows his own name." After hanging up, he told me that Gigi was a wonderful shot—that when he was eleven he had won second place in the shoot championship of Cuba. "Isn't that the true gen, Mouse?" he asked.

"That's right, Papa," said Patrick.

I wanted to know what "true gen" means, and Hemingway explained that it is British slang for "information," from "intelligence." "It's divided into three classes—gen; the true gen, which is as true as you can state it; and the really true gen, which you can operate on," he said. He looked at the green orchids and asked whether anybody had found out who Adeline was.

"I forgot to tell you, Papa," said Mrs. Hemingway. "It's Mother. Adeline is *Mother*." She turned to me and said that her mother and father are in their late seventies, that they live in Chicago, and that they always remember to do exactly the right thing at the right time.

"My mother never sent *me* any flowers," Hemingway said. His mother is now about eighty, he said, and lives in River Forest, Illinois. His father, who was a physician, has been dead for many years; he shot himself when Ernest was a boy. "Let's get going if we're going to see the pictures," he said. "I told Charlie Scribner to meet me here at one. Excuse me while I wash. In big city, I guess you wash your neck." He went back into the bedroom. While he was gone, Mrs. Hemingway told me that Ernest was the second of six children—Marcelline, then Ernest, Ursula, Madelaine, Carol, and the youngest, his only brother, Leicester. All the sisters were named after saints. Every one of the children is married now; Leicester is living in Bogotá, Colombia, where he is attached to the US Embassy.

Hemingway came out in a little while, wearing his new coat. Mrs. Hemingway and Patrick put on their coats, and we went downstairs. It was raining, and we hurried into a taxi. On the way to the Metropolitan, Hemingway said very little; he just hummed to himself and watched the street. Mrs. Hemingway told me that he was usually unhappy in taxis, because he could not sit in the front seat to watch the road ahead.

He looked out the window and pointed to a flock of birds flying across the sky. "In this town, birds fly, but they're not serious about it," he said. "New York birds don't climb."

When we drew up at the Museum entrance, a line of schoolchildren was moving in slowly. Hemingway impatiently led us past them. In the lobby, he paused, pulled a silver flask from one of his coat pockets, unscrewed its top, and took a long drink. Putting the flask back in his pocket, he asked Mrs. Hemingway whether she wanted to see the Goyas first or the Breugels. She said the Breugels.

"I learned to write by looking at paintings in the Luxembourg Museum in Paris," he said. "I never went past high school. When you've got a hungry gut and the museum is free, you go to the museum. Look," he said, stopping before *Portrait of a Man*, which has been attributed to both Titian and Giorgione. "They were old Venice boys, too."

"Here's what I like, Papa," Patrick said, and Hemingway joined his son in front of *Portrait of Federigo Gonzaga (1500–1540)*, by Francesco Francia. It shows, against a landscape, a small boy with long hair and a cloak.

"This is what we try to do when we write, Mousie," Hemingway said, pointing to the trees in the background. "We always have this in when we write."

Mrs. Hemingway called to us. She was looking at *Portrait of the Artist*, by Van Dyck. Hemingway looked at it, nodded approval, and said, "In Spain, we had a fighter pilot named Whitey Dahl, so Whitey came to me one time and said, 'Mr. Hemingway, is Van Dyck a good painter?' I said, 'Yes, he is.' He said, 'Well, I'm glad, because I have one in my room and I like it very much, and I'm glad he's a good painter because I like him.' The next day, Whitey was shot down."

We all walked over to Rubens's *The Triumph of Christ over Sin and Death*. Christ is shown surrounded by snakes and angels and is being watched by a figure in a cloud. Mrs. Hemingway and Patrick said they thought it didn't look like the usual Rubens.

"Yeah, he did that all right," Hemingway said authoritatively. "You can tell the real just as a bird dog can tell. Smell them. Or from having lived with very poor but very good painters."

That settled that, and we went on to the Breugel room. It was closed, we discovered. The door bore a sign that read Now Undertaking Repairs.

"They have our indulgence," Hemingway said, and took another drink from his flask. "I sure miss the good Breugel," he said as we moved along. "It's the great one, of the harvesters. It is a lot of people cutting grain, but he uses the grain geometrically, to make an emotion that is so strong for me that I can hardly take it." We came to El Greco's green *View of Toledo* and stood looking at it a long time. "This is the best picture in the museum for me, and Christ knows there are some lovely ones," Hemingway said.

Patrick admired several paintings Hemingway didn't approve of. Every time this happened, Hemingway got into an involved, technical discussion with his son about it. Patrick would shake his head and laugh and say he respected Hemingway's opinions. He didn't argue much. "What the hell!" Hemingway said suddenly. "I don't want to be an art critic. I just want to look at pictures and be happy with them and learn from them. Now, this for me is a damn good picture." He stood back and peered at a Reynolds entitled *Colonel George Coussmaker*, which shows the colonel leaning against a tree and holding his horse's bridle. "Now, this colonel is a son of a bitch who was willing to pay money to the best portrait painter of his day just to have himself painted," Hemingway said, and gave a short laugh. "Look at the man's arrogance and the strength in the neck of the horse and the way the man's legs hang. He's so arrogant he can afford to lean against a tree."

We separated for a while and looked at paintings individually, and then Hemingway called us over and pointed to a picture labeled, in large letters, "Catharine Lorillard Wolfe" and, in small ones, "By Cabanel." "This is where I got confused as a kid, in Chicago," he said. "My favorite painters for a long time were Bunte and Ryerson, two of the biggest and wealthiest families in Chicago. I always thought the names in big letters were the painters."

After we reached the Cézannes and Degases and the other Impressionists, Hemingway became more and more excited, and discoursed on what each artist could do and how and what he had learned from each. Patrick listened respectfully and didn't seem to want to talk about painting techniques anymore. Hemingway spent several minutes looking at Cézanne's *Rocks—Forest of Fontainebleau.* "This is what we try to do in writing, this and this, and the woods, and the rocks we have to climb over," he said. "Cézanne is my painter, after the early painters. Wonder, wonder painter. Degas was another wonder painter. I've never seen a bad Degas. You know what he did with the bad Degases? He burned them."

Hemingway took another long drink from his flask. We came to Manet's pastel portrait of Mlle. Valtesse de la Bigne, a young woman with blond hair coiled on the top of her head. Hemingway was silent for a while, looking at it; finally he turned away. "Manet could show the bloom people have when they're still innocent and before they've been disillusioned," he said.

As we walked along, Hemingway said to me, "I can make a landscape like Mr. Paul Cézanne. I learned how to make a landscape from Mr. Paul Cézanne by walking through the Luxembourg Museum a thousand times with an empty gut, and I am pretty sure that if Mr. Paul was around, he would like the way I make them and be happy that I learned it from him." He had learned a lot from Mr. Johann Sebastian Bach, too. "In the first paragraphs of *Farewell,* I used the word *and* consciously over and over the way Mr. Johann Sebastian Bach used a note in music when he was emitting counterpoint. I can almost write like Mr. Johann sometimes—or, anyway, so he would like it. All such people are easy to deal with, because we all know you have to learn."

"Papa, look at this," Patrick said. He was looking at *Meditation on the Passion*, by Carpaccio. Patrick said it had a lot of strange animals in it for a religious painting.

"Huh!" Hemingway said. "Those painters always put the sacred scenes in the part of Italy they liked the best or where they came from or where their girls came from. They made their girls the Madonnas. This is supposed to be Palestine, and Palestine is a long way off, he figures. So he puts in a red parrot, and he puts in deer and a leopard. And then he thinks, This is the Far East and it's far away. So he puts in the Moors, the traditional enemy of the Venetians." He paused and looked to see what else the painter had put in his picture. "Then he gets hungry, so he puts in rabbits," he said. "Goddamn, Mouse, we saw a lot of good pictures. Mouse, don't you think two hours is a long time looking at pictures?"

Everybody agreed that two hours was a long time looking at pictures, so Hemingway said that we would skip the Goyas, and that we would all go to the museum again when they returned from Europe.

It was still raining when we came out of the museum. "Goddamn, I hate to go out in the rain," Hemingway said. "Goddamn, I hate to get wet."

Charles Scribner was waiting in the lobby of the hotel. "Ernest," he said, shaking Hemingway's hand. He is a dignified, solemn, slow-speaking gentleman with silvery hair.

"We've been looking at pictures, Charlie," Hemingway said as we went up in the elevator. "They have some pretty good pictures now, Charlie."

Scribner nodded and said, "Yuh, yuh."

"Was fun for country boy like me," Hemingway said.

"Yuh, yuh," said Scribner.

We went into the suite and took off our coats, and Hemingway said we would have lunch right there. He called room service and Mrs. Hemingway sat down at the desk to finish her letter. Hemingway sat down on the couch with Mr. Scribner and began telling him that he had been jamming, like a rider in a six-day bike race, and Patrick sat quietly in a corner and watched his father. The waiter came in and passed out menus. Scribner said he was going to order the most expensive item on the menu, because Hemingway was paying for it. He laughed tentatively, and Patrick laughed to keep him company. The waiter retired with our orders, and Scribner and Hemingway talked business for a while. Scribner wanted to know whether Hemingway had the letters he had written to him.

Hemingway said, "I carry them every place I go, Charlie, together with a copy of the poems of Robert Browning."

Scribner nodded, and from the inner pocket of his jacket took some papers—copies of the contract for the new book, he said. The contract provided for an advance of twenty-five thousand dollars against royalties, beginning at fifteen percent.

Hemingway signed the contract and got up from the couch. Then he said, "Never ran as no genius, but I'll defend the title again against all the good young new ones." He lowered his head, put his left foot forward, and jabbed at the air with a left and a right. "Never let them hit you solid," he said.

Scribner wanted to know where Hemingway could be reached in Europe. Care of the Guaranty Trust Company in Paris, Hemingway told him. "When we took Paris, I tried to take that bank and got smacked back," he said, and laughed a shy laugh. "I thought it would be awfully nice if I could take my own bank."

"Yuh, yuh," Scribner said. "What are you planning to do in Italy, Ernest?"

Hemingway said he would work in the mornings and see his Italian friends and go duck hunting in the afternoons. "We shot three hundred and thirty-one ducks to six guns there one afternoon," he said. "Mary shot good, too."

Mrs. Hemingway looked up. "Any girl who marries Papa has to learn how to carry a gun," she said, and returned to her letter writing.

"I went hunting once in Suffolk, England," Scribner said. Everyone waited politely for him to continue. "I remember they gave me goose eggs to eat for breakfast in Suffolk. Then we went out to shoot. I didn't know how to get my gun off safety."

"Hunting is sort of a good life," Hemingway said. "Better than Westport or Bronxville, I think."

"After I learned how to get my gun off safety, I couldn't hit anything," Scribner said.

"I'd like to make the big Monte Carlo shoot and the Championship of the World at San Remo," Hemingway said. "I'm in pretty good shape to shoot either one. It's not a spectator sport at all. But exciting to do and wonderful to manage. I used to handle Wolfie in big shoots. He is a great shot. It was like handling a great horse."

"I finally got one," Scribner said timidly.

"Got what?" asked Hemingway.

"A rabbit," Scribner said. "I shot this rabbit."

"They haven't held the big Monte Carlo shoot since 1939," Hemingway said. "Only two Americans ever won it in seventy-four years. Shooting gives me a good feeling. A lot of it is being together and friendly instead of feeling you are in some place where everybody hates you and wishes you ill. It is faster than baseball, and you are out on one strike."

The telephone rang, and Hemingway picked it up, listened, said a few words, and then turned to us and said that an outfit called Endorsements, Inc., had offered him four thousand dollars to pose as a Man of Distinction. "I told them I wouldn't drink the stuff for four thousand dollars," he said. "I told them I was a champagne man. Am trying to be a good guy, but it's a difficult trade. What you win in Boston, you lose in Chicago."

(MAY 13, 1950)

Movement

Fawcett publications invited us to a party last week to celebrate the publication of a paperback anthology entitled *The Beats* and containing poems, essays, and stories by a couple of dozen writers who are now leading (according to Fawcett) the Beat (with, according to Fawcett, a capital *B*) movement. The party was held in the lobby of the Living Theatre, a second-floor walk-up at Fourteenth Street and Sixth Avenue, a couple of hours before curtain time of that conspicuously living play called *The Connection*, which is housed there. As we climbed the stairs, we found copies of *The Beats* pasted to the walls. Some displayed the front cover, which has on it a photograph of a pretty young girl and a bearded young man wearing shell-rimmed eyeglasses, plus warnings that read, "Here are the most vital and controversial writers on the American scene," and "Raw, penetrating stories, poems and social criticism by JACK KEROUAC, NORMAN MAILER, ALLEN GINSBERG, LAWRENCE FERLINGHETTI, and many others. Edited by Seymour Krim." Other copies of the book showed the back cover, which added, "The drive, the fury, the frankness they bring to their writing has made the Beat Generation the most hotly discussed literary movement of this century."

Upstairs, the party seemed slow in getting started. Several lovely young ladies, all of them wearing conservative black dresses, were putting up more copies of *The Beats* at the corners of a square bar in the middle of the lobby and helping bartenders open bottles of whiskey. We approached a young man, impeccable in Ivy League oxford gray and a knitted black tie, who was putting up still more copies of *The Beats* on the walls. "Nobody here yet who's authentic Beat," he told us. "All of us are from Fawcett. We're here to inspire confidence. How do you like the girl on the cover? She's an associate editor on our books.

She's not Beat at all. We put her on because she looked so typical." He paused. "Ah, at last! Seymour Krim!"

With this, the Fawcett man turned us over to Mr. Krim, a tall, skinny young man, friendly and wide-eyed, who was sporting a dark-maroon shirt, a black four-in-hand, a brown V-necked pullover, dark-gray trousers, and a silvery coat.

"I'm so nervous," Mr. Krim told us. "I never presided over a cocktail party before. What am I supposed to do? Introduce people? Mix drinks? Offer them cheese crackers? I wish I didn't feel so nervous. Would you like some Scotch? I think it's real."

We moved over to the bar, and the bartender poured Krim and us some Scotch. "Tell me something, will you, kid?" the bartender said to Krim. "What are you kids calling this a movement for? You make it sound like the Communists, when all you are, you're a bunch of not-too-brainy, warmhearted kids."

"Fawcett calls it a movement," Krim said. "Actually, it's sort of a wave. Actually, it's sort of an attitude in anybody who's young or young in heart. It's a posture of rebellion. It's for anybody unwilling to put up with older compromises."

"OK, OK, kid," said the bartender. "I only thought any writer worth his salt, he stuck to his attic all by himself and wrote."

"We're like the French Impressionist painters, that whole group, although the analogy is a little square," Krim said. "Actually, there's less competitiveness among us than you find among most other writers. The wave brings ideas useful to all of us interchangeably. We turn each other on."

"A writer should be like an island," the bartender said. "Alone."

The party was warming up, with a number of informally attired youthful guests arriving in twos and threes. We were joined by a young man wearing chino trousers, a wrinkled khaki shirt open at the collar, and brand-new white sneakers, who had a small, childlike face and shining eyes. "Where's Norman Mailer?" he asked Krim. "I want to meet Norman Mailer. He's the only really good writer in the whole room."

"He's not here yet," said Krim.

"He's the only writer here with major talent," the young man said.

"What about yourself?" Krim asked, plucking a copy of *The Beats* from the wall, introducing the young man to us as Dan Propper, and opening the book to a page headed "Dan Propper—The Fable of the Final Hour."

"I don't regard myself as a great writer," said Propper. "Norman Mailer has made it; he's there. This is my wife, Eunice," he added, introducing a little, round-faced, black-haired girl wearing a black shirt, black pants, and white sneakers as clean as her husband's.

"Where's Norman Mailer?" Eunice asked.

Another young man, handsome and confident, came by and waved a manuscript packed between black hard covers at us.

"Got a carbon copy?" Krim asked. "I never make carbons," said the young man.

"You'll regret it someday," said Krim.

"I don't even belong here," said the young man. "I'm a senior at Harvard. This party looks like any old party at Harvard."

"Is that Norman Mailer?" Eunice asked Krim, standing on her toes and pointing to a nearby man of at least thirty.

"That's Leonard Bishop," Krim said, loudly enough for Bishop to hear. "He's sort of a William Styron type."

"I'm only a sicknik!" Leonard Bishop called over.

"What's Herbert Gold doing in your book? What's the idea?" asked the Harvard man.

"Well, he's really anti-Beat," said Krim. "He's still finding his way. He'll get there."

"You've got hope here," said the Harvard man. "That's more than we've got at Harvard."

"Where's Jack Kerouac?" a chic, attractive lady asked. "My son told me if I came to this party I'd see Jack Kerouac."

"He plays hard to get," said Krim. "Too bad Ginsberg is in Chile, or we'd have had ten good arguments already. Nobody has opened up yet. The party's tame. Anyway, here's Ted Joans."

We shook hands with a bearded young Negro who had a midwestern accent and was wearing a heavy sweater with brown and gray horizontal stripes. "I'm splitting Friday," Joans told us. "That means leaving town. Going on a trip around the world. Getting on a boat. Going to read my poems in the middle of the Atlantic. Going to read all over the world—in Liverpool, London, and Brussels. No matter where I am, I always find a place to read."

"You make a lot of money getting rented?" Krim asked him.

"Enough to get me on that boat to Liverpool," Joans said, and held us by the sleeve. "My friend put this ad in the *Village Voice* offering to rent Beatniks for your party," he said. "I'm the one got rented. People always ask me don't I feel commercial letting myself get rented? What I always reply is 'There's nothing wrong with a Cadillac if you don't let it drive you.' I tell them it's the same as renting yourself out as a capitalist. Nothing wrong with that, long as you get paid."

As we made our way back to the bar, we ran into Mr. and Mrs. Propper. "Norman Mailer is here!" they said happily. Sure enough, in a few seconds we came upon Norman Mailer, looking very conservative in a business suit and very much the elder statesman. We introduced him to the Proppers, whose beaming faces were a joy to see.

"Boy!" said Propper. "I read the scenes from your play! It's a groovy play."

"I read your fable," Mailer said, a fatherly twinkle in his eye. "I liked your fable."

"I was young, rebellious, and adolescent when I wrote that fable," said Propper.

"His current stuff is much better," said Eunice.

Mailer gave them a fatherly nod. "It's a good fable," he said.

"Your play is a groovy play," said Eunice. "That part where the atom bomb goes off."

"That part's all right," said Mailer. "Then I've got two more scenes after that, they're even better."

Ted Joans joined us. "Norman Mailer!" he said. "In one of my poems, I tell them to buy your book."

"Say, thanks," Mailer said, looking bashful.

"I'm splitting Friday," said Joans. "Leaving on a trip around the world. Going to tell everybody, all over, to buy your book."

"I've never heard so many non sequiturs in my life," the bartender told us when we got back to him. "What kind of writers are they, they all talk the same? These kids, they are not Tolstoy."

"Kerouac isn't here yet," the chic, attractive lady said to us. "But I met this cute little Dan Propper. He gave me a copy of the book. I asked him for his autograph. I told him, 'I'm going to take it home, where I can read it properly.' He didn't get it."

We came upon Propper and Eunice a few minutes later.

"Nobody asked Norman Mailer for his autograph," Eunice said.

"That's a mark of his skill," said Propper.

We started to shove off and, on our way to the door, passed Krim. "Fawcett is putting water in the drinks," he told us. "But the party is opening up."

(APRIL 16, 1960)

Life Line

One evening last week, the uproar about coffeehouses in Greenwich Village having died down, we headed for the Figaro, on the corner of Bleecker and Macdougal, to get the latest on *caffè espresso*. The streets were teeming when we arrived—motorcycles, sports cars, Cadillacs, Larks, bicycles, tricycles, little kids, bigger kids, boy gangs, man gangs, girl gangs, young couples, old couples, middle-aged couples, loners, black-garbed Italian ladies in their seventies, panhandlers, book carriers, and Beats of various shapes, sizes, and natures. Paperback books, handwrought jewelry, antiques, sandals, pottery, straw objects, paintings, simmering Italian sausages, onions, and pizzas, and freshly boiled sweet corn were being marketed in neighboring stalls and shops, with enough customers apparently, for everybody. Out of this festival, like a ghost, there suddenly loomed a distinguished and formerly subdued artist we know, who was now wearing boots and a T-shirt (a fancy kind, with an inlaid panel at the throat). "Greetings," he said coolly. "I have just moved down here from the upper East Side. If you want to see something peculiar, go to the Cedar Street Tavern, on University Place. It's full of painters."

"You Beat?" we asked.

"It's a legitimate thing to be a Beatnik, even though most of the time it's the provincial thing," he said. "It draws me. It's the power of innocence."

Inside the Figaro, the power of innocence was going full blast—a jukebox playing Bach's *Toccata and Fugue in D Minor*, two espresso machines hissing, a white-aproned, blond-bearded dishwasher playing chess with a customer, an old Chaplin film flickering on a movie screen in a corner, abstract paintings hanging on the walls, a collection of Tiffany lamps hanging from the ceiling, a grand piano (quiet) to one side, the customers brooding, reading, or buzzing with discussions,

83

polemics, and harangues on faith and life. It drew us. We cornered Tom Ziegler, the owner, a clean-cut man of thirty-one, whose hair was slicked back on his head with water, and whose T-shirt showed faintly under a conventional white one, open at the collar.

"We're sometimes called the square coffeehouse, but we don't mind, because we know we're not square," Ziegler told us. "It's simply that when you come here you have to behave. We don't permit the weekend tourist Beatniks—a lot of them come down from the Bronx sporting day-old beards—or any would-be Beatniks who read about press-created-image Beatniks and try to be like them, to work out their psychic difficulties here. Look around. You'll see plenty of Beatniks, but they're nothing like the exhibitionists exploited in stories in the *News*. Our Beatniks are the real, true, old-fashioned, wonderful bohemians. There's been some harassment of coffeehouses that didn't meet fire-law standards despite the fact that hundreds of eating places in town with the same conditions weren't bothered. But I maintain that the market for coffeehouses is unlimited. This is just the beginning of the boom. It's going on all over. In London two years ago there were two hundred coffeehouses; now there are twice the number. In 1956, when my wife and I started the Figaro, there were a few coffeehouses around, and I wondered whether the Village could stand another coffee place. Last month, there were more than two dozen new ones since we'd started, and I've stopped counting. The coffeehouse fills a real need; people have to congregate. There are two possibilities for a young girl, say, who comes to New York and doesn't know anybody—YWCA dances and coffeehouses. She doesn't want to make the bar scene. For a young man, a coffeehouse is a place for him to sit down and talk to people without being jostled by drunks. One of the things we enjoy is Europeans who find their way here. Americans they've met in Europe tell them the best place for a stranger to go is to the Figaro. Here they have a place they feel they belong in, where they can exchange ideas, talk, carry on a social life. In a way, it follows the high-school corner drugstore for a lot of kids. Where did I go when I was eighteen? I went up to Hell's Kitchen and hung out on street corners and eventually got into trouble. Here we keep an eye on the teenagers. They play chess or checkers, or just talk, and we get them to drink milk. And we don't let them hang around too long. Some of them I ration to three visits a night. Look around. See them? Nice kids."

Mr. Ziegler drew a deep breath and did some looking around himself. "Coffeehouses have been under attack down through history," he said, turning back to us. "I recently came across an article that reported there was hostility to coffeehouses at Oxford in the seventeenth century. They were criticized as being gathering places of students and teachers, who consequently lost respect for each other and frittered away their study time. I don't agree. I'm sure there were people then who benefited tremendously from coffeehouse life, as there are now."

We asked Mr. Ziegler for his coffeehouse background.

"I didn't know a thing about it, and neither did my wife, when we started," he replied. "It was probably a good thing that we didn't have any restaurant experience, because to run a coffeehouse as a restaurant is impossible. We got into the business to make some money to pay my way at NYU; I started college when I was twenty-five. I've lived in the Village all my life—except for two years in Hell's Kitchen—and I went to school here. My father is a painter. One thing I know—in the Village, you can find somebody who knows about anything. Originally, the Figaro was in a former barbershop across the street. That's how it got named: I bought it from a friend for three thousand dollars that I borrowed. He'd had it a couple of months and was tired of it, or so he told me. We put another two thousand dollars into it across the street, and then we took this corner, the site of two former stores—dry goods and instrument repairs. I practically built the place with my own broken hands—put up the walls with a friend who is a writer, who also helped me put in this floor. Marble scraps. My own idea. Cost me twenty dollars, and the marble man I bought the scraps from thought I was crazy. I bought the furniture at auction. I dropped out of college when I discovered that the coffeehouse was more complicated and more enjoyable than I had expected. We filled the place up with chess players during the week and made our money on weekends. My wife and I worked a sixty-hour, seven-day week. We invested an additional twelve thousand dollars here. We had trouble finding an old espresso machine, because these machines haven't been made since the nineteen forties. The Italians don't like them, and now make those hydrocompression ones, which I think are ugly. I got a beautiful old one through a bookie who had a brother-in-law in the old-style Italian coffeehouse business. Now there are about a dozen wholesale places that import newfangled push-button machines from Italy. We have twelve waitresses and two waiters, from all parts of the world. Our dishwasher is from Texas. He's a writer. One of my managers is a high-school English teacher who likes working here better. We have other people who should be out building their careers but can't stand doing that. I make it a point to avoid hiring any girl who just left home to get away from her parents or her husband. I don't mind boasting that each of our waitresses is an adult woman, even though she might be only twenty-two years of age. By that I mean they all have plenty of understanding of themselves and of other people. On Sundays, we have afternoon chamber-music concerts that cost a hundred dollars and that I lose money on, but I don't care."

The conversation was interrupted by a mime in whiteface, selling flowers. "He's a pretty good mime, but there's a better one at the Cafe Wha?, on Macdougal," Ziegler said. "There are all kinds of coffeehouses, with all kinds of attitudes. The venerable ones, the Rienzi and the Manzini, cater to tourists. The Phase 2 and Limelight don't cater to tourists, but if you're a tourist you're acceptable anyway. The upper West Side has the First Born, at Amsterdam and a Hundred and Eleventh; the East Side has the Right Bank, at Madison and Sixty-Ninth. In between, at Orsini's, you have to wear a necktie."

We were joined by Ziegler's wife, a pretty girl with bangs, whom he introduced as Royce, and by one of his part-time assistants, a wide-eyed young man named Alan Eisenberg. "Royce and Alan can testify to the fact that we're known as the only swinging coffeehouse," Ziegler said.

"This place is what Beatism is all about," Royce said. "It's an authentic old-fashioned bohemian place, the kind of place Edna St. Vincent Millay would have liked."

"A truer bohemia than the Montparnasse of the late twenties," a chess player next to us threw in.

"I hate to use the word *rapport*," Eisenberg said, "but that's what we have here. After all, what is true Beatism but an awareness of life? It sounds corny, but that's what the basic meaning is. Trying to feel things. Instead of getting all tied up with things that distort the meaning of life. People come here to look at us and laugh, but we're laughing right back. There's a Beatism that's destructive, but that should have a different name. The coffeehouse is a life line against compromise, which some people think is a great thing. Compromise to me is a synonym for defeat. Admittedly an anticonformist, adolescent attitude, but a good one."

"Alan is a lawyer," Royce said, "but he can't stay away from the Figaro."

"Look around," Ziegler said. "What you see is a young society reacting."

(AUGUST 6, 1960)

Theatre
(Edward Albee)

It had been a long time since we'd enjoyed listening to talk about the theatre as much as we did the other day, when a ninth grader at St. Bernard's (all boys) School invited us to sit in on a meeting of his English class with Edward Albee, the playwright (*The Zoo Story, The Death of Bessie Smith, The Sandbox, The American Dream, Who's Afraid of Virginia Woolf?, Tiny Alice, Malcolm, A Delicate Balance, All Over*, and some others). Also invited were some students from the Brearley (all girls) School and a few teachers from both schools. We all met in the St. Bernard's library, a cozy, wood-paneled refuge with a red carpet, group and individual tables, many posters urging LIVE! READ!, oil paintings of the school's former headmasters, and, thank God, lots of books. We were happy to find that Mr. Albee, whom we hadn't seen for a few years, still looked youthful (he's forty-six) and trim. He now has long hair and a black mustache. He wore a brown suede jacket, tweed slacks, a beige turtleneck shirt, and brown leather boots. The boys and girls—there were about twenty of them—settled down at the group tables facing Mr. Albee, who sat alone, his legs stretched out and crossed.

Mr. Albee got the talk on the move by saying a few words about himself: "Now I write only plays; I used to write novels. I wrote one novel when I was fifteen, and I wrote one when I was seventeen. I wrote poetry when I was six, which is before the age of reason. I stopped writing poetry when I was twenty-six. I wanted to be a writer because I wanted to be my own boss, primarily. I decided I was a writer when I was very young. In fifteen years, I've written fourteen plays. Some of them were critical successes but not commercial successes. Some of them were commercial successes but not critical successes. Some were neither commercial nor critical successes. I'll be happy to answer any

questions. We can talk about anything you like. Or nothing." Mr. Albee
shifted a bit in his chair, looking friendly and sympathetic, and waited
expectantly.

The teachers looked pleased. The students looked attentive and
polite. There was a self-conscious minute-long pause. Then the questions started popping.

BOY: Are the characters in *Who's Afraid of Virginia Woolf?*
based on people you know?

ALBEE: All the characters I make up are always a combination of things. You might start out with some real
people, but then you distort them to suit yourself.
You adjust them. Your characters have a life of
their own. The separate world of reality is always
available to you if you should want it. I usually start
with an idea. By the time I'm finished, as often
as not, nothing is left of the original idea. This is
what is laughingly called the unconscious process.
I do most of the work in my head. For me, the
actual writing procedure is the last part. But there
is always something that starts a play. When I was
going to school, I spent most of my time talking
to teachers and to their wives. My idea was: With
how much honesty and honor do people deal with
their lives? Then, one day, I went into a bar that had
a huge mirror behind it. On the mirror someone
had scrawled in crayon "Who's afraid of Virginia
Woolf?" Meaning, Who's afraid to face life without
false illusions? It all comes together from many different places.

BOY: How do you start to write a play?

ALBEE: The way I start is with the sense of an idea. My next
play is about Attila the Hun. I felt it's time to write
about a second-rate would-be dictator. The play
builds and changes. Theoretically, a play is supposed
to get more interesting as it goes on.

GIRL: Did you think that *Who's Afraid of Virginia Woolf?* was
translated satisfactorily into film?

ALBEE: I doubt whether any play can be translated into film. A play and a film are different. The sense of reality is different. The way the audience approaches a play or a film is different.

BOY: Were the characters in *The Zoo Story* related to anyone you knew?

ALBEE: When I wrote the play, in 1959, I was making a living delivering telegrams, and I did quite a bit of walking around the city. I was always delivering telegrams to people living in rooming houses. I met all those people in the play in rooming houses. Jerry, the hero, is still around. He changes his shape from year to year. Today, he's more politically committed, perhaps. The one person I forgot to mention in any character you make up is yourself. It's very difficult to say where one stops and the other starts. And it's probably a mistake to try to find out.

GIRL: How do audiences in other countries react to your plays?

ALBEE: It's interesting to go from country to country and to see the way the reaction varies from country to country. You learn something about the psychology of a country by seeing the different reactions. I've seen *Who's Afraid of Virginia Woolf?* in London, Paris, Rome, Oslo, Stockholm, Helsinki, Munich, Prague, and Budapest. The differences in reaction are very subtle, but they're there.

BOY: How can you tell if a play has been changed in a country whose language you don't understand?

ALBEE: You hold a copy of the play in one hand and the translation in the other, and you try to tell if one weighs more than the other.

BOY: What authors have influenced you?

ALBEE: Everybody I've ever read. Let's take Samuel Beckett, who is probably the best playwright around today. There's no self-respecting playwright writing today who hasn't been influenced by Samuel Beckett. He's changed the entire nature of playwriting.

BOY: Isn't it easier to write a novel than it is to write a play? In writing a play, it's so hard to show what the characters are thinking.

ALBEE: You can do the whole thing in dialogue in a play. Discovering that was one of the joys of my life.

GIRL: How big a part do you play in the production of your plays?

ALBEE: I choose the actors and the director. After about two weeks of rehearsal, I come in and make sure they're going the way I want them to. You must allow for other people's creativity. But you want to help the actor become the character, not become the star. The better the play, the less opportunity the actor has to improve it. The actor just dissolves into the part.

BOY: Does it bother you when people don't like your plays?

ALBEE: I guess being a playwright is somewhat more optimistic than going to school. You assume what you're doing is going to be good. Every single play of mine has had mixed critical reactions. I've never had a play that has had unanimous acclaim. I'm glad about that. Otherwise, I'd know I was doing something wrong.

BOY: How long does it take you to write a play?

ALBEE: Some plays take a few months. Some have taken five or six years. *The Sandbox* took about an hour to write. They float around in my head before they're out. Once I get a play out of my head, I've emptied my mind of it. It doesn't clutter my head anymore.

BOY: Does writing a play cause you pain?

ALBEE: Both pain and pleasure. Plays are like your kids, in a way. It's hard to be objective about them.

BOY: How long do you work each day when you're writing a play?

ALBEE: If I'm writing well, I work four hours a day. I type. With two fingers. After four hours, I get a headache.

BOY: Do you get sudden artistic impulses, so to speak?

ALBEE: Artistic flashes take place in your head, sometimes.

BOY: How much do you really care whether people like your plays?

ALBEE: I try to teach people. I try to change people. To that extent, it matters a great deal. The responsibility of a serious playwright is to instruct.

SAME BOY: What if people are not listening to what you are teaching?

ALBEE: You have to assume that people are listening. My best audiences seem to be people under thirty and over sixty.

GIRL: Why?

ALBEE: The over-sixties don't have to accommodate anymore, and the under-thirties don't have to accommodate yet.

GIRL: Why do you think there's so little serious theatre here?

ALBEE: It's here. But you have to seek it out. It's Off Broadway, and Off Off Broadway. In this country, we're a movie culture. We're a television culture. I'm told that three percent of our population goes to the theatre. It's there if you want it. We might try to get people started early going to the theatre. I think that anybody who gets to the age of ten can go to see the plays of Samuel Beckett.

(JUNE 3, 1974)

Oprah's Understudy
(Gayle King)

No need to worry about Oprah Winfrey, founder and editorial director of the new magazine *O*, who is staying put in Chicago while her fifty-odd underlings hole up in the Hearst Magazines headquarters, on Broadway. Gayle King, the editor-at-large and the boss's forty-five-year-old best friend, is on the job as staff liaison to Oprah. Miss King is a statuesque, superconfident, cheery former news anchor, with a perfect face and perfect teeth, auburn hair worn straight to the collar, and the immediately chummy, quick-talking, eager, breathy rhythms of the Rosie-Barbara-Katie sisterhood.

"Make no mistake, *O* is Oprah's magazine, and it's going to have the stamp and spirit of Oprah all over it. She wants themes of self-improvement and self-empowerment. As Oprah's oldest and closest friend, I know what Oprah likes and what Oprah wants, and I'm here to see that she gets it," Miss King said last week, sitting in a large conference room at the Hearst corporate offices, on Eighth Avenue (carpeted corridors and Robert Motherwell paintings on the walls), a block away from where the *O* staff works.

Miss King had on a navy tailored suit with light-blue pinstripes and wore navy silk Donna Karan pumps. As she talked, she wiggled a pinkie with a diamond ring on it. "Oprah gave me this—it's actually a toe ring," she said. "Oprah had two very, very large diamond earrings, and she had them made into several toe rings. She gave another one to Steadman's daughter, Wendy. Steadman, as you know, is Oprah's longtime beau."

Miss King talked about how she came to work at *O*. "I told the Hearst people that I didn't want a made-up job, in case they were saying, 'Let's get her something; she's Oprah's friend.' I don't have a magazine background. Oprah doesn't have a magazine background. But we have others for that. My dad was an electrical engineer, and we lived in Turkey and traveled all over Europe. Much different background from Oprah's. She was molested as a child, raped at fourteen, gave birth to a baby who died after ten days. But everybody knows Oprah is tops.

"Oprah and I have been friends since 1977. I was twenty-one and she was twenty-two. She was the anchorwoman at WJZ-TV in Baltimore, and I was a lowly production assistant. I barely knew her. I had an Oldsmobile Cutlass, a much better car than her Chevy Chevette. Even so, one night there was a bad snowstorm, and she said—typical of her—'Why don't you stay over at my place?' I said, 'I have no clothes.' She said, 'We're the same size. I'll give you clothes.' I said, 'I have no underwear.' She said, 'I'll give you underwear.' So we stayed up all night talking. We told each other all the gossip, who was going out with whom. Some people just click. We clicked. We haven't stopped talking since. Oprah knows all the dirt. We never run out of things to talk about. We have so much in common. Our shoe size is the same, ten. Our contact lenses have the same prescription. Our phone numbers—it just happened—are the same, backward.

"Why me in this job? A: I can get to Oprah quickly, late at night, early in the morning, whenever. B: I make a contribution. I know a good story. I'm smart. Oprah really works as the editorial director, harder than she ever thought. She's putting in five hours a day after she does both of her TV shows. She comes up with all the creative ideas, like the Something to Think About page, where we ask questions like 'How would I change my life if I only had one year to live? One month? One day?' and leave space for the reader to write things down. Or The *O* List, the list of things she likes: for instance, a particular Burberry dog collar, because she's nuts about her dogs—two cocker spaniels— and the Rocket eBook. Another one of Oprah's ideas is the Who Knew? department, stuff like 'Did you know that Tina Turner likes scary stories?' On that one, I said no to a particular celebrity, because I know that this celebrity is not a good person.

"Now I'll tell you something that we were arguing about for days, about the cover: whether to put the *O* on top and *The Oprah Magazine* under it, or leave it *The Oprah Magazine* on top and the *O* underneath." Miss King drew a sketch of the choices on a scrap of paper. "Which do you prefer?" she asked.

"*O* on top."

Miss King gave a squeal of delight. "That's what I said! And everybody else was against it. But that's what I told Oprah, and that's what she chose.

"I work with the others at the magazine as an ensemble. If I disagree with them about sending something on to Oprah, I say, 'Go ahead, send it to her.' But I know what Oprah thinks. I even sound like her. It's funny. When my three sisters hear Oprah on her show, they can't tell who's talking. They think it's me."

(SEPTEMBER 24, 2000)

III

YOUNGSTERS

Lillian and J. D. Salinger in Central Park in the late sixties, with Erik Ross, Matthew Salinger, and Peggy Salinger.

Symbol of All We Possess

There are thirteen million women in the United States between the ages of eighteen and twenty-eight. All of them were eligible to compete for the title of Miss America in the annual contest staged in Atlantic City last month if they were high-school graduates, were not and had never been married, and were not Negroes. Ten thousand of them participated in preliminary contests held in all but three of the forty-eight states. Then, one cool September day, a miss from each of these states, together with a Miss New York City, a Miss Greater Philadelphia, a Miss Chicago, a Miss District of Columbia, a Miss Canada, a Miss Puerto Rico, and a Miss Hawaii, arrived in Atlantic City to display her beauty, poise, grace, physique, personality, and talent. The primary, and most obvious, stake in the contest was a twenty-five-thousand-dollar scholarship fund—a five-thousand-dollar scholarship for the winner and lesser ones for fourteen runners-up—which had been established by the makers of Nash automobiles, Catalina swimsuits, and a cotton fabric known as Everglaze. The winner would also get a new four-door Nash sedan, a dozen Catalina swimsuits, and a wardrobe of sixty Everglaze garments. The contest was called the Miss America Pageant. The fifty-two competitors went into it seeking, beyond the prizes, great decisions. Exactly what was decided, they are still trying to find out.

Miss New York State was a twenty-two-year-old registered nurse named Wanda Nalepa, who lives in the Bronx. She has honey-blond hair, green eyes, and a light complexion, and is five feet three. Some other statistics gathered by Miss America Pageant officials are: weight, 108; bust, 34; waist, 23; thigh, 19; hips, 34; calf, 12¼; ankle, 7½; shoe size, 5; dress size, 10. She was asked in an official questionnaire why she had entered the Atlantic City contest. She answered that her friends had urged her to. The day before the contest was to start, I telephoned Miss Nalepa at her home to ask when she was leaving for Atlantic City.

She said that she was driving down the next morning and invited me to go along.

Miss Nalepa lives in a second-floor walk-up apartment in a building near 164th Street on Sherman Avenue, a couple of blocks from the Grand Concourse. At eight the following morning, I was greeted at the door of the Nalepa flat by a thin young man in his late twenties wearing rimless glasses. "Come right in, miss," he said. "I'm Teddy, Wanda's brother. Wanda's getting dressed." He led me into a small, dim living room, and I sat down in a chair next to a table. On the table were two trophies—a silver loving cup saying "Miss Sullivan County 1949" and a plastic statuette saying "Miss New York State 1949"—and a two-panel picture folder showing, on one side, Miss Nalepa in a bathing suit and, on the other, Miss Nalepa in a nurse's uniform. Teddy sat on the edge of a couch and stared self-consciously at a crucifix and a holy picture on the wall across the room. I asked him if he was going to Atlantic City. He said that he was a tool-and-die maker and had to work. "Bob—that's Wanda's boyfriend—he's driving you down," he said. "Bob can get more time off. He's assistant manager for a finance company."

One by one, the family wandered into the room—Mr. Nalepa, a short, tired-looking man who resembles Teddy and who works in a factory making rattan furniture; Mrs. Nalepa, a small, shy woman with gray hair; and Wanda's younger sister, Helen, a high-school senior. Each of them nodded to me or said hello, but nobody said anything much after that. Then a pair of French doors opened and Wanda came in and said hello to me. Everybody studied her. She wore an eggshell straw sailor hat set back on her head, a navy-blue dotted-swiss dress, blue stockings, and high-heeled navy-blue pumps. For jewelry, she wore only a sturdy wristwatch with a leather strap and her nursing-school graduation ring.

"I hope this looks all right," Miss Nalepa said in a thin, uncertain voice. "I didn't know what to wear."

"Looks all right," her father said.

The doorbell rang. Teddy said that it must be Bob. It was Bob—a tall, gaunt man of about thirty with a worried face. He nodded to everybody, picked up Miss Nalepa's luggage and threw several evening gowns over one arm, said that we ought to get going, and started downstairs.

"Well, goodbye," said Miss Nalepa.

"Don't forget to stand up straight," her sister said.

"What about breakfast?" her mother asked mildly.

"I don't feel like eating," Miss Nalepa said.

"Good luck, Wanda," said Teddy.

"Well, goodbye," Miss Nalepa said again, looking at her father.

"All right, all right, goodbye," her father said.

Miss Nalepa was about to walk out the door when her mother stepped up timidly and gave her a peck on the cheek. As we were going downstairs together, Miss Nalepa clutched at my wrist. Her hand was cold. "That's the second time I ever remember my mother kissed me," she said, with a nervous laugh. "The first time was when I graduated from high school. I looked around to see if anybody was watching us, I was so embarrassed."

We found Bob and a pudgy, bald-headed man named Frank stowing the bags in the luggage compartment of a 1948 Pontiac sedan. I learned that Frank, a friend of Bob's, was going along, too. Women neighbors in housecoats were leaning out of windows to watch the departure. Frank told Miss Nalepa that a photograph of her taken from the rear had come out fine. "Wanda has a perfect back," he said to me. "I'm getting this picture printed in the *National Chiropractic Journal*. I'm a chiropractor."

I got in front, with Bob and Miss Nalepa. Frank got in back. On our way downtown, Miss Nalepa told me that we were to stop at Grand Central to pick up her chaperone, a Miss Neville. Miss Neville represented WKBW, the radio station in Buffalo that, with the blessings of the Miss America Pageant people but without any official blessings from Albany, had sponsored the New York State contest. A couple of weeks before competing in that one, which was held at the Crystal Beach Amusement Park, near Buffalo, Miss Nalepa had won the title of Miss Sullivan County in a contest held in the town of Monticello, thus qualifying for the state contest, and a week or so before that she had won the title of Miss White Roe Inn, the inn being situated outside the town of Livingston Manor, in Sullivan County. She had gone to the inn for a short vacation at the insistence of a friend who thought she could win the beauty contest there. Miss Nalepa had heard of such contests and of others held at local theatres but hadn't ever entered one before. "I never had the nerve," she told me. "I always knew I was pretty, but it always made me feel uncomfortable. When I was six, I remember a little boy in the first grade who used to watch me. I was terrified. I used to run home from school every day. At parties, when I was older, the boys paid a lot of attention to me, and I didn't like it. I wanted the other girls to get attention, too." Miss Nalepa went to a vocational high school, to study dressmaking; worked in a five-and-ten-cent store for a while after graduation; considered taking singing lessons but dropped the idea after her two sisters told her she had no singing ability; and went to the Rhodes School, in New York City, for a prenursing course and then to Mount Sinai Hospital, where she got her RN degree in 1948. She didn't like to go out on dates with the hospital doctors. "Doctors are too forward," she said.

At Grand Central, Miss Neville, a pleasant, gray-haired lady, who said she had not been in Atlantic City for twenty years and was very enthusiastic about going there now, got in the back seat with Frank, and they began talking about chiropractic. As we headed for the Holland Tunnel, the three of us in the front seat discussed the contest. "Don't expect much and you won't be disappointed," Miss Nalepa said, clutching Bob's arm. She thought it would be nice to have some scholarship money and said that if she won any, she might use it to learn to play some musical instrument. No money had come with the Miss White Roe Inn title. She had received seventy-five dollars from the Sullivan County Resort Association for becoming Miss Sullivan County, and a picture of her in a bathing suit had appeared in the *New York Daily News* captioned "Having Wandaful Time." When she was named Miss New York State, she was given three evening gowns and two pieces of luggage. She earned ten dollars a day nursing, but she hadn't worked for more than a month—not since she started entering beauty contests—and she had had to borrow three hundred dollars from members of her family for clothes, cosmetics, jewelry, a quick, $67.50 course in modeling, and other things designed to enhance beauty, poise, and personality. She was worried about being only five feet three. The Miss Americas of the preceding six years had all been five feet seven or more. The contestants would be judged on four counts: appearance in a bathing suit, appearance in an evening gown, personality, and talent. Miss Nalepa was wondering about her talent. Her act, as she planned it, was going to consist of getting up in her nurse's uniform and making a little speech about her nursing experience.

"I don't know what else I can do to show I've got talent," she said. "All I know how to do is give a good back rub."

"Listen, what you need right now is a good meal," Bob said.

Miss Nalepa said she wasn't hungry.

"You've got to eat," Bob said. "You're too skinny."

"You've got to eat," Frank repeated. "You're too skinny."

We stopped for breakfast at a roadside restaurant. Miss Nalepa had only half a cheeseburger and a few sips of tea.

In Atlantic City, Miss Nalepa and her chaperone headed for the hotel they had been assigned to, the Marlborough-Blenheim, where they were to share a double room. I said I was going to check in at the Claridge, across the street, and Bob offered to take my bag over. As the two of us walked over, he said that he and Frank were going to hang around for a short while and then go back to New York. "She's not going to win," he said. "I told her she's not going to win. That nursing isn't the right kind of talent. They'll want singing or dancing or something like that."

In the lobby there were large photographs of Miss America of 1948, and of the current Miss Arizona, Miss Florida, Miss Chicago, and Miss District of Columbia, all of whom, I learned from my bellhop, had been assigned to that hotel. "Big crowd comes down every year to see the crowning of Miss America," he said. "This is America's Baghdad-by-the-Sea. The only place on the ocean where you'll find a big crowd relaxing at recreations in the fall."

On my bureau was a small paper cutout doll labeled "Miss America, Be Be Shopp, in her official gown of Everglaze moire for the Miss America Pageant, September 6–11, 1949."

"You seen Be Be yet?" an elevator boy with round shoulders and watery eyes asked me as I was going back down. "Be Be's staying with us. Be Be looks real good. Better than last year. You see Miss Florida yet?" I shook my head. "She's something!" he said.

I went out to the boardwalk, where booths for the sale of tickets to the pageant had been set up in a line running down the middle, between two rows of Bingo Temples, billboard pictures of horses diving into the ocean from the Steel Pier, and places named Jewelry Riot, Ptomaine Tavern, and the Grecian Temple. The roller chairs were rolling in and out among the ticket booths. "Get your ticket now to see the beauties at the parade!" a middle-aged lady called to me from one of them. "Bleacher seats are twenty-five cents cheaper than last year!"

The contestants were registering for the pageant at the Traymore, so I went over there. A couple of dozen policemen were standing outside the registration room. I asked one of them if Miss New York State had arrived. "Not yet, sister," he said. "Stick around. I got my eye on all of them."

A white-haired gentleman wearing a green-and-purple checked jacket asked him how the registration was going.

"You want to see the beauties, buy a ticket to the pageant," the policeman said.

"They got any tall ones?" asked the gentleman.

"Yeah, they got some tall ones," the policeman said. "Utah is five ten. She comes from Bountiful—Bountiful, Utah."

"Hope it won't rain for the parade tomorrow," said the gentleman.

"It don't look too promising," observed the policeman.

Miss Nalepa and her chaperone turned up, and I went inside with them. The contestants were standing in an uneven line, looking unhappily at each other, before a table presided over by a middle-aged woman with a southern accent. She was Miss Lenora Slaughter, the executive director of the pageant. The atmosphere was hushed and edgy, but Miss Slaughter was extravagantly cheerful as she handed out badges and ribbons to the contestants. When Miss Nalepa's turn came to register, Miss Slaughter gave her a vigorous hug, called her darling, handed her a ribbon reading "New York State," and told her to wear it on her bathing suit, from the right shoulder to the left hip. I introduced myself to Miss Slaughter, and she shook my hand fervently. "You'll want to follow our working schedule," she said, giving me a booklet. "All the girls are going upstairs now to be fitted with their Catalina bathing suits, and then they get their pictures taken, and tonight we're having a nice meeting with all the girls, to tell them what's what. The Queen—Miss America of 1948; we call Miss America the Queen—will be there. You're welcome to come. . . . Miss California!" she cried. I moved on and Miss California took my place. Miss New York State clutched at my arm again and nodded toward Miss California, who had a large, square face, long blond hair, and large blue eyes. (Height, 5'6¼"; weight, 124; bust, 36; waist, 24¼; thigh, 20; hips,

36; shoe size 6½-AA; dress size, 12; age, 19. Reason for entering the contest: "To gain poise and develop my personality.") Miss New York State stood still, staring at her. "Come on, Wanda," said her chaperone. "We've got to get you that bathing suit."

The bathing suits were being handed out and fitted in a two-room suite upstairs. The contestants put on their suits in one room while the chaperones waited in the other. The fitting room was very quiet; the other was filled with noisy, nervous chatter.

Miss Alabama's chaperone was saying, "I'm grooming one now. She'll be ready in two years. She's sure to be Miss America of 1951."

"Have you seen Nebraska? She's a definite threat," said Miss New Jersey's chaperone to Miss Arkansas's chaperone.

"What's her talent?" asked Miss Arkansas's chaperone.

"Dramatic recitation," said Miss NJ's.

"She'll never make the first fifteen," said Miss Ark.'s.

"Confidentially," said one chaperone to another, "confidentially, I wouldn't pick *any* of the girls I've seen to be Miss America."

"Some years you get a better-looking crop than others," her companion said. "At the moment, what I've got my mind on is how I can get me a good, stiff drink, and maybe two more after it."

I went into the other room, where Miss New York State was having trouble with her suit. She did not like Catalina suits, she told me; they didn't fit her, and she wished the pageant officials would let her wear her own. Another contestant paused in her struggle with her suit and said it was very important to like the official pageant suits. "There just wouldn't *be* a little old pageant without Catalina," she said severely.

That night, Mr. Haverstick acted as chairman of the meeting of the contestants in Convention Hall, the world's largest auditorium. He is a solid, elderly gentleman with a large, bald head. He introduced the first speaker of the evening, Miss Slaughter, describing her as a friend they all knew and loved, the friend who had been working for the pageant since 1935. Miss New York State and most of the other contestants were wearing suits and hats. They sat attentively, their hands folded in their laps, as Miss Slaughter stood up and shook her head unbelievingly at them. "I see your faces and I see a dream of fifty-one weeks come true," she said. "Now, I want you all to listen to me. I'm going to ask you girls to keep one thought in mind during this great week. Think to yourself, 'There are fifty-one other talented, beautiful girls in this contest besides myself.' Get out of your head the title of Miss America. You're already a winner, a queen in your own right." She announced that a special prize—a thousand-dollar scholarship— would be awarded to the contestant elected Miss Congeniality by her competitors.

An elderly, heavyset woman with a high-pitched, martyred voice, Mrs. Malcolm Shermer, chairman of a group of local hostesses who would escort the contestants from their hotels to the pageant activities and back again, stood up and said that she would personally watch over the girls in their dressing room. "When I wake up on pageant morning, it's like another Christmas Day to me," she said, and went on to list some rules of decorum the contestants would have to follow. The girls were not to make dates with any man, or even have dinner with their fathers, because the public had no way of knowing whether or not a man was a contestant's father; they were not to enter a cocktail lounge or nightclub; they were to stick to their chaperones or their hostesses. "You have reached the top of the Miss America mountain," Mrs. Shermer said in a complaining tone, "so we're making you almost inaccessible, because all good businessmen put their most valuable belongings in a safe place." The contestants looked impressed. Miss New York State sighed. "They don't take any chances," she remarked to me. "This is just like school."

Miss America of 1948, clad in a suit of Everglaze (I later discovered that she had driven over faithfully in a Nash), then welcomed the fifty-two contestants. She smiled and told the contestants to keep smiling from the moment they woke up every day to the moment they fell asleep. Mr. Haverstick nodded solemnly. "Always have that smile on your face," she said. "Your smiles make people feel happy, and that's what we need—happier people in the world." The contestants all managed a smile. They continued to smile as Mr. Bob Russell was introduced as the master of ceremonies of the pageant. He came forward with that lively skip characteristic of nightclub MCs and said, "Girls, this week you're performers, you're actresses, you're models, you're singers and entertainers. Girls, show this great city that you're happy American girls, happy to be in Atlantic City, the city of beautiful girls!" Mr. Haverstick blushed and managed a small smile of his own.

The contestants were instructed to wear evening gowns, but not their best ones, in the parade that was going to take place the next day. Still conscientiously smiling, they filed out of the hall. Miss New York State let go of her smile for a moment and told me that she was returning to her room. She would lie down and elevate her feet for twenty minutes, put pads soaked with witch hazel over her eyes, take two sleeping pills, and go to sleep.

On the way out, Miss Slaughter stopped me and said that I was going to see the best contest in the pageant's history. It had come a long way, she said, from the first one, in 1921, when it was called the Bathers' Revue. The first winner, given the title of the Golden Mermaid, was Margaret Gorman, of Washington, DC, who briefly considered a theatrical career and then went home and married a real-estate man. "In those years, we offered nothing but promises and a cup," Miss Slaughter said. "Now we get real big bookings for our girls, where they can get started on a real big career. This is not a leg show and we don't call the beauties bathing beauties anymore. The bathing part went out in 1945, when we started giving big scholarships." Miss America of 1945—Bess Myerson, of the Bronx—the first winner to be awarded much more than promises and a cup, won a five-thousand-dollar scholarship and bookings worth ten thousand dollars. "Bess went right out and capitalized," Miss Slaughter said. "She went to Columbia and studied music, got married, and had an adorable baby girl, and now she runs a music school and does modeling, too." The next winner—Marilyn Buferd, of Los Angeles—wanted to get into the movies. She got a two-hundred-and-fifty-dollar-a-week job as a starlet with Metro-Goldwyn-Mayer. She is now in Italy, under contract to Roberto Rossellini. Miss America of 1947—Barbara Jo Walker, of Memphis—caused the pageant officials considerable worry. "She upped and announced she wanted to get married; she didn't want to go out and make money and get publicity," Miss Slaughter said. "Well, there was nothing we could do but let her get married to this medical student of hers, and now we've brought her back this year to be a judge." Be Be Shopp, whose term would run out in five days, had been the biggest moneymaker as Miss America. "She just never stopped working at it," Miss Slaughter said. "She set a real good example for our girls." Miss Shopp traveled across three continents, appearing at conventions and similar gatherings with a vibraharp, the instrument with which she had demonstrated her talent at last year's contest by playing "Trees." Miss America of 1944 went back to her home in Kentucky and married a farmer. Miss America of 1943 is singing in a nightclub in Paris. Miss America of 1942 married Phil Silvers, the comedian. Most of the Miss Americas back to 1921 got married soon after winning their titles. Miss America of 1937, however, has neither married nor embarked on a career. "Miss America of 1937 got crowned, and the next morning she just vanished," Miss Slaughter said, looking pained. "Why, she ran right home, someplace in New Jersey, and when we found her, she refused to come out—no explanation or *any*thing. Just the other day, she decided she wanted to be a model or actress or something, but maybe it's too late now."

The following morning, the contestants were photographed again in their Catalina swimsuits. After lunch they were assembled in the ballroom of a hotel near one end of the boardwalk for the American Beauty Parade, which would wind up near the other end, a distance of four and a half miles. Roller chairs and beach chairs were lined up along the route; the supply had been sold out (at $6.15 and $2, respectively) three weeks before. State police had been brought in to help keep order. It was a fine day for a parade—clear, sunny, and brisk. The business streets back of the boardwalk were almost deserted. The boardwalk was packed. Every roller chair was occupied, occasionally by as many as six people. Miss Arizona stood near the door of the ballroom. She would be one of the first to leave. She wore a long skirt of red suede, slit at one side, and a multicolored blouse of Indian design. Miss New York State, looking rested and wearing an aquamarine-colored satin gown, was off in a corner, watching Miss America of 1948, who was wearing a slip and contemplating the original of the dress she was pictured in on the paper doll. The dress lay across the backs of two chairs. It had a large hoop skirt and was decorated on the front with the official flowers, appliquéd, of the forty-eight states. She announced that she had to wear the gown in the parade and every night of the pageant. "It weighs thirty pounds," she said. "How am I ever going to play my vibraharp in it?"

Miss New York State shook her head in speechless marvel. "Will you play every night, Miss Shopp?" she asked.

"Call me Be Be, please," Miss America said, showing a dimpled smile.

"Everybody calls me Be Be. I play my vibraharp every place I go. I've made two hundred and sixty-one appearances with it, opening stores and things. The vibraharp weighs a hundred and fifty pounds, and a man usually carries it for me. They were the only men I got close to all year. I worked so hard I didn't have a chance to have any real dates."

Miss Florida, who was standing nearby, shook her head sadly. "Mah goodness, no dates!" she said.

Two women attendants climbed up on chairs and held the thirty-pound gown aloft while the Queen crawled under it. "Is it in the center of me?" she asked as her head and shoulders emerged. Everybody said that it was in the center of her and that she looked glorious. Miss America was now ready to lead the parade. I went outside and found a place on the boardwalk near a mobile radio-broadcasting unit, where Miss America's father, who is physical-education director at the Cream of Wheat Corporation in Minneapolis, was being interviewed. "I'm just as excited this year as last year," he was saying. "I'm just starting to realize she's Miss America."

The contestants were to rehearse that night with Bob Russell in Convention Hall, and I decided to go over there. Going through the lobby of my hotel, I ran into Miss Florida with her mother.

"Don't forget to smile, honey," her mother said, smiling.

"Ah don't have *any* trouble smilin', Mama," said Miss Florida.

"That's a good girl, honey," her mother said.

The statistics on Miss Florida showed that at eighteen she was already a veteran beauty. She was Citrus Queen of Florida in 1947, Railroad Exposition Queen in Chicago in 1948, Miss Holiday of Florida of 1949, and Miss Tampa of 1949. (Reason for entering the Atlantic City contest: "Because the Chamber of Commerce of Tampa asked me to compete.")

At Convention Hall, Mr. Russell, standing on the stage surrounded by weary-looking contestants, was outlining the procedure for the next three nights. A long ramp ran out into the auditorium at right angles to the stage, and a few of the contestants squatted on it, as though they were too exhausted to move back to the stage with the others. Miss New York State seemed fairly fresh. Her face was flushed, but she appeared to smile without effort. She wanted to know whether I had seen her in the parade. "That was *fun*," she said. "I was standing and yelling things, and people were yelling things to me. That was really a lot of *fun*. I never thought that people would be so *friendly*."

"Please, girls," said the MC. "I need your attention."

"I'm used to a long, hard day from nursing," Miss New York State whispered. "Some of these girls look all done in." Smiling, she gave the MC her attention. He explained that the contestants would be divided into three groups. Each night, one group would compete for points on their appearance in evening dress, another in bathing suits, and the members of the third would demonstrate their talents. The girls would be judged on personality at two breakfasts, when the judges would meet and talk with them. Every girl would be scored in these four categories, and the fifteen girls with the highest total number of points would compete in the semifinals of the contest, at which time the judges would reappraise them and choose the queen and the four other finalists. Miss New York State was assigned to a group that included Miss Florida, Miss California, and Miss Arizona; they would appear the first night in bathing suits, the second in evening gowns, and on the third they would demonstrate their talents. The winners of the bathing-suit and talent competitions would be announced each night, but not the runners-up, and neither the winners nor the runners-up in the evening-gown competition. In this way, it would not be known who the semifinalists were until they were named on the fourth, and last, night of competition. Each day, Mr. Russell said, he would rehearse the girls in whatever they had prepared to do to show their talent that night. He then made the contestants line up in alphabetical order and parade together from the wings onto the stage and off it down the long ramp—the same ramp each would eventually be required to walk alone. The parade would wind up on each of the first three nights with the appearance of Miss America of 1948 in her thirty-pound gown. The other girls would raise empty water glasses in a toast to her while Mr. Russell sang the Miss America Pageant song, which goes:

> Let's drink a toast to Miss America,
> Let's raise our glasses on high
> From coast to coast in this America,
> As the sweetheart of the USA is passing by.
> To a girl, to a girl.

To a symbol of happiness.
To the one, to the one
Who's the symbol of all we possess.

Miss New York State took only an hour to get dressed for the opening night. I stopped by her room before dinner. She was studying herself in a mirror. She wore an ice-blue satin evening gown, her hair was shining, she had on very little makeup, and her face was smooth and pale. She put on a rhinestone necklace, looked hard at herself, wiped a bit of lipstick from a front tooth, and shrugged. "I'm so vain," she said.

"We'd better go down to dinner," Miss Neville said. "You're due at Convention Hall at eight."

The hotel dining room was filled, mostly with elderly ladies in high lace collars, canes hanging from the backs of their chairs. Several of them applauded as Miss New York State made her entrance, and one later sent her a note wishing her good luck. Miss New York State ordered onion soup, filet of sole, a caramel-nut sundae, and tea with lemon. After she had finished her fish, she waited placidly for her sundae, which was not served until almost eight.

I found a seat at the press table at Convention Hall, abreast of the ramp, as Mr. Russell, wearing a dinner jacket, skipped out and announced that the parade was going to begin. Miss Alabama and the fifty-one others came onto the ramp, smiling but shaking with nervousness. My seat was not far from where Miss New York State stood on the ramp, and I could see her trembling with a kind of sick, forced laughter. The judges, all in evening dress, were introduced: Vyvyan Donner, women's editor of Twentieth Century-Fox Movietone News; Ceil Chapman, dress designer; Clifford D. Cooper, president of the United States Junior Chamber of Commerce; Guy E. Snavely, Jr., who was described as a husband, father, and executive secretary of Pickett & Hatcher, an educational foundation in Birmingham, Alabama; Paul R. Anderson, president of Pennsylvania College for Women, in Pittsburgh; Mrs. Barbara Walker Hummell, Miss America of 1947; Conrad Thibault, baritone; Vincent Trotta, art director of the National Screen Service, a company that makes posters and billboards for motion pictures; Coby Whitmore, commercial artist; Hal Phyfe, photographer; and Earl Wilson, columnist. Voting was by ballot, with two certified public accountants acting as tellers of the ballots. From the press table I picked up a brochure about Convention Hall and read that it is 488 feet long, 288 feet wide, and 137 feet high, and that it could be transformed in a few hours into a full-size football field or into the world's largest indoor fight arena. "The place dwarfs," a gentleman seated next to me said with finality.

After the parade, the group competing in evening gowns that night came onstage one by one, modeled before the judges, and walked down the ramp. Then they came out in a group and lined up in front of the judges, who sat in their enclosure, which adjoined the ramp. Miss Illinois, a pert girl with green eyes and blond hair, fixed in a Maggie (Jiggs's Maggie) hairdo, winked saucily at the judges. She wore a strapless white gown with a rhinestone-trimmed bodice. (Height, 5'6¼"; weight, 118; bust, 35; hips, 35½; age, 19. Reason for entering the pageant: "I entered with the sincere hope of furthering my career.") Mr. Russell urged the girls to give big smiles and urged the judges to pay attention to coiffure, grooming, and symmetry of form. The contestants faced front, turned to show their profiles, turned to show their backs, turned to show their other profiles, then faced front again, and retired. The tellers collected the ballots. Next, a group in bathing suits came out, led by Miss Arizona. Miss California, the tall blonde, came next. Miss Florida followed, and, after a few other contestants, Miss New York State. As they stood before the judges, the MC asked them to examine the girls' figures carefully for any flaws. For example, he asked, did the thighs and the calves meet at the right place. Miss New York State stood rigidly, once grasping at the hand of Miss North Dakota. The audience of nine thousand, who had paid from $1.25 to $6.15 for their tickets, sat patiently and stared. The bathing suiters retired, and Mr. Russell announced that he would do impersonations of Al Jolson, Bing Crosby, Eddie Cantor, and Enrico Caruso. After this demonstration of versatility, he said that the curtains were about to open on "our beautiful old-fashioned southern garden." The curtains parted. All the girls, in evening gowns, were seated in chairs on simulated grass. Here and there were potted palms. For some reason, Miss New York State sat behind one of them.

The talent competition began. Miss Alabama, a mezzo-soprano, led off by singing "Neath the Southern Moon," accompanied, more or less, by a pit orchestra. Miss Nevada's talent, it seemed, was raising purebred Herefords; she had wanted to bring one of her cows, she said in a brief speech, but the officials wouldn't let her. Miss Colorado gave a monologue from *Dinner at Eight*. Miss Hawaii danced a hula. Miss Indiana showed a movie demonstrating her talent in swimming. Miss New Jersey sang "Mighty Lak' a Rose." Miss Minnesota, a small version of Be Be Shopp, played some gypsy airs on a violin. While the judges marked their ballots, Miss Shopp entertained by playing "Smoke Gets in Your Eyes" on her vibraharp, evidently not handicapped by the thirty-pound gown. Then the preliminary winners were announced: bathing suit, a tie between Miss Arizona and Miss California; talent, Miss Minnesota.

The contestants got back to their hotels late, because Miss Michigan was given a party backstage in honor of her nineteenth birthday. This had come about because she had decided early in the evening that she wanted to drop out of the pageant and go home at once. I had been advised of the circumstance by an official of the pageant. "This little brat wants to run out on us," he had said, stuffing some chewing tobacco into his mouth. "We're taking a gamble and blowing a sawbuck on a cake for her. It better work." It worked. Miss Michigan decided to stay in Atlantic City. Everybody appeared to enjoy the party, and everybody made a determined effort to be Miss Congeniality. Miss New York State showed no disappointment at not having won first place in the swimsuit competition. "California is so *tall*," she said to me.

At my hotel the next afternoon, I ran into Miss Arizona's chaperone in the elevator. "I thought I would die last night before they announced that my girl had won," she said. "I've been with her ever since she won her first contest, three years ago, but I've never been through anything like *that* before." Three years ago, she told me, Miss Arizona had won a teenage beauty contest sponsored by Aldens, a mail-order house in Chicago; she had then attended a modeling school and had modeled teenage clothes for Aldens catalog. The business people of Arizona (Arizona has the largest man-made lake in North America and the largest open-pit copper mine in the world, and it is great to live in Arizona, a brochure entitled "Miss Arizona, 1949—Jacque Mercer," put out by the contestant's sponsor, the Phoenix Junior Chamber of Commerce, and handed to me by the contestant's chaperone, said) had given her twenty-five hundred dollars to prepare for the Atlantic City contest. The chaperone invited me to come up to her room to look at

Miss Arizona's wardrobe. It was a spectacular wardrobe, put together with taste. Miss Arizona was an only child. Her mother had married at fifteen and had named her daughter Jacque after a doll she had had. "Jackie's parents are here, but I'm making them stay away from her," the chaperone said. "They're schoolteachers. Schoolteachers don't know what to do with children." Miss Arizona came into the room.

"The pageant asked Jackie what kind of car she likes and I said to put down Nash," said the chaperone.

"I like Cadillacs," Miss Arizona said.

I told Miss Arizona and her chaperone that I had to get along, in order to look in on Miss New York State. Miss Arizona immediately said she liked Miss New York State. "*She* doesn't giggle, the way some of the others do," she explained. "I don't care for girls who giggle." She flicked a speck of dust off one of her new shoes. "I'll be glad when this is over and I can frown at people if I feel like it," she said. "I sometimes feel as though my face is going to crack. But I keep that bi-ig smile on my face." She laughed.

When I joined Miss New York State, she was wearing her nurse's uniform—white dress, white stockings, and white shoes. She was going, she said, to the Atlantic City Hospital. Two photographers covering the pageant had heard that she had no way of demonstrating her talent, and had arranged to make a movie short showing her in professional action. She looked crisp and efficient. She had had a busy morning, she said, having been examined for personality at the first of the two breakfasts with the judges. The contestants sat at small tables, with a couple of judges at each. After each course, a bell rang and the judges changed tables, which gave them an opportunity to talk with all the contestants. Miss New York State said that most of the girls had trouble getting their breakfast down but that she had had orange juice, bacon and eggs, toast, marmalade, and tea. "I wasn't going to sit there and let all that good food go," she said. She didn't know whether she had made a favorable impression on the judges. "I told Conrad Thibault I had never heard of him," she said. "He didn't seem to like that."

Before the pageant's second-evening program began, some of the judges wandered about Convention Hall, presumably judging the new Nash waiting in the lobby for the winner and judging the audience, which was approximately the same size it had been the first night. Earl Wilson stopped at the press table and said he had been reading an essay on beauty by Edmund Burke. "He says that an object of beauty should be comparatively small and delicate, bright and clear, with one section melting neatly into the other," he said. "The essay didn't affect me any. I like 'em big." He was joined by a gentleman from Omaha, who listened to him impatiently for a while. "I tell you what you're gonna pick, Earl," he finally broke in. "You're gonna pick the kind of girl *I* would pick for my own wife or daughter. That's what we got this contest for." Mr. Wilson nodded respectfully and moved on.

In front of the dressing room, Miss Florida was taking leave of her mother.

"Smile, now, honey," said her mother.

"Ah *am* smilin', Mama," said Miss Florida.

Inside, Miss New York State was standing with her back right up against an ironing board while a lady attendant pressed the skirt of the gown she was wearing for the evening's competition. It had a white net skirt and a white satin bodice. She had bought it at a New York wholesale house for $29.75. She looked around admiringly and objectively at the dresses of the other girls. "What beautiful *gowns*," she said.

Miss Florida was smiling at no one in particular. The city of Tampa had given her her gown—ruffled champagne-colored lace (a hundred and fifty yards)—and matching elbow-length gloves. Miss California sat gravely before a mirror in a dress of blue satin trimmed with black lace on the bodice and a black lace bow at the waist. Miss Arizona stood in a corner, a tense smile on her face, in a gown with a hoop skirt of ruffles of white organdy eyelet (a hundred and sixty yards) with a bouquet of red carnations at one side.

Miss Missouri came in, and Miss New York State waved to her. "Missouri is going to dance tonight," she told me. "I like dancing. It always makes me feel good. You know," she went on rapidly, "I found out today I'm photogenic. One of those photographers told me I could be a model, and my picture is in all the papers. One of the papers said I was *outstanding*." She grabbed my arm. "Nobody ever called me *outstanding* before."

Mrs. Shermer, the chief hostess, called out that the girls were to line up in the wings, and that they should be careful not to step on each other's dresses. Miss New York State took her place in line and the contestants started to move onto the stage, big smiles on their faces.

"Mind my horse!" Miss Montana said cheerily to her hostess.

"I *would* get the one with the horse," the hostess said to me.

I went out front and again sat down at the press table, next to a man whose badge said he was Arthur K. Willi, of RKO Radio Pictures. Throughout the evening-gown and bathing-suit parades, he held a pair of opera glasses to his eyes, then he put them down with a groan. "I look and I look and I look, and what do I see?" he said. "If Clark Gable walked out on that stage right now, he would fill it up, or Maggie Sullavan, or Dorothy Maguire. There's nothing here, nothing—not even when I look at these kids with the eyes of the masses."

The MC brought out two platinum blondes and introduced them as Miss Atlanta of 1947 and Miss Omaha of 1947. They did a tap dance to "I Got Rhythm." "Those poor kids," Willi said. "Those poor, poor kids. Look at them. They look as though they had been knocking around Broadway for fifteen years." When the talent session began, he put the glasses back to his eyes. Miss Kansas, who was twenty-two, sang "September Song" with a deliberately husky voice. Miss Canada sang "Sempre Libera" from *La Traviata*. Miss Connecticut recited "Jackie, the Son of the Hard-Boiled Cop." Miss Montana, wearing a conventional riding coat and frontier pants, rode her horse, a nine-year-old mare named Victory Belle, out onto the stage. Miss Illinois grinned confidently at the judges, and in a strong soprano sang "Ouvre Ton Cœur" as though she meant it. Miss Wisconsin wound up with a baton-twirling act. The winners: bathing suit, Miss Colorado; talent, Miss Canada.

"The pageant wants publicity in the Canadian papers," a newspaperman near me said.

Willi put his opera glasses in his coat pocket. "They've all lost their youth already," he said. "They come down here for what? To lose their youth!"

Miss New York State's picture was in the New York, Philadelphia, and Atlantic City newspapers the next morning. She was shown at the Atlantic City Hospital, wearing her uniform and holding a two-year-old girl who had just had her tonsils out.

Miss Arizona had dark circles under her eyes when I encountered her in our hotel lobby after lunch, and she said that she was going to spend the afternoon thinking about Shakespeare and listening to a recording of Tchaikovsky's *Romeo and Juliet* overture, to get in the mood for her talent demonstration that night—Juliet's potion scene. She had stayed up all the night before talking about it and other pageant matters with her chaperone. Miss Arizona had played Juliet at Phoenix Junior College, having been chosen from five hundred girls who had tried out for the part. She wanted to be an actress; she wouldn't go to Hollywood until she had attended drama school and spent several years in the theatre. "Hollywood would try to make me be something *they* wanted me to be," she said.

That night, Miss Arizona came out in a wispy white nightgown and, in the auditorium that could be transformed in a few hours into a full-size football field, called up the faint, cold fear thrilling through her veins that almost freezes up the heat of life. The audience was restless and noisy as she expressed her fear that she would die ere her Romeo came. She was followed by Miss Greater Philadelphia, playing "I'm in the Mood for Love" on an electric guitar. Miss Mississippi did Hagar berating Abraham, in a dramatic reading popular with elocution teachers. Miss California acted the part of a girl who had been wronged by a man, in a reading even more popular with elocution teachers. Miss Florida sang "Put Your Shoes On, Lucy," which was announced in a release to the press as "Put Your Shoes on Lucy." Miss New York State, wearing her ice-blue evening gown, gave a short talk on nursing. She spoke without any expression at all, as though she were reciting something she had memorized with difficulty. "Ever since I was a little girl, I was taught that people were here for the purpose of serving others," she said. The audience shifted unsympathetically in their seats. Somebody muttered that Miss Illinois ought to stop flirting with the judges. Miss New York State said she had decided to become a nurse when she visited a friend who was a patient in a veterans' hospital during the war. She had been shocked by the men's helplessness. She would now show a film of herself going about her usual duties. She was pictured in the children's ward, in the maternity ward, and assisting a surgeon at an operation. At the end of the picture, the audience applauded half-heartedly. The winners: bathing suit, Miss Illinois; talent, Miss Arizona.

I was awakened at seven by the sound of gunfire. Some former Seabees had arrived in the city for a convention, and the Navy was welcoming them with a mock assault landing on the beach. It was the last day of the pageant, and the boardwalk seemed to sag with the crowds.

The auditorium that night had a capacity audience, including standees, of twenty thousand. The Seabees came en masse. Most of the police at the hall felt that Miss California would be the winner, but the captain in charge of the detail was indifferent. "All you can do is look, and you get tired looking," he said. "I been guarding the beauties since 1921. An old lady come up to me during the parade the other day and says hello. I must have looked at her strange, because she says she was Miss Maryland of 1924. She was a grandmother! That kind of thing don't make me feel no better."

The contestants arrived and were counted. No one was missing; no one had walked out on the pageant. The girls had had breakfast that morning with the judges again and then had voted for Miss Congeniality; Miss Montana and Miss New Jersey had tied for the honor and split the thousand-dollar scholarship. An only fairly congenial miss wanted to know what kind of education you could get with a five-hundred-dollar scholarship. "Why, same as you can do with a bigger one," said Miss New Jersey. "Take voice lessons, or go to tap-dance school, or even go to Europe and learn something." Miss Slaughter nodded staunchly in approval. Also at the breakfast, Miss America of 1948 had made all fifty-two misses members of the pageant sorority—Mu Alpha Sigma, whose letters stand for Modesty, Ambition, and Success—and each girl had been given a gold-filled pin. "The most thrilling thing a girl could have," Miss America had said. "It means that all of you are queens. Remember that when the fifteen semifinalists are named tonight, *all* of you are queens." Miss New York State had asked if the sorority high sign was a big smile, a remark that didn't get much of a laugh. She had voted for Miss Montana as Miss Congeniality. "I knew that I would never be elected," she told me. "In nursing, I got to know too much about human nature to be able to *act* congenial."

Mrs. Shermer was looking very pleased. She told Earl Wilson she had a hot item for his column—she had discovered some contestants putting on false eyelashes. Mr. Wilson looked pleased, too. He had spent the afternoon autographing copies of his latest book at a department store in town. Miss Arizona had received a wire from her father (who was staying at a nearby hotel) saying that she had made first base, second base, and third base and concluding, "Now slide into home!"

Mr. Russell was in tails for the big night. The curtains opened on the "beautiful old-fashioned southern garden" again. One by one, the fifteen semifinalists stood up as their names were called: Miss Arizona, Miss Arkansas, Miss California, Miss Canada, Miss Chicago, Miss Colorado, Miss Hawaii, Miss Illinois, Miss Kansas, Miss Michigan, Miss Minnesota, Miss Mississippi, Miss New Jersey, Miss New York City, and Miss Wisconsin. Each of them was now sure of at least a thousand-dollar scholarship. The losers sat motionless in the southern garden, some smiling, some in tears, others trying unsuccessfully to look indifferent. Out front, Miss Florida's mother cried softly, but Miss Florida was still smiling. Miss New York State, this time only half hidden behind a potted plant, looked puzzled but interested in what was going on.

The semifinalists paraded before the judges once again, then withdrew to change into bathing suits. Mr. Russell asked the losers to walk the ramp, one by one, for the last time. "Give the valiant losers a hand, folks," he said. "They've got what it takes. They are your future wives and mothers of the nation." The valiant losers got a big hand. Miss New York State walked very gracefully—better than she had walked in competition. She waved cheerfully as she passed me and with her lips silently said, "Bob—is—here." She received more applause than any of the other losers and quite a few whistles from the gallery. Then Miss Omaha of 1947 and Miss Atlanta of 1947 did their tap dance. Miss New York State watched them with a look of resigned but genuine appreciation.

The semifinalists paraded in bathing suits and then demonstrated their talent all over again. While the judges marked their ballots, a six-year-old girl named Zola May played Chopin's "Minute Waltz" on a piano. The MC then spoke glowingly of the three donors of the prizes and introduced the president of the company that makes Everglaze, the president of Catalina, and a delegation of three stout men in white linen suits from Nash. They all took bows. Then the MC asked Eddie Cantor to come out of the audience and up on the stage. Cantor did, and said hoarsely and passionately, "Communism hasn't got a chance when twenty thousand people gather to applaud culture and beauty."

Then the five big-prize finalists were announced: Miss Arizona, Miss California, Miss Colorado, Miss Illinois, and Miss Mississippi. Mr. Russell interviewed them, and their manner in replying was supposed to help the judges measure them for poise and personality. Each girl was asked three questions: "How do you plan to use your scholarship?"

"Do your future plans include marriage, a career, or what?" "What did you get out of the pageant?" Miss New York State peeked attentively around the potted plant as Miss Arizona, leading off in alphabetical order, replied tersely but politely that she planned to study dramatics at Stanford University, that she wanted marriage first and a career second, and that the pageant had given her a chance to test herself before a new audience in a new part of the country. Miss California wanted to study interior decorating at the University of California and then go into the furniture business with her father; she wanted a career, so that she could help whomever she married; she was grateful to the pageant for giving her the opportunity to meet so many wonderful girls from all over the country. Miss Illinois said that music was her first ambition. Mr. Russell, breaking the routine, asked her if she had ever been in love. She replied that she *was* in love but that music was still her first ambition. Miss New York State watched and listened carefully.

The winners were announced in reverse order: Fifth place, Miss California ($1,500); fourth place, Miss Colorado ($2,000); third place, Miss Illinois ($2,500); second place, Miss Mississippi ($3,000); first place, Miss Arizona ($5,000, plus the new four-door Nash sedan, the dozen Catalina swimsuits, and the wardrobe of sixty Everglaze garments), now Miss America of 1949. There were hoots and boos, as well as cheers, from the audience. The governor of New Jersey, who had arrived after Miss Arizona had done her Juliet scene, awarded her a gilt statue, half as high as she was, of a winged miss and said, "The world needs the kind of beauty and talent you have." Most of the losers then straggled out of the southern garden into the wings, and a number of chaperones, hostesses, parents, and press people crowded onto the stage. I went along. Miss New York State came forward to watch Miss America of 1948 crown her successor. Miss America of 1948 wept, and her mother, standing nearby, wept with her. The new Miss America, tremulous but happy, said, "I only hope you'll be half as proud of me as I am of the title Miss America." *Her* mother, who had suddenly been surrounded by a group of admiring strangers, was much too occupied with her own emotions to notice her daughter coming slowly down the ramp, crown on her head, purple robe over her shoulders, and scepter in her hand. The orchestra (the violinist holding a cigar in a corner of his mouth) played "Pomp and Circumstance," and Miss America of 1949 walked the length of the ramp, smiling graciously.

"This is the beginning," a reporter said to me. "She's going to spend the rest of her life looking for something. They *all* are."

"She is now the most desirable girl in the United States," another said.

When the Queen got back to the stage, Miss New York State offered her her solemn congratulations. "I'm glad you won, kid," she said. "I was rooting for you."

Then the new Miss America was engulfed by still photographers, newsreel men, and interviewers.

"Everybody wants my autograph because I'm her father," Miss America's father was saying.

Her mother wanted to know whether the parents were to get a badge or ribbon, too.

"We got to get her in the Nash!" one of the Nash triumvirate in white suits was saying.

A group of people were asking Miss Slaughter about the new Queen's plans. "She's going to have breakfast with all the newspaper people in New York," Miss Slaughter said. "Then she gets outfitted with a whole new wardrobe by Everglaze, and she wears Everglaze whenever she goes out in public—it's in her contract. She's got to fly to California to preside at the Catalina swimsuit show, and after that she's got to make a couple of screen tests in Hollywood. I've been going mad arranging for those screen tests."

Miss New York State shook her head at the wonder of it all. "Going to Hollywood!" she said. "She'll probably be in the movies."

The two of us walked back to the dressing room, where we found Miss Missouri tearfully folding up her Catalina swimsuit. Miss New York State looked puzzled at her tears and said that *she* hadn't cried, because when you don't expect very much, you're never disappointed. She was returning to New York with Bob the next morning. She had the name of a photographer who wanted to take a lot of pictures of her to sell to magazines, and another man wanted to talk to her about becoming a model. She was not going back to nursing if she could help it. "You *get* more when you're a model," she said.

(OCTOBER 22, 1949)

The Yellow Bus

A few Sundays ago, in the late afternoon, a bright-yellow school bus, bearing the white-on-blue license plate of the State of Indiana and with the words BEAN BLOSSOM TWP MONROE COUNTY painted in black letters under the windows on each side, emerged into New York City from the Holland Tunnel. Inside the bus were eighteen members of the senior class of the Bean Blossom Township High School, who were coming to the city for their first visit. The windows of the bus, as it rolled out into Canal Street, were open, and a few of the passengers leaned out, deadpan and silent, for a look at Manhattan. The rest sat, deadpan and silent, looking at each other. In all, there were twenty-two people in the bus: eleven girls and seven boys of the senior class; their English teacher and her husband; and the driver (one of the regular bus drivers employed by the township for the school) and his wife. When they arrived, hundreds of thousands of the city's eight million inhabitants were out of town. Those who were here were apparently minding their own business; certainly they were not handing out any big hellos to the visitors. The little Bean Blossom group, soon to be lost in the shuffle of New York's resident and transient summer population, had no idea of how to elicit any hellos—or, for that matter, any goodbyes or how-are-you's. Their plan for visiting New York City was divided into three parts: one, arriving; two, staying two days and three nights; three, departing.

Well, they had arrived. To get here, they had driven eight hundred and forty miles in thirty-nine and a half hours, bringing with them, in addition to spending money of about fifty dollars apiece, a fund of $957.41, which the class had saved up collectively over the past six years. The money represented the profits from such enterprises as candy and ice-cream concessions at school basketball games, amusement booths at the class (junior) carnival, and ticket sales for the class (senior) play, *Mumbo-Jumbo*. For six years, the members of the class had talked about how they would spend the money to celebrate their graduation. Early this year, they voted on it. Some of the boys voted for a trip to New Orleans, but they were outvoted by the girls, all of whom wanted the class to visit New York. The class figured that the cost of motels and hotels—three rooms for the boys, three rooms for the girls, one room for each of the couples—would come to about four hundred dollars. The bus driver was to be paid three hundred and fifty dollars for driving and given thirty for road, bridge, and tunnel tolls. Six members of the class, who were unable to participate in the trip, stayed home. If there should be any money left over, it would be divided up among all the class members when the travelers returned to Bean Blossom Township. The names of the eighteen touring class members were R. Jay Bowman, Shelda Bowman (cousin of R. Jay), Robert Britton, Mary Jane Carter, Lynn Dillon, Ina Hough, Thelma Keller, Wilma Keller (sister of Thelma), Becky Kiser, Jeanne Molnar, Nancy Prather, Mike Richardson, Dennis Smith, Donna Thacker, Albert Warthan, Connie Williams, Larry Williams (not related to Connie), and Lela Young.

It was also a first visit to New York for the English teacher, a lively young lady of twenty-eight named Polly Watts, and for her husband, Thomas, thirty-two, a graduate student in political science at Indiana University, in Bloomington, which is about twelve miles from the Bean Blossom Township school. The only people on the bus who had been to New York before were the driver, a husky, uncommunicative man of forty-nine named Ralph Walls, and his wife, Margaret, thirty-nine and the mother of his seven children, aged twenty-one to two, all of whom were left at home. Walls was the only adviser the others had on what to do in New York. His advice consisted of where to stay (the Hotel Woodstock, on West Forty-Third Street, near Times Square) and where to eat (Hector's Cafeteria, around the corner from the hotel).

The Bean Blossom Township school is in the village of Stinesville, which has three hundred and fifty-five inhabitants and a town pump. A couple of the seniors who made the trip live in Stinesville; the others live within a radius of fifteen miles or so, on farms or in isolated houses with vegetable gardens and perhaps a cow or two. At the start of the trip, the travelers gathered in front of their school shortly after midnight, and by one in the morning, with every passenger occupying a double seat in the bus (fifty-four passenger, 1959 model), and with luggage under the seats, and suits and dresses hung on a homemade clothes rack in the back of the bus, they were on their way.

The senior-class president, R. (for Reginald) Jay Bowman, was in charge of all the voting on the trip. A wiry, energetic eighteen-year-old with a crew haircut, he had been president of the class for the past five years, and is one of two members of the class who intend to go to college. He wants to work, eventually, for the United States Civil Service, because a job with the government is a steady job. Or, in a very vague way, he thinks he may go into politics. With the help of a hundred-and-two-dollar-a-year scholarship, he plans to pay all his own expenses at Indiana University. The other student who is going to college has also chosen Indiana University. She is Nancy Prather, an outdoorsy, freckle-faced girl whose father raises dairy and beef cattle on a two-hundred-and-fifty-acre farm and who is the class salutatorian. As for the valedictorian, a heavyset, firm-mouthed girl named Connie Williams, she was planning to get married a week after returning home from New York. The other class members expected, for the most part, to get to work at secretarial or clerical jobs, or in automobile or electronic-parts factories in Bloomington. The New York trip was in the nature of a first and last fling.

Ralph Walls dropped the passengers and their luggage at the Woodstock and then took the bus to a parking lot on Tenth Avenue, where he was going to leave it for the duration of the visit. His job, he had told his passengers, was to drive to New York, not in it. He had also told them that when he got back to the Woodstock he was going to sleep, but had explained how to get around the corner to Hector's Cafeteria. The boys and girls signed the register and went to their rooms to get cleaned up. They all felt let down. They had asked Walls whether the tall buildings they saw as they came uptown from the Holland Tunnel made up the skyline, and Walls had said he didn't know. Then they asked him which was the Empire State Building, and he had said they would have to take a tour to find out. Thus put off, they more or less resigned themselves to saving any further questions for a tour. Jay Bowman said that he would see about tours before the following morning.

Mrs. Watts and her husband washed up quickly and then, notwithstanding the bus driver's advice, walked around the Times Square area to see if they could find a reasonably priced and attractive place to have supper. They checked Toffenetti's across the street from the hotel, but they decided that it was too expensive (hamburger dinners at two dollars and ten cents, watermelon at forty cents) and too formidable. When they reconvened with the senior class in the lobby of the Woodstock, they recommended that everybody have the first meal at Hector's. The party set out—for some reason, in Indian file—for Hector's, and the first one inside was Mike Richardson, a husky, red-haired boy with large, swollen-looking hands and sunburned forearms. A stern-voiced manager near the door, shouting "Take your check! Take your check!" at all incomers, gave the Indiana group the same sightless once-over he gave everybody else. The Bean Blossom faces, which had been puzzled, fearful, and disheartened since Canal Street, now took on a look of resentment. Mike Richardson led the line to the counter. Under a sign reading BAKED WHITEFISH, a white-aproned counterman looked at Mike and said, "Come on, fella!" Mike glumly took a plate of fish and then filled the rest of his tray with baked beans, a roll, iced tea, and strawberry shortcake (check—$1.58). The others quickly and shakily filled their trays with fish, baked beans, a roll, iced tea, and strawberry shortcake. Sweating, bumping their trays and their elbows against other trays and other elbows, they found seats in twos and threes with strangers, at tables that still had other people's dirty dishes on them. Then, in a nervous clatter of desperate and noisy eating, they stuffed their food down.

"My ma cooks better than this," said Albert Warthan, who was sitting with Mike Richardson and Larry Williams. Albert, the eldest of seven children of a limestone-quarry worker, plans to join the Army and become a radar technician.

"I took this filet de sole? When I wanted somethin' else, I don't know what?" Mike said.

"I like the kind of place you just set there and decide what you want," said Larry, who is going to work on his grandfather's farm.

"My ma and pa told me to come home when it was time to come home, and not to mess around," Albert said. "I'm ready to chuck it and go home right now."

"The whole idea of it is just to see it and get it over with," Mike said.

"You got your money divided up in two places?" Albert asked. "So's you'll have some in one place if it gets stolen in t'other?"

The others nodded.

"Man, you can keep this New York," said Larry. "This place is too hustly, with everybody pushin' and no privacy. Man, I'll take the Big Boy any old day."

Frisch's Big Boy is the name of an Indiana drive-in chain, where a hamburger costs thirty cents. The general effect of Hector's Cafeteria was to give the Bean Blossom Class of 1960 a feeling of unhappiness about eating in New York and to strengthen its faith in the superiority of the Big Boys back home.

Jay Bowman went from table to table, polling his classmates on what they wanted to do that evening. At first, nobody wanted to do anything special. Then they decided that the only special thing they wanted to do was go to Coney Island, but they wanted to save Coney Island for the wind-up night, their last night in New York. However, nobody could think of anything to do that first night, so Jay took a revote, and it turned out that almost all of them wanted to go to Coney Island right away. Everybody but three girls voted to go to Coney Island straight from Hector's. Mrs. Watts was mildly apprehensive about this project, but Mike Richardson assured her it was easy; somebody at the hotel had told him that all they had to do was go to the subway and ask the cashier in the booth which train to take, and that would be that. Mrs. Watts said she was going to walk around a bit with her husband. The three girls who didn't want to go to Coney Island explained that they firmly believed the class should "have fun" on its last night in the city, and not before. The three were Ina Hough, whose father works in an RCA television manufacturing plant in Indianapolis (about fifty miles from Stinesville); Lola Young, whose foster father works in a Chevrolet parts warehouse in Indianapolis; and Jeanne Molnar, whose father is a draftsman at the Indiana Limestone Company, in Bloomington. All three already knew that they disliked New York. People in New York, they said, were all for themselves.

At nine o'clock, while most of their classmates were on the Brighton BMT express bound for Coney Island, the three girls walked to Sixth Avenue and Fiftieth Street with Mr. and Mrs. Watts, who left them at that point to take a walk along Fifth Avenue. The girls stood in a long line of people waiting to get into the Radio City Music Hall. After twenty minutes, they got out of the line and walked over to Rockefeller Plaza, where they admired the fountain, and to St. Patrick's Cathedral, which looked bigger to them than any church they had ever seen. The main church attended by the Bean Blossom group is the Nazarene

Church. No one in the senior class had ever talked to a Jew or to more than one Catholic, or—with the exception of Mary Jane Carter, daughter of the Nazarene minister in Stinesville—had ever heard of an Episcopalian. At ten o'clock, the three girls returned to the Music Hall line, which had dwindled, but when they got to the box office they were told that they had missed the stage show, so they decided to skip the Music Hall and take a subway ride. They took an Independent subway train to the West Fourth Street station, which a subway guard had told them was where to go for Greenwich Village. They decided against getting out and looking, and in favor of going uptown on the same fare and returning to their hotel. Back at the Woodstock, where they shared a room, they locked themselves in and started putting up their hair, telling each other that everybody in New York was rude and all for himself.

At Coney Island, the Indiana travelers talked about how they could not get over the experience of riding for forty-five minutes, in a shaking, noisy train, to get there.

"The long ride was a shock to what I expected," said Albert Warthan.

Nancy Prather said she didn't like the looks of the subway or the people on it. "You see so many different people," she said. "Dark-complected ones one minute, light-complected ones the next."

"I hate New York, actually," Connie Williams said. "I'm satisfied with what we got back home."

"Back home, you can do anything you please in your own back yard any time you feel like it, like hootin' and hollerin' or anything," said Larry Williams. "You don't ever get to feel all cooped up."

"I sort of like it here in Coney Island," said Dennis Smith. "I don't feel cooped up."

Dennis's buddies looked at him without saying anything. His "sort of liking" Coney Island was the first sign of defection from Indiana, and the others did not seem to know what to make of it. Dennis is a broad-shouldered boy with large, beautiful, wistful blue eyes and a gold front tooth.

"I hate it," Connie said.

Jay Bowman organized as many of the group as he could to take a couple of rides on the Cyclone. Most of the boys followed these up with a ride on the Parachute Jump and then complained that it wasn't what they had expected at all. Some of the boys and girls went into the Spookorama. They all rode the bobsled, and to top the evening off they rode the bumper cars. "The Spookorama was too imitation to be frightening," Albert said. Before leaving Coney Island, Jay got to work among his classmates, polling them on how much money they were prepared to spend on a tour of the city the next day. They stayed in Coney Island about an hour. Nobody went up to the boardwalk to take a look at the ocean, which none of the class had ever seen. They didn't feel they had to look at the ocean. "We knew the ocean was there, and anyway we aim to see the ocean on the tour tomorrow," Jay said later.

When Ina, Lela, and Jeanne got in line for the Music Hall, the Wattses took their stroll along Fifth Avenue and then joined a couple of friends, Mike and Ardis Cavin. Mike Cavin plays clarinet with the United States Navy Band, in Washington, DC, and is studying clarinet—as a commuter—at the Juilliard School of Music. At Madison Avenue and Forty-Second Street, the two couples boarded a bus heading downtown, and while talking about where to get off, they were taken in hand by an elderly gentleman sitting near them, who got off the bus when they did and walked two blocks with them, escorting them to their destination—the Jazz Gallery, on St. Mark's Place. Mike Cavin wanted to hear the tenor-saxophone player John Coltrane. The Wattses stayed at the Jazz Gallery with the Cavins for three hours, listening, with patient interest, to modern jazz. They decided that they liked modern jazz, and especially Coltrane. Leaving the Jazz Gallery after one o'clock, the two couples took buses to Times Square, walked around for twenty minutes looking for a place where they could get a snack, and finally, because every other place seemed to be closed, went to Toffenetti's. Back at the hotel, the Wattses ran into one of the Coney Island adventurers, who told them that Ina, Lela, and Jeanne were missing, or at least were not answering their telephone or knocks on their door. Mr. Watts got the room clerk, unlocked the girls' door, and found them sitting on their beds, still putting up their hair. Everybody was, more or less unaccountably, angry—the three girls who hadn't gone to Coney Island, the girls who had, the boys who had, the Wattses, and the room clerk. The Wattses got to bed at 3:30 a.m.

At 6:30 a.m. Mrs. Watts was called on the telephone. Message: One of the anti–Coney Island trio was lying on the floor of the room weeping and hysterical. Mrs. Watts called the room clerk, who called a doctor practicing in the Times Square area, who rushed over to the hotel, talked with the weeping girl for twenty minutes, and left her with a tranquilizing pill, which she refused to take.

By the time everybody had settled down enough to eat breakfast in drugstores and get ready to start out, it was after nine in the morning, half an hour behind time for the scheduled (by unanimous vote) all-day tour of the city by chartered sightseeing bus, at six dollars per person. The tour was held up further while Mrs. Watts persuaded the weeper to take a shower, in an effort to encourage her to join the tour. After the shower, the unhappy girl stopped crying and declared that she would go along. By the time the group reached the Bowery, she felt fine, and in Chinatown, like the other boys and girls, she bought a pair of chopsticks, for thirty-five cents. The Cathedral of St. John the Divine was the highlight of the tour for many of the students, who were delighted to hear that some of the limestone used in the cathedral interior had very likely come from quarries near Stinesville. Mrs. Watts, on the other hand, who had studied art, had taught art for five years at Huntington College, in Huntington, Indiana, and had taken an accredited art tour of Europe before her marriage, indignantly considered the cathedral "an imitation of European marvels."

Mrs. Watts took the Bean Blossom teaching job, at thirty-six hundred dollars a year, last fall, when her husband decided to abandon a concrete-building-block business in Huntington in order to study for a PhD in political science, a subject he wants to teach. Since he had decided that Indiana University was the place to do this, they moved from Huntington—where Mr. Watts had won the distinction of being the youngest man ever to hold the job of chairman of the Republican Party of Huntington County—to Bloomington. Mrs. Watts drives the twelve miles from Bloomington to Stinesville every day. She teaches English to the tenth, eleventh, and twelfth grades, and, because the school had no Spanish teacher when she signed up for the job, she teaches Spanish, too. She considers the Bean Blossom Township school the most democratic school she has ever seen. "They vote on everything," she says. "We have an average of two votes on something or other every day." Having thus been conditioned to voting as a way of life, Mrs. Watts left the voting on day-to-day plans for the group visit in the capable hands of Jay Bowman. He solved the problem of the tour's late start that morning by taking a vote on whether or not to leave out the Empire State Building. It was promptly voted out of the tour, and voted in for some later time as a separate undertaking.

The tour included a boat trip to the Statue of Liberty, where the group fell in with crushing mobs of people walking to the top of the torch. Mrs. Watts found the experience nightmarish and quit at the base of the torch. Most of the boys and girls made it to the top. "There are a hundred and sixty-eight steps up the torch, and there were forty thousand people ahead of me, but I was determined to climb up it," Jay Bowman reported to Mrs. Watts. "It took me twenty minutes, and it was worthwhile. The thing of it was I had to do it."

For the tour, Jay, like the other boys, had put on dress-up clothes bought specially, at a cost of about twenty-five dollars an outfit, for the trip to New York—white beachcomber pants reaching to below the knee, white cotton-knit shirt with red and blue stripes and a pocket in one sleeve, white socks with red and blue stripes, and white sneakers. The girls wore cotton skirts, various kinds of blouses, white cardigan sweaters, and low-heeled shoes. Mrs. Watts wore high-heeled pumps, even for sightseeing. Everyone else on the tour was astonished at the way New York City people dressed. "They look peculiar," Nancy Prather said. "Girls wearing high heels in the daytime, and the boys here always got a regular suit on, even to go to work in."

"I wouldn't trade the girls back home for any of the girls here," Jay Bowman says. "New York girls wear too much makeup. Not that my interests are centered on any of the girls in the senior class. My interests are centered on Nancy Glidden. She's in the junior class. I take her to shows in Bloomington. We eat pizzas, listen to Elvis Presley—things of that nature—and I always get her home by twelve. Even though my interests are centered on the junior class, I'm proud to say my classmates are the finest bunch of people in the world."

Jay lives with his parents and two brothers in an old nine-room house on thirty acres of land owned by Jay's father, who works in the maintenance department of the Bridgeport Brass Company, in Indianapolis. His mother works in Bloomington, on the RCA color-television-set assembly line. Jay's grandfather, who has worked in limestone quarries all his life, lives across the road, on five acres of his own land, where he has a couple of cows and raises beans and corn for the use of the family. The Bowman family had no plumbing in their house while Jay was a child, and took baths in a tub in the kitchen with water from a well, but a few years ago, with their own hands, they installed a bathroom and a plumbing system and did other work on the house, including putting in a furnace. Jay's parents get up at four in the morning to go to work. Jay, who hasn't been sick one day since he had the mumps at the age of twelve, never sleeps later than seven. He is not in the least distressed at having to work his way through college. He plans to get to school in his own car. This is a 1950 Chevrolet four-door sedan, which he hopes to trade in, by paying an additional four hundred dollars for a slightly younger model before the end of the year.

"The thing of it is I feel proud of myself," Jay says. "Not to be braggin' or anything. But I saved up better than a thousand dollars to send myself to college. That's the way it is. I scrubbed floors, put up hay, carted groceries, and this last winter I worked Saturdays and Sundays in a country store on the state highway and got paid a dollar an hour for runnin' it."

The Bowman family has, in addition to a kind of basic economic ambition, two main interests—basketball and politics. Jay, like most of the other boys on the trip, played basketball on the school basketball team, which won the first round in its section of the Wabash Valley tournament last season. Jay talks about basketball to his classmates but never about politics. Talk about the latter he saves for his family. His grandfather is a Democrat. "If it was up to my grandpa, he'd never want a single Republican in the whole country," he says. "And my dad agrees with him. I agree with my dad. My dad thinks if Franklin D. Roosevelt was still president, this country wouldn't be in the trouble it finds itself in."

At 5 p.m. of this second day in the City of New York, the members of the Bean Blossom senior class returned to their hotel and stood in the lobby for a while, looking from some distance at a souvenir-and-gift stand across from the registration desk. The stand was stocked with thermometers in the form of the Statue of Liberty, in two sizes, priced at seventy-nine cents and ninety-eight cents; with silver-plated charm bracelets; with pins and compacts carrying representations of the Empire State Building; with scarves showing the RCA Building and the UN Building; and with ashtrays showing the New York City skyline. Mike Richardson edged over to the stand and picked up a wooden plaque, costing ninety-eight cents, with the Statue of Liberty shown at the top,

American flags at the sides, and, in the middle, a poem, inscribed "Mother," which read:

> To one who bears the sweetest name
> And adds a luster to the same
> Who shares my joys
> Who cheers when sad
> The greatest friend I ever had
> Long life to her for there's no other
> Can take the place of my dear mother.

After reading the poem, Mike smiled.

"Where ya from?" the man behind the stand asked him.

"Indiana," Mike said, warming up. "We've been on this tour the whole day."

"Ya see everything?" the man asked.

"Everything except the Empire State Building," said Mike.

"Yeah," said the man, and looked away.

Mike was still holding the plaque. Carefully, he replaced it on the stand. "I'll come back for this later," he said.

Without looking at Mike, the man nodded.

Mike joined Dennis Smith and Larry Williams, who were standing with a tall, big-boned, handsome girl named Becky Kiser. Becky used to be a cheerleader for the Bean Blossom Township basketball team.

"We was talkin' about the way this place has people layin' in the streets on that Bowery, sleepin'," Larry said. "You don't see people layin' in the streets back home."

"I seen that in Chicago," Dennis said. "I seen women layin' in the streets in Chicago. That's worse."

The others nodded. No argument.

Mike took a cigarette from his sleeve pocket and lit it with a match from the same pocket. He blew out a stream of smoke with strength and confidence. "I'll be glad when we light out of here," he said. "Nothin' here feels like the farm."

Becky Kiser, with an expression of terrible guilt on her attractive, wide-mouthed face, said, "I bet you'd never get bored here in New York. Back home, it's the same thing all the time. You go to the skating rink. You go to the Big Boy. In the winter, there's basketball. And that's all."

"When I was in Chicago, I seen a man who shot a man in a bar," Dennis said. "I stood right across the street while the man who was shot, the people drug him out." He looked at Becky Kiser. The other boys were also looking at her, but with condemnation and contempt. Dennis gave Becky support. "In Stinesville, they see you on the streets after eleven, they run you home," he said. "Seems like here the city never closes."

"Man, you're just not lookin' ahead," Mike said to Dennis, ignoring Becky.

"You like it here?" Larry asked, in amazement. "Taxes on candy and on everything?"

The Nazarene minister's daughter, Mary Jane Carter, came over with Ina Hough.

"Dennis, here, likes New York," Mike announced.

"I don't," said Ina. "I like the sights, but I think they're almost ruined by the people."

"The food here is expensive, but I guess that's life," said Mary Jane, in a mood of forbearance.

"Oh, man!" said Mike.

"Oh, man!" said Larry. "Cooped up in New York."

Ina said stiffly, "Like the guide said today, you could always tell a New Yorker from a tourist because a New Yorker never smiles, and I agree with him."

"After a while, you'd kinda fit in," Dennis said mildly.

Before dinner that night, Mr. Watts walked through the Times Square area checking prices and menus at likely restaurants. He made tentative arrangements at the Californian for a five-course steak or chicken dinner, to cost $1.95 per person, and asked Jay Bowman to go around taking a vote on the proposition. Half an hour later, Jay reported to Mr. Watts that some of the boys didn't want to go to the Californian, because they thought they'd have to do their own ordering. So Mr. Watts talked to the boys in their rooms and explained that the ordering was taken care of; all they had to say was whether they wanted steak or chicken. On the next ballot, everybody was in favor of the Californian. The class walked over. When the fifth course was finished, it was agreed that the dinner was all right, but several of the boys said they thought the restaurant was too high-class.

After dinner, it started to rain, and it rained hard. The Wattses and

seven of the girls decided that they wanted to see *The Music Man*. The
four other girls wanted to see *My Fair Lady*. None of the boys wanted
to see a musical show. In the driving rain, the Wattses and the girls ran
to the theatres of their choice, all arriving soaked to the skin. By good
luck, each group was able to buy seats. At *The Music Man*, the Wattses
and the seven girls with them sat in the balcony, in the direct path of
an air-conditioning unit that blew icy blasts on their backs. At *My Fair
Lady*, the four girls sat in the balcony, where an air-conditioning unit
blew icy blasts at their legs. The girls liked their shows. The *My Fair
Lady* group was transported by the costumes. Ina Hough, who went to
The Music Man, thought that it was just like a movie, except for the way
the scenes changed.

The boys split up, some of them taking the subway down to Greenwich Village, the others heading for the Empire State Building, where
they paid a dollar thirty for tickets to the observatory and, once up
there, found that the fog and rain blotted out the view completely. "We
stood there about an hour and a half messin' around, me and my buddies," Jay later told Mrs. Watts. "Wasn't no sense in leavin' at that price."
In Greenwich Village, Mike Richardson, Dennis Smith, and Larry Williams walked along the narrow streets in a drizzling rain. All were still
wearing their beachcomber outfits. Nobody talked to them. They didn't
see anybody they wanted to talk to. They almost went into a small coffeehouse; they changed their minds because the prices looked too high.
They went into one shop, a bookstore, and looked at some abstract
paintings, which appealed to them. "Sort of interesting the way they
don't look like nothing," Mike said. Then they took the subway back to
Times Square, where they walked around for a while in the rain. Toward
midnight, Mike and Dennis told each other they were lonesome for
the smell of grass and trees, and, the rain having stopped, they walked
up to Central Park, where they stayed for about an hour and got lost.

The next morning, a meeting of the class was held in the hotel lobby
to take a vote on when to leave New York. Jay Bowman reported that
they had enough money to cover an extra day in the city, plus a side
trip to Niagara Falls on the way home. Or, he said, they could leave
New York when they had originally planned to, and go to Washington,
DC, for a day before heading home. The bus driver had told Jay that it
was all one to him which they chose. The class voted for the extra day
in New York and Niagara Falls.

"I'm glad," Becky Kiser said, with a large, friendly smile, to Dennis Smith. Several of her classmates overheard her and regarded her with a uniformly deadpan look. "I like it here," she went on. "I'd like to live here. There's so much to see. There's so much to do."

Her classmates continued to study her impassively until Dennis took their eyes away from her by saying, "You get a feelin' here of goin' wherever you want to. Seems the city never closes. I'd like to live here, I believe. People from everyplace are here."

"Limousines all over the joint," Albert Warthan said.

"Seems like you can walk and walk and walk," Dennis went on dreamily. "I like the way the big buildin's crowd you in. You want to walk and walk and never go to sleep."

"I hate it," Connie Williams said, with passion.

"Oh, man, you're just not lookin' ahead," Mike Richardson said to Dennis. "You got a romantic notion. You're not realistic about it."

"This place couldn't hold me," Larry Williams said. "I like the privacy of the farm."

"I want to go to new places," said Becky, who had started it. "I want to go to Europe."

"Only place I want to go is Texas," Larry said. "I got folks in Texas."

"There's no place like home," Mike said. "Home's good enough for me."

"I believe the reason of this is we've lived all of our lives around Stinesville," Dennis said. "If you took Stinesville out of the country, you wouldn't be hurt. But if you took New York out of the country, you'd be hurt. The way the guide said, all our clothes and everything comes from New York."

Becky said, "In Coney Island, I saw the most handsome man I ever saw in my whole life. I think he was a Puerto Rican or something, too."

Albert said, "When we get back, my pa will say, 'Well, how was it?' I'll say, 'It was fine.'"

"I'd like to come back, maybe stay a month," Jay Bowman said diplomatically. "One thing I'd like to do is come here when I can see a major-league baseball game."

"I'd like to see a major-league baseball game, but I wouldn't come back just to see it," Mike said.

"I hate New York," Connie said.

"Back home, everybody says 'Excuse me,'" Nancy Prather said.

"I like it here," Dennis said stubbornly.

This day was an open one, leaving the boys and girls free to do anything they liked, without prearranged plan or vote. Mike passed close by the souvenir-and-gift stand in the hotel lobby, and the proprietor urged him to take home the Statue of Liberty.

"I'd like to, but it won't fit in my suitcase," Mike said, with a loud laugh.

A group formed to visit the zoo in Central Park, got on the subway, had a loud discussion about where to get off, and were taken in hand by a stranger who told them the zoo was in the Bronx. Only the boy named Lynn Dillon listened to the stranger. The others went to the zoo in Central Park. Lynn stayed on the subway till it reached the Bronx, and spent the entire day in the Bronx Zoo by himself. The rest of the zoo visitors, walking north after lunch in the cafeteria, ran into the Metropolitan Museum of Art and went in. "It was there, and it was free, so we did it," Nancy Prather said. "There were these suits of armor and stuff. Nothin' I go for myself."

That morning, the Wattses had tried to get some of the boys and girls to accompany them to the Guggenheim Museum or the Museum of Modern Art, but nobody had wanted to pay the price of admission. "Why pay fifty cents to see a museum when they got them free?" the class president asked. Mrs. Watts reported afterward that the Guggenheim was the most exciting museum she had ever seen, including all the museums she had seen in Europe on her accredited art tour. "There aren't big crowds in there, for one thing," she said. "And I don't think the building overpowers the paintings at all, as I'd heard." From the Guggenheim, the Wattses went to Georg Jensen's to look at silver but didn't buy anything. Then they went to the Museum of Modern Art and had lunch in the garden. "Lovely lunch, fabulous garden, fabulous sculpture, but I'm disappointed in the museum itself," Mrs. Watts said. "Everything jammed into that small space! Impossible to get a good view of Picasso's *Girl Before a Mirror*."

By dinnertime, more than half of the Bean Blossomers had, to their relief, discovered the Automat. Jay Bowman had a dinner consisting of a ham sandwich (forty cents), a glass of milk (ten cents), and a dish of fresh strawberries (twenty cents). Then, with a couple of buddies, he bought some peanuts in their shells and some Cokes, and took them up to his room for the three of them to consume while talking about what to do that night. They decided, because they had not yet had a good view of the city from the Empire State observatory, that they would go back there. They were accompanied by most of the girls and the other boys, and this time the group got a cut rate of sixty-five cents apiece. Dennis went off wandering by himself. He walked up Fifth Avenue to Eighty-Fifth Street, over to Park Avenue, down Park to Seventy-Second Street, across to the West Side, down Central Park West to Sixty-Sixth Street, over behind the Tavern on the Green (where he watched people eating outdoors), and down Seventh Avenue to Times Square, where he stood around on corners looking at the people who bought papers at newsstands.

The Wattses had arranged to meet anybody who was interested under the Washington Arch at around nine thirty for an evening in Greenwich Village. The boys had decided to take a walk up Broadway after leaving the Empire State Building, but the girls all showed up in Washington Square, along with two soldiers and three sailors they had met in the USO across the street from the Woodstock. The Wattses led the way to a coffeehouse, where everybody had coffee or lemonade. Then the girls and the servicemen left the Wattses, saying they were going to take a ride on the ferry to Staten Island. The Wattses went to the Five Spot, which their jazz friend had told them had good music.

After breakfast the following morning, the bus driver, Ralph Walls, showed up in the hotel lobby for the first time since the group's arrival in New York and told Jay Bowman to have everyone assembled at five forty-five the following morning for departure at six o'clock on the dot. The driver said that he was spending most of his time sleeping, and that before they left he was going to do some more sleeping. He had taken his wife on a boat trip around Manhattan, though, he said, and he had taken a few walks on the streets. After reminding Jay again about the exact time planned for the departure, he went back upstairs to his room.

Mrs. Watts took nine of the girls (two stayed in the hotel to sleep) for a walk through Saks Fifth Avenue, just looking. Mr. Watts took three of the boys to Abercrombie & Fitch, just looking. Everybody walked every aisle on every floor in each store, looking at everything on the counters and in the showcases. Nobody bought anything. The two groups met at noon under the clock in Grand Central; lunched at an Automat; walked over to the United Nations Building, where they decided not to take the regular tour; and took a crosstown bus to the Hudson River and went aboard the liner SS *Independence*, where they visited every deck and every lounge on the boat, and a good many of the staterooms. Then they took the bus back to Times Square and scattered to do some shopping.

Mike Richardson bought all his gifts—eleven dollars' worth—at the hotel stand, taking not only the plaque for his mother but a set of salt and pepper shakers, with the Statue of Liberty on the salt and the Empire State Building on the pepper, also for his mother; a Statue of Liberty ashtray for his father; a George Washington Bridge teapot for his sister-in-law; a mechanical dog for his niece; a City Hall teapot, cup, and saucer set for his grandparents; and a cigarette lighter stamped with the Great White Way for himself. At Macy's, Becky Kiser bought a dress, a blouse, and an ankle chain for herself, and a necklace with matching bracelet and earrings for her mother, a cuff link and tie clasp set for her father, and a bracelet for her younger sister. Albert Warthan bought a miniature camera for himself and a telephone pad and pencil set stamped with the George Washington Bridge and a Statue of Liberty thermometer, large-size, as general family gifts, at the hotel stand. Jay Bowman bought an unset cultured pearl at Macy's for his girlfriend in the junior class, as well as silver-looking earrings for his married sister and for his mother, and at a store called King of Slims, around the corner from the hotel, he bought four ties—a red toreador tie (very narrow) for his older brother, a black toreador tie for his younger brother, a conservative silk foulard for his father, and a white toreador tie for himself. Dennis Smith bought a Statue of Liberty ashtray for his mother and a Statue of Liberty cigarette lighter for his father. Connie Williams bought two bracelets and a Statue of Liberty pen for herself. The bus driver and his wife spent sixty dollars on clothes for their children, six of whom are girls. Nancy Prather didn't buy anything. The Wattses spent about a hundred dollars in the course of the visit, most of it on meals and entertainment.

On their last evening in New York, all the boys and girls, accompanied by the Wattses, went to the Radio City Music Hall, making it in time to see the stage show. Then they packed and went to bed. The bus driver, after an early dinner with his wife at Hector's Cafeteria, brought the yellow school bus over from Tenth Avenue and parked it right in front of the hotel, so that it would be there for the early start.

Next morning at five forty-five, the Bean Blossomers assembled in the lobby; for the first time since the trip had started, nobody was late. The bus pulled out at exactly 6 a.m., and twenty minutes after that, heading west over the George Washington Bridge, it disappeared from the city.

(AUGUST 20, 1960)

From
Dancers in May

The morning of Wedesday, February 5, was bleak. Rain was threatening. Miss Marion Ross White, a pretty, soft-voiced woman in her twenties, who teaches a fifth-grade class at Public School 31, on the Lower East Side, left home for school carrying—in addition to an umbrella, some notebooks, and an overstuffed two-foot-long pocketbook of black patent leather—a record album of folk-dance tunes to use in preparing a group of sixty P.S. 31 fifth graders and sixth graders to take part in the fifty-seventh annual festival of folk dancing late in the spring on the Sheep Meadow in Central Park. This yearly ritual, which is duplicated in each of the four other boroughs of the city, is known officially to the Board of Education as the Park Fête. It is sponsored jointly by the Girls' Branch of the Public Schools Athletic League and the Bureau for Health Education. In Manhattan, on the Sheep Meadow, this year's fête would include nearly three thousand boys and girls of eleven and twelve, from fifty public schools. At lunchtime, for one hour, the children would dance around fifty maypoles, as their counterparts had done each May for the past fifty-six years. (For forty-six Park Fêtes, only girls danced; boys were first included ten years ago.) Miss White was starting her preparations three and a half months before the event. With two other teachers, she was going to teach her own class of twenty-seven children, plus thirty-three more, from a couple of other classes, eight international folk dances, the climactic one being the "Maypole Dance," which had been danced in every one of the past fifty-six Park Fêtes.

Miss White lives on West Eighth Street, in Greenwich Village, in a one-room, third-floor, ninety-two-dollar-a-month walk-up that does not have an air conditioner but does have a wood-burning fireplace. She lives ten doors west of the Eighth Street Playhouse and directly over a Riker's restaurant. Her apartment measures roughly twelve by fourteen feet, and in it, besides the working fireplace, she maintains a working upright piano, a small working pump organ, a clarinet, a guitar, eight recorders of various sizes, an Israeli clay-and-canvas drum, a flute, a sagging daybed, a blue canvas butterfly chair, a couple of shelves of books (mainly paperbacks), and an ironing board. On the ironing board, which is usually stationed, open, between the back of the organ and the front of a four-by-four-foot wall kitchen, Miss White has her daily breakfast, of toast and instant coffee. She eats it standing up at the ironing board and facing the piano, which is against the far wall, between two small windows looking out on Eighth Street.

Miss White knows how to play all the instruments she has, but her main instrument is the flute, and she is still studying it. . . . She went to Hunter College, majored in music, and decided in her senior year that she wanted to become a teacher. She originally wanted to teach in the high-school system, but she was somewhat intimidated by teenagers, and while she was getting up the courage to take them on, she became a "permanent substitute" teacher in the elementary-school system. She came to P.S. 31 six years ago. Her salary for this past school year was sixty-six hundred dollars. In addition to teaching her class (which has, like all the other classes at the school, a mixture of Negro and white children, with a large percentage of Puerto Ricans) such regular fifth-grade subjects as social studies, reading English, spelling, mathematics, geography, and science, Miss White teaches a subject known as band. First, she teaches her fifth graders how to play one or more instruments— clarinet, tuba, trumpet, trombone, saxophone, flute, bass drum, and snare drums—and then she teaches them to play in the band, of which she is the conductor. On her own time, and using her own piano, she gives free piano lessons to half a dozen children from the school. In the evening, often working past midnight, she writes her own arrangements for the band to play. In a recent concert given at P.S. 31, her band had played her arrangements of such numbers as "Tonight," from *West Side Story,* and "St. James Infirmary," along with a Bach chorale. . . .

Last year, Miss White's class put on its own production of *My Fair Lady,* also with book and music rearranged by Miss White. It came as no surprise to anyone at P.S. 31 when the principal, a cheerful, enthusiastic, hardworking man named Hyman Terner, asked Miss White to serve again, as she had several times before, as the grade teacher responsible for the plans for the Park Fête.

As Miss White, wearing a heavy black raincoat and no hat, left home for school with the folk-dance album that Wednesday morning, she looked thoughtful, serious, and controlled. Her expression remained immobile as she glanced routinely at the clock inside Riker's and checked the time—seven thirty—on the watch on her wrist. She skirted a Sanitation Department sweeping truck on the street, her expression still fixed, and walked quickly to the subway entrance around the corner. Her route took her on a D train of the Independent subway to East Broadway; upstairs to Madison Street; north along a block of ancient tenements, their stoops littered with refuse, and past clusters of Negroes and Puerto Ricans standing or sitting on the curb, who appeared to be completely indifferent to Miss White as she walked quickly by; past a pink stucco synagogue at the corner of Madison and Montgomery Streets, from which a lone worshipper, a bearded Moses in a broad-brimmed hat and a black robe reaching to the ground, emerged (he, too, seemingly indifferent to Miss White); and, on the next block, past a new middle-income housing cooperative smelling of wet cement and bearing a banner that read GOUVERNEUR GARDENS—APTS. AVAILABLE, 1-2-3 BEDROOMS. A garbage truck passed by, with the message "A Cleaner New York Is Up to You" on its side. A skinny Negro boy ran up behind Miss White, calling to her. She stopped and turned, and for the first time since she had left her walk-up, twenty minutes before, her expression broke. She gave the boy a sudden, open grin—something like his own. He waved to her and ran off. She turned down Montgomery Street, and P.S. 31, which is on Monroe Street, came into view—a dirty-gray stone building five stories high, with baroque windows and a roof playground enclosed by a wire-mesh fence and covered with a grilled canopy of iron beams. . . .

By the time she reached the fifth floor, she was alone. In front of her door, which was marked at the top with a black-and-white enamel plate reading 506, the corridor was deserted except for one small figure, seated opposite the door. He sat on a rectangular instrument case, and he was wearing high black canvas sneakers trimmed with white rubber; torn trousers a couple of sizes too large for him; and a dungaree jacket over a green knit shirt. He had freckles, and his hair, light brown, fell over his forehead. His face was pale, and there were dark circles under his eyes. He sat drumming with his fingers on his knees and staring at the brass doorknob of Room 506's door, which, like all the other door-knobs in sight, was embossed with the words Public School. His name was Willy Crespo, and he was in the sixth grade. Miss White had been his teacher in fifth grade. His present teacher was Mr. Allen Guskin, whose room, 504, was right next door to Miss White's. Back when Willy was in Miss White's class, he had been found to possess musical talent; a saxophone owned by the Board of Education had been entrusted to him for the school year, and then he had won a Henry Street Settle-ment House music scholarship for additional lessons. When Willy was a year old, his father had died, at the age of thirty, of diabetes. Willy now lived, with his mother and four older children, in the Vladeck housing project, across the street from the school. . . . He regularly came to school three-quarters of an hour early and waited for Miss White, so that he might spend half an hour or so practicing his saxophone in her room, with her as his audience. Several weeks earlier, he had informed Miss White that before he was given his instrument he had felt like nothing, and that now he cared about music more than anything else.

As soon as Miss White appeared on the fifth floor, Willy greeted her with a wave of the hand, and they exchanged smiles. She unlocked her door, and Willy picked up his saxophone case and followed her into her room. Still carrying the case, Willy automatically trailed her as she got the room ready for her class—switching on the lights, hanging up her coat in a corner closet, arranging papers on her desk. Her desk, which was cluttered with—in addition to the papers—confiscated comic books, a volume entitled *Our Country's Story*, and a small metal bust of Abraham Lincoln fixed to a wooden base, was in the corner of the room opposite the door and was surrounded by music stands, used by the band. An American flag hung over the blackboard at the front of the room. The far side of the room was taken up by four large win-dows, their small, square panes decorated with paintings of flowers in various colors. On the doors of the coat closets along the wall opposite the windows, and on bulletin boards around the room, and over the blackboards at the front and back of the room, were drawings done by the children, along with pictures, clipped from books and magazines, of various historical figures, such as George Washington, Abraham

Lincoln, Louis Armstrong, John F. Kennedy, Mahatma Gandhi, the Beatles, and Martin Luther King. As Miss White picked up some chalk and started to write "Lesson Plan" on the blackboard, Willy opened his case, attached the mouthpiece to his saxophone, and started to practice an arrangement that Miss White had written for him of the song "Moon River." On the blackboard, Miss White wrote:

1. Salute to the Flag
2. Band
3. Current Events
4. Phonetics—adding ER, EST, ING to words ending in LE and one-syllable words
5. Social Studies—Lewis and Clark Expedition

Then Miss White paused and turned around. Willy paused, too, and Miss White said that rehearsals were going to start that day for the Park Fête. "I'd like you to be in it," Miss White said.

"Sure, I'll be in it," Willy said, with a small, pleased shrug and a quick smile. "What is it?"

"You remember. You were in it last year," Miss White said. "We fixed the maypoles, and we all went to Central Park and did all the dances."

"Sure," Willy said, with another little shrug. "I liked the one where we yelled '*Olé! Olé!*'"

Miss White laughed. "'Fado Blanquita,'" she said. "That's the name of *that* dance." They exchanged looks of understanding, and Miss White turned back to the blackboard, and Willy started in again on "Moon River.". . . .

The day before the Park Fête, Miss White came to school wearing a pretty blue linen dress with a matching jacket. Her pupils reminded her that the day was Teacher Recognition Day and presented her with an orchid, which she pinned to her lapel.

After lunch, Mr. Guskin came into Miss White's room, looking, as usual, for Willy. Miss White said that Willy would be there in a few minutes to practice his saxophone. Mr. Guskin asked about the Park Fête, and Miss White told him that they had suddenly discovered the day before that they were short four vests. She had rushed over to Orchard

Street and bought some extra parakeet-blue material, and she was cutting some last-minute patterns; Mrs. Zablidowsky was going to make
the vests overnight. "And tonight," Miss White announced, "I'm taking
my oral exam to become permanent as an elementary-school teacher."

"Congratulations!" Mr. Guskin said, with a grin. "Welcome to the
club. What made you decide to do it?" He had been a permanent elementary teacher from the start.

"I guess I felt I could do more for the younger children," Miss White
said. "In elementary school, it's important to find the children with talent
and develop that talent. Like Willy. And I guess you usually find out that
the age you want to work with is the age you were happiest at yourself."

The two teachers exchanged looks of understanding.

Miss White gave Mr. Guskin a small, controlled smile. "One of the
hardest things, at the beginning, was when the time came for the term
to end and the children left me," she said. "The first couple of years,
every June, when they left me, I'd cry. Then, in the fall, when I saw
them again, I found, to my surprise, that they hardly knew me."

"It still comes as a shock, every time," Mr. Guskin said, with a grin.

"Now I don't cry," Miss White said hastily.

"You worried about the exam?"

"Yes," Miss White said. "When they give an oral exam, they make
faces at you. I find it difficult to speak to people who make faces at you."

"Don't worry about that," Mr. Guskin said. "The main thing is to
just act natural. Be yourself. Answer everything just the way you're now
speaking to me. Be the way you are, and you'll have it made."

Miss White smiled. "All right," she said. . . .

[After the maypole dance] most of the school groups started walking
away from the Sheep Meadow, each led by a boy carrying the maypole
top. A few, including the group from P.S. 31, lingered awhile. The
children bought more Cracker Jack and offered it to the pigeons and
to each other. Yvonne Palmer chased Louis Feldman across the grass.
David Gomez, Irod Daley, John Sidoti, and Quentin Holley piled on
top of each other, and Arturo Vanderpool came over and flung himself
on top of them.

Miss White, standing by herself with a contented look on her face,
leaned against a bench. Willy came over to her, looked up, and waved.

Magdalena walked over from the refreshment stand, carrying paper cups of orange soda. She offered a cup to Willy. He thanked her and drank it.

Then Miss White said they ought to start back. Slowly, they wandered toward the Tavern on the Green. . . .

Before leaving the Park, they paused for a few minutes on benches near the Tavern on the Green. Yvonne and David ran over to Willy, Magdalena, Lois, and Irod carrying boxes of Cracker Jack. The contents were shared out. The prizes were discovered and held up to view. Willy leaned against a tree and impatiently loosened his yellow string tie. Magdalena watched him. He took off the tie and held it out toward Magdalena. She accepted it, and smiled, and tied it under the collar of her blouse.

The P.S. 31 group returned to Monroe Street straggling, with Michael carrying the maypole top on his head. They reached P.S. 31 at about three thirty. School had let out, but they all had to go in and be dismissed in the yard. Inside, another teacher put the maypole top away in the storeroom.

Miss White ran into Mr. Terner, who was just about to leave the building. He asked her how things had gone in the park. She said that the children had been wonderful. Then he asked her how she had made out with her oral exam the night before. She replied that one of the examiners had made strange faces at her but that she hadn't minded too much. On the whole, she had found the exam quite stimulating, she said. "But I don't know if I passed," she added. "I just said what I thought."

"If you said what you thought, you did fine, I know," Mr. Terner said cheerfully.

"OK," Miss White said.

They said good night, and Mr. Terner left. . . .

Most of the children scattered in a hurry. Willy and Magdalena waited. Magdalena was wearing Willy's yellow string tie under the collar of her blouse. She and Willy walked out with Miss White. On the school steps, Willy and Magdalena each gave Miss White five. Then the two of them went off toward Gouverneur Street together. Miss White started in the direction of her subway, turned around once to look at the two children, and then went on her way alone.

(JULY 18, 1964)

Mays at St. Bernard's
(Willie Mays)

A young friend of ours in the fifth grade at St. Bernard's School, on East Ninety-Eighth Street, called us up the other day to tell us that Willie Mays was coming there that afternoon to talk to the students about baseball. Our friend offered to cover the story for us and to write it after he came home from the dentist. His report arrived, as promised, and here it is:

Willie Mays spoke to the boys in the gym, where about a hundred and twenty-five of us sat around on the floor. Willie Mays stood up, looking very individual. He has great posture. He wore a beautiful suit of blue-and-white checks and a bright-blue shirt with a tie of many colors. Our headmaster, who usually wears a tweed jacket, was standing on the sidelines, and he kept smiling happily at Willie Mays. One of our older teachers stood at the entrance to the gym, peeking in, and she looked puzzled but terribly interested. Willie Mays said he loved to talk about baseball and the best way of talking about baseball now would be for him to answer questions. Everybody in the place, almost, raised his hand to ask a question, so Willie Mays started with a guy on one side, and then seemed to work his way over to the other side. The first question was "How come you don't use an aluminum bat?" Willie Mays said he liked wood better. He has a surprisingly light-sounding voice. He talked so fast, and the guys asked so many questions so fast, I caught about one question in five. I'll give you the questions I caught with the answers Willie Mays gave:

Q: What's the greatest play you ever made?
A: The greatest play I ever made was in high school or kinder-garten. It was my first hit.

Q: Do you think you could beat Babe Ruth's record?

A: I don't think I could beat anybody's record with my shoulders and legs in the shape they're in now.

Q: Did you ever make a triple play?

A: Not yet.

Q: When did you first know you were good?

A: Every time the ball went up in the air, I felt I could catch it.

Q: What was your longest home run?

A: Well, I always felt this way—I never worry as long as the ball goes over the fence.

Q: Did you want to get traded?

A: I don't have anything to say about it. My gosh, man! Do you want to get homework? You don't have anything to say about it—right, man?

Q: Who is your favorite pitcher?

A: It never made any difference to me as long as I could hit the balls.

Q: Who'd you hit your six-hundredth home run off of?

A: Mike Corkins, of San Diego. Now, you didn't think I'd remember that, did you?

Q: What made you become a baseball player?

A: I just liked baseball.

Q: How many kids do you have?

A: One. He's thirteen.

Q: How many good seasons have you had?

A: Eight.

Q: Which do you like better—grass or that composition stuff they play on?

A: I like grass better. I know my legs and what they do according to the way the ball bounces. But on this new stuff you find the ball bounces all kinds of ways. It's not reliable. On grass, you know.

Q: Do you feel sorry about anything you ever did in baseball?
A: The way I feel about anything I've ever done, I feel you can't look back. Always look forward.

Q: How do you keep yourself in such good condition? (Our gym teacher asked this one.)
A: I sleep a lot. I don't eat too much. I eat a big breakfast—three eggs, sausage, coffee, juice. All that kind of stuff. But I eat only two meals a day. Most guys eat three. Some eat four. I play golf. I walk a lot. But eating and sleeping, those are the main things. I sleep during the day. I don't mean you have to sleep. Just lie down. Rest. Relax yourself. Do you guys realize how old I am?

"Forty-two!" (This was yelled by almost everybody in the gym.)

Q: What do you do when you're sitting on the bench?
A: We talk a lot.

Q: How long did it take before you got famous?
A: I never think about things like that. When you're playing a sport, you don't worry about being famous. You think about catching the ball, doing the best you can at that particular moment.

Q: Do you think baseball is a rough sport?
A: It is a rough sport, man! That ball is coming at you at ninety miles per hour. Man, that's rough.

Willie Mays wrote a lot of autographs after he stopped answering questions. Then he drove away in his car, which is a pink limousine with a white roof.

(JUNE 9, 1973)

The Shit-Kickers
of Madison Avenue

The tenth graders heading up Madison Avenue at 7:30 a.m. to the private high schools are freshly liberated from their dental braces, and their teeth look pearly and magnificent. They are fifteen years old. During the week, they arrive, by bus or on foot, singly or in pairs or in clusters, and they make their way up the west side of Madison—they call it the "cool" side—toward their schools: Dalton, on East Eighty-Ninth; Sacred Heart and Spence, on East Ninety-First; Nightingale-Bamford, on East Ninety-Second; the Lycée Français, on East Ninety-Fifth. Brearley and Chapin are farther east; Collegiate, Columbia Prep, and Trinity are in the west; Browning is south; Horace Mann, Riverdale, and Fieldston are in the north. On the weekends, the tenth graders from all points will find a way to get together. Today is only Tuesday.

Boys and girls spill out of the Eighty-Sixth Street crosstown buses at Madison Avenue and join the flow of their counterparts heading north. The walking tenth graders greet one another in soft, kindly rhythms, in polite, gentle tones. The boys greet one another with high fives. Girls with girls and girls with boys bestow quick, sweet kisses on one another's cheeks—some cheeks still not completely rid of hints of baby fat. No routine air kisses from these kids. Their kisses are heartfelt, making their unity, their devotion to and trust in one another, palpable. Kisses from their mouths are like the cool little first nippy smacks of a very young baby.

Most of the tenth graders are in the habit of leaving home without eating any breakfast. Still in clusters, with fifteen minutes to get to school, they pause in doorways. One girl in a cluster of five takes out a pack of Marlboro Lights—the brand favored at the moment—and

each member of the cluster participates in lighting the cigarette—
striking the match, guarding the flame, offering a propane lighter.
They share. The lighted cigarette is passed from mouth to mouth. They
all inhale, the girls twisting their mouths like thorough pros, exhaling
the smoke from a tiny corner opening on one side of the lips.

One angelic-looking blond beauty with raw, red nostrils takes a puff,
inhales deeply, and says wearily, "I've like got the fucking flu or something."

"Fuck the you know fucking germs," another says smoothly, reassur-
ingly, a positive reinforcer.

"I got home like three?" another member of the cluster says, making
her statement in the form of a question. "I sweat Henry? Who do you
sweat? Anybody?"

The others regard her skeptically. "Nobody," one says.

"I sweat the shit out of Henry," the one who got home at three says
mildly.

On the feet of all the members of this cluster are boots, not quite
Timberland. The girls, some wearing black panty hose or black knee-
socks, have on chic black lace-ups, all with Vibram soles, all with steel
tips. One girl wearing lace-ups two feet high lifts a knee, turning the
booted foot this way and that. "New shit-kickers!" she squeals, but in
subdued, ladylike tones.

"Cool," the angelic-looking one with the flu says. "Cool shit-kickers."

They crush out their shared cigarette with the heels of their shit-
kickers, and they go to school.

Whenever the tenth graders have a break in their school program,
and daily at 12:35 p.m., they head for one of their hangouts. The
second floor of Jackson Hole, at the southwest corner of Ninety-First
and Madison, is in at the moment. On this Tuesday, at 12:36 p.m. six
four-place tables and a couple of two-place tables, accommodating
twenty-eight customers, are filled. Ketchup bottles absolutely full are
at the ready on every table. A teenage Al Pacino look-alike waiter serves
them their first meal of the day: lone platters of ketchup-doused french
fries or fried onion rings, or combo french fries and onion rings, and
Cokes. A late arrival, dark-eyed, and smaller and chubbier than the
ones settled in, turns up, and a place is found for her. Tearfully, she
reports that her French teacher sprang a surprise test on her class, and
she thinks she did badly on it.

"Don't like get fucking stressed out," a girl says, offering that same kindly positive reinforcement.

"Fucking teachers," a companion says, chewing on a fry and simultaneously taking a drag on a cigarette and passing it on. "I'm on my way you know to lunch, and the fucking teacher asks where I'm going?" The statements continue to sound as though they were questions. "I don't want teachers being like into my you know business?"

"I miss the teacher who used to be a model and then left the school and went to Africa to be a nun?" someone says. "She would like talk you know about her experiences? She was very like open to everybody?" The others at the table and the girls at all the other tables agree that they miss the teacher who went to Africa to be a nun.

One of the girls, very pretty, with long dark hair, is "presenting" a party and hands out printed invitations. She has dark glasses pushed on top of her hair. She wears silver loop earrings, a double in the left ear, a single in the right. The invitation shows a picture of Stonehenge on one side, and the other side has a long list of names of people supporting the party, which has a title: "The Farside."

"I can't go to the party?" one of the fifteen-year-olds says. "My father grounded me? Because I was smoking?"

"My mom is trying to like ship me off to a fucking school in fucking Spain?" another girl says. "Unless I you know quit smoking?"

"I want to quit, but I can't? I don't have a choice? It's too late?" one fatalist says.

The party entrepreneur explains that she is working with six other presenters to spread the invitations around, to telephone friends at the schools to the east, west, north, and south, and to obtain the services of a really topnotch DJ. They are working with a well-to-do party producer, whose take of the proceeds will be forty percent, the balance to be divided evenly among the seven presenters. Admission to the party will be twelve dollars per person.

"This rich, older guy is like experienced you know?" she says. "He's twenty-nine?"

The mention of the number draws forth gasps.

"Fucking twenty-nine," one of the girls says. "That's the age of those actors in the mindless *90210* or that mindless *Melrose Place*. They're twenty-nine, and they're like playing our age."

At any rate, there are plans to be made. The party is going to start at 10 p.m. The girls will spend the afternoon before in preparations.

"Here's what we'll do," the entrepreneur says. "We need five hours. You three come to my house you know at five? You bring all your clothes? I take everything out of my closet and spread everything out on the floor? We try on all the stuff? Depending on what kind of mood we're in, we make our selection?"

"We have to be fucking blunt," one of the potential guests says. "About what like looks good on us."

"Then we take showers? Half an hour? Then we like shave our legs? Half an hour? Then we like put cream on our legs? Half an hour? Then we call up everybody who's been like grounded? We talk to them for at least an hour? Maybe we give them an hour and a half? Then we go out and buy a quart of vodka and some orange juice and cranberry juice? Then we go to somebody else's house and drink vodka with orange juice or vodka with cranberry juice? Then we get dressed? Then we get another quart of vodka and go to somebody else's house? We become like outgoing? And we make calls to friends and invite them over? By then, we'll be ready to go?"

On the first school day after the weekend, promptly at 12:36 p.m., the tenth graders are back in place at Jackson Hole, smoking, chewing gum, eating fries and onion rings, and reviewing the party. "I like feel real ripped off?" the young Farside presenter-entrepreneur is saying. "Too many people came to the party, which was at this nice club on West Forty-Seventh Street? There were hundreds pushing and shoving and clogging the street, and the police came? And they said we had to be carded, because they had a bar? And we we you know didn't like have cards, so this twenty-nine-year-old rich guy said the fee for getting the club had to be raised from three thousand dollars to eight thousand dollars, because they had to close the bar and were not allowed you know to sell us drinks? And everybody had to pay twenty dollars instead of twelve dollars just to get in? So, but even so, nobody like wanted to leave? And it was so crowded you couldn't even dance? And at the end of it the twenty-nine-year-old rich guy took forty percent, and all I got was about fifty fucking dollars, after I did all the fucking work and made a million phone calls?"

She chews on a french fry, accepts a glowing Marlboro Light from the girl beside her at the table, and takes a quick puff. The chubby, dark-eyed girl who was stressed out by her French teacher comes over from another table and gives the entrepreneur a soft, comforting kiss on the cheek, and one by one all the other tenth graders in the area come over and do the same.

(FEBRUARY 20, 1995)

IV

NEW YORKERS

Lillian and William Shawn on the streets
of New York in the nineteen sixties.

From
El Único Matador

The best bullfighters in the world have come, traditionally, from Spain or Mexico. The old Spanish province of Andalusia has contributed more bulls and more bullfighters to the bullring than all the rest of Spain. Manolete, probably history's top-ranking matador, who, at the age of thirty, was fatally gored in the summer of 1947, was an Andalusian. Carlos Arruza, who retired last year, at twenty-eight, with a two-million-dollar fortune and the reputation of fighting closer to the bull than any other matador had ever done, was born in Mexico, of Spanish-born parents. Belmonte, an Andalusian, and Joselito, a Spanish gypsy, were the leading figures in what is known in bullfight countries as the Golden Age of Bullfighting, which ended with Belmonte's retirement to breed bulls, in 1921, a year after Joselito's death in the arena. The only Mexican who ranked close to Belmonte and Joselito in their time was Rodolfo Gaona, an Indian, who, in 1925, retired a millionaire with large real-estate interests in Mexico City. Some years ago a Chinese bullfighter named Wong, who wore a natural pigtail, turned up in Mexico as El Torero Chino, and a Peruvian lady bullfighter, Conchita Cintrón, is active today. Only one citizen of the United States has ever been recognized as a full-fledged matador. He is Sidney Franklin, who was born and raised in the Park Slope section of Brooklyn.

Franklin, who is now forty-five, estimates that he has killed two thousand bulls so far. Last winter, in Mexico, he killed thirteen. He is planning to go to Spain this summer to kill as many bulls as he can get contracts to fight, although he is much older than the usual bullfighter is at his peak. "Age has nothing to do with art," he says. "It's all a matter of what's in your mind." He hopes someday to introduce bullfighting to this country, and, if he succeeds, expects it to become more popular than baseball. Ernest Hemingway, who became an authority on bullfighting, as well as on Franklin, while preparing to write *Death in the Afternoon*, maintains that to take to bullfighting, a country must have an interest in the breeding of fighting bulls and an interest in death, both of which Hemingway feels are lacking in the United States. "Death, shmeath, so long as I keep healthy," Franklin says. When *aficionados*, or bullfight fans, charge that Americans born north of the border are incapable of the passion necessary for bullfighting, Franklin replies passionately that coldness in the presence of danger is the loftiest aspect of his art. "If you've got guts, you can do anything," he says. "Anglo-Saxons can become the greatest bullfighters, the greatest ballet dancers, the greatest anything." When, in 1929, Franklin made his Spanish début, in Seville, the aficionados were impressed by the coldness of his art. "Franklin is neither an improviser nor an accident nor a joker," wrote the bullfight critic for *La Unión*, a Seville newspaper. "He is a born bullfighter, with plenty of ambition, which he has had since birth, and for the bulls he has an ultimate quality—serene valor. Coldness, borrowed from the English, if you please. . . . He parries and holds back with a serene magnificence that grandly masks the danger, and he doesn't lose his head before the fierce onslaughts of the enemy." "Franklin fought as though born in Spain; the others fought as though born in Chicago," another critic observed a year later, in comparing Franklin's manner of dispatching two bulls with the work of the Spanish matadors who appeared on the same bill in a Madrid bullring. One day early in his career, Franklin killed the two bulls that had been allotted to him, then, taking the place of two other matadors, who had been gored, killed four more. This set off such an emotional chain reaction in the ring that another bullfighter dropped dead of excitement. Today, many aficionados, both Spanish and Mexican, disparage Franklin's artistry. "Manolete made you feel inside like crying, but Franklin does not engrave anything on your soul," a Spanish aficionado of thirty years' standing complained not long ago. "Franklin has no class," another Spaniard has said. "He is to a matador of Spanish blood what a Mexican baseball player is to Ba-bee Ruth." "I am A Number One," Franklin says. "I am the best in the business, bar none."

Franklin was nineteen when he saw his first bullfight. He was in Mexico, having recently run away from home after a quarrel with his father. As he recalls this particular bullfight, he was bored. In Brooklyn, he had belonged, as a charter member, to the *Eagle*'s Aunt Jean's Humane Club and to the old *New York Globe*'s Bedtime Stories Club, which devoted itself to the glorification of Peter Rabbit. "At that time, the life to me of both man and beast was the most precious thing on this planet," he says. "I failed to grasp the point." The following year, he fought his first bull—a twelve-hundred-pound, four-year-old beast with horns a foot and a half long—and was on his way to becoming a professional. In the quarter of a century since then, Franklin has come to feel that the act of dominating and killing a bull is the most important and satisfying act a human being can perform. "It gives me a feeling of sensual well-being," he has said. "It's so deep it catches my breath. It fills me so completely I tingle all over. It's something I want to do morning, noon, and night. It's something food can't give me. It's something rest can't give me. It's something money can't buy." He is certain that bullfighting is the noblest and most rewarding of all pursuits. He often delivers eloquent discourses on his art to men who are more interested in power, money, love, sex, marriage, dollar diplomacy, atomic energy, animal breeding, religion, Marxism, capitalism, or the Marshall Plan. When his listener has been reduced to acquiescence, or at least bewilderment, Franklin will smile tolerantly and give him a pat on the back. "It's all a matter of first thing first," he will say. "I was destined to taste the first, and the best, on the list of walks of life." The triumph of man over bull is not just the first walk on Franklin's own list; it is the only one. There are no other walks to clutter him up. "I was destined to shine," he adds. "It was a matter of noblesse oblige."

The expression "noblesse oblige" is one Franklin is fond of using to describe his attitude toward most of his activities in and out of the bullring, including the giving of advice to people. He is an unbridled advice giver. He likes to counsel friends, acquaintances, and even strangers to live in a sensible, homespun, conventional, well-tested manner, in line with the principles of saving nine by a stitch in time, of finding life great if one does not weaken, of gathering moss by not rolling, of trying and trying again if success is slow in arriving, and of distinguishing between what is gold and what merely glitters. He is convinced that he thought up all these adages himself. In order to show how seriously he takes them, he often pitches in and helps a friend follow them. He takes credit for having helped at least a half-dozen other bullfighters make hay while the sun shone; for having proved to habitués of saloons and nightclubs that there is no place like home; for having taught a number of ladies how to drive automobiles, after telling them emphatically that anything a man can do, a woman can do; for having encouraged young lovers to get married, because the longer they waited, the more difficult their adjustment to each other would be; and for having persuaded couples to have babies while they were still young, so that they might be pals with their children while they were growing up. "I was destined to lead," Franklin states. "It was always noblesse oblige with me." Some Americans who have watched Franklin dispose of bulls on hot Sunday afternoons in Spain believe that he is right. "Sidney is part of a race of strange, fated men," says Gerald Murphy, head of Mark Cross and a lover of the arts. Franklin has a special category of advice for himself. "I never let myself get obese or slow," he says. "I make it a point never to imbibe before a fight. I never take more than a snifter, even when socializing with the select of all the professions. I am always able to explain to myself the whys and wherefores. I believe in earning a penny by saving it. By following the straight and narrow path, I became the toast of two continents. My horizon is my own creation."

Franklin, who has never married, is tall—five feet, eleven and a half inches—thin, fair-skinned, and bald except for a few wavy bits of sandy-colored hair at the base of his skull. The backs of his hands and the top of his head are spotted with large tan freckles. His eyebrows are heavy and the color of straw. His ears are long. His eyes are brown, narrow, and lacking in depth, and there are a good many lines around them. There is a small scar at the tip of his nose. His build is considered good for bullfighting, because a tall bullfighter can more easily reach over a bull's horns with his sword for the kill. Franklin's only physical handicap is his posterior, which sticks out. "Sidney has no grace because he has a terrific behind," Hemingway says. "I used to make him do special exercises to reduce his behind." When Franklin walks down a street, he seems to dance along on his toes, and he has a harsh, fast way of talking. He sounds like a boxing promoter or a cop, but he has many of the gestures and mannerisms of the Spanish bullfighter. "Americans are taught to speak with their mouths," he likes to say. "We speak with our bodies." When the parade preceding the bullfight comes to a halt, he stands, as do the Mexicans and Spaniards, with the waist pushed forward and the shoulders back. When he becomes angry, he rages, but he can transform himself in a moment into a jolly companion again. In the company of other bullfighters or of aficionados, he glows and bubbles. Last winter, at a hotel in Acapulco, he discovered that the headwaiter, D'Amaso Lopez, had been a matador in Seville between 1905 and 1910. "Ah, Maestro!" cried Franklin, embracing Lopez, who grabbed a tablecloth and started doing *verónicas.* "He is overjoyed to see me," Franklin told his host at dinner. "I'm a kindred spirit." At parties, he likes to replace small talk or other pastimes with parlor bullfighting, using a guest as the bull. (Rita Hayworth is considered by some experts to make his best bull.) Claude Bowers, former United States ambassador to Spain, used to invite Franklin to his soirées in Madrid. "Sidney loved to perform," an embassy man who was usually Franklin's onrushing bull has said. "He'd give the most fascinating running commentary as he demonstrated with the cape, and then he'd spend hours answering the silliest questions, as long as they were about bullfighting. He was like a preacher spreading the gospel."

Franklin gets along well with Mexicans and Spaniards. "On the streets of Seville, everybody talks to him," a friend who has seen a good deal of him there says. "He knows all the taxi drivers and lottery vendors, and even the mayor bows to him." Franklin claims that he has made himself over into an entirely Spanish bullfighter. "I know Spain like I know the palm of my hand," he says. "I happen to be much more lucid in Spanish than in English. I even *think* in Spanish." Franklin's lucidity in Spanish has been a help to other Americans. Rex Smith, former chief of the Associated Press bureau in Madrid, occasionally used him as a reporter. During a rebellion in 1932, he commissioned Franklin to look into a riot near his office. "Suddenly, I heard a great hullabaloo outside my window," Smith says in describing the incident. "I looked out, and there was Sidney telling the crowd, in Spanish, where to get off." "Sidney is fabulous on language," Hemingway has said. "He speaks Spanish so grammatically good and so classically perfect and so complete, with all the slang and damn accents and twenty-seven dialects, nobody would believe he is an American. He is as good in Spanish as T. E. Lawrence was in Arabic." Franklin speaks

Castilian, *caló* (or gypsy talk), and Andalusian. The favorite conversa-
tional medium of bullfighters in Spain is a mixture of *caló* and Andalusian. Instead of saying *"nada"* for "nothing" to other bullfighters, he
says *"na', na', na',"* and he says *"leña,"* which is bullfight slang, instead
of the classical *"cuerno,"* in talking of an especially large horn of a bull.
In conversing with a lisping Spanish duke, Franklin assumes a lisp that
is far better than his companion's, and he is equally at home in the
earthy language of the cafés frequented by bullfighters. The Spanish
maintain that Franklin never makes a mistake in their tongue. One
day, he went sailing in a two-masted schooner. A Spanish companion
called a sail yard a *palo.* "You ought to know better than that," Franklin
told him, and went on to explain that the sail yard he had spoken of
was a *verga,* that *palo* meant mast, and that there were three terms for
mast—one used by fishermen, another by yachtsmen, and the third
by landlubbers.

When Franklin first went to Mexico, in 1922, he did not know any
Spanish. A few years later, while he was training for bullfighting on a
ranch north of Mexico City, he started a class in reading and writing for
forty illiterate peons, of all ages. After three months, sixteen of Franklin's pupils could read and write. "They idolized me for it," he says. In
any restaurant—even a Schrafft's, back home—he follows the Spanish
custom of calling a waiter by saying "Psst!" or clapping the hands. His
Christmas cards say, *"Feliz Navidad y Próspero Año Nuevo."* Conversation
with bulls being customary during a fight, he speaks to them in Spanish. *"Toma, toro! Toma, toro!"* he says, when urging a bull to charge.
"Ah-ah, toro! Ah-ah-ah, toro!" he mutters, telling a bull to come closer.

In putting on his coat, Franklin handles it as though it were a bullfighter's cape, and his entire wardrobe is designed to express his idea
of a bullfighter's personality. "Sidney always took a long time to dress
in the morning," says Hemingway, who often sleeps in his underwear
and takes a half minute to put on his trousers and shirt. "I always had
to wait for him. I don't like a man who takes a long time to dress in the
morning." Most of Franklin's suits were tailored in Seville. "Genuine
English stuff—nothing but the best," he tells people. His wardrobe includes a transparent white raincoat, several turtleneck sweaters, some
Basque berets, a number of sombreros, and a purple gabardine jacket
without lapels. His bullfighting costumes are more elegant and more
expensive than those of any other matador in the business. He has

three wigs—two parted on the left side, one parted on the right—which are the envy of bald bullfighters who have never been to Hollywood or heard of Max Factor. A bullfighter's looks have a lot to do with his popularity, especially in Mexico, where a bald bullfighter is not esteemed. A Spanish matador named Cayetano Ordóñez, professionally called Niño de la Palma, who was the prototype of Hemingway's young bullfighter in *The Sun Also Rises*, lost a good part of his Mexican public when he lost his hair. In 1927, when he appeared in Mexico City and dedicated one of the bulls he was about to kill to Charles A. Lindbergh, he was young, slender, and graceful, with dark, curly hair. "An Adonis," Franklin says. "Niño had a marvelous figure. All the sexes were wild about him." Eight years later, Niño, who had been fighting in Spain, returned to Mexico heavier and partially bald. The moment he took off his matador's hat in the ring, the ladies in the audience transferred their affections to a slimmer and handsomer matador, and the men turned to the bulls. One day, Franklin showed his wigs to Niño. "Poor Niño was flabbergasted," says a witness. "He put on a wig and stood in front of the mirror for an hour, tears in his eyes. My God, what a scene when Sidney tried to take the wig away from him!" Franklin used to wear his wigs whenever he appeared in public, but lately he has worn them only in the bullring, at the theatre, and when having his picture taken. He says that someday, if the action in the ring gets dull, he is going to hang his wig on the horn of a bull.

In accordance with his belief in noblesse oblige, Franklin feels that he can afford to be generous toward his fellow man. "Sidney doesn't envy his neighbors a thing," says a friend. "He is the extreme of what most men like to think of themselves, so much so that he never thinks about it. He doesn't want things. He thinks he has everything." Although Franklin does not carry noblesse oblige so far as to forgive enemies, he is tolerant of those whose friendship for him has cooled. He has rarely seen Hemingway, whom he had come to know in 1929, since leaving him in Madrid in 1937, in the middle of the civil war. Franklin had been doing odd jobs for Hemingway, then a war correspondent.

"I weighed Ernest in the balance and found him wanting," Franklin remarks. "When he began coloring his dispatches about the war, I felt it was time for me to back out on the deal."

"Obscenity!" says Hemingway in reply.

"Ernest got to the point where I knew his mind better than he did himself. It began to annoy him," Franklin says.

"Obscenity!" says Hemingway.

"I may disagree with Ernest, but I'll always give him the benefit of the doubt, because he is a genius," Franklin says.

"Obscenity obscenity!" says Hemingway.

Franklin is highly critical of most of his confreres, but there are a few he praises when he feels they deserve it. After a bullfight in Mexico City a year ago, a friend commented to him that one of the matadors looked good only because he had been given a good bull to kill—a good bull being one that has perfect vision and is aggressive, high-spirited, and, from a human point of view, brave. Franklin said no—that the bull was a bad bull. "The fellow had the guts to stand there and take it and make a good bull out of a lemon," he said. "You can't understand that, because you have no grasp of noblesse oblige." Because of his own grasp of noblesse oblige, Franklin is determined to go on fighting bulls as long as his legs hold out, and he would like to see Brooklyn continue to be represented in the bullring after he retires. To this end, he took under his wing for a while a twenty-six-year-old Brooklyn neighbor of his named Julian Faria, nicknamed Chaval, meaning "the Kid." Chaval, whose parents are of English, Spanish, and Portuguese descent and whose face resembles a gentle, sad-eyed calf's, made his début as a matador in Mexico in the fall of 1947, fighting with Franklin in some of the smaller rings. On the posters announcing the fights, Chaval's name appeared in letters an inch high, beneath Franklin's name in letters two inches high, along with the proclamation that Franklin was "El Único Matador Norteamericano."

"There are two kinds of people," Franklin repeatedly says. "Those who live for themselves and those who live for others. I'm the kind that likes to serve mankind." He believes that he would have made a wonderful doctor, and he acts as a general practitioner whenever he gets a chance. One afternoon, a bull ripped open one of his ankles. "I took a tea saucer and put some sand in it and mixed it up with tea leaves and manure and applied it to the injured member," Franklin says, with a look of sublime satisfaction. "I was then ready to get right back in the ring, functioning perfectly to a T." Once, when he was working on the

ranch in Mexico, a peon accidentally chopped off two of his, the peon's, toes. Franklin claims that he sewed them back on with an ordinary
needle and thread. "I put a splint underneath the foot, bandaged it,
and told him to stay off it for a few days," he says. "In no time at all, the
man was as good as new." In Mexico a few years ago, Franklin stood by
as an appendectomy was performed upon his protégé, Chaval, advising
Chaval, who had been given a local anesthetic, not to show any fear or
sign of pain, not even to grunt, because other bullfighters would hear
about it. Chaval didn't make a sound. "I saw to it that the appendectomy was performed according to Hoyle," Franklin says.

Franklin considers himself an expert on mental as well as physical
health. At a bullfight in Mexico City, last winter, he sat next to a British
psychiatrist, a mannerly fellow who was attending the Unesco conference. While a dead bull was being dragged out of the ring, Franklin
turned to the psychiatrist. "Say, Doc, did you ever go into the immortality of the crab?" he asked. The psychiatrist admitted that he had
not, and Franklin said that nobody knew the answer to that one. He
then asked the psychiatrist what kind of doctor he was. Mental and
physiological, the psychiatrist said.

"I say the brain directs everything in the body," Franklin said. "It's
all a matter of what's in your mind."

"You're something of a psychosomaticist," said the psychiatrist.

"Nah, all I say is if you control your brain, your brain controls the
whole works," said Franklin.

The psychiatrist asked if the theory applied to bullfighting.

"You've got something there, Doc," said Franklin. "Bullfighting is
basic. It's a matter of life and death. People come to see you take long
chances. It's life's biggest gambling game. Tragedy and comedy are so
close together they're part of each other. It's all a matter of noblesse
oblige."

The psychiatrist looked solemn. Another bull came into the ring,
and a matador executed a *verónica*. It was not a good one. The matador
should hold the cape directly before the bull's face, one hand close
to his own body, the other away from his body, stretching the cape,
then pull it away from the bull's face in such a manner that when
the animal follows it, he passes directly in front of him. This matador
held both hands far away from his body, and the bull passed at some
distance from him. The crowd whistled and shouted insults. "Look at

that, Doc," said Franklin. "There's a guy who doesn't have the faintest grasp of noblesse oblige."

The psychiatrist cleared his throat. The bullfight, he said, might be looked upon as a plastic model of Freud's concept of the mind and its three divisions: the id, the uncivilized brute in man; the ego, a combination of environment, which has tamed the id, and of the id itself; and the superego, the conscience, often represented by the father or the mother, who approves or disapproves. He suggested that the id might be represented by the bull, the ego by the bullfighter, and the superego by the whistling and hooting crowd. "Many things you do in life," he added, "are a projection, or model, of what is going on in your mind. For instance, you might be fighting bulls because internally you have a conflict between your id and ego, id and superego, or ego and superego, or possibly a conflict between your combined id and ego and your superego. The bullfight, then, might be a good model of your state of mind."

"Nah," said Franklin. "If I had my life to live all over again, I'd do exactly the same thing. Do you grasp my point?"

The psychiatrist thought it over for a while, then said yes, he believed he did.

After the bullfight, Franklin, in saying goodbye to the British psychiatrist, advised him to take care of himself. "If you can't be good, be careful, Doc," he said.

In general, Franklin says, he likes the life of a bullfighter because of the number of things he can pack into it. "You come into a town, and the moment you arrive, be it by plane, ship, train, or car, everybody is there to receive you," he says. "You barely have time to change your clothes before it's a high old round of banquets and dinners. You don't pay for a thing; others consider it a privilege to pay for you. You're yanked out to go swimming, hunting, fishing, and riding, and if you don't know how to do those things, others consider it a privilege to teach you, to satisfy your every whim and desire. The select of all the professions like to be seen with you." "They're never alone," Hemingway says morosely of bullfighters. "What Ernest has in mind when he says that is that all the sexes throw themselves at you," Franklin explains. "I never went in for that night-owl stuff. I never let myself become detoured. Many of them allow themselves to become so detoured they never get back on the main highway."

Chaval's attitude toward the bullfighter's life is rather different. "I just like to scare girls," he says. "Boy, I bring the bull so close to me, the girls, they scream. Boy, I get a kick out of making girls scream."

Franklin used to lecture Chaval on the significance of noblesse oblige in bullfighting to help the young man stay on the main highway. "I am alive today only because I was in *perfect* condition when I had my accidents in the ring," he sternly told Chaval, who had night-owl inclinations.

"Jeez, Sidney, all you gotta do in the ring is show you're brave," said Chaval. "That's what girls like, when you're brave."

Most bullfighters agree with Chaval, but they state their case with more dignity. A young woman who once met Carlos Arruza at a party in Mexico City complimented him on his bravery in fighting so close to a bull. "You think I am going to be killed, but for you I am courageous in the face of death," Arruza replied gallantly. "This is manliness. I fight to make money, but I like very much to bring the bull to his knees before me." The fearlessness of Manolete is legendary. He specialized in the most difficult and dangerous maneuver in bullfighting—the *pase natural*, which, properly executed, requires the bull to pass perilously close to the body. He had no worthy competitors, but he always tried to outdo himself. "Manolete was a tremendous personality," a Mexican aficionado said recently. "He never smiled." He was gored several times before he received his fatal wound. On more than one occasion, he might have saved himself by moving an inch or two. "Why didn't you move, Manolo?" he was asked after suffering a leg wound one afternoon. "Because I am Manolete," he replied somberly. Lack of fear has been attributed by some people simply to lack of imagination. Franklin disagrees with this theory. "I believe in facing facts," he says. "If you're a superman, you're a superman, and that's all there is to it." Few of the critics who hold to the opinion that Franklin lacks artistry believe that he lacks *valentia*, or bravery. "Nobody ever lives his life all the way up except bullfighters," Franklin says, quoting from *The Sun Also Rises*.

In giving advice to Chaval on how to live his life all the way up, Franklin once said, "You've got to be the sun, moon, and stars to yourself, and results will follow as logically as night follows day."

"Jeez, Sidney! I don't get it," Chaval replied. "All I know is I gotta kill the bull or the bull kills me."

"Bullfighting taught me how to be the master of myself," Franklin said. "It taught me how to discard all that was unimportant."

"Jeez, Sidney!" said Chaval.

Franklin began to make history in the bull ring at his Spanish début, on June 9, 1929, in Seville. Aficionados who saw him fight that day wept and shouted, and talked about it for weeks afterward. "On that day, I declared, 'Bullfighting will never again be the same,'" Manuel Mejías, the bullfighting father of five bullfighting sons, has said. "Sidney Franklin introduced a revolutionary style in the bull ring." "Sidney was a glowing Golden Boy," recalls an American lady who was at the fight. "He was absolutely without fear. He was absolutely beautiful."

"I was carried out on the shoulders of the crowd through the gates reserved for royalty," Franklin told Chaval ecstatically not long ago. "The history of the ring was then a hundred and ninety-nine years old. All that time, only four fellows had ever been carried out of the ring on the shoulders of the crowd. I was the fifth. Traffic in the streets of Seville was wrecked. The next day, they passed a law prohibiting the carrying of bullfighters through the public streets. I was taken out of the ring at seven and deposited at my hotel at twelve-twenty that night. I didn't know what I was doing or what had happened to me. I was so excited I took all my money out of a dresser drawer and threw it to the crowds on the street. The die was cast that day. I was riding on the highest cloud in this or any other world. I felt so far above anything mundane that nothing mattered. I didn't hear anything. I didn't see anything. I looked, but I didn't see. I heard, but nothing registered. I didn't care about food. I didn't care about drink. I was perfectly satisfied to lay my head on the pillow and pass out."

Terrific

The Junior League of the City of New York, Inc., a fifty-three-year-old club for women under forty, gave its third annual Mardi Gras Ball—"a brilliant assemblage of those prominent in society, stage, screen, and television," the *Herald Tribune* called it—on Tuesday evening, March 2, 1954, in the Grand Ballroom of the Hotel Astor. About eight hundred Junior League members and husbands, and friends of members and friends of husbands, attended, paying fifteen dollars a head for the privilege, and one and all agreed that it was quite a do. Emil Coleman's twenty-four-piece, two-piano orchestra played for dancing, and the highlights of the evening were the crowning of a Queen of the Mardi Gras by Mayor Robert F. Wagner, Jr., and a parade of fifteen Junior Leaguers and two professional models who wore costumes more or less expressing the spirit of seventeen commercial firms (including Pepsi-Cola and United States Steel) that had sponsored the ball by donating fifteen hundred dollars each to the New York Junior League's Welfare Trust Fund. The New York League has fifteen hundred members (it is one of 183 chapters, with a total membership of sixty-three thousand), who dedicate themselves, upon joining, to serving the social, economic, educational, cultural, and civic interests of the community, and the League spends the money in its Welfare Trust Fund for the operation of volunteer services it carries on in hospitals, settlement houses, and similar worthy centers. A week after Mardi Gras night, the treasurer of the Junior League Mardi Gras committee reported to her forty-five glinting-eyed co-members that by the time the books were balanced, the ball would net a profit for the Welfare Trust Fund of something over eighteen thousand dollars.

Preparations for the ball began more than a year before it was held. At eleven fifteen on the morning of February 18, 1953, the day after the second annual Mardi Gras Ball, which was also held at the Astor and

which, sponsored by only fourteen commercial firms (including Flamingo Orange Juice and Pepperidge Farm Bread), netted $11,517.02,
the chairman of the second Mardi Gras committee, Mrs. Thomas D.
Luckenbill, turned up at the League's headquarters and clubhouse—a
five-story building, at 130 East Eightieth Street, that was formerly the
town house of Vincent Astor. Mrs. Luckenbill immediately set to work
writing thank-you notes to sponsors, celebrities, and others who had
helped with the second Mardi Gras Ball. She was joined a few minutes
later by Mrs. Stirling S. Adams, one of the four vice chairmen of the
committee. Mrs. Adams, looking cool and satisfied with everything
around her, said she had got to bed at five that morning and had got up
again at eight, to go down to the Astor and pick up the Queen's throne
and some trumpets, and return them to a rental company. By noon,
more than half the members of Mrs. Luckenbill's committee were on
hand to help write the thank-you notes, many of them coming in after
laboring all the morning at volunteer jobs in clinics or day nurseries.
Everybody was already enthusiastically looking ahead to the 1954 ball.
They rehashed the previous night's ball and determined to improve
on it in certain ways the third time around. There was the problem of
the Astor's public-address system, for example (it had conked out just
as the Queen was being crowned), and the problem of guarding the
dressing room of the models. (Newspaper photographers had wandered in while the girls were putting on their costumes.) Mrs. Adams
said that Mrs. Henry I. Stimson, the committeewoman in charge of
costumes, had done a terrific job, and that the costume she herself
had admired the most was the one worn by Mrs. Wickliffe W. Crider,
who had appeared as a chicken sandwich, to represent Pepperidge
Farm Bread. Mrs. Crider had worn two giant slices of bread and had
been carried in by four gentlemen dressed to look like toothpicks.
"Next year, we might have someone dressed up as an olive if we have
the sandwich again," Mrs. Adams said. "But then I suppose Pepperidge
will want something different costumewise."

Mrs. Luckenbill told Mrs. Kevin McLoughlin, the liaison member
between the Mardi Gras committee and the League's board of managers, that she was recommending Mrs. Stimson for the job of Mardi
Gras chairman for the next year. Mrs. McLoughlin looked delighted.
"Louise Stimson is a nifty gal," she said. "That pink-clown drawing
she made for the program could be our permanent motif for all fu-

ture Mardi Gras. Mrs. Luckenbill agreed, and suggested that someone should make a motion endorsing the clown drawing at the next
meeting of the League's board of managers. "I'm sure everyone will
be for it policywise," Mrs. McLoughlin said. Mrs. Albert C. Santy, who
had been in charge of reservations for the ball, said that everyone was
happy about the selection of Mrs. Oliver Rea as Queen the night before. There had been five candidates, known as Maids, for the crown,
and the Queen had been chosen by three civic-minded men in public
office, on the basis of her personality and the work she had done for
the Junior League and for the community at large. Mrs. Rea had served
as chairman of the League's Volunteer Social Work Aides, chairman
of its placement committee, and chairman of a rehabilitation project
it set up at Bellevue Hospital. As Queen of the Mardi Gras the night
before, she had sat on her throne on a stage and ruled over the ball.
Now, with no further regal duties, she was up at Riverside Hospital,
an institution for adolescent narcotics users on North Brother Island,
in the East River, doing her regular volunteer work with the patients
there. "Betty Rea is a nifty gal," McLoughlin said. "All five Maids were
nifty, but *somebody* had to be Queen."

Mrs. John C. Carrington, who is vice president of the New York Junior League, joined the group. "Wasn't Betty Rea a doll as Queen!" she
said. "My only suggestion for improvement next year is to get escorts
and Maids to match. Tall for tall. Short for short."

Mrs. W. Mahlon Dickerson, a tall, broad-shouldered woman, who
had been one of the four Maids not chosen for the throne, remarked
good-naturedly that her escort had been short but very charming. Her
only complaint was that the room upstairs reserved for the Maids had
been so well guarded that she herself had a good deal of trouble getting admitted. "Next year, we ought to have smoother functioning of
who gets in and who stays out," she said. "Next year, we ought to do a
really bang-up job." Mrs. Paul H. Raymer, another committee member,
observed that the models had been left stranded on the stage after
the show and that no one had seemed to know what to do with them.
"My husband grabbed Flamingo Orange Juice and danced with her,"
she said, and everybody laughed. "Next year, we ought to have more
of a proper conclusion to things." Everybody agreed that for the third
Mardi Gras Ball there would be smoother functioning of who got in
and who stayed out, as well as more of a proper conclusion to things.

During the following month, in accordance with Mrs. Luckenbill's suggestion, the New York Junior League's board of managers, presided over by Mrs. Samuel Wilson Moore, the New York president, voted unanimously to appoint Mrs. Stimson chairman of the third Mardi Gras Ball. In addition, it also voted unanimously to make Mrs. Stimson's pink-clown drawing a permanent fixture on the program. In April, Mrs. Stimson, a serious and efficient woman who has belonged to the League for six years and is a past president, and present member, of the board of the Manhattanville Day Nursery, began organizing her committee to prepare for the ball. She named Mrs. Adams chairman of the subcommittee in charge of the pageant, Mrs. Crider chairman in charge of costumes, and Mrs. Santy chairman in charge of hotel arrangements and reservations, and put Mrs. Raymer and Mrs. McLoughlin in charge of special invitations and publicity, respectively. At 10:30 a.m., on May 6, these members, along with two others—Mrs. Dickerson and Mrs. Robert Cooke, who were as yet unassigned—were called to order by their chairman at a preliminary meeting of the 1954 Mardi Gras committee.

The women assembled in the boardroom, on the third floor of the League building, walking to it through a corridor whose walls are hung with photographs of the twenty-five past presidents of the New York League—a new one is elected every second year—beginning with Mrs. Charles C. Rumsey, the former Mary Harriman, who in 1901 conceived the idea of founding an organization to be called the Junior League for the Promotion of Settlement Work. (The name was shortened in 1912.) At the outset of the meeting, everybody agreed that the coming ball should be a dinner affair. The previous ball had been a supper dance, and the general feeling was that it had made Mardi Gras night too expensive for the individual members of the League, because so many of them had felt it mandatory to give dinner parties at home before going to the Astor. Everybody also agreed that the charge for the next Mardi Gras should be fifteen dollars a head, eight of which, it was hoped, would cover the cost of the dinner and other expenses, so that the remaining seven could be turned over to the Welfare Trust Fund. There was some discussion about a date for the ball. The two previous ones had been held on the night of Shrove Tuesday, the actual Mardi Gras. Some of the committee members thought that a weekend might be better, but the majority insisted that the traditional night was the best, and that this was one time when people would simply have to stay up late in the middle of the week. Once that had been settled, Mrs. Stimson explained that she was going to delay awhile before naming someone to the critical post of chairman of sponsors, because she wanted to be sure of finding a woman with some understanding of the problems of the business world. "Let's not be afraid to face facts, girls," said Mrs. Dickerson. "We're out to make money. We want sponsors who will fork over money." Her fellow members nodded in agreement that she had a sound point there. Mrs. Adams said that she thought the Astor had the best ballroom for the purposes of the Mardi Gras, and she proposed that, provided the hotel had fixed up the public-address system, the ball be held there again. Then she looked at her wristwatch, gave a little cry, and asked to be excused from the meeting because a quartet of Junior League members, in which she sang second soprano, was scheduled to sing in one of the wards at St. Luke's Hospital in half an hour. She went on to explain breathlessly that they wanted to have at least one run-through of "Tulip," "Daisy," and "Easter Parade" before singing for the patients. Mrs. Stimson adjourned the meeting.

The first official meeting of Mrs. Stimson's committee was held at ten thirty on the morning of June 3, at the Junior League clubhouse. Mrs. Santy and Mrs. Raymer had visited the Astor's banquet department a few days before, and Mrs. Santy reported that a roast sirloin of beef dinner would cost the League seven dollars a person, plus a fifteen percent service charge—a total of eight dollars and five cents. It was a good dinner, Mrs. Santy said, and it didn't have what she called "that hotel-chicken-dinner personality." Mrs. Raymer put in hastily that the dinner started with clear green-turtle soup, instead of what she called "that hotel-chicken watery stuff." She looked around at her fellow members and went on, "The soup is more important than you might think. If we're going to have a dinner, we must keep in mind that discouragement everybody feels if the soup is cold and dishpanny. If they get that discouraged feeling at the outset, the party is sunk moralewise." Mrs. Stimson said all that was true, but the price of the dinner was about two dollars more than the price of the supper at the last ball. In a rather weak voice, Mrs. Adams pointed out that the extra cost of the meal might mean a loss of as much as sixteen hundred dollars to the Welfare Trust Fund.

After a few moments' silence, Mrs. Santy said loudly, "Let me read you the entire menu for the roast sirloin of beef dinner." She cleared her throat and read. "'Clear green-turtle soup, celery, palettes of corn, olives, roast sirloin of beef Chevreuse, mushroom sauce, potatoes dauphine, new peas, salad chiffonade, peach Melba, petits fours, demitasse.'" Mrs. Santy stopped reading and sighed.

"It does sound *so* good," said Mrs. Stimson. She looked around encouragingly at her committee members.

"Well," Mrs. Adams said, "it would be nice to have roast beef and all that, but I do think we ought to pause and consider the fundamental objective of Mardi Gras. I move that we postpone our decision until Mrs. Santy and Mrs. Raymer have an opportunity to obtain other menus at lower prices."

"Second that motion," said Mrs. Santy.

A low moan rose in the committee room, but everybody voted to postpone the decision on the menu.

Mrs. Stimson said that this year there ought to be more emphasis in the *Observer*, the League's monthly magazine, and, if possible, in general publications, of how the five Maids who are candidates for Queen are chosen, and a lot more about how their service to the League and the community qualifies them for that honor. Mrs. McLoughlin, in her capacity as publicity director, agreed. The point ought to be driven home once and for all to the whole membership, she said, that the Maids are picked from among twenty candidates who are selected by the League's placement committee on the basis of the time and energy they have devoted to worthwhile services. "They're chosen by sensible, serious-minded gals," she went on. "Those gals do a terrific job studying the records of all the active members except the board of managers, and the membership ought to know that everybody's record gets examined seriously."

"And that only active members are eligible," said Mrs. Stimson.

Mrs. Santy wanted to know whether the provisional members—those newly elected to the League—wouldn't feel left out.

"You can't be provisional forever, dear girl," Mrs. Stimson said, with a little laugh. She added that she hoped Mrs. McLoughlin would make it clear that the placement committee submits the names of all its candidates to the board of managers. "We're counting on you to point up the fact that if the board feels some deserving member has been overlooked, it can say, 'Heavens, why isn't So-and-So a candidate?'" she continued, and Mrs. McLoughlin replied that she would and that she would also try to impress upon the membership the fact that five judges not connected with the League make the final selection of the Maids, on the basis of interviews with the twenty candidates and a study of their service records. This year, she said, the judges were to be James F. Macandrew, director of broadcasting at the Board of Education's radio station; Miss Helen M. Harris, the executive director of the United Neighborhood Houses of New York; Mrs. Joseph P. Lash, the executive director of the Citizens' Committee on Children of New York City; Stanly P. Davies, the general director of the Community Service Society of New York City; and Clyde E. Murray, executive director of the Manhattanville Neighborhood Center.

"Very good," Mrs. Stimson said. "Now—costumers?" She turned to Mrs. Crider, who after consulting a sheaf of papers, announced that her preliminary investigation of the matter of the models' costumes had been very encouraging. She thought that instead of having each costume made in a different place, as in the past, it might be feasible to have them all made in Brooks Costume Company. She said she had spoken with James Stroock, the head of the company, and he had estimated that each costume would cost about seventy-five dollars, or nearly twenty dollars less than the average cost of the costumes for the previous ball. Furthermore, Mrs. Crider said, she thought it would be a fine idea to ask Gunther Jaeckel, which had placed an advertisement in the most recent issue of the *Observer*, to contribute gowns for the five Maids. The other members applauded Mrs. Crider, and the committee then turned to a general discussion of a number of questions: Could the Astor provide the master of ceremonies with two microphones, so that all the guests could hear the program? Could the Astor take the hum, whistles, and squeaks out of the public-address system? Could the Astor be enlisted as a sponsor of the ball, and perhaps be represented by a Miss Astor, who might hold a large numeral 50 to commemorate the fiftieth anniversary of the hotel, which was coming the following year? Could Jo Mielziner, the theatrical designer, be persuaded to do the staging for the Mardi Gras show? Could Rodgers and Hammerstein be enlisted to contribute a score written specially for the Mardi Gras? Or, failing that, could Rodgers and Hammerstein do at least one special song for the Mardi Gras? Mrs. Stimson said the committee now had some meaty questions to work on before its first meeting in the fall.

The first fall meeting of the committee was held on November 4 at 10:30 a.m. The members looked authoritative and eager. To start things off, Mrs. Stimson asked Mrs. Santy to give her report on the question of the menu. Mrs. Santy asked if the committee wanted to hear the $8.05 roast sirloin of beef menu again, and said that if so, she would read it first and then read the menus of two less expensive dinners. Everybody wanted to hear the roast sirloin of beef menu again, so Mrs. Santy started with the clear green-turtle soup and went right on through the petits fours and demitasse. Everybody sighed, and then Mrs. Santy read the menu of a six-dollar roast turkey dinner. This one was greeted with cold silence. Mrs. Santy went on to read a third menu: fruit cocktail, celery, olives, broiled breast of chicken Virginie, Virginia ham, broiled mushrooms, candied yams, asparagus tips, hearts of lettuce with Roquefort dressing, baked Alaska with bing cherries flambées, demitasse. This dinner would cost $6.50, plus the fifteen percent service charge, which would bring the cost to $7.48. Mrs. Adams said that menu sounded pretty good, even if it did include chicken, and other members agreed without enthusiasm that when you came right down to it, a chicken-and-ham dinner was better than a turkey one. Mrs. Dickerson wanted to know if the fruit cup would be made of canned fruit or fresh fruit. Fresh, Mrs. Santy said, and pointed out that the chicken was *breast* of chicken and that this automatically raised it above the level of many hotel dinners.

Mrs. Dickerson's expression was that of a person who has reached a decision. "If it's a *breast* of chicken, I'd say it's a darn nice dinner and we needn't worry about the word *chicken*," she said cheerfully. "We might aim for a seafood cocktail, though—or anything but fruit cup. Fresh or canned, fruit cup is rather downbeat, partywise."

"I move we ax the fruit cup and take the third menu," Mrs. McLoughlin said. The motion was seconded and carried. Everybody applauded.

"All right, then," Mrs. Stimson said sternly. "Now we must buckle down and get those sponsors. Mrs. Correa will be chairman of sponsors. Mrs. Correa?"

Mrs. Henry A. Correa stood up and asked all the committee members to get after everybody they knew in a big business who might be influential in producing a sponsor. There were three sponsors so far, she said—WNBC, WNBT, and Liggett & Meyers. "Caroline Burke spoke to Pepsi-Cola, and she thinks they will be a sponsor," she went on. "But so far only the other three are absolutely definite."

Mrs. Luckenbill suggested that it wasn't a bit too early to put the heat on everybody to get sponsors.

"Sponsors are basic," Mrs. Adams said.

Mrs. Crider said that she was having a bit of a problem with Liggett & Myers over its model's costume.

"Liggett and Myers apparently wasn't too happy at the last Mardi Gras," she said. The Liggett & Myers costume at the 1953 ball had been a tube of white felt, mounted on a wire frame, that glowed at the tip.

"Liggett and Myers was unhappy about the way the girl was hidden inside the tube, instead of looking glamorous or something," said Mrs. Stimson. "We did the best we could with a limited budget."

"Liggett and Myers wants a Parade of Quality," Mrs. Crider said. "They want their four cigarettes—Chesterfield, king-size Chesterfield, Fatima, and L and M—represented by *four* models with perhaps a man lighting their cigarettes."

Mrs. Adams, looking alarmed, said that to go along with this request might raise problems in dealing with other sponsors who made more than one product. After a half-hour discussion, it was decided that if any sponsor wanted to pay the cost of additional costumes, and if it didn't require more parade time than any other sponsor got, it could have additional models.

Mrs. Stimson then said that she had met a number of gentlemen from the National Broadcasting Company and they had all agreed that Faye Emerson and Skitch Henderson would be ideal for mistress and master of ceremonies. A motion to try to get Faye and Skitch to lend their services was made, seconded, and carried, and everybody applauded again.

Mrs. Stimson blushed slightly at this tribute to her enterprise and frowned at her agenda. "Since the last Mardi Gras, a new mayor has been elected," she said. "Would someone make a motion to the effect that Betsy Carrington, who knows Mayor Wagner, contact him and invite him to crown the Queen at the next Mardi Gras?" A motion to that effect was then made, seconded, and carried.

Mrs. Adams rose and said that everybody ought to set to work getting famous people to submit sketches for costumes. Mrs. Dickerson added that everybody also ought to be thinking of somebody famous to serve as King.

"Let's have some famous names suggested now," said Mrs. Stimson. The members decided to ask Fannie Hurst, Irving Berlin, Hedda Hopper, Red Barber, and Dale Carnegie to submit sketches for costumes. Then, as possible Kings, they nominated Adolphe Menjou, Robert Montgomery, Conrad Thibault, Charles Boyer, John Cameron Swayze, James Stewart, Fredric March, Douglas Fairbanks, Jr., and Lawrence Tibbett. Mrs. Stimson looked satisfied. "Kingwise we don't have anything to worry about," she said.

At the beginning of December, Mrs. Stimson stood before her committee with a budget—drawn up by Mrs. John R. Stevenson, the treasurer of the committee, and approved by the New York Junior League board of managers—that, based on a thousand paying guests and fifteen paying sponsors and an expenditure of $16,500, showed a profit of $17,535 for the Welfare Trust Fund. Mrs. Stimson was prepared to place an order for sixty-five hundred invitations, to be printed at a cost of $438. She had already worked out one design for these and had brought it along for the members to look at. On the outside of the invitation, a folded affair, were two gay faces—one of a clown and the other of a devil—smiling down at the words "You Are Invited to the New York Junior League Mardi Gras." On the inside, the invitation read, GLAMOUR, FUN, GAYETY, FROLIC, MELODY, AND PAGEANTRY. Beneath these words were inscribed: "A PAGEANT WITH COSTUMES OF FANTASY—A Glamorous Parade of Junior League Models in Fabulous Costumes." To the left of this boast was a large pink star with a blue question mark in its center and the words "QUEEN OF THE MARDI GRAS." All Mrs. Stimson's committee members thought that her design was terrific, and it was swiftly adopted.

By mid-December, the committee had signed up five more sponsors—TWA, the Moore-McCormack Lines, Fuller Brush, Philco, and the Astor Hotel. Shortly thereafter, consternation set in, for Mrs. Correa had to accompany her husband on a business trip to South America and would not be back until after the ball. An emergency meeting of the committee was called, and Mrs. Stimson named Mrs. Dickerson, who had just nabbed Moore-McCormack and the Packard Motor Car Company, to carry on as chairman of sponsors. Mrs. Dickerson got to work at once. At a brief committee meeting shortly before Christmas, she announced, "I want to put up a poster on the main floor of the clubhouse with a thermometer on it showing that we have nine sponsors, and then as the list grows, the thermometer will be filled in. And we've simply got to make it grow. I knew some of the Moore-McCormack people and that helped me get them as sponsors. But, on the other hand, I sold Packard cold. Just went in there and said I had something that might interest them, and that was *that*." There was a prolonged hum of approval from the other committee members, and Mrs. Dickerson acknowledged it with a nod. "Pepsi-Cola looks good," she said. "Miss Burke is still after them. The only other thing I want to ask is whether there is any objection to approaching None Such Mince Meat in addition to Borden's, since None Such Mince Meat is a Borden product." The committee unanimously sanctioned going after anybody and everybody who might be a sponsor, instead of worrying about who owned what.

On January 7, the five judges interviewed twenty Junior Leaguers whose names had been put up by the placement committee as potential Maids of the Mardi Gras Ball and, after conferring among themselves for more than three hours, submitted a list of the five indefatigable winners.

Three weeks before the date of the ball, Mrs. Stimson held a meeting of the executive committee of the Mardi Gras Committee—Mrs. Adams, Mrs. McLoughlin, Mrs. Dickerson, Mrs. Santy, Mrs. Raymer, Mrs. Crider, and Mrs. Stevenson—at which she regretfully announced that it didn't look as if any of the Kings who had been nominated would ever reach the throne: Adolphe Menjou was in Hollywood, James Stewart was in Hollywood, Robert Montgomery would be on his way to Washington, and the others were too busy. Everyone looked downcast. Then Mrs. Stimson said, "But Henry Fonda is in town now, with a new play. I think Henry Fonda would make a charming King." The committee responded with energetic approval and voted to ask Mrs. Douglas Leigh, a committee member who knew Fonda, to invite him to serve as King.

"I regret to say that Rodgers and Hammerstein can't do a special score for us," Mrs. Stimson next announced. "But I'm sure that Emil Coleman will provide whatever we need in the way of music." The board expressed understanding and agreement.

Mrs. Santy reported that applications for tickets to the ball were pouring in. "Martha Wadsworth sent out over six thousand invitations on January 25," she said. "She stamped, stuffed, addressed, and mailed them practically all by herself. There's no beating Martha when it comes to that hideous job."

Two weeks before the date of the ball, a clipping from the *World-Telegram & Sun* was posted on a bulletin board beside the elevator at League headquarters. It was a photograph showing the five Maids grouped around Fonda, who, with a royal smile, was holding a diamond tiara that Napoleon had once given to the Empress Josephine and that the jewelry firm of Van Cleef & Arpels was going to lend to the League for the crowning of its Queen.

On the afternoon the clipping was posted, Mrs. Cooke, the chairman of models, and her assistants, Mrs. Frederick R. Hanson and Mrs. Kilner Husted, were seated in a corner of the Pine Room—a large lounge on the second floor of the clubhouse, with a fireplace and comfortable armchairs arranged around several small cocktail tables. With them were two of the League members who were going to serve as models at the ball—Miss Polly Ann Bryant and Mrs. David Drew Zingg. "We want our sponsors to be happy," Mrs. Cooke was saying to Miss Bryant, a pretty dark-haired girl with large blue eyes, who had agreed only a few hours before to be the Philco model. "It was very nice of you to come on such short notice, Miss Bryant."

"Mardi Gras is two weeks from tonight," Mrs. Hanson said. "I'm exhausted. I hope somebody reminds all the models and Maids to get enough sleep."

Mrs. Cooke asked Miss Bryant to stand up, so that she could show her how to move when she had the Philco costume on. "You're a refrigerator and you're all filled with stuff," Mrs. Cooke said. "Now, you're all in white as you walk in and your white robe comes to a kind of V in front. You fling one arm out"—Miss Bryant flung one arm out—"and inside there's the tomato juice and soft drinks and oranges. Then you open the other side"—Miss Bryant flung out her other arm—"and there's the eggs and butter and milk and cream. Do you think you get the idea?"

Miss Bryant nodded eagerly. "Oh yes," she said. "All I do is open the doors and I have all the stuff inside the costume."

"Right," Mrs. Cooke said crisply. "Now Mrs. Zingg." The other model stood up. She was tall and very slim, with long, slender legs. Mrs. Cooke explained that she would model for the American Express Company, a newcomer. "You're just terrific," Mrs. Cooke said. "You simply wear the company's uniform—jacket and cap, that is—and tights."

"Just tights?" Mrs. Zingg said, rather proudly. "Not trousers?"

"American Express prefers tights, and thank goodness you have the figure for them," Mrs. Cooke said. "Do you think you've got the idea, Mrs. Zingg?"

Mrs. Zingg said it sounded like a cinch. Then Mrs. Cooke told the two models that Mrs. Hanson would make an appointment for each of them for a costume fitting and would telephone them in a day or so, and Miss Bryant and Mrs. Zingg left. Mrs. Cooke told Mrs. Husted that Fannie Hurst, Irving Berlin, Hedda Hopper, Red Barber, and Dale Carnegie had not come across with designs for costumes. An auxiliary list of celebrities had been got up, and as a result of it Bing Crosby had agreed to let his name be used as the designer of the American Express Company's costume—coat, cap, tights and all; Rosalind Russell had suggested that the American Viscose Corporation, another newcomer, have Queen Guinevere escorted by a white knight in shining armor, just like its trademark; Perry Como had suggested that the Liggett & Myers girl wear a slinky evening gown and a necklace of Liggett & Myers cigarettes; and Charles Boyer had authorized the use of his name as the designer of a costume that included a spool hat and a dressmaker's dummy, for Singer Sewing Machine, which had recently signed up. "Groucho Marx gave us a peach for Fuller Brush," Mrs. Cooke said. "He came up with something real dreamy. One of our girls will be dressed as Groucho and smoking a long cigar with gold ashes that she'll drop as she walks down the aisle, and she'll be followed by a tall blonde who'll sweep up the ashes with a Fuller brush. Jo-Jeanne Barton is going to be Groucho. All she does all day, she says, is practice her walk. And she just had a baby two weeks ago, too."

Mrs. Husted asked if Pepperidge Farm Bread was a sponsor again this year, and Mrs. Cooke said no, adding that Pepperidge somehow felt last year's sandwich had everything and there just wasn't anything else to say. But among the new sponsors the League did have were

Pepsi-Cola, United States Steel, Cities Service, and Rheingold Beer, which was going to send its own Miss Rheingold to represent it.

"That Pepperidge sandwich last year was a dream," Mrs. Husted said wistfully.

"Wait'll you see Moore-McCormack's fruit salad," said Mrs. Cooke.

That same afternoon, on the fifth floor of the clubhouse, in a small office shared by the editor of the *Observer* and Mrs. McLoughlin, the latter was having a conference with Miss Margaret Roberts, a serious, quiet-spoken young lady who had been engaged by the League as a professional producer of the Mardi Gras show and whose job included, among many other things, keeping the pageant within the time limit set by the television people. Miss Roberts told Mrs. McLoughlin that the television people were giving the League only forty minutes. "They've preempted our time, but it will really be a much better show that way," she said. Mrs. McLoughlin did not question the point, and Miss Roberts continued, "This is what we call the rundown—the sequence of events as they will be filmed by the cameras. We open with balloons falling from the ceiling and everybody dancing. Then we go to Faye and Skitch sitting at a small ringside table, and they say 'The Junior League—' "

"The *New York* Junior League," Mrs. McLoughlin said.

Miss Roberts accepted the correction and went on to tell her that after saying hello, Faye and Skitch would explain the purpose of the ball. "Then Faye and Skitch go over to the mayor's table," Miss Roberts said, "and there we meet Mayor and Mrs. Wagner, and Mrs. Moore and her husband, Dr. Moore, and they talk about the history of the Junior League."

"The *New York* Junior League," said Mrs. McLoughlin.

Miss Roberts nodded. "And the New York Junior League's accomplishments of the past year," she said. "Now, what should Faye and Skitch say about the volunteer work?"

Mrs. McLoughlin said Faye and Skitch ought to mention the work of the Volunteer Social Work Aide Project, which was set up by the League to pay tuition at the New York School of Social Work not only for League members but for members of other welfare agencies, and to place the League volunteers trained there at Riverside Hospital. Miss

Roberts assured Mrs. McLoughlin that she would pass this information along to Faye and Skitch. They were leaving for Europe that evening, she said, but they would be back a day or two before the Mardi Gras. She then outlined the rest of the television program—the costume parade, the introduction of the five Maids, the announcement by the mayor of the name of the Maid chosen as Queen, and the march through the ballroom by the King and Queen. "With only forty minutes, it's going to be very tight," Miss Roberts said.

"Well," said Mrs. McLoughlin, "It's the *New York* Junior League. Let's be sure to get *that* in, anyway."

At ten the next morning, there was a meeting of the executive committee of the Mardi Gras Committee, presided over by Mrs. Stimson, who started out briskly by announcing that this year there would be about eight hundred people at the ball—a hundred more than had come the year before; this would probably mean turning some people down, but it had been decided that the one thousand originally figured on would make things too crowded. The members of the executive committee were beginning to wear a look of combined worry, distraction, and great expectation. One after another, problems were disposed of: Had the Astor been advised that the hum, whistles, and squeaks from the mikes last year had made it difficult to hear and that the public-address system ought to be fixed? (Mrs. Adams said that the Astor had promised to have all the mikes in good working order.) Did all the sponsors know that each sponsor would be given only a few seconds for commercials, to be delivered by Faye and Skitch? (Mrs. Dickerson said she had personally informed them all of this fact.) Had tables been allocated to all the sponsors? (Mrs. Santy said American Express had had no table until a quarter of an hour ago, but now an entire table was reserved for American Express and it was ringside.) Where was Pepsi-Cola sitting? (Mrs. Santy said with Miss Burke, who had nabbed Pepsi-Cola.)

Mrs. Adams—tall, cool, and self-possessed—reported on the matter of prices. "We'll just skimp by under the budget," she said. "I told the Astor they've simply got to come down on some of the prices, and they may, but the fact remains that in order to make the ballroom look right, you've got to do certain things that cost money." The rest of the committee looked glum. "It isn't the *things* that are so expensive," Mrs. Adams continued. "It's all in the *labor*." The pageant designer, Lester

Gaba, had all sorts of wonderful ideas for decorating the ballroom, she said, but they would cost money. The rest of the committee looked glummer. Mrs. Adams picked up a sheet of paper and rattled it. "Lester thinks we should have an underwater theme," she said. "Lester wants to do the stage up in sea-blue satin drapes and have it all sort of bubbly-looking, with balloons held up by mermaids."

"Mmm, yummy!" said Mrs. Stimson, and then blushed and looked apologetically at the rest of the committee. Mrs. Adams went on to extend the undersea theme of the stage all through the ballroom, which would mean an additional $375 for labor. She read off a list of other costs, including $55 for robes and scepters for the King and Queen, $5 for a page's trumpet, $150 for balloons, $50 for hoops (wooden frames with canvas spread loosely across them to hold balloons near the ceiling until the time for their release), $150 apiece for two papier-mâché mermaids, and $100 for a pink-and-blue papier-mâché shell, ten feet high, to hold throne chairs. The mermaids, she explained, would be faceless and silvery-looking.

"Oh, let's have them flicker," said Mrs. Dickerson.

"Well, the light to make them flicker costs twenty-five dollars extra," said Mrs. Adams.

"Oh dear!" said Mrs. Dickerson.

"We must be strong, girls," said Mrs. Stimson. "Of course, we're ahead of last year on sponsors. We just got Forstmann Woolens today. And with the eight hundred people we expect—"

"I'd rather see that money go into the Welfare Trust Fund," said Mrs. McLoughlin.

"Of course," said Mrs. Adams. "And if we drape just one tier of the ballroom, instead of both, we'll save a hundred and fifty dollars."

"Rosie, take one more crack at seeing if you can get the Astor to shave the price," Mrs. Dickerson said to Mrs. Adams. "We're not getting anywhere with None Such Mince Meat."

Mrs. Adams nodded. "Another thing," she said. "Lester Gaba wants these long candles for the tables. That's fifty dollars."

"I tried to talk him out of it," Mrs. Stimson said. "Last year, we spent a hundred and fifty for extra-long candles—long *pink* candles. The Astor wanted to give us those little beaded mushroom things, and if we have those this year, Lester is just going to be *sick*."

A couple of mornings later, with the ball hardly a week away, Mrs.

Santy called on Robert Howard, the Astor's banquet director, in his office at the hotel. Howard is a patient, hoarse-voiced man, with a round,
pink face and a small mustache. Mrs. Santy was accompanied by three
other members of the Mardi Gras committee—Mrs. Dickerson, Mrs.
J. Calhoun Harris, and Mrs. Edmund Johnstone—and by Miss Eva M.
Scism, assistant to the Junior League treasurer. All five women had on
little hats with little veils, and three-strand chokers of pearls, and they
sat around Howard's desk in a semicircle.

"Well, ladies," Howard said, somewhat nervously, "are you all set for
the big night?"

"You're never really set until it's all over," Mrs. Santy said.

Howard laughed wanly.

"If you'll take some notes on what I tell you . . . ," Mrs. Santy began.
Howard drew up a pad and seized a pencil. Mrs. Santy asked him to
have the models' room properly guarded, and the Maids' room, too,
because the year before, Mrs. Dickerson, a Maid herself, had had trouble getting in; to have a waiter on hand to take food to the models,
who hadn't been able to get anything to eat the last time until after
the show was over, and had starved, and to bear in mind the names
of judges who would choose the Queen—Mrs. Oswald B. Lord, the
United States representative to the United Nations Commission on
Human Rights; Dr. Howard A. Rusk, the chairman of the Department
of Physical Medicine and Rehabilitation at the New York University
College of Medicine; and Russel Crouse, the playwright—because they
would have to be passed by the guards and admitted to the Maids'
room.

"Everything will be taken care of, ladies," Howard said.

Mrs. Santy brought up the question of cocktails before dinner, and
Howard told her that the Coral Room was very good for cocktails. "It's
really green," he said, and laughed.

Mrs. Johnstone wanted to know if there would be peanuts on the
table there.

Howard made a note. "Now I'd like to ask you some questions," he
said.

"Yes, sir," said Mrs. Santy.

"What about cigarettes?" Howard asked.

Mrs. Dickerson started: "Nothing but Chesterfields," she said. "Liggett and Myers is one of our sponsors. And there must be Pepsi-Cola.

If Mr. Steele, the Pepsi-Cola man, asks for Pepsi-Cola, he mustn't get Coca-Cola."

Howard made another note. "You want *pink* tablecloths, ladies?" he asked.

"What did Mrs. Adams say?" asked Mrs. Santy.

"She said to use as many as we have but not to *buy* any," Howard replied. He shrugged wearily. "As soon as I get through with one committee, another comes in," he said. "I don't think we'll be able to cover more than half the tables with pink cloths."

Mrs. Santy nodded and looked worried. "There was something else, but I've forgotten it," she said.

"I write everything down," said Mrs. Dickerson.

"Well, ladies," Howard said cheerfully, "shall we go in and take a look at the tables?"

Everybody rose and walked into the ballroom. The floor was bare, and the tables, their brown wooden tops exposed, looked dark and dreary in the dimly lit room. The stage was deserted. The balconies were undraped. There were no blue satin draperies and no sign of an underwater theme. Mrs. Santy took a list of table reservations out of her pocketbook and Howard produced a chart, and they went to work on the problem of who's going to sit where.

The last general meeting of the 1954 Mardi Gras committee was held the following morning, five days before the ball. It was a tense session.

Mrs. Adams said that she had bargained with Mr. Howard over the price of the hanging blue satin draperies and gold fishnet that would produce a bubbly, undersea effect and had succeeded in getting him to knock fifty dollars off the price, but that, even so, she had decided they might do better without the draperies entirely and just use balloons or some other less expensive bubbly device. "So I canceled the drapes, at least for the time being, and left Mr. Howard feeling a bit angry," she said. "I'm meeting with Lester Gaba and a balloon man this afternoon. And if you feel you can leave it up to me, I'll decide between the drapes and the balloons, or possibly some cellophane fringe we just heard about. Anyway, we're going to have a ballroom that looks pretty." The committee members decided to leave it to Mrs. Adams.

After lunch that day, Mrs. Adams went to a room behind the Astor ballroom for a meeting with Gaba and P. Raymonde Warny, a bald, mournful balloon salesman, who was wearing heavy shell-rimmed glasses. As she joined them, Warny pulled a fistful of balloons from a briefcase and blew up a silver one.

"Doesn't it look like a pearl?" Gaba asked Mrs. Adams.

"Well . . . ," said Mrs. Adams.

Warny held up the balloon to the light.

"You certainly get the biggest effect for the least money with balloons," Gaba said. "Now, remember, we want them to look like bubbles and pearls."

Warny lugubriously blew up a green balloon.

"Pretty," said Gaba. "But we don't want to get off the track."

Mrs. Adams asked how much it would cost to drape the balconies with balloons. Warny replied that at least three thousand balloons would be needed for the balconies and, at $12 a hundred, the price would come to $360, in addition to the $198 for the balloons he had already planned to use for the ceiling and tables.

"Pretty expensive," Mrs. Adams said thoughtfully.

"The draped tiers got kicked out because *they* were too expensive," said Gaba irritably.

Just then, a young man came in carrying a large suitcase and introduced himself as the cellophane-fringe salesman. He opened his suitcase and displayed the fringe—gleaming, transparent stuff. He could drape the balconies with it for $180.20, he said.

"We can't afford it," said Gaba. "Unless we kick out the balloons."

Warny looked unhappy.

"The fringe has that watery, bubbly look," Gaba said.

Mrs. Adams agreed that it looked pretty.

"If we have just balloons, it ends up looking like a high-school dance," Gaba said.

Gaba told the cellophane-fringe salesman that he would let him know their decision, and the salesman packed up his fringe. Mrs. Adams said that the League had some giant harlequin masks left over from the previous year's ball, and suggested using them again, to cover the second tier of balconies.

"I'm not mad about those masks," said Gaba.

"It's just that we have them," said Mrs. Adams.

"I really think we need the balloons if we're going to have a truly bubbly and watery effect," said Gaba.

Warny nodded, and started blowing up a pink balloon.

"Do a *clear* one," Gaba said. "I think we'll stick to clear, watery-looking ones only."

Warny dropped the pink balloon and blew up a clear one. Gaba stared moodily at it. "Without the blue satin draperies, the theme is neat but it certainly isn't the spirit of Mardi Gras," he remarked.

Mrs. Adams looked dismayed. "Oh, Lester!" she said. "Come on, now!"

"There was no reason for picking the undersea motif except that we were counting on the blue satin draperies and stuff," Gaba said. "Now that that's all kicked out, what's the point? We might just as well have another theme."

Mrs. Adams reminded him that anyway the King and Queen would have a large seashell for their throne.

"But what's the *point?*" Gaba asked.

Then Mrs. Adams made up her mind. They would decorate the ballroom, stage, and balconies with blue satin draperies, she said firmly, and give the ball an undersea motif. And they would have a large seashell for their throne. And they would have some bubbly-looking balloons, too.

At three o'clock on the afternoon of March 1, the day before Mardi Gras, most of the committee members, together with the five Maids and all the models, gathered in the ballroom for a dress rehearsal. The stage and both tiers were draped with sequined blue satin, and interspersed here and there along the tiers were branches of coral made of sparkling papier-mâché. Gaba stood on the stage surveying the scene. Everybody looked dazed. Mrs. Barton, wearing striped pants and a long coat, after the fashion of Groucho Marx, was practicing her walk. The Singer Sewing Machine model, with a gold spool on her head, was urging her to bend her knees more, with more of a side-to-side waddle. Mrs. Zingg, wearing black tights, high-heeled shoes, and an American Express Company coat and cap, joined them just as Anita Colby, who appears on television for Pepsi-Cola, walked on the stage wearing an old-fashioned pink tulle gown and carrying a fan with "Pepsi-Cola" written on it.

"Professional competition," said Mrs. Zingg. "Pepsi-Cola is *so* particular."

"I can't sleep at night," said one of the Maids to nobody in particular. "I have a steady feeling of being sick to my stomach."

Mrs. Adams arrived and asked if anybody had seen her husband. "Stirling is supposed to be here to try on his knight's armor," she said. "He's escorting Guinevere for American Viscose."

Mrs. Dickerson came up to her and said she had reserved three tables for a total of fifty-six people and she was sure she'd never have a chance to get her place cards properly distributed. "I've got forty people coming to my house for cocktails earlier in the evening," she said, sitting down on a table. "I've hired a bus to bring them over." They were joined by Mrs. McLoughlin, who said she was late because she had tried on her ball gown that morning and found she had lost so much weight working on the Mardi Gras that she had to have it taken in two inches at the waist.

Mrs. McLoughlin then wandered off again and, a minute later, shouted to Mrs. Adams, "Here's Stirling!"

"Bless you!" cried Mrs. Adams, and hustled her husband backstage to try on his armor.

Half an hour later, Mr. Adams, who is assistant vice president of Commercial Investment Trust, Inc., had succeeded in putting it all on, even to long, pointed sollerets, or flexible steel shoes, and a helmet. "Now, don't go off and leave me here!"

"Stick your chin in, Stirling," Mrs. Adams said soothingly.

"You're convinced you want it worn?" Mr. Adams said. "You're convinced the party won't come off unless it's worn?"

"We'll stop by Brooks on the way home and get it fixed," Mrs. Adams said. "Now try to walk."

"I wish you'd stick your hands in and put my ears where they belong," said Mr. Adams. "And I can't see a darn thing. Holy cow! Now I'm stuck to the floor! Heck! Get a pair of pliers!" he shouted wildly. "Somebody bend up my toes!"

"Walk sideways, Stirling," Mrs. Adams said gently. "Like we do going uphill skiing."

On the morning of the day of the ball, the first person to show up at the ballroom, around nine o'clock, was Warny, the balloon man, who had brought along an assistant named Leroy Williams and a machine for blowing up balloons. Soon handymen and League members began to arrive, and at noon some truckmen hauled in the blank-faced mermaids, the pink-and-blue shell for thrones, and quite a bit of gold fishnet. Gaba appeared and began arranging the stage set. The Astor keeps a Bahama sea grotto on hand for just such occasions as Mardi Gras balls, and he ordered it installed on the stage. After it was in position, he ordered it taken down. "Too corny," he said. "We don't want it. It gives the scene a gooked-up character. I'd rather keep it simple."

"Lunch," Warny said suddenly. Williams dropped a half-filled balloon and, as it sputtered into a state of collapse, the two hurried out.

Mrs. McLoughlin came over to Gaba and said the mermaids looked just dreamy. Mrs. Adams came over and said the balloons looked just divine. Mrs. Stimson came over and said everything looked just peachy.

Faye Emerson and her husband, Skitch Henderson, arrived and were soon joined by a number of television men, one of whom handed them a sheaf of papers outlining the rules of master and mistress of ceremonies.

"What's all this—*commercials*?" Henderson said, leafing through the script.

"This is a *commercial* show?" Miss Emerson said incredulously.

"Kids, this is very important," one of the television men said. "If we get messed up here, we're dead."

"Who's going to be the Queen?" one of the television men asked Mrs. Stimson.

"Nobody knows," said Mrs. Stimson.

"G'wan!" said the television man.

"Oh dear!" said Mrs. Stimson.

"Faye, you grab the mayor, and you say, 'Look who I found!'" the television man said. "Then he gives the official ad-lib rehearsed greeting to the throng."

"Go, man! Go!" said Miss Emerson.

Henry Fonda arrived and tried on the King's robes. "Lord, these are warm!" he said.

"Hank's costume looks tacky," said a television cameraman.

Emil Coleman, a heavyset, distraught-looking man wearing thick eyeglasses, turned up with his twenty-three musicians and tried out one of the pianos. "This is awful!" he cried. "Out of tune! No pitch! Where are my pianos?"

Miss Roberts began alerting everybody to prepare for a television-time dress rehearsal. "Play 'Everywhere You Go'!" she called to Coleman.

"Lady, please get me a piano tuner!" Coleman shouted back, clasping his hands in supplication.

"Everything looks *so* lovely," Mrs. Luckenbill said to Mrs. Stimson.

"Everybody *couldn't* be nicer," Mrs. Stimson replied.

By seven thirty that night, the tables had been set in the ballroom. Two-thirds of them glowed with pink cloths; the others had white cloths. There were no tall pink candles on any of the tables; instead, there were small candle lamps like mushrooms, with fringed shades. An aquamarine program, with Mrs. Stimson's pink clown on the cover, lay at each guest's place. Helium-filled clear balloons floated above the tables, held fast to them by strings. Clusters of clear balloons were held in their hoops close to the ceiling, ready to drop. The blue satin draperies on the stage and hanging from the ballroom's two tiers of balconies sparkled with sequins in the rays of multicolored spotlights. The pink-and-blue shell, with two thrones in it, stood in the center of the stage, and the two faceless mermaids, almost swamped in bubbly balloons, clutched at gold fishnet. Everything looked soft and gleaming and quiet. The only people in the ballroom were Coleman and the members of the orchestra. Coleman was wearing white tie and tails, and he had exchanged his glasses for a monocle in his right eye. He sat at the piano, gloomy and silent, his elbows on the keyboard and his fingertips at his temples. All at once, he looked at his watch and came to life. He took his elbows off the keyboard, sighed loudly, adjusted his monocle, and started to play "Young at Heart," and the members of his orchestra joined in. At the end of the number, Coleman struck a loud chord and stood up. "*Why* can't they get me a tuner?" he said plaintively.

The green Coral Room was doing a lively business in mixed drinks at a dollar apiece.

"So nice to see you," Mrs. Adams said to Mrs. Stimson.

"So nice to see you," Mrs. Stimson said to Mrs. Adams.

Mr. Adams was at the bar buying drinks for a party of five. Mrs. Cooke asked him why he wasn't wearing a suit of armor.

"I get into it at ten," he said heartily. "I've been repairing the goldarn thing. You might say I'm getting canned tonight! Ha!"

In the hotel florist shop, a young man asked for a white camellia, and the clerk had to turn him down. The young man was the clerk's twenty-first disappointed white-camellia customer this evening. "You going to that thing, *too?*" the clerk said. "Well, they're all gone. They were all gone at six o'clock."

The ballroom was filling up. A couple of television technicians wearing tweeds and limp bow ties wandered in appraising the scene. Most of the male guests were wearing black tie, even though white tie was preferred.

Upstairs, in a well-guarded private room, the five Maids were putting on their ball gowns.

"My shoes actually fit!" one of them cried joyfully.

"Are you relaxed?" asked another. "Or do you wish it was tomorrow?"

Downstairs a uniformed guard stood at the entrance to the models' dressing room backstage. A waiter was on hand to take orders for food if any of the models wanted food. None did. At nine, waitresses in the ballroom started serving dinner to the guests. Instead of fruit cup, there was seafood cocktail, and it looked upbeat, partywise, Mrs. Dickerson said.

Just before coffee was served, Mrs. Moore, as the League's president, corralled the three judges preparatory to escorting them up to the Maids' room to pick the Queen. "Did you get a chance for any coffee?" Russel Crouse asked Dr. Rusk, who replied that he had not. Crouse sighed. "I'm not too good before coffee," he said. "I *live* for coffee."

Dr. Rusk cleared his throat. "We'll do our best," he said.

"It's a difficult assignment," Mrs. Lord said.

On the way to the elevators, Mrs. Moore and the judges ran into a small woman who was wearing a flowered hat and carrying a brown paper bag.

"Where's the Queen?" the woman in the flowered hat asked.

Mrs. Moore told her the Queen had not yet been chosen.

"Well, I've got the crown," said the woman in the flowered hat. "I'm Van Cleef and Arpels."

"Backstage," said Mrs. Moore.

"After the Queen is crowned, have them take her picture fast, and then give me back the crown," said Van Cleef & Arpels. "You get about one hour with the crown, that's all."

Mayor Wagner arrived late and was ushered to a ringside table. People were already dancing. "I got up to the good seats the hard way," he said.

"OK, let's get on with the show!" one of the television men called out.

The lights dimmed and a spotlight played on the dance floor. Someone shouted for balloons, and a few of them floated down from the ceiling.

"The hoops aren't working right," Gaba said nervously.

At Miss Burke's table, a Pepsi-Cola man asked for Pepsi-Cola and got it. Miss Emerson and her husband sat at a ringside table and talked into microphones about the work of the New York Junior League. Everything went off the way Miss Roberts, the professional producer, had said it would. Miss Emerson went over to the mayor's table and said into a microphone, "Look who I found in the audience!" The mayor made a speech thanking the League on behalf of the City of New York for giving help to those who needed help so badly. He referred to the League members as "wonderful young ladies" and told them that "with the help of you young ladies we'll leave a better heritage for our children." Then a page blew a trumpet, accompanied by a fanfare from the orchestra, and unfurled a banner that read "Parade of Fabulous Costumes." The parade started with Mrs. Zingg, who made her way from the stage down an aisle cleared through the center of the ballroom, to the strains of "Everywhere You Go" for the American Express Company. The people at the American Express Company applauded fervently. Miss Emerson and her husband read off the commercial for each sponsor. Mrs. Dickerson observed that the Liggett & Myers people looked happier this year than they had the year before, and Mrs. Stimson observed that the Liggett & Myers girl, wearing a slinky gown and a necklace of Liggett & Myers cigarettes, looked glamorous. Mrs. Barton got quite a laugh as Groucho Marx, and the blonde following her swept up her cigar ashes with a brush labeled "Fuller." Miss Bryant opened up as a refrigerator on cue, and all the fruit and dairy products were clearly displayed. Mr. Adams stepped lightly along in his shining armor beside Guinevere. Then Henderson introduced each of the five Maids. The judges handed a scroll bearing their decision to a page, who handed it to the mayor, and the mayor announced that the Maid who had been chosen for Queen of the 1954 Mardi Gras was Miss Joan Gray. Everybody applauded.

"How dreamy!" Mrs. McLoughlin said. "Joan's a nifty gal."

Henry Fonda and Miss Gray paraded in the royal robes and took their places on the thrones in the pink-and-blue shell. The mayor placed the tiara on Miss Gray's head, saying it was a privilege to crown her Queen on behalf of the Junior League and the people of the City of New York. "I know you'll carry on this work even after this—the ultimate in honor—tonight," he concluded. All the Maids and models gathered around the King and Queen and were photographed, and then Van Cleef & Arpels stepped forward and took back the crown.

The guests got up to dance, and a few more balloons floated down on their heads. On the stage, several of the models looked as if they felt stranded. Mr. Raymer went up and grabbed the model representing Moore-McMormack Lines, took a basket of fruit off her head, and led her gallantly onto the dance floor.

Coleman looked at his watch. "One hour and thirty-five minutes to go," he said. "There's *still* time to get me a tuner."

Early the next morning, Mrs. Stimson turned up at the League's headquarters and immediately started writing thank-you notes to sponsors. She had already read with delight several lengthy accounts of the ball in the newspapers. She was presently joined by Mrs. Adams, who said she had got to bed at five that morning and had got up at eight, to arrange to have the costumes returned to the Brooks company. By noon, about half of Mrs. Stimson's committee had turned up to help with the thank-you notes. Mrs. Stimson said she was recommending Mrs. Dickerson for chairman of the 1955 Mardi Gras, and everybody said that that was wonderful. The committee members were full of enthusiasm for plans for the 1955 Mardi Gras Ball, and they talked about improvements that should be made. Next year, they would make sure the hoops released all the balloons at the right time. Next year, they ought to have the Astor get the hum, squeaks, and whistles out of the microphones of its public-address system, because some of the guests hadn't been able to hear the program. Next year, they ought to have a supper dance instead of a dinner dance, so that people wouldn't feel so rushed. Next year, they would make a determined effort to let no one get left stranded on the stage and to have more of a proper conclusion to things. Next year they would really do a bang-up job.

(APRIL 24, 1954)

The Big Stone
(Harry Winston)

Harry Winston, a short, round, bushy-haired man of fifty-four, who owns the jewelry establishment of Harry Winston, Inc., at 7 East Fifty-First Street, and who is regarded by his rivals and his associates alike as the world's most daring dealer in precious stones, has for forty years been making his way to the top of his hotly competitive profession, inspired principally by a passionate devotion to diamonds. It has been estimated that he sells twenty-five million dollars' worth of jewels a year, and it is generally conceded by those in a position to know that he does a greater dollar volume of business, and has a bigger and more varied stock of diamonds on hand at any given time, than any other independent diamond dealer in the world. Among big-time diamond dealers, who constitute a small, intimate, and not always charitable group, Winston, a cool-eyed man who is nevertheless tense and given to high-powered histrionics, is sometimes referred to as "our little Napoleon," but even those who use the term most disparagingly do not deny having a certain admiration for him. And as for the several thousand small-time dealers in New York City who eliminate overhead by carrying their wares in their pockets, they look upon Winston, who started out from scratch himself, as the outstanding example of how far a man can go, given luck, intelligence, and sure instinct in just the right proportions.

"Harry Winston is *the* genius of our time," one of these sidewalk salesmen often says. *Genius* is a word that is subjected to a good deal of kicking around when diamond men get to talking about Winston. "Harry Winston started with nothing and became the biggest man in the business," a man working for a rival firm said not long ago. "He copies no one. He goes on his own. He's a gambler and he's got the guts to gamble. Why, he's got *salesmen* making twenty, forty thousand a year. He's a genius." One such fortunate salesman recently recalled an occasion when he told his employer that he thought a certain diamond Winston owned was worth seven hundred thousand dollars. "And what was his answer?" the salesman said. "He turned to me and he said, 'Why not a million?' And why *not?* Only a genius can think like that." Walter Lehman, the secretary and treasurer of Eichberg & Co., which was founded in 1867 and is one of the oldest New York importers and cutters of rough diamonds, says, "Harry Winston is a brilliant man. He has the nerve to buy in tremendous quantities, and his courage and foresight help the entire industry. He's a true genius." An official of I. Hennig & Co., Ltd., a London firm of diamond brokers, says, "He's the only man in the diamond business who has no fear of spending a million dollars in cash at a time. Clearly, an authentic genius." And a Belgian diamond salesman who has operated in Cairo, Rome, Paris, and Madrid, as well as in New York, puts it this way: "In life, if you are fifty-one percent right, you are ahead. If you are more than fifty-one percent right, you are a genius. Harry Winston is always more than fifty-one percent right."

The chorus is, however, by no means unanimous. Among retailers of diamonds who are in competition with Winston, the word *genius* is seldom, if ever, applied to him. Indeed, at some of the big houses, even the word *Winston* is taboo. "Tiffany is interested in Tiffany," an official of that firm said not long ago, in a five-word summary of what it thought of Winston. A Cartier man sized Winston up similarly by saying, "Once you know Cartier style, you want Cartier style and you don't want anything else." A Van Cleef & Arpels man was equally pithy. "Van Cleef is tops in the retail field," he said, referring to Winston. Back in the days when Winston was a struggling wholesaler of jewels, both Tiffany and Cartier occasionally bought from him, and more recently Van Cleef & Arpels, which is a French firm that has had a branch here only since 1938, did some business with him, but nowadays all three are competitors of his, and each goes its own individualistic way. Another voice that seldom joins in the chorus of praise is that of Lazare Kaplan, who learned the art of cutting diamonds as a child in Antwerp and has been a wholesale diamond dealer here since 1914. Nineteen years ago, Kaplan cut up the famous 726-carat Jonker diamond for Winston, who owned it, and, while the press of the nation reported his every move, converted it into twelve smaller diamonds, ranging in weight from 5 to 140 carats. Kaplan isn't so sure there would be a Harry Winston, Inc., today if Winston had not commissioned him to cut the diamond. "I saved Winston a fortune," Kaplan said a while back. "In 1935, when he brought the Jonker to me, I agreed to cut it for him, but only if he took the entire responsibility. In cutting diamonds, you must know the grain, in order to determine the softest direction to cut in. Winston brought the stone to me with a cutting plan that someone in Europe had given him, and it would have meant disaster. He had invested a fortune in the Jonker, and if it had been cut according to his plan, he would have lost it. Instead, my staff and I spent a year making a new cutting plan and then cutting the Jonker. That stone was worth seven hundred thousand dollars when we started and two million when we finished." Kaplan paused and sighed. "And what did Winston do?" he went on. "A few years later he advertised that he was the one who had cut the Jonker diamond." Kaplan sighed again, and said, "But Winston is fabulous. He is a remarkable gambler and a brilliant salesman, and he is the only real showman we have in the diamond business." Winston has a rather different version of the cutting of the Jonker. "I didn't give Kaplan a plan for cutting it," he says. "Afterward, following a plan of my own, I recut ten of the diamonds Kaplan had cut. I paid him thirty thousand dollars to cut the stone, right in the middle of the Depression. I even put his picture in the paper." Winston also resents being referred to as a gambler—by Kaplan or anybody else. "When the other man doesn't know what you're doing, he calls you a gambler," he says. "I'm no gambler, because I know what I'm doing. It's because they know so damn little about me and what I do that they call me a gambler."

After Winston had recut the big 140-carat stone from the Jonker, it weighed 125 carats. "Keeping one even that large was risky," he has since said. "I priced it at a million dollars and it took me fourteen years to sell it. In the end, it took a king—Farouk of Egypt—to buy it. That's why I wanted the Jonker cut up in the first place. If I'd kept it as a single stone, it would have turned out to be a four-hundred-carat one, impossible to sell at its true value. A million dollars is about as high a price as you can ask for a diamond." The Jonker was one of the six largest high-grade diamonds in the world; the five others have also been cut into a number of smaller stones, and their weights when found

were the Cullinan, 3,106 carats; the Excelsior, 995.5 carats; the Vargas
(which Winston has also owned), 726.6 carats; the Jubilee, 650.8 carats;
and the Victoria, 464 carats. Four smaller but almost equally famous
stones that Winston owns or has owned, together with their weights
after polishing (no record of their original weights exists), are the Star
of the East, 94.8 carats, and the Hope, 44.5 carats, both of which were
owned by Mrs. Evelyn Walsh MacLean; the Idol's Eye, 72 carats; and
the Nassak, 43 carats. (The diamond in the average thousand-dollar
engagement ring weighs from 1 to 3 carats, depending on its quality.)

Although Winston derives his greatest aesthetic pleasure from the
company of large, expensive, perfect stones, he takes a kindly paternal
interest in diamonds both good and bad, all the way—to use the idiom
of the trade—from top blue-white diamonds; through fine white diamonds; white diamonds; top silver Cape; top light-brown, light-brown,
and silver Cape; to Cape, or yellow. Unlike the ancient Hindus, who
believed that flawed diamonds brought on jaundice, pleurisy, leprosy,
lameness, and similar misfortunes, Winston is also tolerant of diamonds that contain imperfections, such as bubbles, clouds, cracks,
carbon spots, and the white, crack-like markings known as feathers.
"Diamonds are like your children," he says. "No matter how bad they
are, if they're yours, you can't help being fond of them. Once you get
them, you don't want to give them up." Winston's relationship to his
diamonds is as nearly like that of a parent to a child as he can make it;
he tries to superintend every stage of their development. He buys diamonds in the rough, imports them, cuts them, polishes them, designs
their settings, sells them, and, whenever possible, follows their careers
after they leave his hands. And he does this not with just a few stones
but, insofar as is practicable, with thousands of them every year. He
also exports diamonds wholesale and buys diamonds from the heirs
of estates. Nor is Harry Winston, Inc., by any means his only outlet in
this country; department stores, other retail jewelers, and installment
houses sell Winston diamonds, and readers of the Montgomery Ward
catalog may buy them through its pages. While other diamond men are
content to specialize in one—or, at most, two or three—of these many
and varied activities, Winston thinks that his parental relationship is
still not quite all it should be; as matters stand, he feels he is in the
position of a foster parent, for he doesn't so much as hear about a new
diamond until weeks, or even months, after it has left the mine. This is

because ninety-five percent of the world's diamond supply is controlled by De Beers Consolidated Mines, Ltd., a closemouthed British-owned company, commonly known as the Syndicate, which has held a monopoly on the mining of diamonds in South Africa since 1889.

The Portuguese colony of Angola, in southwest Africa, produces about a million carats of rough diamonds—or fifteen million dollars' worth—a year from mines that are owned jointly by the Angola Diamond Corporation and the Portuguese government. The Angola Diamond Corporation—which is owned by American, British, and Portuguese interests—has been selling its output to De Beers, under a contract that was signed in 1950, without sanction of the Portuguese government, and that expires in 1955. Winston is currently negotiating with the Portuguese government to purchase the total Angola diamond output over the next ten years—a bid for independence that the Syndicate considers so presumptuous that it has tried, without much success, to cut him off from obtaining any diamonds at all. "De Beers might make me a preferred client if I'd pass up the Portuguese deal," Winston said the other day. "But I'd rather have an independent diamond supply, and I'm going to try to get it." Winston's ambitious scheme has been received with admiration and without surprise—and also without support—by the rest of the diamond men in this country. "I wouldn't lift a finger to help him in this deal," one of his bitterest rivals said recently, "but if he comes out a winner again, he'll not only be a genius, he'll be more so."

"There's a calculated risk in every business," Winston once said. "The only way to keep the risk down is to know what you're doing. I happen to have been born with the gift of knowing what I'm doing. I also happen to have been born with the gift of courage to do what I want to do." Thus doubly gifted, Harry Winston was born in New York City on March 1, 1900, on the third floor of a five-story walk-up apartment on West 106th Street, the third son of a jeweler who owned and ran an unpretentious shop on Columbus Avenue. His father was an unworldly, idealistic man; once, when a customer whom he knew could not afford jewelry came into the shop and asked to buy an eight-dollar ring, the elder Winston declined to sell it to him and advised him to spend the money on groceries for his family instead. When Harry was seven, his mother died, and a year or so later his father, who suffered severely from asthma, moved to Los Angeles for his health, taking Harry and a younger daughter with him, while the two older sons—Charles and Stanley—found jobs as salesmen with antique-and-crystal dealers in New York. They later opened an antiques-and-crystal-chandelier store on West Forty-Fourth Street. It has since moved to Fifty-Third Street and Madison Avenue and is run by Stanley, Charles having died in 1942. Harry went to public school in Los Angeles, quitting at fifteen to go into business with his father, who had opened a jewelry store on Figueroa Street, in the city's central business section. Right from the start, Harry kept the store going. From time to time, the boy would take a satchelful of jewelry and, wearing a visored cap that he rarely removed from his head, go on the road, peddling his wares to oil prospectors in boomtown saloons. After ten years in California, the father moved back to New York, where he opened another jewelry shop, on upper St. Nicholas Avenue, which he ran until a few years before his death, in 1929.

Not long after returning to New York, Harry Winston, who was then nineteen, felt that he knew enough about the business to branch out on his own, and with a capital investment of two thousand dollars, which he had saved while working in California, he rented an office at 535 Fifth Avenue for a hundred dollars a month and founded a one-man firm called the Premier Diamond Company. He took his first big step forward when, shortly afterward, he succeeded in winning the confidence of the directors of the New Netherlands Bank of New York—which has since been absorbed by the Chase National Bank— to such a degree that they consented to lend him money with little more than his demonstrably sound judgment as collateral. He got off to a shaky start with the bank when he arrived late at the meeting of the board of directors at which his first application for a loan was to be considered; walking in with his cap on his head, he was taken for a messenger boy and ordered to go back and inform his boss that he would have to appear in person if he wanted the money. Once he had established his identity, he was granted the loan, but for many years thereafter he kept a front man on his payroll—a tall, white-haired, distinguished-looking gentleman who accompanied him to all business conferences and did the talking, while Winston kept an eye on the jewels and the sums of money involved.

More loans from the New Netherlands Bank followed, and with its backing Winston set about buying jewels from estates, recutting and resetting them along modern lines, and reselling them to retailers. He sent out letters announcing that he was in the market for jewels from estates. He used the Social Register as his mailing list, supplementing it with the names of leading judges and attorneys throughout the country, who, he felt, were in a position to hear about estates that were about to be liquidated. If an estate he was interested in was a small one, with jewels that could be bought for five or ten thousand dollars, Winston would borrow the money outright from the bank and repay the loan with the proceeds from his sales. In the case of estates involving a larger investment, the bank would buy the jewels and turn them over to Winston, and he would freshen them up and dispose of them. Five years after starting out on his own, he had interested other banks in backing him and was engaging in deals in which as much as a million dollars changed hands. "They call me a gambler," he says. "But if I was a gambler, how could I have got that kind of credit from banks? The first fifty thousand dollars was the hardest—lots harder than it would be borrowing five million today. I bought everything—crowns, tiaras, dog collars. I had a knowledge of everything—rubies, pearls, emeralds, diamonds. I worked a seven-day week. I never stopped. I loved it. I got a thrill out of every deal. If a bank I went to for credit wasn't in a position to give me the amount of money I needed, the directors would get together and raise the money among themselves. In addition to knowledge, ability, courage, and imagination, I've always had the financing."

Winston believes that he was the first jeweler in this country to realize the full potentialities of estates as sources of supply. One of the first large estates he tackled was that of Arabella Huntington, the wife of Collis P. Huntington, the railroad builder, and later of his nephew, H. E. Huntington; it involved the investment of a million and a half dollars by the New Netherlands Bank. Subsequently, Winston took over the jewels in the estates of such people as Lucky Baldwin, a farm boy who struck gold in California, and Emma T. Gary, the widow of Judge Elbert H. Gary, for many years chairman of the board of United States Steel. (Mrs. Gary's jewels, which included the Lord Dudley pearl—a hundred-grain pear-shaped gem that is considered one of the finest of its kind in the world—were left to the Metropolitan Museum of Art, but the museum found them too expensive to care for and got the courts to permit it to sell them.) Winston has especially fond memories of the Huntington jewels. "Mrs. Huntington had a necklace with a hundred and sixty-one pearls in it," he says. "It reached from my neck to my toes—and I'm five feet four. That rope of pearls cost her more than a million to assemble. It was sixty inches long. Poor old Mrs. Huntington! By the time her rope of pearls had been assembled, she was blind and couldn't see them. I split up most of the jewels in her estate, of course. There are at least two dozen women, in various parts of the world, who are now sharing Mrs. Huntington's pearls."

Confident though Winston is of his ability, he has learned from experience that he is not infallible. "I've made mistakes, and when I make a mistake, it's a big one," he told a dinner-table companion at a party not long ago. "But I don't think I've ever made a mistake in judging people. A man came into my office one morning last week and wanted to take two pieces of jewelry to show his wife. Worth three hundred thousand dollars. He asked for a receipt to sign. I said, 'Your signature isn't necessary.' You should have seen the look on his face! The way he walked out! I wouldn't let anybody else in the house use judgment in a matter like that. Not everybody knows how to judge people that way. Why, I've let people go out of my place with a million dollars' worth of jewels! No deposit. No receipt. Once, a couple of years ago, I gave a man four pieces of jewelry to take home, so he could decide which he liked best. Next morning, he was back at nine sharp, waiting for me. He said, 'Tell me, Mr. Winston, did you have someone follow me home?' I said no. He said, 'You don't know me. Suppose I'd given you a false name?' I said, 'Well, that would have been my mistake.' He said, 'Did you sleep last night?' I said I'd slept like a baby. He said, 'I didn't get a wink of sleep. I was up all night worrying about you worrying.'

"When I was in London a couple of years ago, I showed a lady a ring. Then we went to the Savoy for tea, and took the ring along. She kept putting it on and taking it off. Then she had to leave, and she forgot she had it on. I didn't say anything. By dinnertime, she was calling all over the West End, trying to get in touch with me. She finally reached me at a restaurant and asked me if I'd realized she had the ring on when she left. I said certainly. She said, 'You're just a damn fool.' 'No,' I said. 'I know how to evaluate people.'

"A couple of years after I sold King Farouk the hundred-and-twenty-five-carat stone from the Jonker, I sold him the Star of the East for a

million, and some other pieces for three hundred thousand. He gave
me a hundred and fifty thousand on account. Now he says he doesn't
have the rest of the money and doesn't know what's happened to the
jewels. The last time I talked to him was in Capri, in the summer of
1952, just after he'd abdicated. He said he'd left the diamond in his
palace. I'll visit him this summer. The night I sold him the Star, I gave
a small dinner party at La Reserve, in Beaulieu-sur-Mer, near Monte
Carlo. It cost me about five hundred dollars. At four a.m., I got Farouk
alone out on the terrace and I closed the deal for the Star and the other
stones. That party may yet cost me an extra one million one hundred
and fifty thousand dollars. Maybe I made a mistake with Farouk, but I
don't think so. I still feel it will come out all right. Anyway, I'm the kind
of man who, no matter what happens, can go to sleep at night and wake
up feeling that life is worth living. I love the diamond business. It's a
Cinderella world. It has everything! People! Drama! Romance! Precious stones! Speculation! Excitement! What more could you want?"

At noon on Tuesday, January 13, 1953, Winston was sitting alone
in his office on the second floor of the six-story granite building that
his firm occupies, a building that was the town house of the late Mrs.
Marius de Brabant, a daughter of Senator William A. Clark, the mining millionaire. Seated at a Louis XV desk, Winston looked bleakly
through his window at the people filing steadily in and out of St. Patrick's Cathedral, directly opposite. He was wearing, as usual, a neat,
dark, impeccably tailored double-breasted suit and no jewelry at all.
Before him on the desk was a large square of black velvet, on which
lay a gauge for estimating the weight of stones in settings, a pair of
tweezers for picking up small stones, a couple of yellow pencils with
sharp points, a silver pillbox, a jeweler's loupe, a pad of white paper,
on which he had been doodling, and a couple of his diamonds—a
blue-white 60-carat stone set in a ring and the 44.5-carat Hope, a deep-
blue oval stone set in a pendant. Also on the desk was a telephone,
connected with the house switchboard; on a stand behind him was a
second telephone, this one a private wire. Several framed photographs
of Winston's wife and their two sons—Ronald, thirteen, and Bruce,
ten—stood on a small desk in a corner, and an oil painting of the trio
hung on the wall. A couple of love seats faced each other before a
fireplace, and several chests, tables, and chairs of the same period were
scattered about the room.

The door to Winston's office opened, and his secretary, a young, pleasant blonde named Polly Rowe, came in, carrying a delicately flowered china cup and saucer. "Your coffee, Mr. Winston," she said.

Winston sighed deeply and nodded. "Why everybody goes out to lunch, I never understand," he said. "All that eating. Why?"

"I really don't know, but everybody does it," Miss Rowe said respectfully.

Winston took a saccharin pill from the silver box. He sighed again as he dropped the pill into the cup. While sipping his coffee, he put his forefinger through the 60-carat diamond ring and looked thoughtfully at its stone. Then he wrenched the ring off, tossed it impatiently toward Miss Rowe, and told her to put it away. "And the Hope, too," he said. "I don't feel very well. I think I'm coming down with one of those virus things."

Winston's private telephone rang, and as he answered it, he suddenly became alert. He lowered his voice to a tone of confidential intimacy and spoke more and more softly as the conversation went on. After he hung up, he motioned to Miss Rowe to hand the Hope diamond and the ring back to him. "I'll play with them awhile," he said. "And would you ask Ludel to come down as soon as possible?" As Miss Rowe left the room, he put the ring on his forefinger again and looked at it with admiration.

"You have to go to London," Winston said a few minutes later to Bernard Ludel, a bald, square-faced, amiable man who has been Winston's buyer of rough diamonds for the past seven years, during which time he has enthusiastically spent thirty million Winston dollars. Ludel has been in the diamond business for forty years. Born in Amsterdam, he was trained there by his father to be a diamond cleaver. He came to the United States in 1916, at the age of twenty, and in the ten years that followed he cleaved approximately fourteen thousand diamonds, ranging in size from six carats to eighty. Then he became an independent buyer and seller of diamonds. After some twenty years of that, he gave up his own business to join Winston.

"I am ready," Ludel replied now. The previous week, he had returned from his forty-sixth trip to Europe, his eighth in six months. He and his wife were living in a small hotel on the West Side, where they were expecting a visit any day from a married daughter living in Panama. "I am always ready," Ludel added.

"I just got a call from London," Winston said sharply. "Prins tells me he's got a one-hundred-fifty-four-and-a-half-carat stone from Jagersfontein. Prins says it's perfect. A perfect stone."

Ludel smiled and said nothing.

"Take a look at it," Winston said, his voice soft and low again. "See if it's perfect."

"I can take the plane tomorrow," Ludel told him.

"Good luck," said Winston. He put his head in his hands and closed his eyes. "I think you're coming down with something, Harry," he said aloud to himself. "You'd better go home and go to bed." He put on a black cashmere overcoat and a black homburg, and as he was leaving his office, his secretary handed him, as she does every day, a crisp new dollar bill—he hates to carry money around with him—for his taxi fare to his apartment, on upper Fifth Avenue.

As soon as Ludel's plane landed in London, on Thursday, he took a taxi directly from the airport to the diamond-brokerage offices of I. Hennig, on the third floor of Audrey House, a gray stone Edwardian building on Ely Place, in the city's jewelry district. It was late afternoon when he arrived. George F. Prins, a thoughtful, scholarly gentleman, who is one of the two directors of the firm and the man who sold Winston the Jonker diamond, told Ludel that the light wasn't right for looking at the stone then and suggested that he come back in the morning. Ludel drove to a hotel, where, after an early dinner, he went to bed and lay awake all night thinking about the 154½-carat diamond. At nine thirty, he was back at the Hennig establishment. Prins told him that the vault in which the diamond was kept could not be opened until ten. Ludel stood around waiting and smoking one cigarette after another. At three minutes after ten, Prins took the diamond out of the vault. It was in a small folder of heavy white paper lined with a sheet of thin waxed paper. Prins handed the folder to Ludel, who smiled slightly as he unwrapped the stone. It was a little more than an inch and a half long and an inch thick at one end, tapering to about a third that thickness at the other, and, like most rough diamonds, it had a frosted coating that made it look rather like a wad of frozen absorbent cotton. Its avoirdupois weight was a bit over an ounce. Ludel held the stone between his thumb and forefinger and continued to smile. Prins left the room and returned in a few minutes with a cup of lukewarm coffee, with milk, which he handed to Ludel. Then, without saying anything, he left the room again. Ludel sat down at a table near a window facing north over the roofs of several fine old Georgian houses. He put a loupe to his eye and looked at the diamond through it. Despite its coating, he could tell with reasonable certainty that there were no imperfections in the interior. Ludel sat there silently studying the diamond through the loupe for two hours. Then he returned the stone to Prins, went back to his hotel room, and, sitting on his bed, put in a call to his employer on East Fifty-First Street.

"Ludel!" Winston said.

"The biggest sensation of my life," Ludel said, without preliminaries. "The stone is absolutely perfect, I feel sure. I could never dream of a stone like that—it's the finest I have ever seen. So magnificent in color. Blue-white."

"Ludel, is it clean?" Winston asked impatiently. "Is it absolutely clean?"

"I am convinced that it is absolutely clean," said Ludel. "Also, it is an ideal shape for a pear-shaped diamond. You should own this stone."

"Is it perfect, Ludel?" Winston asked.

"Perfect, perfect," Ludel assured him.

Winston and Ludel went on to discuss the price Hennig was asking—a quarter of a million dollars—and ways of persuading Hennig to knock twenty-five thousand dollars off that figure. They talked for thirty-eight minutes, and the cost of the call came to a hundred and ninety dollars. It was the first of thirteen transatlantic telephone calls Ludel made to Winston during ten days of intensive negotiations. Then Ludel told Winston that there was nothing further he could do in the way of bargaining and that he would wait in London until he received orders, one way or the other, from New York. On the evening of February 3, Winston went to bed early with a virus infection and a high fever. At midnight, he suddenly made up his mind about the 154½-carat diamond. He picked up the telephone at his bedside and sent a cable to Ludel, via Western Union. The cable consisted of one word—"BUY." Winston thereupon fell into a deep sleep, and when he awoke in the morning, his fever was gone.

As soon as Ludel received the cable, he notified Prins that Winston was going to buy the big diamond and that Winston's bank in New York would make arrangements with a London bank to pay I. Hennig, Ltd., $230,807—the price agreed upon, plus the broker's commission.

The next day, Ludel left London for Amsterdam, to see about buying some other diamonds for Winston. On February 6, Winston received the following cable:

> LONDON VIA CABLES FEB 6 316P
> HARWINSTON (HARRY WINSTON)
> NYK.
> 154-½ CARATS AIRMAILED TODAY
> HENNIG
> 110.8A.

The 154½ carats were fully insured on their flight. Winston regards the mails as the safest way of moving diamonds from one place to another. He does not like to have his employees carry valuable jewels on long journeys alone, because of the obvious risks involved.

Embedded in a fragment of blue ground, or kimberlite—the volcanic rock formation in which most diamonds are found—the 154½-carat stone was brought up out of a De Beers mine at Jagersfontein, in the Orange Free State, during the latter part of 1952. The African natives who were working the mine were then drilling and blasting in a rain of blue ground located at a depth of about thirteen hundred feet. It is doubtful whether any of the miners who were responsible for getting the big stone to the surface were aware that they had done a particularly valuable day's work, for diamonds are rarely visible in the pieces of shattered blue ground that are hauled up—ten tons at a time—in huge skips, or steel buckets. These buckets are raised and lowered in the mine shafts at a speed greater than man can endure, and there is good reason for speed, since it takes ten thousand tons of blue ground from the average South African mine to produce one pound of diamonds. Each skipful, as it comes up out of the earth, is dumped into a bin, from which a conveyor belt hauls it to a mill. There the blue ground is crushed, screened, and washed to cull out all but the very heaviest particles, known as the diamondiferous concentrate. The concentrate is then placed on an oblong table that has been coated with petroleum jelly. The table is flooded with water and made to shake violently from side to side, and as it shakes, all the remaining waste rock is washed away and the diamonds, which have the peculiar property of shedding water, remain stuck in the jelly. Finally, the jelly is scraped off the table and boiled, setting the diamonds free.

The 154½-carat stone was found in the normal course of mining operations, and recovered on the grease table like any run-of-mine stone. Despite its large size, no special record was made of its discovery. It was simply listed in De Beers's record of all stones over ten carats, in accordance with the diamond laws of the Union of South Africa. De Beers, through its distributing organization called the Diamond Trading Company, sold the diamond in London to Diamond Realizations, Ltd., wholesalers of rough diamonds. Diamond Realizations placed it with Hennig for resale.

In New York, the afternoon of February 11 was gray, damp, and bone-chilling. At four thirty that afternoon, a large, white-haired man, hatless and wearing rimless spectacles, got out of a taxi in front of 7 East Fifty-First Street. He wore a dark overcoat belted in the back, and he was chewing gum. The taximeter registered a dollar and ninety cents. The white-haired man gave the driver three dollars.

"Take it easy, Mac," he said.

"Same to you, Mr. Siegel," said the driver. Sam Siegel, an employee of Meadows Wye & Co., which acts as Custom House brokers for Winston, touched a forefinger to his temple in farewell. When he has a valuable package to deliver, he makes a point of taking taxis whose drivers he knows and trusts. On this occasion, the package he was delivering was a small one that he had enclosed in a manila envelope. As the taxi drove off, Siegel went up to the iron-grilled door leading to the foyer of the Winston establishment, a door that is kept locked at all times. He rang the doorbell and was recognized by a broad-shouldered, prematurely gray man, wearing a gray business suit and an automatic pistol in a holster, who was standing just inside and who guards the house of Harry Winston, Inc., against all comers. The guard nodded to a receptionist seated at a desk on the left side of the foyer, and she pushed a button that unlocked the door.

"Hello, Mr. Chaplin," Siegel said to the guard upon entering, and then he nodded to the receptionist and said, "Miss Shaw, how are you?"

Just beyond the receptionist's desk was a circular marble staircase, leading to Winston's office. Siegel glanced into a mirror on the wall opposite and straightened his tie.

"You're looking well, Mr. Siegel," the receptionist said. Siegel smiled, glanced into the main salon, beyond the foyer, and then, escorted by Chaplin, entered a small elevator next to the staircase. The two men rode up to the third floor, where they made their way to the comptroller's office through a series of doors that were unlocked for them by the clerks and secretaries. There Siegel handed the manila envelope to the comptroller, Bertram Barr, a thin, worried-looking man, who removed the package from it. It was wrapped in blue paper, tied with brown string, and sealed with red wax, which had been stamped by a customs inspector with the words "US Appraiser of Mdse." It was addressed, in longhand, to Winston, and had three British stamps on it, totaling one pound five shillings and sixpence—a mailing cost of three dollars and sixty-one cents.

Siegel remarked to Barr that the weather was rotten and offered him a stick of chewing gum. The comptroller unwrapped the gum and put it in his mouth. A secretary came forward and handed Siegel a receipt specifying that he had delivered one parcel, with the United States customs seal intact, containing one rough diamond weighing 154½ carats and costing $230,807. She also handed him a check for $28.75, to cover the brokerage fee; because the diamond was in its rough state, it had been admitted to this country duty-free. Siegel folded the check, slipped it into an inside coat pocket, and left. Barr placed the blue package, still unopened, in a huge, electrically controlled safe, and hurried away to attend a meeting of the Federal Government Accountants Association of New York, of which he is a director.

The next morning, Winston saw the 154½-carat diamond for the first time. He arrived at his office at eight fifty-five and immediately asked Miss Rowe to tell Barr to bring the diamond in. Before he had time to do more than glance through a few of the letters in his morning mail, the comptroller came in and put the package on the desk in front of him. It was just nine o'clock.

"Turn out the light, so I can see the color," Winston said as he cut the string. Barr flicked the switch. There was a happy and expectant smile on Winston's face. Quickly, he broke the seal, unwrapped a plain white cardboard box, and opened it. Inside the box, on a bed of cotton, lay the diamond, done up in white tissue paper. Winston held his breath and his smile grew numb. Then he drew back the edges of the tissue paper. His smile vanished. He took the stone out of the wrapping and looked at it, and his face froze. Without saying a word, he held the stone up to the light, grasping it between thumb and forefinger. Then he stood up, kicked his chair back, and took the stone over to the window. Putting his loupe to his eye, he studied the stone for some time. "I suppose I've got to take Ludel's word for it," he said at last, in a flat, cold voice. "He should know what he's talking about. Otherwise he'd be getting twenty dollars a week instead of what he's getting. But a piece is missing from this stone. An important piece. A third of the stone is missing. Maybe a million years ago some sort of volcanic disturbance broke it off. It might be fifty miles away from where this was found." Turning the diamond slowly in his fingers, he went on, talking to himself, "It's a fine stone, all right. It's a great stone, Harry. But I'm not sure I agree with Ludel that it's the finest color." He was silent for a few moments. Then he said abruptly, "Perhaps we're being unfair to the stone. The light is bad here. I want to look at it upstairs."

Leaving Barr standing in the office, Winston went out and waited briefly for the elevator, and then turned impatiently and ran up four flights of stairs to the sixth floor, where loose diamonds are sorted according to color, size, and quality. He walked over to one of a row of desks standing under several windows that faced north and sat down at it. "Now we see the purity of it," he said, looking at his diamond again. With a faint smile, he tossed the stone on a piece of white tissue paper. "It does look a little bluer on the paper," he said, without spirit.

A young man, one of the sorters, came up and saw the diamond lying on the paper. "Oh, my!" he said, leaning over to get a closer look at the diamond but not touching it. "Oh, my!" he repeated. "Beautiful!"

"Do *you* like it?" Winston asked crossly.

"Oh, it's beautiful!" said the sorter.

"A piece is missing," Winston said. "Isn't that criminal?"

"But it's a glorious stone," said the sorter. "There aren't many like that one."

Winston said, "Let me have some of the silver Capes." The sorter brought over a paper folder full of rough diamonds. "Do you see the contrast?" Winston said. "This stone looks so superior now. But that's just because of these silver Capes. A small jeweler would rate them as first-class, of course, but they're fourth-class by our standards." Talking as much to himself as to the sorter, he went on, "Ludel says it's the finest he's ever seen. Well, I think it's a fine stone, all right, but we'll wait and see how fine. Ludel says the yield will be sixty-five carats after it's been cut. That's a big diamond. The average broker says you've got to have a prospective client when you spend a quarter of a million on a stone. I don't know whether I'm crazy or not, but at the present time I haven't even a dream of a client." He picked up the diamond, and it slipped from his fingers and fell to the floor. He stooped quickly and retrieved it.

"Mr. Winston, that means good luck, dropping a diamond," the sorter said.

"Maybe, maybe not," Winston said, with a dry laugh.

"It's got the beauty of a miniature Jonker," the sorter said.

"Maybe by the time it's finished it'll be much more brilliant," Winston said. "The more I look at it, the better I like it. I'm beginning to feel closer to it. Yes, I do believe it's going to be a beautiful stone after all."

Still clutching the diamond, Winston headed back downstairs. The sorter accompanied him. "I kept asking Ludel over the phone, if it's so perfect, why is the yield going to be so low?" Winston said in the elevator. "He didn't tell me anything about the missing piece, and I think he should have, but I suppose he had so much confidence in the stone that he didn't feel it was necessary." He shrugged.

At the second floor, the sorter complimented Winston again on his new acquisition and went on downstairs. Back in his office, Winston sat down at his desk and tossed the diamond on the velvet pad. Miss Rowe came in and said that Daniel Frey, the general manager of the company, wanted to see him, and Winston told her to send him in. "And get a cable off to Ludel in Amsterdam," he added. "Say, 'Stone beautiful.' That's all." He looked at the diamond again. "It is going to be beautiful," he said, almost in a whisper. "Nature produces so few perfect stones. I hope this stone will turn out to be perfect."

When Frey came in, he looked first at the diamond, and whistled. Then he looked at Winston. "That's quite a piece," Frey said. He is a friendly, hardworking man of forty-six who, twenty-eight years ago,

while a student at City College, took a summer job with Winston as
an errand boy. After he graduated in 1928, he was given a full-time
job with the firm, and he has been with Winston ever since. (When
Winston bought the Huntington necklace, it was Frey's job to take all
the worn or cracked pearls in it over to a pearl doctor, who peeled
their skins to bring out the proper shape and color. "I was very fond
of pearls," Frey says. "Too bad pearls have come upon bad days.") Now
he picked up the diamond and studied it against the light from the
window. "Spectacular," he said, and handed it to Winston, who held it
up, turning it this way and that. "Here will be the table, and this will be
the culet, and this the girdle," he said, indicating in succession where
he thought the diamond's large, flat upper facet should be cut, and its
small lower facet, and the edge that would be grasped by the setting.
"We'll tilt it just like that."

"Beautiful," said Frey.

"It may turn out to be perfect," Winston said softly, looking at the
diamond through his loupe. "If it does, maybe we'll sacrifice a little
of it to get a better slope. It looks to me as if the heart of this stone is
clean." He put aside the loupe, held the diamond at arm's length, and
looked at it thoughtfully. "No two diamonds are alike," he said. "Each
diamond has a different nature. Each diamond has different problems.
Each diamond must be handled as you handle a person."

At nine thirty the next morning, right after arriving at his office, Winston called in Frey and Bernard De Haan, who is the head of Winston's
diamond-cutting-and-polishing department. De Haan, a good-natured,
steady, solid-looking man, is a cousin of Ludel's, and their careers have
for the most part followed parallel lines. He was born fifty-six years ago in
Amsterdam, where he started learning to be a diamond cutter and polisher at the age of fourteen. His father and one of his great-grandfathers
were diamond polishers, and one of his grandfathers was a diamond set-
ter. De Haan came to this country at eighteen and had had a business of
his own for some years when Winston asked him to take over the cutting
department, in 1952. This morning, De Haan was wearing Army suntans
and a pair of shell-rimmed spectacles with large, round, steamy lenses.
De Haan and Frey entered the office together, and Winston immediately
handed the 154½-carat diamond to De Haan.

De Haan's spectacles grew even steamier as he stood facing the light and studying the stone. "You certainly got something special with this one," he said.

"As you can see, there's a piece missing," Winston said. "What a stone it would have been if that piece hadn't shot off! Isn't it criminal." The telephone on his desk rang. It was a salesman calling from downstairs. "Yes," Winston said. "I remember the man. He's looking for a pair of earrings. Let Joe work with him on it." He hung up and took the diamond from De Haan. "There isn't any question of trying to get more than one stone out of it, and the loss shouldn't be over fifty-five percent," he said. "Or do you think we might go through here and make two stones?" He pointed to what looked like a ridge in the stone.

"Oh, no," De Haan said. "This should be one stone. One pear-shaped stone."

"That's what I thought," Winston said, looking satisfied.

"This is going to be your stone," said De Haan. "A stone like this comes once in a lifetime." He held his hand out for the diamond, but Winston did not give it to him. He was busy rubbing it with his thumb and rolling it around in the palm of his hand. The door opened and a young salesman came in with a black velvet jewel box containing a diamond necklace. "You wanted to see this," he said to Winston.

Winston handed the diamond to De Haan and, turning his attention to the necklace, sighed, put his fingertips to his temples, and said wearily, "When we designed this necklace, she said she wanted to be able to wear it as a bracelet, too. So Eddie delivered it to her yesterday, and she said it was too long to wear as a bracelet. She asked Eddie if he'd make it shorter. Eddie said no, he couldn't, and she became hysterical. It was hardly discreet of him to say no."

"You want to take out a few stones?" the salesman asked.

"Yes," Winston said. "And you'll have to air-mail it to her in Palm Beach. She wants to wear it to a party there Wednesday night."

The salesman picked up the box with the necklace and left. "My God!" Winston said. "What we go through to adorn women. What we have to do in this business! The talking I have to do! I'm constantly hoarse from the talking. These people take everything out of you. For two hours yesterday afternoon, I pleaded with a woman to choose a forty-thousand-dollar necklace of round diamonds instead of a mar-quise-diamond one for sixty-five thousand dollars. She's fifty years old, and she's had a mean life. The round diamonds would have softened her, but she insisted on the long, tapered ones. No matter how successful you are, you still must bow to the whims of these people." He took the big diamond from De Haan and put it on the velvet pad. After looking at it for a few moments, he said hopefully, "You know, I wouldn't be surprised if we get a seventy-three-carat stone out of it."

"It's easier to visualize the stone than the customer," Frey remarked.

"Well, seventy-three-carat diamonds aren't sold every day," Winston said, holding his loupe to his lips.

"This will be much more brilliant than the Jonker," said De Haan.

"Prins claimed it was bluer," Winston said.

"The Jonker had more of an icy color," De Haan said. "When I first saw it, I was really a little let down. It didn't have as much life as I'd expected. Now I look at this and I don't feel a bit let down. I never liked the Jonker. It was a colder color."

"I'll be satisfied if this is the same color," Winston said. He rang for Miss Rowe and asked her to get him a photograph of the Star of the East, the diamond he had sold to Farouk eighteen months earlier and had not yet been paid for.

"Don't get me wrong," Frey said while they were waiting. "You'll sell this stone. It'll just be a matter of time."

"I'll sell it, all right," Winston said. "No matter what it costs us by the time we're through. Some people want the finest." Miss Rowe brought in the photograph. After studying it intently, he said that when the new diamond was finished, it would be smaller than the Star of the East but it would also be a finer stone. With that, he rewrapped the diamond in its original tissue paper, gave it to De Haan, and asked him to take it upstairs and register it in stock.

Then De Haan went upstairs with Frey to the accounting department, where he turned the stone over to a girl clerk, who weighed it. It weighed exactly 154½ carats. It was then registered as No. 20118. "Anyone superstitious?" the girl said. "It's Friday the thirteenth." Pointing to a page in a loose-leaf folder, she turned to De Haan and said, "Sign here." De Haan signed for the diamond, and the girl rewrapped it in the tissue paper and handed it back to him. Then he went upstairs to the polishing room, where rough diamonds are ground to give them the facets, or windows, that admit and reflect light and produce the characteristic sparkle. The polishing room was dominated by a couple of long tables on which stood perhaps a dozen machines somewhat resembling record players. On each machine a cast-iron disc, coated with a paste of diamond dust and olive oil, was spinning at the rate of 2,200 revolutions a minute, and pressed against each disc was a diamond, held in a dop, or metal cup, that was supported by a wood-and-metal arm. Four men—dressed, like De Haan, in suntans—were watching the machines; from time to time, they made tiny adjustments in the dops as the discs gradually ground the diamonds to the desired shape. De Haan stood silently in the doorway for a while. Then he coughed ostentatiously. His colleagues looked up and immediately gathered around him. Still without speaking, he unwrapped the diamond and showed it to them.

"What a terrific piece," said one.

"Nice color," said another.

"Beautiful stuff," said the third. The fourth nodded and said, "That is a diamond."

"Now I get to work," De Haan said.

"I make a little window or two in the stone, so we can look inside to be sure there is no blemish." One of the cutters asked De Haan how long he expected to have to work on the diamond.

"What's the rush?" De Haan said. "It took millions of years to make this diamond. Why hurry now!"

One morning a few weeks later, Frey stopped in at the polishing room to ask De Haan how the big stone was coming along. De Haan showed it to him. The skin had been removed from the table of the diamond, revealing the interior, and lines had been inked on the exposed surface as a guide in polishing. "No grave internal problems?" Frey asked. De Haan said no—none. As a matter of fact, he went on, he was about to take the diamond down and show it to Winston. He removed the stone from the dop and held it up to Frey, tantalizingly waving it this way and that just out of his reach. Then both men took the elevator to Winston's office, and De Haan placed the diamond before Winston, who was seated at his desk. The diamond was beginning to show a blue-white brilliance.

Winston smiled as he looked at it. "There's your diamond, Harry," he said. "No pinpoint marks. No little white flaws. We've seen the heart, and the heart is pure. This diamond is going to be like a glorious woman. It's going to have everything—form, grace, beauty, and perfect health." He told Frey and De Haan that he had been afraid that an imperfection would be found in the diamond, and it was a relief that none had been. There had been no accidents so far during the polishing of the stone, either, and that was a relief, too. Winston is generally philosophical about accidents. Only the week before, there had been a slip while an eighty-carat stone was being cleaved and ten carats had been lost. It was, as he had remarked at the time, fifty thousand dollars down the drain. Frey asked Winston whether he would soon be showing the diamond to a prospective buyer. Winston looked horrified. "You can make a great thing common by showing it at this stage," he said. "That's the last thing I want to do. I'm going to keep this stone quiet. I want to keep it to myself. I'll put it in the safe for a while after it's finished. I may play with it for a while"—he rolled the stone across his desk like a marble—"or I may just look at it. This stone is like a great painting. You want to keep on looking at it." He put his loupe to his eye and scrutinized the diamond. "This is one of the finest stones in the world," he said, with a catch in his voice. Then he handed the stone back to De Haan, saying, "I want to look at the stone again when this little flaw in the skin here has been removed!" De Haan nodded and left. "Fastest man in the world—De Haan," Winston said to Frey. "Yet he's like a first-class chess player. He works slowly on the dangerous moves."

Winston turned to a black jewel box on his desk, opened it, and took out a necklace set with fourteen marquise diamonds, and a matching bracelet. "What beautiful eyes!" he said, admiring the elliptical stones. "This is that bracelet I sold the Princess a few years ago," he went on. "Later, I made the necklace to match it. She's calling me this morning about it. She and I are thinking of taking this necklace and combining it with the bracelet to make two bracelets. Then she'll have twenty-eight beautiful eyes as well as her own two." He added, with a short, low laugh, "She'll have a bracelet on each arm, and she'll be continually raising her arms—first one, then the other—as she smokes cigarettes." He raised his arms to show what he meant. "Twenty-eight marquises like that!" he said softly to himself. "All the same color! It's a dream! Where else could you get such stones? You could sort your way through fifty million dollars' worth of diamonds and never find anything like them. I can tell you—" His private telephone rang.

"Your Highness, good morning!" Winston said into the phone, his voice coaxing and gentle. "How are you, Your Highness? . . . Did you have a good sleep? . . . Am I going to have the pleasure of seeing you today, Your Highness? . . . You'll have a pair of bangles, each with fourteen beautiful eyes. Wait till you see the designs." The conversation ambled along for ten minutes or so. After hanging up, Winston called Miss Rowe and told her that the Princess would be around late that afternoon and that she should be shown up to his office as soon as she arrived. "She'll have two of the most elegant bangles in the world," he said to Frey. "Fit for a princess!"

At ten o'clock on the morning of April 16, Winston went upstairs to the polishing room with Frey to check on the progress of his big diamond. De Haan, smiling but silent, took the diamond out of the dop, where it had been running on the wheel, and handed it to Winston. Then, folding his arms, he cast a significant glance at a couple of his polishers. Winston held up the diamond and gave a low hum of pleasure. He quickly fished his loupe from his coat pocket and examined the stone more closely. Then he looked unbelievingly at De Haan, who grinned at him but still said nothing. The two polishers grinned at each other. Winston, his hands trembling as he started to take another look at the diamond, dropped his loupe. The polishers laughed as it rolled across the floor.

"I told you it was better than the Jonker," De Haan said.

When Winston finally spoke, he spoke to himself. "The softness!" he said, his voice tremulous. "Harry, the brilliance!"

He handed the diamond back to De Haan. Winston and Frey returned to Winston's office. "When that diamond first arrived, I really did think it was wonderful, but you can never he sure until a stone is finished," Winston said. "I have seen rough diamonds that seemed full of promise, but when they were finished they looked yellow. I thought this stone was beautiful in the rough. But now the coating is off and—well, I've seen some great stones, but this one looks to me as though it will be the finest diamond in the world." He suddenly groaned and covered his eyes with his hands. "I'm so tired," he said. "Last night, my wife and I went to Barney Balaban's daughter's wedding. The tension! The women parading to show off their jewels! The gowns! The drinking and the smoking! I can't do it. It kills you. If it weren't for my wife, I'd never go to a party. When you're with people, they take everything out of you." He rubbed his eyes for a moment or two and then started to talk about the diamond again. "De Haan has been saying all along that this stone is the finest diamond he's ever worked on. I thought it was because he was new here and hadn't seen some of our diamonds in the past. Now I see he was right. It's turning out to be a perfect pear shape. This stone will go down in history."

Miss Rowe came in and announced that he had a visitor, a woman from Fort Worth. Winston said, "Bring her in," and the secretary retired. Almost at once, the door burst open and in strode a smartly dressed middle-aged woman wearing a mink stole and carrying a violet umbrella. "Harry, you rascal, you had a beautiful girl in here yesterday!" she said, in a loud, hoarse voice. Winston stood up, smiling, and held out his hand. The woman shook his hand, laughing, and the laugh turned into a brief fit of coughing. "I've just come from Saint Patrick's," she went on, tapping him on the shoulder with her umbrella. "Here's what I do, Harry. I go in to see the Blessed Mother and I come out the side door and look right up into your office, and that way I know whether you're here and what you're doing."

Winston laughed dutifully, and they both sat down.

"I'm having lunch with Cardinal Spellman tomorrow," the woman said.

"And how is His Eminence?" Winston asked.

"He's just as busy as can be," said the woman. "But every time I'm in town, he makes it a point to have lunch with me."

"You're such good friends," said Winston. "And did you see Bishop Sheen?"

"No, not this trip. Harry, I've decided to take the big sapphire."

"It's a glorious stone," Winston said, lowering his voice. "You'll look glorious with it."

"You don't think it's too big for me, Harry? You think I can wear it?"

"You certainly can wear it," said Winston. "It's glorious on you."

"Harry, here's what I think. Nobody would ever think it's just a piece of costume jewelry—not seeing it on me—so I guess I can get away with wearing it."

Winston leaned across the desk and, in a still lower voice, said, "I've got a new stone, a diamond."

"What you going to call it?" the woman asked.

Winston said he didn't know yet.

"What's this heart-shaped diamond they're all yelling and screaming about?" the woman asked. "And comparing it with the Hope, only it's not as blue."

Winston waved a hand disparagingly. "Oh, that's a good diamond, all right," he said. "But wait till you see this diamond. It will be one of the great stones of the world."

The woman's eyes gleamed.

"And how are your poodles?" Winston asked. The woman laughed. "We've got a new one we call Lover Boy," she said. "He makes love to everybody who crosses his path. Harry, I want you to promise me you'll show that diamond to me before anybody else."

Winston gave her a knowing smile, and she smiled back.

"I'm counting on you, Harry," she said.

The next day, Winston was conferring in his office with one of his polishers about several diamonds that had been partly cut, when De Haan came in with the 154½-carat stone. Winston was holding a diamond about a tenth its size up to the window. "Lengthen your culet a little," he told the polisher. "The stone should have more brilliance. The color is magnificent, but it lacks a kick. With that color, it should live! It should talk to you!" The polisher nodded, took the stone, and left.

"I don't like this business of expecting to get fifteen carats out of a stone and getting ten," Winston said to De Haan when the polisher was out of earshot. "We took a terrific beating on that stone, Bernard." On his desk lay a ring set with a large marquise diamond. Winston picked it up and tried it on his forefinger. He held the finger out and looked at the ring blankly. Then he put it aside and reached for the big stone. After studying it through his loupe for a while, he held it up to the window, turning it around and around between his fingers.

"It's beginning to talk," he said finally, with a sigh of pleasure.

"That stone is in a class all by itself," said De Haan.

"I visualized the brilliance, but I didn't visualize the color," said Winston. "It shows there's no limit to beauty. It's more beautiful than the Star of the East." De Haan said that the stone now weighed 126 carats. Polishing had already taken off 28½ carats.

"And to think it's absolutely perfect!" Winston said, looking at it fondly. "The delicacy and softness of the blue! You feel like diving right into it! This is no hard, cold blue. I see the Jonker blue but much more brilliant. God, this is glorious!" Then the light caught the stone at a new angle, and he grew tense. "I think the bottom lacks brilliance," he said in a sharp, angry voice.

"That's not the fault of the bottom," De Haan said indulgently. "It's the top. There's still some work to be done on top."

Winston's face relaxed. "Hmmm," he said, and now he gave the diamond a friendly, affectionate look. Then he abruptly handed it back to De Haan. "I don't even know the value of the stone you're holding," he said. "I don't know how to put a price on it. All right, Papa, go to work." As De Haan started for the door, Winston said, "You know, I'm beginning to feel elated."

Early one afternoon in May, Winston was sitting in his second-floor office discussing with Frey the prospects of the big stone. He impulsively picked up the telephone on his desk to ask De Haan to bring it down from his workshop. He was told that De Haan was at lunch but should be back any minute.

"How the Dutch do love to eat!" Winston said peevishly.

Frey smiled placatingly. "He'll be back soon," he said. "Most people like to eat."

Winston appeared mollified. "Every time I look at that diamond now, I get excited," he said.

"The thrill you'll get when somebody buys that stone!" Frey said.

Winston looked gloomy. "I hate to think of parting with it," he said.

Frey did not seem to have heard him. "The thrill I get every time I sell an engagement ring!" he said. "Just from looking at a kid who's getting married and is seeing his diamond for the first time!"

"I hate to think of that stone going to some of the women I know," Winston said. In front of him, on a black velvet pad, lay a number of round diamonds that had been set in wax on a square of cardboard to indicate the way they were going to be mounted for a necklace, which he planned to price at fifty thousand dollars. "These round stones are good for women over forty or fifty," he said idly to Frey. "When women get that hard look from all the smoking and the drinking, they need the softness and roundness of these stones." Suddenly angry, he gave the cardboard square a shove. "Adornment!" he said. "They'd wear diamonds on their ankles if it was stylish! They'd wear them in their noses! They have no real feeling for diamonds."

"Some of these women don't appreciate half the stuff they're given," Frey said. "But I must say most of the people I sell diamonds to really get the thrill of a lifetime."

Winston's anger subsided. "What can you do?" he said philosophically. "You can't control them." A faraway look came into his eyes. "I have no worries about our big stone," he said. "The child is healthy. It has ten toes." He smiled faintly.

"You've got more than toes in that stone," Frey said. "You've got a great stone."

"Where's De Haan?" Winston demanded. "He can't still be at lunch." He picked up the telephone, and this time De Haan answered. After a brief conversation, Winston hung up.

"He's got Ludel with him," he told Frey.

"Ludel just got back this morning," Frey said. "I guess he can't tear himself away from the diamond." A moment later, De Haan and Ludel came in. They are cousins—both of them Dutch and solidly built, with large, square faces. De Haan held out the diamond to Winston, who took it with his left hand while rising and holding out his right to Ludel, who shook it heartily.

"Well, Ludel, how do you like our baby?" Winston said, holding the diamond up.

"I never dreamed of a stone like that," Ludel said, grinning broadly.

De Haan stood by with a proud smile. "I was bringing it along so nicely," he said. "Now maybe it'll be days before I get it back. Mr. Winston likes to hold on to it."

"Yes, yes," Ludel said, still grinning. Winston sat down and looked at the stone through a loupe. "The child is healthy," he said. "Healthy and pure."

"Pure," said Ludel. "I was saying as we came down in the elevator that in forty years I never dreamed of a stone like it. The moment I saw it, I knew I was going to buy it for you."

"The stone was not misrepresented," Winston said, turning the diamond around and around on his fingertips. "But I might as well tell you, Ludel, that for a while I was worried. That piece that cracked off. You should have mentioned it to me."

"I felt as confident as anyone can feel, with a rough diamond, that in

itself it was a perfect stone," Ludel said. "I didn't want to raise doubts
in your mind. Doubts can be very upsetting when there is an ocean
between us. And I wanted you to have that stone. When you finally
decided to buy it, I was the happiest man in the world. It's the biggest
stone I've ever bought. And the highest in price. When I went to Antwerp from London, and walked into the Diamond Club on Pelikaans-
traat, every diamond man in town came up and wanted to know what
the stone looked like. Everybody asked me, 'Is it really so magnificent,
Ludel?' And I said to everybody 'Don't ask so many questions.'" Ludel
slapped his thigh and laughed long and loud.

"It's coming along," Winston said, studying the diamond. By this time
De Haan, after removing most of the stone's skin, had started to rough
out sixteen basic facets that would give the stone a pear-shaped con-
tour; later on, the basic facets would be broken up into smaller facets,
to provide greater brilliance—a process known as brillianteering. "We're
centering it up," Winston went on. "Getting the girdle a little thinner.
There's a slight surface defect—just like a little scab—on the side here.
But it's going to come off and everything will be beautiful. Just now our
diamond looks a trifle clumsy. It looks too short and round and fat and
thick and heavy in the belly—it looks a little bit like me." He gave a quick,
hoarse laugh, and went on, "And the girdle's too heavy on the bottom.
There's too much of a behind. So we'll just take the fat off the hips. And
we'll make the table larger, Bernard. There's still a lot to be done, but
there aren't any major problems left. I want to see this stone have grace
and form and beauty. I'd rather lose ten carats and have a perfectly pro-
portioned stone. This isn't the kind of diamond that should be sold by
the carat. It's too great for that." Winston put the diamond on a sheet of
white paper and pushed it roughly back and forth.

Ludel asked Winston if he had shown the diamond to any prospective buyers. Winston curtly said that he hadn't, and picked up the stone
again. "I may keep it to play with for a few months," he added. "I don't
want to show it for a while yet."

"In the meantime, I'd like to take it back upstairs and go to work
on it," De Haan said, holding out his hand.

Winston made no move to give it to him.

Ludel turned to his cousin and asked who was working on the stone
with him. Frey laughed. "If his job was at stake, he wouldn't let anyone
else touch that stone," he said.

"As long as I have two hands, I'll do it all myself," De Haan said. Again he asked for the stone, but Winston shook his head. "I want to keep it close to me," he said.

The following week, Winston surprised De Haan by not calling for the big diamond for his usual Monday morning inspection. The entire week passed, and Winston spent each day in his office and did not ask to see the stone. Most of the time, he had been busy with Ludel, buying up some large diamonds that had just become available, in an effort to protect what he calls "the big-stone market." He had been made apprehensive by talk in the diamond business that the prices of large diamonds might drop.

"We've been offering fair prices for them," Winston said to Ludel on Friday afternoon. "I want to treat everybody fairly. I don't want to cut any throats."

"You never cut throats," Ludel assured him. "I don't want to see great things cheapened," Winston said. "That new big stone of ours! My God, a thing like that! We've got to protect it." Ludel nodded.

"Of course, buying this way is extremely speculative," Winston said. "I've already spent a million dollars today on rough diamonds. If things work out right, we'll do fine. But you can get hurt very badly doing what I'm doing if you don't know the market. The risks I've taken! Look at King Farouk. Last July, when Farouk already owed me more than a million dollars for the Star of the East and some other jewels, he heard I had a certain emerald that he wanted. Worth a quarter of a million dollars. I sent him the stone and then I told my son Ronnie about it. My little fella is only thirteen, but I talk everything over with him. Ronnie is like a sponge. He soaks up everything about the business. The conversations I have with him! He talks like a jewel merchant. Anyway, I said to Ronnie, 'I sent His Majesty the emerald even though he owes me more than a million.' My little fella listened and finally he said, 'Daddy, if he still owed you the money, I wouldn't have sent him the emerald.' The stone arrived in Alexandria two days before His Majesty abdicated. Just before he went aboard ship to flee from Egypt, he handed the emerald to an American embassy man, and it came back to me. With all his problems, he took the time when he arrived in Naples to send me a cable saying, 'Article you are interested in given to your embassy.' I told Ronnie about it, and I said, 'When dealing with royalty, you must remember you're dealing with people who are brought up with honor. And a king, of course, is above the law anyway.'" Ludel asked Winston if he had heard anything from Farouk about the million dollars still due on the Star of the East, and Winston replied that he hadn't.

"Most of the time I don't try to fathom the people in that part of the world," he said. "Once, I made a deal to sell an Indian prince five hundred thousand dollars' worth of jewels, to be paid for over a period of a year. A few days later, he called and said he wanted to sell me some other jewels, for two hundred and fifty thousand dollars—cash. He said he wanted the money to bet on the horses. Well, I bought the jewels, and he bet on three horses. The first two came in. The third ran out of the money, and he lost the entire quarter of a million. I had to comfort him through his ordeal. His ordeal! But I must say he paid the five hundred thousand on schedule." Winston's secretary, Miss Polly Rowe, came in with some papers, and he asked her whether she had heard from a woman who had called earlier to say she'd be in to see him. Miss Rowe said she hadn't.

"She's a good customer, if she ever gets here," Winston said to Ludel. "She went to the hairdresser's four hours ago. Said she'd be over as soon as she was finished there. I'm selling her a pair of earrings for a hundred and fifty thousand." After a moment, he added, "She has unusually small earlobes. I've been trying for months to get her a pair of earrings that will do something for her lobes."

The telephone rang. Winston answered it and talked to someone for a few minutes about an oil well, remarking that forty barrels a day seemed rather low. After he had hung up, he grimaced and said, "Dull business, Ludel. So you drill a hole and you strike oil. I don't know why I let myself be talked into buying an oil well. I'm not even interested." He sighed and picked up his telephone and asked to speak to De Haan. "Bernard!" he said. "Before you go home, bring down the big stone. You can go home, but I want the baby."

All the next week, up in the polish A room, on the sixth floor, De Haan happily kept the big diamond running on the polishing wheel that was taking the fat off, making the table wider and the girdle leaner. On Friday afternoon, an industrial-diamond man named Daniel S. de Rimini dropped in for a visit, and De Haan took the diamond out of the dop, or cup, at the end of the metal arm holding the diamond to the wheel, and showed it to him. De Rimini whistled. "That's really something!" he said. At the time, he was the general manager of a tool corporation in Tuckahoe, which uses diamonds in precision-tool work. "If I had a wife, I wouldn't let her wear that stone," de Rimini said. "Somebody might steal it—and her, too."

De Haan looked flattered.

"I once held the Cullinan in my hands," de Rimini went on. (The Cullinan, which weighed 3,106 carats before it was cut up into smaller stones, was the largest diamond ever mined.) "I was a little boy at the time. My father worked for Asscher's Diamond Works, in Amsterdam, and they were cutting the Cullinan. My father let me hold it. I'll never forget how I felt. If you'd let me hold this stone, I'd feel the same way—I know it."

A slow grin spread over De Haan's face. "You'll remember to give it back?" he said. Then he laughed loudly and handed the diamond to de Rimini. De Rimini hefted the stone in the palm of his hand. "I'm telling you the truth, Bernard," he said. "I feel more impressed than I did when I held the Cullinan."

De Haan took the diamond back and put it in the dop. "The Cullinan was all cut up," he said. "Our stone will never be cut up."

A few days later, Winston had the big diamond in his office again. It was lunchtime, and his customary cup of coffee, with its milk and saccharin tablet, was in front of him on the desk. Beside it lay three pairs of platinum earrings; each earring was set with ten diamonds, weighing from five to twenty carats. Winston had been rolling the big diamond between his fingers, and now he laid it down on the other side of his coffee cup. Its girdle had been slimmed and its table had been made larger. The sun was shining that day, and its rays, coming through the window, were reflected with more intensity and emphasis by the big stone than by the diamonds in the earrings. In a few moments, Miss Rowe came in and asked what jewels Winston wanted to lend Mrs. William K. Carpenter, who was about to be photographed with some Winston jewels for an advertisement of the annual flower show in Wilmington. Winston put his hands to his head for a moment. Then he got up and took a large black leather box from his safe, and from among the jewels in it he selected a long diamond necklace, which he handed to his secretary. "We want Mrs. Carpenter to look beautiful, don't we?" he said.

"What about a bracelet, Mr. Winston?" Miss Rowe asked.

Winston gave her a diamond bracelet, and then a pair of diamond ear clips. He told her he thought that would be enough. "What ads are we in this week?" he asked.

"Cadillac, Parliament, Tabu, Maximilian Furs, Lucky Strike, and Revlon Nail Enamel," the secretary told him.

"Good," Winston said. "Don't keep Mrs. Carpenter waiting for her jewels," he said. As Miss Rowe was putting the box back in the safe, he picked up the big diamond and smiled at it, and then, with his other hand, picked up the cup and took a sip of coffee. "There, now, Harry," he said to himself. "There we are."

Miss Rowe went out, closing the door. It opened again almost immediately, and Richard Winston, a handsome, soft-spoken man of twenty-seven who is Harry Winston's nephew and works for his uncle as a salesman, came in, carrying a large black suede-covered jewel box.

"Did you get the necklace, Dick?" Harry Winston asked, closing his hand over the big diamond. Dick opened the jewel box and showed his uncle a diamond necklace. Winston gave it a quick glance, still holding on to the big stone. "Who's going to take it over to her?" he asked. A prospective customer—a woman—had asked to have the necklace brought to her hotel, so she could make her final decision.

Dick said he would take it over himself, and that he hoped to return with a check for seventy-five thousand dollars. "She was in this morning with her husband," he said.

"What happened?" Winston asked.

"I'm not sure how we stand," Dick told him earnestly. "Her husband said to her. 'What occasion would you have to wear a necklace like that? We don't go anywhere.' So she said, 'Don't worry. First buy the necklace, and then we'll make the occasion.'"

Winston smiled. "Those two need to be educated," he said. "We'll educate them."

"Suppose she changes her mind again?" Dick asked.

"Leave the necklace with her overnight," Winston said casually.

"Leave it?"

Winston laughed. "Sure," he said. "She ought to get used to having important jewels around. She ought to get used to living with them. It's all part of her education."

Just then, Winston's wife, Edna, came in. A slim, attractive woman, she was wearing a smart black suit that had large round buttons, each set with twenty tiny round diamonds. The Winstons were married in 1933. They had met on a train to Atlantic City four years earlier, when Winston was taking some diamonds there to sell; his bride-to-be had just had her tonsils out, and was on her way to the resort to recuperate, accompanied by her father, a physician and sociologist who was head of a settlement house on the lower East Side called the Educational Alliance. Edna greeted Winston and Dick warmly and sat down across the desk from her husband. Winston asked Dick to tell her what the woman customer had said in the salesroom that morning. Dick told the story again, and Mrs. Winston laughed. "Oh, Dick, that's a funny story," she said.

"I hope she buys the necklace," Dick said.

"She'll buy it," Winston said. "I've told Dick to leave it with her overnight. She'll buy it."

"The way you handle jewels!" Mrs. Winston said. "It seems so careless."

"I never lose one," Winston said.

"Only because you're lucky," his wife said. "You weren't so sure about that the time you lost the hundred-thousand-dollar diamond when the Windsors were here."

"I never heard about that," said Dick.

"That was before you were with me," Winston said, still keeping his hand closed over the big diamond. "I never even mentioned it to the Duke and Duchess. About seven years ago, they were in here one day and I was showing them some things. This whole desk was covered with jewels—diamonds, rubies, emeralds, pearls, everything. After they left, my secretary came in and cleared the stuff away. Well, I went home to dinner, and about nine o'clock that night I got a call from Frey. He was in a terrible state. Said the nightly inventory had showed a fifty-five-carat diamond was missing. We called the Holmes company to arrange for reopening the safe in my office. Not a sign of it. What we went through! The next day, the insurance people wanted to go ask the Duke and Duchess if they remembered seeing the diamond, but I said no—they could talk to anybody else they wanted to but not to the Duke and Duchess. I told them I'd take the responsibility for the loss—if it was lost—and the insurance company wouldn't have to make good. Anything, so long as they didn't bother the Windsors. We searched the entire building. We went through all our wastepaper. Fifty-five carats! It couldn't be missing! It was big enough to trip over! We all went through agony for weeks. It was a reflection on everyone in the building. My secretary, of course, was a nervous wreck. Three months later, a customer came in here and bought a pearl necklace, and I asked my secretary to bring in an empty jewel case to put it in. She brought the case in, and when I opened it, there was the diamond. It had fallen in there by mistake while I was showing all those things to the Duke and Duchess. So you see I was right. It would have been a dreadful thing if we'd let the insurance investigators go around and bother the Duke and Duchess of Windsor."

With his free hand, Winston held up the three pairs of diamond earrings.

"Which do you like, Edna?" he asked.

"For a woman with very small earlobes?" Mrs. Winston tried the various earrings on, and her husband watched her with admiration. "I hate to see the woman get any of them," he said.

Mrs. Winston laughed. "Oh, Harry!" she said. "Always complaining about selling your babies. Dick, did I ever tell you about the time Harry sold two million dollars' worth of diamonds all at once? When he came home that night, I said to him, 'Harry, you must be awfully happy.' You know what he said? 'I'm miserable,' he said, and what's more, he looked it. He's always been that way. He never could stand to see anything get away from him, even before we were married. There never really was anyone else for me, but Harry was in love with his diamonds, so I got engaged to another man. Two days before I was supposed to marry this other man, I got a call from Palm Beach. It was Harry. He'd been selling jewels down there. We hadn't seen each other for a year, but after we'd talked for a minute or two he said, 'Why don't you marry me instead?' I told him I would if he'd come back to New York and marry me right away. He came up the next day and we got married. Then he took me to Palm Beach and he went straight back to selling jewels. He spent most of our honeymoon talking about the big diamonds he hoped to buy. We've been chasing diamonds ever since." Mrs. Winston laughed again, and went on, "Harry just can't forget about a diamond once he's made up his mind he wants it. A few years ago, while we were in Paris, he saw a diamond he liked and decided to buy it. But it was awfully hot, and before he got around to it, I persuaded him to take me to Deauville for the weekend. By the time we got back, the diamond had been sold to someone else. Six months later, in New York, Harry saw the same stone and paid sixty thousand dollars more for it than he could have got it for in Paris. He just had to have that diamond."

"It was an expensive weekend," Winston said. Smiling, he slowly unclenched the hand that held the big diamond.

"Oh, Harry!" Mrs. Winston said, as her husband began rubbing the stone against his coat sleeve. "Is that it?"

Winston held the stone away from her.

"My mouth is watering," Mrs. Winston said. "Do you know what you're going to do with it?"

Winston did not reply, and his wife asked the question again.

"I may sell it in two weeks," Winston said. "Or I may sell it in ten years."

In May, Ludel had to go to Europe on another buying trip. The day before he left, he met his brother, a diamond broker, in front of the Winston establishment at noon and walked with him to the Diamond Dealers Club, at 36 West Forty-Seventh Street, which is one of the local centers for buying, selling, and talking about diamonds. On the way down Fifth Avenue, Ludel's brother asked him if he had seen the big diamond recently.

"Of course," said Ludel.

"I hear it is a perfect stone," his brother said.

Ludel grinned. "Don't ask so many questions," he said.

As the two men turned west on Forty-Seventh Street, Ludel nodded to an elderly gentleman who was hurrying in the opposite direction. "I saw that man in Antwerp a few weeks ago," he said. "Did you notice his pockets? They're bulging with diamonds." The block between Fifth and Sixth Avenues was lined with one jewelry shop or exchange after another. Since it was the lunch hour, the sidewalks were packed with small groups of men who were standing around and showing one another diamonds. Uniformed police were patrolling the street, and in almost every second doorway stood a plainclothes detective. Here and there among the people entering and leaving the shops and exchanges were men with long beards and earlocks, who were wearing the black round-brimmed hat and the long black frock coat often worn by Hasidic Jews. As businessmen, they attracted no particular attention from the others, who had long taken their dress for granted.

Ludel and his brother entered the building where the club had its quarters, and took an elevator to the ninth floor, where, after being waved on by a receptionist sitting in a small glass cage who knows every one of the club's fifteen hundred members by sight, they were admitted to a long room whose north wall consisted almost entirely of large windows. At the windows were rows of long tables on which paper packets of diamonds were spread out. Dealers and brokers were sitting at the tables and bargaining in several languages—English, Dutch, French, Flemish, German, and Yiddish. Against the opposite wall was a small lunch counter, and between the tables and the counter stood groups of members who were waiting their turn at the tables.

Ludel strolled past the tables, smiling and nodding at the men seated there. He seemed to be enjoying himself. Looking around the crowded room, he said to his brother, "Diamond clubs all over the world are alike. Some people making peanuts on a sale, others making millions. It is hard to realize that Harry Winston used to work this way, too."

A small man with a Vandyke beard and bright-blue eyes elbowed his way through the crowd to Ludel and, without saying anything, opened a small packet of diamonds and showed them to him.

Ludel looked at the stones without interest but picked one up and examined it politely. "Very nice," he said, and returned it.

Apparently satisfied, the small man rewrapped his packet and beamed at Ludel. "How's the big stone you bought?" he asked. Ludel looked pleased. "Don't ask so many questions," he said.

A few days later, Winston was assembling a collection of his most famous historical jewels with the help of a four-man crew of his employees, who were to take them to Oklahoma City, where they would be displayed at a Junior League charity ball. The collection, an assortment of a dozen or more museum-piece items known to the Winston staff as the Court of Jewels, had been shown at benefits in a number of other cities during the past year. People had paid something like a million dollars to see it, and the money had been donated to charity. Winston handed several jewel boxes to a young man named Julius, while Dick and the two other members of the crew looked on.

"In a few minutes, four salesmen will walk out of here with millions of dollars' worth of jewels," Winston said jovially.

"We're not salesmen," Julius said. "We're *promoters*." He removed the jewels from the boxes and began calling off the items to Dick, who checked them against an inventory list required for insurance purposes. "The Catherine the Great sapphire," Julius said, holding up a 337-carat stone. "When I travel with the Court of Jewels, I always wrap this one up in my socks. How much?"

"Two hundred and fifty thousand dollars," Winston said, and Dick checked off the Catherine the Great sapphire.

Julius held up a 44½-carat diamond, of a freakish midnight-blue color, that was suspended from a diamond chain. "The Hope diamond," he said. "Once owned by Louis XV and stolen with the rest of the French crown jewels in 1793—that's the sort of thing people want to hear about. How much?"

"A million dollars," Winston said, and Dick checked off the Hope diamond.

"There's always somebody in the crowd who's ready to swear it's a sapphire," he remarked.

Julius said the Hope had just come back from the Munsey Park School, in Manhasset, where he had sent it to be shown to his ten-year-old daughter's class. All her classmates were crazy about the Hope diamond, he said, and the teacher had asked them to write poems to Winston about it. Julius took a sheet of paper from his coat pocket.

"Listen to this one," he said. "It's called 'The Hope Diamond.'" Then he read:

> A diamond is beautiful
> That is true
> And the prettiest ever
> Is owned by you.

"Better finish the inventory," Winston said.

Julius dutifully held up a pair of gold-and-silver anklets set with emeralds and diamonds, once the pride of an Indian maharajah. Winston set their value at a hundred and twenty-five thousand dollars. Julius held up a diamond diadem.

"From the Austrian crown jewels," he said. "Over a hundred years old. How much?"

Winston said two hundred thousand dollars.

"I could make more money selling Bulova watches, but I wouldn't be happy selling Bulova watches," Julius said.

The following month, Winston sat at his desk with the big stone in the palm of his hand. The diamond had three new basic facets. As Winston stared thoughtfully at it, De Haan walked in. "When am I going to get it back?" De Haan asked, nodding toward the diamond. "I haven't been able to get any work done on it for almost two weeks."

"I like to keep it down here with me," Winston said, almost timidly. "You've got other stones to work on, Bernard. You don't really need it."

De Haan looked helplessly at Winston. Then he said, "At this rate, the stone won't be finished before you go to Europe."

"There's no rush," Winston said.

"I thought you wanted to take it with you," De Haan said.

"Well, I'll give it to you tomorrow morning," Winston said. At that moment, Frey entered, and Winston looked relieved.

"I just had a letter from another one of those nuts," Frey said. "This time, it's someone who says he's found a twenty-two-hundred-carat diamond in his backyard in Nashville. The letters we get! Last week, somebody thought he'd found the treasure of the Incas. In Brooklyn!"

Neither De Haan nor Winston seemed to be listening. De Haan looked around reproachfully and left the office. Frey looked at the diamond in Winston's hand. "It's shaping up," he said.

Winston smiled sadly at the diamond. "I started in this business when I was fourteen years old," he said. "My father was always afraid that jewels would someday possess me. He was satisfied with just a small neighborhood jewelry furnishers business uptown, but I was always interested in large stones. He used to say to me, 'Harry, you're the master of your jewels now, but if you keep on buying such big stones, someday your jewels will master you.' Sometimes I think he was right."

In the main salesroom, on the ground floor of the Winston establishment, where clients who do not see Winston personally are waited on, a salesman was displaying some jewelry to a young lady and her mother. "I'm going to show you the heart that practically beats," the salesman said, and brought out a platinum-mounted diamond clip in the shape of a heart. "Mother, it does look as if it might beat at any moment, doesn't it?" the young lady said. The price, said the salesman, was forty thousand dollars.

It was quiet in the room. The two women were the only customers. Two other salesmen stood in a corner talking about Winston.

"I saw him with that big stone of his," one of the salesmen said. "Why is he taking such a long time finishing it, I wonder."

"The way he looks at that stone!" said the second. "I doubt if he's thought about anything else around here since it came in."

Winston planned to go to Europe about the middle of the summer. He was sitting at his desk late one afternoon studying a schedule of transatlantic sailings when Frey came in and asked how soon he was leaving. Winston said he wasn't sure exactly when he would go. He called Miss Rowe in and asked her to have De Haan come down with the big diamond.

"You're not taking it with you, are you?" Frey inquired anxiously. "It's not finished."

"I'm not taking it with me," Winston said.

Frey asked Winston if he was going to Portugal, and Winston said yes. He hoped to sign a contract with the government of that country that would enable him to buy the production of the diamond mines in the Portuguese colony of Angola, in East Africa. "Our government wants an independent source of industrial diamonds, and I've been talking to Portugal about it on the telephone all day," Winston said. "England is against it. I'm fighting the whole British government—not just De Beers."

The door opened and De Haan came in. As he handed the diamond to Winston, he remarked that he was just about to start brillianteering it. "And then you'll mount it?" he asked Winston.

Winston examined the diamond, and the two other men watched him gravely. "Beautiful," he said, in a low, hoarse voice. "It's beautiful."

"Wait till you see it after we've brillianteered it," said De Haan.

"I hate to see it finished," Winston said.

"You're not taking it to Europe?" De Haan asked. He seemed worried. Winston said no, he wasn't, and De Haan's face brightened. He held out his hand for the stone, but Winston did not give it to him. He looked embarrassed and apologetic. "I can't bear to see it finished," he said.

Winston returned from his European trip early in October, and on his first morning back in the office De Haan came down and presented him with the diamond. It was finished and it had been mounted in a simple temporary setting of platinum wire. The diamond weighed 62.05 carats. More than half of the original stone had been lost. What remained was a pear-shaped diamond an inch and a half long and about an inch across at its widest point. Glass replicas of the diamond—in both its rough and its finished form—had been made, and sets of them were going to be sent to the Smithsonian Institution and to the American Museum of Natural History to be added to their collections of replicas of great diamonds. Winston held the stone in the palm of his hand and for more than a minute looked at it tenderly, without speaking. De Haan waited, his arms crossed over his chest.

"It's like a soft, beautiful day in June," Winston said, finally. "It's like a June day when the sky is absolutely clear and the color of the sky is that delicate blue, that brilliant—and pure, absolutely pure." His voice broke, and he cleared his throat. "So soft, so blue," he said.

"It's a greater stone than the Jonker," De Haan said.

"It isn't cold like the Jonker," said Winston. "It lives. It talks to you. In fact, now it sings to you."

"A perfect pear shape," De Haan said. "Fifty-eight facets, and every facet perfect." Winston was not listening. "Isn't it beautiful, Harry?" he said as he stared at the diamond. "Harry, it's a mass of brilliance."

Frey came into the office, and whistled when he saw the diamond. "What a lovely piece!" he said.

"That's what man has done to perfect nature," Winston said.

"Do you know yet what you're going to call the baby?" Frey asked.

"We don't need a name," Winston said. "We'll probably leave that up to whoever buys it." Then he added with a smile, "But it's great enough to be called the Winston diamond."

One morning early in November, Winston called Frey into his office and handed him a small case made of smooth black leather. Frey opened the case. In it, on a white doeskin lining, lay the big diamond, still in its temporary setting. Winston, obviously dispirited, told Frey that a European count wanted to see the stone, and that he had agreed to send it to him in Zurich. Frey asked what price Winston had set on it, and Winston said he was asking six hundred thousand dollars. Frey nodded, lifted the diamond from the case, and took it upstairs to the shipping room. There the stone was wrapped in tissue paper, placed in a cardboard box with four gummed flaps, and sent off to Zurich that same day—by registered air mail, fully insured, in line with Winston's belief that this is the safest way of sending jewels overseas. A few hours later, Winston instructed one of his salesmen, a man named Oberlander, to fly to Zurich to answer any questions the count might have. Eighteen days later, the diamond was returned by registered air mail, beating Oberlander back by twenty-four hours. When Oberlander reported to Winston, he found his employer holding the black leather case that contained the big stone. "The little fella has done some traveling," Winston said, looking fondly at the diamond. He shook hands with Oberlander, a neat, gray-haired man of fifty who wears tortoise-shell spectacles and speaks with a Viennese accent.

"If he had had the money, he would have written a check on the spot," Oberlander said. "He wants the stone. He goes around Europe talking about 'my diamond.'"

Winston grunted.

"Now he's getting divorced," Oberlander said. "His divorce is costing him a great deal—I believe he just gave his wife a couple of million dollars—so he's a bit short of cash right now. But he's got a new girl and he wants to give the diamond to her."

"I know the girl," Winston said angrily. "One of those Continental glamour girls." He snapped the lid shut over the diamond. "We can wait until he raises the money," he said. "We'll keep the little fella right here."

One afternoon about two weeks later, Winston showed the diamond to another prospective buyer—a middle-aged businessman from Texas, who had recently made quite a bit of money in oil and whose wife, a client of Winston's, had asked him to stop in and take a look at the diamond. The businessman sat in Winston's office for an hour and a half, staring at the big stone. Neither he nor Winston spoke very much.

The businessman asked an occasional question about such matters as the quality of the stone, how long Winston had worked on it, and how it might be worn. Winston answered the questions briefly, making no attempt to influence his client's decision. The businessman held the open case in his hand most of the time, looking at the diamond without touching it. Finally, he snapped the case shut, handed it back to Winston, and stood up. "I'll let you know," he said. Winston nodded and went to the door with the man. A few minutes later, Frey came in and found Winston with his fingers pressed against his temples.

"You look exhausted," Frey said.

Winston told him that he had been showing the big diamond to a possible customer. "I sat here for an hour and a half while he looked at it," he said. "I was afraid he was going to take it."

"Is he going to take it?" Frey asked.

Winston opened the jewel case and snapped it shut with a gesture of finality. "He closed the case this way and said, 'I'll let you know,' which means he's interested," he told Frey glumly.

A few days before Christmas, at seven thirty in the evening, Winston, in his apartment on upper Fifth Avenue, was having dinner with his wife and their two sons—Ronald, thirteen, and Bruce, ten, when he was summoned to the telephone. After a few minutes, he returned to the dining room and told his wife that a client had called him and that he was going down to the office. He telephoned his nephew Dick, and then he took a taxi to his office, where he found two Holmes detectives waiting on the sidewalk; they had been sent around after Dick had informed their headquarters that one of the Winston safes was about to he opened. Winston identified himself, went in, and opened the safe in his office, setting off an alarm at the Holmes headquarters. While one of the detectives called in and reported that all was well, Winston removed from the safe the leather case containing the big diamond. A few minutes later, Dick arrived, breathless and looking excited. He was, as always, carefully dressed, washed, and brushed, and his face had the perpetual glow that comes from enthusiasm and good circulation. Winston handed him the case and told him to take it up to the Hotel Pierre, where the wife of a Detroit industrialist was waiting to see the diamond.

It was half past eight when Dick hailed a cab and headed for the Pierre. He was wearing a light overcoat, and he carried the jewel case in the right-hand pocket, keeping his hand on it the whole way. Upon reaching the Pierre, he took an elevator to the thirty-ninth floor, where he rang a bell and was admitted by a maid to the foyer of a suite. In the middle of the living room, just beyond, stood his client, a slender woman in her late sixties, with a pale, thin face and soft gray hair. She was wearing a housecoat, and, as Dick stepped out of the foyer, she disappeared into an inner room. The maid left, and a moment later a young woman in a tailored suit, who was evidently the older woman's secretary, came in and offered to take Dick's coat. Dick took off his coat but said he'd just as soon hold it. She asked him if he'd care to sit down, and he said he didn't mind standing. She said the weather was unusually warm for December, and he agreed that it was. Then she, too, left. Half an hour later, the maid came back and ushered Dick into the inner room, where the woman from Detroit was waiting for him. Dick noticed that the window shades had been drawn. The woman had changed from her housecoat into a purple satin evening gown with a high neckline and wrist-length sleeves, and she had put on a diamond necklace, diamond ear clips, and a diamond-and-ruby pin at her shoulder. She was standing in front of a full-length mirror, and as Dick entered, she said, "Good evening, Mr. Winston. Where are your detectives?"

Dick smiled, produced the jewel case, opened it, and held it toward her. There lay the big stone, in its temporary platinum setting. Without speaking, she picked up the diamond with her thumb and forefinger, carefully touching only the sides, so as not to blur the facets with fingerprints. She held the diamond to her neck and asked Dick how he thought she could attach it to her dress to get its full effect. He suggested sewing it on. The maid brought a needle and some blue silk thread, and Dick, gently refusing her offer of help, threaded the needle with steady hands and sewed the platinum wire holding the diamond to the neckline of his client's dress. The woman then turned back to the mirror and looked at the reflected diamond, in a way that Dick later told his uncle he considered the typical look of people who really know what they are looking at. A bit of color came to her face, but otherwise there was no change in her cool, gracious, confident manner.

The woman stood in front of the mirror for fifteen minutes, turning this way and that. Then she said she was going into the next room to show it to her husband, and asked Dick to wait in the living room. She was gone nearly another quarter of an hour. At nine forty-five, she came into the living room, and Dick, who had been sitting in an armchair, stood up, and remained standing while she walked about pulling down window shades. Then, for an hour and a half, he stood there while she paced the room and they talked about great jewels.

Back on East Fifty-First Street, Harry Winston sat at his desk waiting for his nephew to return. Across the room from him sat the two Holmes detectives, with their hats on. No one said anything. Winston lighted a cigarette, smoked it a quarter of the way down, and crushed it out. He picked up some sketches he had been working on earlier in the day— designs for jewelry to go with strapless evening gowns—and puttered over them for an hour or so. Then he put them aside.

"Nice quiet building, Harry," he said. "I love it this way."

The detectives said nothing.

At eleven fifteen, at the Pierre, the woman from Detroit looked at her watch and said to Dick, "Oh, my goodness, you must want to get back!" Dick said it was perfectly all right; as far as he was concerned, he wouldn't mind staying and talking about diamonds all night, but his uncle was waiting for him at the office. The woman agreed that he should go, so he telephoned Winston and said he'd be back in about ten minutes. Then he offered to help the woman take off the big diamond. She gave him a pair of scissors, and he cut the blue silk thread. But after the diamond was off, she held it lovingly in her hand and talked on and on about the histories of great stones. It was nearly an hour before she said, "Thank your uncle for being kind enough to send the diamond over."

"It was a privilege," said Dick.

Shortly after midnight, Dick had not returned to the office, and Winston was beginning to worry. He telephoned the woman at the Pierre and was told that his nephew had just left. Then Winston and the detectives went downstairs and out onto the sidewalk, and looked up and down the street. Just as they were starting back inside, a cab drew up and Dick stepped out. Winston and the detectives accompanied his nephew up to the office, and they put the diamond back in the safe. Then the detectives saw them into a cab and left. "She appreciated what a great jewel it is," Dick said as they rode toward his uncle's apartment. "She understands great jewels."

The next morning, the Detroit industrialist called on Winston at his office and looked at the diamond again. The man said his wife liked the stone very much, and Winston smiled faintly. The stone had looked very beautiful on his wife, the man said. Again Winston smiled faintly. The man thanked Winston for sending the diamond over, so that his wife could try wearing it with an evening dress and her other jewels. Winston replied that he had been happy to send it over. The man said he would let Winston know his decision. As he was leaving, he paused and, after a moment's hesitation, said, "Isn't it a shame she couldn't have had that diamond when she was younger?"

Later that day, Winston's son Ronald paid a Christmas holiday visit to his father at the office. He marched in, announcing in a matter-of-fact tone that his dog had eaten a Christmas tree bulb right after breakfast and hadn't been hurt at all. Winston said he was glad to hear that. He seemed happy to see Ronald and pulled up a chair facing his desk. Ronald was wearing a dark-blue suit with long pants, and a blue-and-gray striped tie. He sat on the edge of the chair, his toes just touching the floor, and waited politely and seriously for his father to begin the conversation. Winston smiled at his son and plunged into an account of how he had spent part of the morning showing the big diamond to a very wealthy gentleman from Detroit.

"Get the stone, Ronnie," said Winston. "You know where to find it."

Ronald went to the safe, pulled open the door, and took out the jewel case, which he handed to Winston. "You consider it your best diamond?" he asked earnestly.

Winston said he did. He took the diamond from the case and held it up before the boy. "The little fella has traveled," he said. "Our baby has been to Switzerland and back."

"Is it better than the Jonker diamond?" Ronald asked.

"The Jonker was much harder in color, Ronnie," said Winston. "This diamond is softer. The brilliance didn't come through in the Jonker. I couldn't want a finer stone than this."

"Is it better than the Idol's Eye?" Ronald asked.

"That Golconda stone?" said Winston. "Ronnie, you have the natural reaction of a diamond merchant, the natural reaction of comparing one stone with all other stones. I showed you the Idol's Eye six years ago, and it was an old stone even then. This stone has been cut with a lot more knowledge of the art and science of diamond cutting."

"It took millions of years to make that diamond," Ronald said, solemnly contemplating the stone. "And you cut it and polished it in a few months. Did you get another diamond out of the rough stone?"

"No, Ronnie," Winston said. "The stone weighed a hundred and fifty-four and a half carats originally, and we've got a sixty-two-carat stone now."

Ronald was silent while he did some mental arithmetic. "Then you lost ninety-two and a half carats, just blown into the air," he said presently. "What are you going to call this diamond, Daddy?"

"We may call it the Winston diamond," said Winston.

"Good idea," said Ronald.

"Of course, we may sell the diamond to someone who will want to choose his own name for it," Winston said.

"I think you ought to name it the Winston diamond before you sell it," Ronald said. Winston looked hard at the diamond.

"You may be right, Ronnie," he said.

Ronald asked his father whether he knew of anybody besides the man from Detroit who wanted to buy the diamond and how much it would cost. Winston said that he had shown it to three people, and that the price was six hundred thousand dollars. "All three want the diamond, Ronnie," he went on. "One is a Texas oilman. Another is a European count, and he would have bought the diamond last month, but he was a little short of cash at the time. And the third is the man I saw this morning. His wife's getting quite old, and it may be the last diamond he'll be buying for her."

Ronald asked whether Winston cared which of the three bought the diamond.

"That's very difficult to say," Winston replied. "You know, I like the diamond very much myself."

"Yes, Daddy," said Ronald. "I know. And I like it very much, too."

"Whoever buys the diamond now will buy it over the telephone," Winston said, suddenly assuming a palpably false air of heartiness. "They've all seen it. The preliminaries are over. I'll get a telephone call, and I'll hear that one of the three will take it—and that will be that, Ronnie." Winston's voice trailed off on a note of misery.

"Yes, Daddy," Ronald said, his own voice loyally miserable.

One morning, shortly after the New Year, Ludel, who had just returned from another European trip, was on his way down to Winston's office with De Haan to see the diamond for the first time since it had been finished. In the elevator, he told his cousin about a plane crash he had been in while taking off from Amsterdam for Paris, where Winston had asked him to look at some diamonds. Ludel had suffered six broken ribs and a broken chest bone.

"I called Mr. Winston and told him I was sorry but I was going to be late getting to Paris," Ludel said. "You know what he said? 'The hell with Paris,' he said. 'How are you?' You don't find that sort of consideration among rich men in Europe."

The two cousins entered Winston's office, and he greeted them with a smile. On the black velvet pad on his desk lay the big stone. Ludel stared at it for a long time while Winston waited expectantly for his reaction. "Such a wonderful color!" Ludel said, at last.

"You were right on the weight, Ludel," said Winston. "I was influenced by De Haan, here. He thought it would be bigger."

"I happen to be an optimist," De Haan said.

Apparently, Ludel's response was not all Winston had hoped it would he, for he said a bit sharply, "Ludel, you'd always rather see a stone in the rough, wouldn't you?"

Ludel blushed slightly. "Absolutely right," he said.

Winston's annoyance was soon gone. "Within a period of about a month, I paid over a million dollars for four stones, and I haven't sold any of them yet," he said cheerfully. "This is just one of them. I'm a patient man."

The door opened, and Richard Winston came in, carrying a box that contained necklaces and bracelets that were being set with diamonds. He put the box down on his uncle's desk and told him that the diamond setters were asking for smaller stones that would match the others in color. Winston sighed in mock despair. He had thousands and thousands of diamonds, he said, but he always seemed to be short of the diamonds the setters wanted.

"Still, you can get thousands and thousands of the diamonds they want," Dick said comfortingly. Then he pointed to the big diamond. "But this you get only once in a thousand years."

"What nature and man have combined to make!" Winston said in an awed voice.

"We certainly have the finest diamond nature ever produced," Ludel said.

"And yet you can never be sure," Winston said. "You're always wondering. It's like seeing a beautiful girl and asking yourself, 'Is she as beautiful as that girl?' You're always comparing. You always feel you may be missing something. You're never sure."

Miss Rowe came into the office and said that the count was calling from Zurich. Winston looked flustered as he picked up the telephone. While he waited for the call to be put through to him, he said, in a weak, dazed voice, "Well, Harry, it's all over now."

(MAY 8 AND 15, 1954)

The Sporting Scene
(John McEnroe)

If, during these Sampras–Hingis US Open days, you're missing the tennis playing of good old (thirty-eight-year-old) John McEnroe (four singles championships and four men's-doubles championships), console yourself: he's missing himself. In his current incarnation, as an announcer-commentator on the USA Network and CBS, he not only describes the action; he can tell you, with a lot of instructive discourse, what the players are thinking and feeling before and after each shot.

Last week, on the Opens day three, McEnroe arrived, a huge black Nike carrying bag slung over a shoulder, at the USA broadcast booth in the Arthur Ashe Stadium a few minutes before airtime. He grabbed a hot dog, took a couple of big bites, and called for makeup to powder his face, especially the sunburned and peeling top of his nose. He looked like the early puckish, vigilant McEnroe—the one with the audible mouth, ready to wake up myopic umpires—but with modestly graying and thinning hair. He wore a slate-blue silk designer suit, a navy shirt, an elegant gray print necktie, shiny black shoes, and white tennis socks. He had an exceptionally handsome gold loop attached to his left ear.

"Six years ago, I was having difficulty going to a tennis match," he told me. "I wanted to be there, but I had no reason to be there. I have to give credit to Vitas Gerulaitis. He was here." McEnroe put on his headphones with mouthpiece and took his position, facing several TV monitors, alongside Ted Robinson, his co-announcer. "Vitas got me doing this. The producer Gordon Beck said, 'Hey, you guys are great together.' So I started doing it with Vitas. Lately, I've been doing Wimbledon, the French Open, and this. It's been good for me. I feel comfortable now at tennis matches. I hang out with the guys in the locker room. It's an opportunity for me to get the feel for the way the intensity is affecting them. I sort of try to be there for them. I know what it is. I've been there."

The broadcast began. McEnroe and Robinson started talking. First, they talked over a replay of an earlier match—Thomas Muster (Austria) vs. Tim Henman (England)—that had not got on the air. McEnroe said that Henman, who won the second set in a tiebreaker, was very talented. Robinson talked about both players' stats and histories. McEnroe started looking intense. "Muster has a tendency to try to hit the ball too hard," he said. "Henman can be in the top ten if he gets himself a little bit stronger."

During a commercial, Robinson had a hot dog. McEnroe turned down a second hot dog. He said, "Vitas didn't digest hot dogs; he just ate them, four or five at a time."

Back on the air, McEnroe said, "If you go at an opponent, be like Lendl—go right at him." On the monitor, Muster was smiling. At one point, Henman made a great exchange of volleys, and Muster pretended to go running after him, racquet raised. Big laughter in the crowd. McEnroe drummed on the table with a pen, holding it, like his racquet, in his left hand. "The way I was brought up, if you joke around, you lose your concentration," he said. Henman made some magnificent passing shots. "Henman's showing he has plenty of gas left in the tank," McEnroe said.

Muster flubbed a backhand shot. "Such a basic thing—but not as easy as it sounds—to keep your eye on the ball till the ball hits the racquet," McEnroe observed. "That's the only reason he missed it." Henman sent a deadly drop shot just out of Muster's reach. "Henman is playing great tennis," Robinson said. "And that's doing it without bending your knees at all," McEnroe added.

Then Henman won. "He's showing absolutely no emotion," McEnroe said. "Looking ahead, I suppose, to Wayne Ferreira"—his next opponent.

Another commercial break. McEnroe said, "I could always tell what my opponents were thinking; then I'd be imposing my will on them. That's how I got to be number one."

Former Mets first baseman Keith Hernandez, a McEnroe pal, entered the booth grinning. No. 17. Also missed.

(SEPTEMBER 8, 1997)

Camaraderie
(Ralph Kiner)

Ralph Kiner, the Hall of Fame ballplayer who has been a Mets broadcaster for four decades, showed up at Shea Stadium early the other day for one of the interleague games against the Yankees. He stopped in at his usual center of operations—the Mets' broadcast area has been designated the Ralph Kiner Television Booth—but didn't stay long.

"I'm not going to work announcing this one, just visit some of the guys," he said. "I miss the camaraderie of the old days, the way it used to be." Kiner is eighty-one years old, more than six feet tall, and sturdy-looking, with erect posture, a calm, courtly manner, and an earnest sun-beaten face. He had on a burnt-orange sports jacket, a multicolored silk shirt, cream-colored pants, and spotless white shoes. His 1975 Hall of Fame ring was on his wedding-ring finger.

Baseball fans know that Ted Williams put Kiner on his list of the twenty best hitters of all time; that Kiner was a Navy pilot in the Second World War; that, as a rookie outfielder with the Pittsburgh Pirates, in 1946, he led the National League in home runs, and that he did so again for the next six seasons; and that he retired at the age of thirty-two because of back problems. He joined the Mets in 1962, their first season, to do both radio and television broadcasting, and for what seems like forever, with a hiatus or two, he has hosted a postgame show called *Kiner's Korner*, which is as raffish as always but which, sadly, no longer features Kiner pouring a glass of Rheingold Extra Dry beer.

Kiner dropped by the main broadcast booth to say hello to the guys calling the game, then made his way downstairs to the tunnel that leads to the visitors' dugout. Groundskeepers, ball boys, players, and sportswriters stopped to call out "Hi, Ralph!" Someone pushing a cart full of bats said, "Ralph! What do you think Yogi said when Piazza was honored

the other night for his record number of home runs as a catcher?" Kiner
smiled. Several people chorused, "'I knew my record would stand until
it's broken!'" Kiner continued onward, the field coming into view over
the lip of the dugout, a lovely thing to see. The Yankees were out there,
taking batting practice. "We used to be fined if we were caught talking
to players on the opposing team," Kiner said. "But I always wanted to
talk to all the guys who knew baseball. I still find camaraderie with some
of the guys. Joe Torre is an old friend." An elderly man sat alone on
the Yankee bench, out of uniform. He resembled a wilting leprechaun.
A credential hanging on a ribbon around his neck identified him as
"Arthur Richman—Senior Advisor." Kiner greeted him cordially.

Richman looked sad. "You not doing the game?" he asked.

Kiner said, "Not today. I'll do it next in a week or so. What's new,
Arthur?" Kiner regarded him with affection and went on, "Arthur, the
guys say you're the most pessimistic person in the world. You always
say to everybody, 'You have no chance to win.'"

"I go way back with you," Richman said. "I know everybody."

"You know more people in baseball than any man alive," Kiner said.
"You're the one who recommended Torre to Steinbrenner. You knew
Casey Stengel as well as anyone."

"Stengel never slept," Richman said. "He'd stay up all night, talking."

"That's why you'd see him sleeping on the bench," Kiner said. "Arthur," he added quickly, "you've got your funeral all planned?"

"Eight pallbearers—you and seven others, every one a Hall of
Famer," Richman said, perking up.

"You got us our plane tickets, hotel accommodations, everything,"
Kiner said. "That's very considerate."

"I'm not sick or anything, but everything's taken care of," Richman
said.

Kiner walked quickly out onto the field, to the batting cage, where
Joe Torre was conferring with Don Mattingly, who is now one of his
hitting coaches. When Torre spotted Kiner, he came over and grinned
majestically.

"You gonna remind me again about my brief career with the Mets?"
Torre asked.

"You mean when you hit into four straight double plays in one
game?" Kiner replied. "It tied the record! And you blamed it on Felix
Millan, the man in front of you."

"It was his fault," Torre said. "How's your golf, Ralph?"

"Good," Kiner said. "Remember when we started playing together? You weren't any good. But I made you better."

Torre lifted his eyebrows and laughed.

"Thanks for the expensive wine you sent me for my birthday," Kiner said. "When is your birthday?"

"This month," Torre said. "I'll be sixty-four."

Kiner pretended to look impressed.

"Yep! Sixty-four," Torre said. "But I've got an eight-year-old daughter. I like to boast about that."

(SEPTEMBER 26, 2004)

Ellen Barkin at Home

L ast week, Ellen Barkin was flitting around town promoting *Palin-dromes*, a new movie directed by Todd Solondz, in which she plays the unctuous mother of a pregnant thirteen-year-old girl.

Simultaneously, she was carrying on her real life, as a wife (to Ronald Perelman, the Revlon billionaire) and mother (to two children from her previous marriage, with Gabriel Byrne, and to two stepkids), in the Perelmans' five-story town house in the East Sixties.

On Monday morning, she was at home, looking trim in a couple of layered T-shirts worn under a saffron-colored hand-knit cardigan, snug jeans, and brown Christian Louboutin boots with tall, spiky red heels. "I have four herniated disks," she said, flashing her squinty eyes. "With a bad back, it's easier to walk on high heels." She was also wearing big diamond earrings and two rings—a vintage Deco diamond on her right hand and a wedding band of diamonds set with a rose-cut nineteenth-century jar diamond on her ring finger—along with a briolette diamond pendant on a platinum-and-diamond chain. "I sleep in them," she said, as she toured the premises with a visitor. She checked in with a driver in the foyer (one of Andy Warhol's famous Maos hung on the wall), nodded to various security men, and consulted with two housekeepers and a chef. She paused in a small sitting room. It had a flat-screen TV on the wall. "The children aren't allowed to have television in their rooms; we all watch in here," she said. "We also have four dogs—a miniature Yorkie, a Maltese, a Wheaten terrier, and a King Charles spaniel. And," she added cheerfully, "I hate them all."

The Yorkie, named Scruffy, blew frantically into the room and jumped into her arms. He was impeccably groomed, and he wore a pink leather collar. "My daughter, Romy Byrne, wants him to be a her, in pink," Barkin said. "Romy is twelve, laid back, listless. She'll look at you like this." Barkin slouched back, flopped her arms, pantomimed an imitation of her daughter, just as Romy herself, listless, very pretty, with long light-brown hair, sauntered in, a perfect reflection of her mother's impersonation. After being introduced, she sauntered out with Scruffy. "Romy is beautiful," Barkin said matter-of-factly, but with a corner-of-the-mouth grin. "My fifteen-year-old son, Jack, is sweet. He's a guitarist, who reads only books from the nineteen sixties and before, and listens only to music from the sixties and before, but Romy is like all the girls who would never speak to me in high school."

The tour continued. "All the beautiful French modern furniture you see here now is the replacement of what I found when I first came to live here, six years ago," she said. "The house was full of eighteenth- and nineteenth-century Russian furniture. Everything was gold. Ronald and I lived together for a year before we got married. After another year with all the gold furniture and gold carpets and gold walls and gold floors, and the dining room all done in navy-blue cashmere, I got to work. It was easy. I had eight billion dollars to spend. When I came, there was no kitchen to speak of. Now we have a huge kitchen with a wall of refrigerators—one dairy, one meat. Ronald is one-hundred-percent kosher. I make the brisket on Passover." Laughing, she said, "Ronald has me buy the meat from a kosher butcher shop where everything costs three times as much."

She went on. "The first piece of furniture we bought was for Ronald's bedroom, a Giò Ponti desk and the old matching chair." She pointed them out in the bedroom. At one end stood a high, king-size bed, done up in white Pratesi linens. "All the little kids like to sleep with us—Patricia's ten-year-old, Caleigh, and my Romy," Barkin said. "Today, Ronald and I are ninety-nine percent in agreement about all the furniture and stuff in the house. I'm home alone so much—I love to sit with a book in the living room. I sit there and read and look at what's on the walls. That Modigliani!" She pointed to the wall opposite the entrance to the living room (about the size of a Versailles ballroom), to the famous *Tête de Jeune Fille (L'Italienne)*. "It was the first thing I saw on the walls when I first came here," she said. "I said to Ronald, 'Are you joking me?' I can sit for hours in the library or in the living room and look at the Picassos, the Matisses, the Lichtensteins, the Mirós, the de Koonings, the Rothkos.

"Before Ronald, I never dated a man who wore a suit and tie. Ronald used to put on the suit and tie to go to his office, even though it's here—he goes out the back door to his office building across the courtyard. Now he just wears a cashmere sports jacket." She said, "I met Ronald at a party, when he came up to me and asked me for a date. Then he kept leaving messages for me on the machine. Finally, I went to dinner with him. What was I doing with him? I was afraid he would be one of those megalomaniac guys who would bore me to death. He came from Philadelphia. I came from the Bronx and Queens. My father was a Fuller Brush man. Ronald lived in a big house. He went to private schools." She pointed to a marble table. On it was a book about two feet square. On the cover was a photograph of a cute, solemn-faced thirteen-year-old wearing a dark suit and a yarmulke. It was entitled "Ronald's Bar Mitzvah. January 1956." "I found it in the basement and brought it up here to be with the other pictures," she said.

Near the dining room—which holds a long, polished Ruhlmann table seating twenty-four ("Sometimes, for the seder, we squeeze in up to twenty-eight," she said)—is a bookshelf piled high with yarmulkes. "Look at this," Barkin said, and pulled from under the yarmulkes a book of writings by Allen Ginsberg. She patted the yarmulkes and patted the book of poems. "There you have it, Ronald and me," she said.

She went on. "I told Ronald, 'I don't understand anything you do.' He said, 'You're smart. You'll learn.' I said, 'I'm forty-five. I'm already who I am.' I was very concerned about the effect of all of it on my kids. As it is, my kids don't even like my being in the entertainment business. They find it embarrassing. But Ronald is down to earth."

She stopped herself suddenly, looking alarmed. "My class!" she said. "I teach an acting class this afternoon, down at the Actors Studio Drama School at the New School."

She grabbed a brown crocodile Birkin bag ("Ronald got it for me"), heavy with books and papers, added a can of Diet Coke, two bottles of Evian, and a package of Twizzlers to the lot, and got into her waiting sedan. Half an hour later, she chomped on a Twizzler and listened intently as two students did a scene from Ionesco's *The Lesson*. At the end of it, she looked disappointed. She tried to explain to the students what they were doing wrong. "When you do one of those absurdist plays," she said firmly, "you still have to find the emotional core."

(APRIL 25, 2005)

V

BIG CHEESES

Lillian, John Huston, and Audie Murphy on the
set of John Huston's *The Red Badge of Courage,*
outside Los Angeles, 1950.

Feeling Lost
(Charlie Chaplin)

Charlie Chaplin has been spending a few days at the Plaza, and we found him in his suite there, handing soiled laundry to a maid. The first words we heard him speak were "Here's a very dirty shirt." He looked in fine shape—pink-cheeked, with pure-white hair, bristling white eyebrows, and freckled hands. The problem of the laundry left him slightly distraught, and as soon as the maid departed, he turned around once or twice, in a sort of dance, then motioned us to a chair and lighted on the edge of a couch. Mrs. Chaplin came in from the next room to say that she was going shopping, and Chaplin asked her to pick up a couple of hundred dollars for him. "I don't like to cash checks at the desk in the lobby," he told us, after Mrs. Chaplin left. "At the same time, I hate to slash into a place with no money at all. It makes me feel lost." He gazed thoughtfully at a toy on a nearby table. "There's something I got for the kids," he said. "I have three from the age of four down, besides the two grown boys, Charles, Jr., and Sydney. They're both actors. Sydney is a good comedian, whimsical, with an excellent lilt, and he has size and stature. For one thing, he's over six feet. But I'm not sending him the toy. You put in the penny . . ." Chaplin searched his pockets. "There's me—haven't a cent," he said. "Anyhow, you put in a penny and out comes a colored ball of chewing gum. My kids love chewing gum. This toy will be wonderful for them. I found it yesterday, along Forty-Second Street. There was this little squashed-in place, with the toy in the window. There was a toy for chocolates, too, but I wasn't sure about giving the children chocolate."

Chaplin told us he has been walking around town a lot, to take the place of tennis, which is how he gets his exercise at home. "The other day, I walked all up and down Tenth Avenue, and I loved it," he said. "But, oh, the dirt and the ash cans!" He sat silent a moment, and then suggested that we go downstairs and have lunch. The two of us adjourned to the restaurant, where, walking just like Charlie Chaplin, Chaplin led the way to a table by a window. He sat down and looked at Central Park. It was snowing. "What beautiful snow!" Chaplin said. "I remember sitting here in this room, just like this, in the winter of 1916, after my first success. I registered as Charles Spencer—Spencer's my middle name—and I stayed here because I didn't know any other place where you could dine. The police had sent me word on the train that I wasn't to go into Grand Central, because of the crowds waiting to see me there, so I had to get off at 125th Street—and all I was coming here for was to look for a job."

Chaplin said that he hoped in the course of his current visit to find a leading lady for a movie he's planning to make, but that he didn't know how to go about finding her. "I see shows and interview a certain number of people, out of a sense of duty, but all the people I've found I've always found by luck," he said. "This new role is a very difficult one. The girl will have to be able to act and dance ballet. I said something about the role a while ago, jokingly, and it came out in one of the gossip columns that I was looking for a person who could act like Duse and dance like Pavlova, and some agent called me up and said, 'I've got her!'—really quite humorlessly. I'm going to see the poor dear after lunch."

Chaplin said, over lunch, that it had taken him two years to prepare the script of his new movie, that he had composed the music for it, and that he will, as usual, direct it, produce it, and act the leading role. He's anxious to get it under way as quickly as possible. "I can't afford to wait too long on it, because I use my own money," he said. "I don't want to say much about it, but I've poured my guts into the script and I mean it to be the best thing I've ever done." His role will be different from the roles he played in his early films and from his role in *Monsieur Verdoux*, which he considers his best work. "I lost money on that one," he said. "The people who came to see me came to see the funny man. They were shocked. They couldn't adjust. They wanted to know where the big shoes were." Though *Monsieur Verdoux* was a failure in this country, it won several prizes elsewhere, including the Danish equivalent of an Oscar.

Chaplin recalled that when he entered the movies, in 1913, his contract called for three pictures a week. They used to make a picture in half a day then. Chaplin told us that he acts without any conscious intellectual activity. "All you feel while you're acting is ebullience," he said. "You intellectualize when you go into the projection room and say, "Now, why isn't that funny?" When you get older, you know how to approach humor. The best definition of humor I ever heard is that it's getting people in and out of trouble. That's what I try to do. I'm emotional about most things but objective about my work. I don't get satisfaction out of it, I get relief." Chaplin said he doesn't have time for much of anything besides his work and his family. "I live in my very secure house of cards," he said. "I'm a self-educated man and don't get everything I'd like to get out of reading. Oh, maybe I browse through my Burton's *Anatomy of Melancholy*, but I leave most of the reading to my wife. Besides, I've an odd quirk in my sight. I see only the first word and the last in a line on a page. Must be something psychological in that, don't you think?" A man hurried up, whispered something in Chaplin's ear, and hurried away. "That's the girl's agent," he said, as we got up to go. "This will be very embarrassing. I never know what to say to them. Usually, you know, I just look at them from a distance."

(FEBRUARY 25, 1950)

Picture, Part I:
Throw the Little Old
Lady down the Stairs!

The making of the Metro-Goldwyn-Mayer movie *The Red Badge of Courage*, based on the Stephen Crane novel about the Civil War, was preceded by routine disclosures about its production plans from Louella Parsons ("John Huston is writing a screen treatment of Stephen Crane's classic, 'The Red Badge of Courage,' as a possibility for an M-G-M picture."); from Hedda Hopper ("Metro has an option on 'The Red Badge of Courage' and John Huston's working up a budget for it. But there's no green light yet."); and from *Variety* ("Pre-production work on 'Red Badge of Courage' commenced at Metro with thesp-tests for top roles in drama."), and it was preceded, in the spring of 1950, by a routine visit by John Huston, who is both a screenwriter and a director, to New York, the headquarters of Loew's, Inc., the company that produces and distributes M-G-M pictures. On the occasion of his visit, I decided to follow the history of that particular movie from beginning to end, in order to learn whatever I might learn about the American motion-picture industry.

Huston, at forty-three, was one of the most admired, rebellious, and shadowy figures in the world of motion pictures. I had seen him a year before, when he came here to accept an award of a trip around the world for his film contributions to world unity. He had talked of an idea he had for making a motion picture about the nature of the world while he was going around it. Then he had flown back to Hollywood, and to the demands of his employers, Metro-Goldwyn-Mayer, and had made *The Asphalt Jungle*, a picture about a band of criminals engaged in pursuits that Huston described somewhere in the dialogue of the movie as "a left-handed form of human endeavor." Now, on this visit, shortly after the sudden death, in Hollywood, of his father, Walter Huston, he telephoned me from his Waldorf Tower suite and said he was having a terrible time trying to make *The Red Badge of Courage*. Louis B. Mayer and most of the other top executives at M-G-M, he said, were opposed to the entire project. "You know something?" he said, over the telephone. He has a theatrical way of inflecting his voice that can give a commonplace query a rich and melodramatic intensity. "They don't want me to make this picture. And I want to make this picture." He made the most of every syllable, so that it seemed at that moment to lie under his patent and have some special urgency. "Come on over, kid, and I'll tell you all about the hassle," he said.

The door of Huston's suite was opened by a conservatively attired young man with a round face and pink cheeks. He introduced himself as Arthur Fellows. "John is in the next room getting dressed," he said. "Imagine getting a layout like this all to yourself! That's the way the big studios do things." He nodded with approval at the Waldorf's trappings. "Not that I care for the big studios," he said. "I believe in being independent. I work for David Selznick. I've worked for David for fifteen years. David is independent. I look at the picture business as a career. Same as banking, or medicine, or law. You've got to learn it from the ground up. I learned it from the ground up with David. I was an assistant director on *Duel in the Sun*. I directed the scene of the fight between two horses. Right now, I'm here temporarily on publicity and promotion. David—" He broke off as Huston strode into the room. Huston made his entrance in the manner of an actor who is determined to win the immediate attention of his audience.

"Hel-lo, kid," Huston said as we shook hands. He took a step back, then put his hands in his trouser pockets and leaned forward intently. "Well!" he said. He made the word expand into a major pronouncement.

Huston is a lean, rangy man, two inches over six feet tall, with long arms and long hands, long legs and long feet. He has thick black hair, which had been slicked down with water, but some of the front strands fell raffishly over his forehead. He has a deeply creased, leathery face, high cheekbones, and slanting, reddish-brown eyes. His ears are flattened against the sides of his head, and the bridge of his nose is bashed in. His eyes looked watchful, and yet strangely empty of all feeling, in weird contrast to the heartiness of his manner. He took his hands out of his pockets and yanked at his hair. "Well!" he said, again as though he were making a major pronouncement. He turned to Fellows. "Art, order some martinis, will you, kid?"

Huston sat down on the arm of a chair, fixed a long brown cigarette in one corner of his mouth, took a kitchen match from his trouser pocket, and scraped the head of the match into flame with his thumbnail. He lit the cigarette and drew deeply on it, half closing his eyes against the smoke, which seemed to make them slant still more. Then he rested his elbows on his knees, holding the cigarette to his mouth with two long fingers of one hand, and looked out the window. The sun had gone down and the light coming into the suite, high in the tower, was beginning to dull. Huston looked as though he might be waiting—having set up a Huston scene—for the cameras to roll. But, as I gradually grew to realize, life was not imitating art, Huston was not imitating himself, when he set up such a scene; on the contrary, the style of the Huston pictures, Huston being one of the few Hollywood directors who manage to leave their personal mark on the films they make, was the style of the man. In appearance, in gestures, in manner of speech, in the selection of the people and objects he surrounded himself with, and in the way he composed them into individual "shots" (the abrupt close-up of the thumbnail scraping the head of a kitchen match) and then arranged his shots into dramatic sequence, he was simply the raw material of his own art; that is, the man whose personality left its imprint, unmistakably, on what had come to be known as a Huston picture.

"I just love the light at this time of the day," Huston said as Fellows returned from the phone. "Art, don't you just love the light at this time of the day?"

Fellows said it was all right.

Huston gave a chuckle. "Well, now," he said, "here I am, spending the studio's money on this trip, and I don't even know whether I'm going to make the picture I'm here for. I'm auditioning actors at the Loew's office and talking production up there and doing all the publicity things they tell me to do. I've got the *Red Badge* script OK'd, and I'm going down South to pick locations for the picture, but nothing is moving. We can't make this picture unless we have six hundred Confederate uniforms and six hundred Union uniforms. And the studio is just not making those uniforms for us. I'm beginning to think they don't *want* the picture!"

"It's an offbeat picture," Fellows said politely. "The public wants pictures like *Ma and Pa Kettle*. I say make pictures the public wants. Over here," he said to a waiter who had entered with a tray holding six martinis in champagne glasses. "No getting away from it, John," Fellows went on, handing Huston a drink. "Biggest box-office draws are pictures catering to the intelligence of the twelve-year-old."

People underestimated the intelligence of the twelve-year-old, Huston said. He said he had an adopted son in his early teens, a Mexican-Indian orphan, Pablo, whom he had found while making *The Treasure of the Sierra Madre* in Mexico a few years ago, and his boy had excellent taste in pictures. "Why, my boy Pablo reads Shakespeare," he said. "Do you read Shakespeare, Art?"

"Television, John," said Fellows. "The junk they go for on television."

Huston asked him vaguely what the talk was in New York about television.

Television was booming, Fellows said, and all the actors, singers, dancers, directors, producers, and writers who hadn't been able to get work in Hollywood were going into television in New York. On the other hand, all the actors, singers, dancers, directors, producers, and writers who had gone into television in New York were starving and wanted to go back to Hollywood. "Nobody really knows what's happening," said Fellows. "All I know is television can never do what pictures can do."

"We'll just make pictures and release them on television, that's all. The hell with television," Huston said. "Do you kids want the lights on?" The room was murky. It made a fine tableau, Huston said. Fellows and I agreed that it was pleasant with the lights off. There was a brief silence. Huston moved like a shadow to a chair opposite mine and lit another brown cigarette, the quick glow from the match lighting up his face. "Been to the races out here, Art?" he asked.

A few times, Fellows said, but David Selznick had been keeping him so busy he hadn't had much time for horses.

"The ponies have me broke all the time," Huston said. "You know, I can't write a check for five hundred dollars. I am always broke. I can't even take an ordinary vacation. But there's nothing I'd rather spend my money on than a horse, especially when the horse is one of my own. There's nothing like breeding and raising a horse of your own. I've got four horses racing under my colors right now, and in a couple of years I'll have more, even if I have to go into hock to support them. All I want is one good winner of my own. Everybody I know is conspiring to take my horses away from me. Someday I'll have one good winner, and then I'll be able to say, 'Well, you bastards, this is what it was all about!' "

Financial problems, Huston said, had prevented him from taking the trip around the world. Although his M-G-M salary was four thousand dollars a week while he was making a picture, he had had to get the company to advance him a hundred and fifty thousand dollars, which he was paying off in installments. He was bound by his contract to make at least one picture a year for the next three years for M-G-M. He was a partner in an independent company, Horizon Pictures, which he had started a couple of years before with a man named Sam Spiegel, whom he had met in the early thirties in London. Huston had directed one picture, *We Were Strangers*, for Horizon, but it had lost money. He was scheduled to direct another—*The African Queen*, based on the novel by C. S. Forester—as soon as he had completed *The Red Badge of Courage* for M-G-M. Huston said he thought *The African Queen* would make money, and if it did, he could then make some pictures on his own that he wanted to make as much as he did *The Red Badge of Courage*. The reason L. B. Mayer and the other M-G-M executives did not think that *The Red Badge of Courage* could be a commercial success, Huston said, was that it had no standard plot, no romance, and no leading female characters, and if Huston had his way in casting it, would have no stars. It was simply the story of a youth who ran away from his first battle in the Civil War, and then returned to the front and distinguished himself by performing several heroic acts. Huston, like Stephen Crane, wanted to show something of the emotions of men in war, and the ironically thin line between cowardice and heroism. A few months earlier, Huston and an M-G-M producer named Gottfried Reinhardt, the son of the late Max Reinhardt, had suggested to Dore Schary, the studio's vice president in charge of production, that they make the picture.

"Dore loved the idea," Huston said. "And Dore said he would read the novel." A couple of weeks later, Schary had asked Huston to write a screen treatment—a rough outline for the detailed script. "I did my treatment in four days," Huston said. "I was going down to Mexico to get married, so I took my secretary along and dictated part of it on the plane going down, got married, dictated some more after the ceremony, and dictated the rest on the plane trip back." Schary approved the treatment, and the cost of making the picture was estimated at a million and a half dollars. Huston wrote the screenplay in five weeks, and Schary approved it. "Then the strangest things began to happen," Houston said. "Dore is called vice president in charge of production. L. B. is called vice president in charge of the studio. Nobody knows which is boss." His voice rose dramatically. "We were told Dore had to OK everything. We got his OK but nothing moved. And we know that L. B. hates the idea of making this picture." His voice sank to a confidential whisper. "He just hates it!"

For the role of the Youth, Huston said, he wanted twenty-six-year-old Audie Murphy, the most-decorated hero of the Second World War, whose film career had been limited to minor roles. Huston said he was having some difficulty persuading both Schary and Reinhardt to let Murphy have the part. "They'd rather have a star," he said indignantly. "They just don't see Audie the way I do. This little, gentle-eyed creature. Why, in the war he'd literally go out of his way to find Germans to kill. He's a gentle little killer."

"Another martini?" Fellows asked.

"I hate stars," Huston said, exchanging his empty glass for a full one. "They're not actors. I've been around actors all my life, and I like them, and yet I never had an actor as a friend. Except Dad. And Dad never thought of himself as an actor. But the best actor I ever worked with was Dad. All I had to tell Dad about his part of the old man in *Treasure* was to talk fast. Just talk fast." Huston talked rapidly, in a startling and accurate imitation of his father. "A man who talks fast never listens to himself. Dad talked like this. Man talking fast is an honest man. Dad was a man who never tried to sell anybody anything."

It was now quite dark in the room. We sat in the darkness for a while without talking, and then Huston got up and went over to the light switch. He asked if we were ready for light, and then snapped the switch. He was revealed in the sudden yellow brightness, standing motionless, a look of bewilderment on his face. "I hate this scene," he said. "Let's go out and get something to eat."

Huston finished his drink in a gulp, set the glass down, and put a gray homburg on his head, and the three of us rode down in the elevator. It was a warm, drizzly evening. The Waldorf doorman got us a cab, and Huston told the driver to take us to "21." He raised one of the jump seats and rested his knees against it. "You know, I just love New York when summer is coming in," he said, emphasizing each word possessively. "Everything begins to slow down a little. And later on, the clatter and hassling sort of comes to a stop. And the city is quiet. And you can take walks!" he said in a tone of amazement. "And you pass bars!" he said, as though this were even more astonishing. "And the doors of the bars are open," he said, holding up his hands, palms toward each other, framing a picture of an open door. "You can go anywhere alone, and yet you're never alone in the summer in New York," he said, and dropped his hands to his lap.

Huston first came to New York in 1919, when he was thirteen, to spend the summer with his father, who had been divorced from his mother several years before. John was born in the town of Nevada, Missouri, and had spent the better part of his childhood with his mother, first in Weatherford, Texas, and then in Los Angeles. His mother, who died in 1938, had been a newspaperwoman. For three years before coming to New York, Huston had been bedridden with what was called an enlarged heart, and he also suffered from an obscure kidney ailment. When he recovered, he went to visit his father. He had a marvelous birthday in New York the summer he turned eighteen, he said. He had come east again from Los Angeles, where he had won the amateur lightweight boxing championship of California, and he had moved into a small fourth-floor apartment on Macdougal Street; the apartment above was occupied by Sam Jaffe (the actor who, years later, played the part of the German safecracker in *The Asphalt Jungle*). Huston's father, who was appearing on Broadway in *Desire Under the Elms*, came to the birthday celebration. Jaffe had asked John what he wanted as a present, and he had said a horse. "Well," he said, "Sam" (and there was great affection in his pronouncing of the name), "the kindest, most retiring guy in the world, had gone out and bought the oldest, saddest, most worn-out gray mare. It was all wonderful. The best birthday I ever had. Art, don't you just love New York in the summer?"

Not to live in, Fellows said, and Huston said, with a sigh, that it *would* be difficult to keep horses in New York, and besides, when you came right down to it, he really liked the way of life in the motion-picture world.

"It's the jungle," he said. "It appeals to my nature. Louella Parsons and her atavistic nonsense. I really like Louella. She's part of the jungle. It's more than a place where streets are named after Sam Goldwyn and buildings after Bing Crosby. There's more to it than pink Cadillacs with leopard-skin seat covers. It's the jungle, and it harbors an industry that's one of the biggest in the country. A closed-in, tight, frantically inbred, and frantically competitive jungle. And the rulers of the jungle are predatory and fascinating and tough. L. B. Mayer is one of the rulers of the jungle." He lowered his voice impressively. "I like L. B. He's a ruler now, but he has to watch his step or he'll be done in. He's shrewd. He's big business. He didn't know a thing about horses, but when he took up horses, he built up one of the finest stables in the country. L. B. is tough. He's never trying to win the point you're talking about. His aim is always long-range—to keep control of the studio. He loves Dore. But someday he'll destroy Dore. L. B. is sixty-five. And he's pink. And healthy. And smiling. Dore is about twenty years younger. And he looks old. And sick. And worried. Because L. B. guards the jungle like a lion. But the very top rulers of the jungle are here in New York. Nick Schenck, the president of Loew's, Inc., the ruler of the rulers, stays here in New York and smiles, watching from afar, from behind the scenes, but he's the real power, watching the pack closing in on one or another of the lesser rulers, closing in, ready to pounce! Nick Schenck never gets his picture in the papers, and he doesn't go to parties, and he avoids going out in public, but he's the *real* king of the pack. And he does it all from New York!" He uttered an eerie, choked laugh through clenched teeth. "God, are they tough!"

The taxi drew up before "21." "Mr. Huston!" the doorman said, and Huston shook hands with him. "Welcome back, Mr. Huston."

It was close to midnight when Huston and Fellows and I emerged. Huston suggested that we walk, because he loved to walk at that time of the night. The drizzling rain had stopped and the air was clear, but the street was wet and shining. Huston said he wanted to go over to Third Avenue, because he liked to see into the bars there and because nobody over there looked like a studio vice president. We headed for Third Avenue.

As we walked down Third Avenue, Huston started to take fast, important strides. "You know what I like about making this picture, Art?" he said. "I'm going to be out in the country. On location." Walking along, he glanced into shop windows displaying silver plate and paintings. He stopped for a moment in front of the dusty window of an art shop and looked at the reproduction of a painting. "Modigliani," he said. "I used to spend hours in this town looking at Modiglianis." He had once done considerable painting himself, he said, but in recent years he had done little. We moved on, and suddenly, in the middle of the wet, glistening walk, we saw a man lying motionless, facedown. He had one arm in the sleeve of a torn, brown overcoat, and the other arm was underneath him, the empty sleeve of the coat folded back over his head. His shoes were scuffed and ragged and they were pointed in toward each other. Half a dozen spectators stood gazing silently at the figure on the sidewalk. Huston immediately took charge. Putting his hands in his trouser pockets, he gave a peculiar quarter twist to his body. He took just a moment to push his hat back on his head, then squatted beside the motionless figure. He let another moment go by without doing anything, while the group of spectators grew. Everyone was very quiet. Huston lifted the hand in the overcoat sleeve and felt for the pulse. The Third Avenue el rattled noisily by overhead, and then there was silence again. Huston held the man's wrist for quite a long time, never looking up at the crowd. Then he took quite a long time putting the man's arm back in its original position. Huston rose slowly to his feet. He fixed his hat forward. He put his hands back in his pockets. Then he turned to the audience, and, projecting his words with distinct care, he said, "He's—just—fine!" He gave a thick, congested laugh through his closed teeth. He tapped his hat forward with satisfaction and jauntily led us away. It was a scene from a Huston movie.

Five weeks later, Huston was back at the Waldorf, in the same suite. When he telephoned me this time, he sounded cheerful. During his absence, *The Asphalt Jungle* had opened in New York and had been reviewed enthusiastically, but he didn't mention that; what he felt good about was that he had just bought a new filly from Calumet Farms. When I went over to see him that evening, he was alone in his suite. Two days before, he had found a superb location for *The Red Badge of Courage* outside Nashville.

When Huston had returned to the studio after his Eastern trip, he told me, he had found that no preparations at all were under way for *The Red Badge of Courage*. "Those uniforms just weren't being made!" he said with amazement. "I went to see L. B. and L. B. told me he had no faith in the picture. He didn't believe it would make money. Gottfried and I went to see Dore. We found Dore at home, sick in bed. The moment we entered, he said, 'Boys, we'll make this picture!' Maybe it was Nick Schenck who gave Dore the go-ahead sign. Anyway, that night Dore wrote a letter to L. B. and said in the letter he thought M-G-M ought to make the picture. And the next morning L. B. called us in and talked for six hours about why this picture would not make any money. You know, I like L. B. He said that Dore was a wonderful boy, that he loved Dore like his own son. And he said that he could not deny a boy who wrote that kind of letter to him. And when we came out of L. B.'s office, the studio was bubbling, and the uniforms were being made!" Huston chortled. He and Reinhardt had found a marvelous actor named Royal Dano to play the part of the Tattered Man, he said, and Dano had that singular quality that makes for greatness on the screen. Charlie Chaplin and Greta Garbo have that quality, he said. "The screen exaggerates and magnifies whatever it is that a great actor has," he said. "It's almost as though greatness is a matter of quality rather than ability. Dad had it. He had that something people felt in him. You sense it every time you're near it. You see it in Audie Murphy's eyes. It's like a great horse. You go past his stall and you can feel the vibration in there. You can feel it. So I'm going to make the picture, kid. I'm going to direct it on horseback. I've always wanted to direct a picture on horseback."

The expenses at the Nashville site, he said, would be less than at the one he had originally hoped to get, in Leesburg, Virginia, and its terrain lent itself perfectly to the kind of photography he wanted—a sharply contrasting black-and-white approximating the texture and atmosphere of the Brady photographs of the Civil War.

"Tell you what," Huston said, in his amazed tone. "I'm going to show you how we make a picture! And then you come out to Hollywood and you can see everything that happens to the picture out there! And you can meet Gottfried! And Dore! And L. B.! And everybody! And you can meet my horses! Will you do it?"

I said I would.

Several weeks later, Huston telephoned again, this time from California. He was going to start making *The Red Badge of Courage* in a month, and the location was not going to be in Tennessee, after all, but on his own ranch, in the San Fernando Valley. He didn't sound too happy about it. "You'd better get out here for the fireworks," he said. "We're going to have the Civil War right here on the Coast."

When I arrived on the West Coast, Huston set about arranging for me to meet everybody who had anything to do with *The Red Badge of Courage*. The day I met Gottfried Reinhardt, the thirty-nine-year-old producer of *The Red Badge of Courage*, he was sitting in his office at the Metro-Goldwyn-Mayer studio, in Culver City, studying the estimated budget for the picture. It would be the 1,512th picture to be put into production since Metro-Goldwyn-Mayer was founded, on May 24, 1924. The mimeographed booklet containing the estimate was stamped Production No. 1512. (The estimate, I learned later on, informed Reinhardt that the picture would be allotted nine rehearsal days and thirty-four production days; the footage of the finished film was expected to come to 7,865 feet; the total cost was expected to be $1,434,789.) Reinhardt's office was a comfortable one. It was a suite, which included a small bath and a conference room furnished with leather armchairs. A brass plate engraved with his name was on the door. In his private office, in addition to a desk and several green leather armchairs and a green leather couch, he had a thick brown carpet, a bookcase with a set of the *Encyclopædia Britannica*, and a potted plant six feet high. The walls were hung with old prints. On his desk, near several large cigarette lighters, a couple of ballpoint pens, and a leather cigar box, stood a framed photograph of Max Reinhardt. The elder Reinhardt had a look of gentle but troubled thoughtfulness. There was a considerable resemblance between father and son.

"Where you have your office is a sign of your importance," Reinhardt told me as we sat around talking. "I'm on the first floor. Dore Schary is two floors up, right over me. L. B. is also two floors up. I have a washbasin but no shower in my office. Dore has a shower but no bathtub. L. B. has a shower *and* a bathtub. The kind of bath facilities you have in your office is another measure of the worth of your position." He smiled sardonically. "An important director is almost as important as a producer," he continued, getting up and straightening one of the prints. "John's office is a corner one, like mine."

Reinhardt is a paunchy man with a thick mane of wavy brown hair; in his cocoa-brown silk shantung suit, he looked like a teddy bear. There was a cigar in his mouth and an expression of profound cynicism on his face. A heavy gold key chain hung in a deep loop from under his coat to a trouser pocket. He speaks with a German accent but without harshness, and his words come out pleasantly, in an even, regretful-sounding way. "We promised Dore we would make our picture for one million five or under, and that we would make it in about thirty days," he said, sitting down at his desk again. He put a hand on the estimate and sighed heavily. "The producer's job is to save time and money." He bobbed his head as he talked. A strand of hair fell over his face. He replaced it and puffed at his cigar in a kind of restrained frenzy. Then he removed the cigar and, bobbing his head again, said, "When you tell people you have made a picture, they do not ask, 'Is it a good picture?' They ask, 'How many days?'" He tapped the ash from his cigar tenderly into a tray and gave another heavy sigh.

Reinhardt, who was born in Berlin, arrived in the United States in 1932, at the age of nineteen, for a visit. He had been over here a few months when Hitler came to power in Germany, and he decided to stay. Ernst Lubitsch, who had worked with the elder Reinhardt in Europe, offered Gottfried a job, without pay, at Paramount, as his assistant on a film version of Noel Coward's *Design for Living*, starring Fredric March, Miriam Hopkins, and Gary Cooper. In the fall of 1933, Reinhardt moved to Metro, as a hundred-and-fifty-dollar-a-week assistant to Walter Wanger, then a producer at that studio. Not long afterward, Wanger left and Reinhardt was made assistant to Bernard Hyman, who was considered a right-hand man of Irving Thalberg. Reinhardt became first a film writer (*The Great Waltz*) and then, in 1940, a producer (*Comrade X*, with Clark Gable and Hedy Lamarr; *Rage in Heaven*, with Ingrid Bergman and Robert Montgomery; *Two-Faced Woman*, with Greta Garbo, the last picture she appeared in). In 1942, he went into the Army. He worked on Signal Corps films for four years, and then returned to Metro and produced pictures featuring some of the studio's most popular stars, including Clark Gable and Lana Turner. His recent pictures, however, had not been regarded as box-office hits by the studio. At the age of seventy-two, Reinhardt's mother, a celebrated German actress named Else Heims, is still appearing in plays in Berlin. His father, who died eight years ago, came to Hollywood in 1934 to direct a stage production of *A Midsummer Night's Dream* at the Hollywood Bowl. (The production became famous because it presented an unknown young woman named Olivia de Havilland, who had never acted in public before, as a last-minute replacement for the star, who, for some reason or other, was unable to go on.) Max Reinhardt was then invited by Warner Bros. to direct a movie production of *A Midsummer Night's Dream*. This picture was not a hit. For the next five years, he ran a Hollywood school known as Max Reinhardt's Workshop; for a short while in 1939, John Huston conducted a course in screenwriting there. Max Reinhardt never got another directorial job in the movies. For many months he tried to obtain an appointment with L. B. Mayer, but Mayer was always too busy to see him.

At Metro-Goldwyn-Mayer, Gottfried Reinhardt had witnessed a succession of struggles for power among the executives at the studio. He had learned many lessons simply by watching these battles, he told me. "M-G-M is like a medieval monarchy," he said. "Palace revolutions all the time." He leaned back in his swivel chair. "L. B. is the king. Dore is the prime minister. Benny Thau, an old Mayer man, is the foreign minister and makes all the important deals for the studio, like the loan-outs of big stars. L. K. Sidney, one vice president, is the minister of the interior, and Edgar J. Mannix, another vice president, is lord privy seal, or, sometimes, minister without portfolio. And John and I are loyal subjects." He bobbed his head and gave a cynical laugh. "Our king is not without power. I found, with *The Red Badge of Courage*, that you need the king's blessing if you want to make a picture. I have the king's blessing, but it has been given with large reservations." He looked at me over his cigar. "Our picture must be a commercial success," he said flatly. "And it must be a *great* picture."

There was a stir in Dave Chasen's Restaurant in Beverly Hills when Dore Schary walked in. Chasen's is run by the former stage comedian whose name it bears, and it is popular with people in the motion-picture industry. The restaurant is divided into several sections. The first one, facing directly upon the entrance, contains semicircular booths. This section leads to a long bar opposite another section of booths. There are additional sections behind and to the sides of the first two. The headwaiter immediately led Schary to a front booth. Two waiters took up sentrylike positions there, facing each other across the table. All the other patrons focused their attention on Schary. They seemed to be looking around at everybody except the people they were with and with whom they were managing to carry on conversations.

"I'll read you Ben's letter," a man near us was saying. "He writes, 'Whenever I think of Byzantium, I remember you. I hope you survive the court intrigues of Hollywood's twilight, and when the place crumbles, may you fall from a throne.'"

"I have news for you," said his companion. "It's not twilight yet. It's only smog."

"I have news for *you*," the first man said, staring without restraint at Schary. "Ben will be back here. He *likes* the court intrigues."

Schary was not a bit self-conscious. He had an aura of immense self-assurance, as though he had reached a point where he could no longer be affected by anything that might happen in Chasen's. He is an optimistic man, and he was talking to me optimistically about the movies. He respected foreign movies, he said, but he believed that the American picture industry provided more entertainment and enlightenment than any other moviemakers in the world. "Our scope is international," he said. "Our thinking is international, and our creative urges and drives are constantly being renewed with the same vigor that renews so many things in the American way of life." The motion-picture community generically referred to as Hollywood, he told me, is no different from any other American community that is dominated by a single industry. "We're the same as Detroit," he said. "We just get talked about more, that's all." He was almost the only man in Chasen's who was not at that moment looking around at someone other than the person he was talking to.

Dave Chasen, a small, solemn man with soft, wistful eyes, came over and told Schary how happy he was to see him there.

"How are you, doll?" Schary said.

"You're looking good," Chasen said sadly.

Schary gave him a genial grin and went on talking to me about the picture industry. A man who seems to be favorably disposed toward the entire world, Schary has a chatty, friendly, homespun manner reminiscent of the late Will Rogers, but there is in it a definite hint of a firm-minded and paternalistic Sunday School teacher. He is six feet tall, and he has a big head, a high, freckled forehead, and a large nose, shaped like a Saint Bernard's. He spoke earnestly, as though trying to convey a tremendous seriousness of purpose about his work in motion pictures.

"A motion picture is a success or a failure at its very inception," he told me. "There was resistance, great resistance, to making *The Red Badge of Courage*. In terms of cost and in other terms. This picture has no women. This picture has no love story. This picture has no single incident. This is a period picture. The story—well, there's no story in this picture. It's just the story of a boy. It's the story of a coward. Well, it's the story of a hero." Schary apparently enjoyed hearing himself talk. He was obviously in no hurry to make his point. "These are the elements that are considered important in determining success or failure at the box office," he said, and paused, as if he felt slightly bewildered by the point he was trying to make. He finally said that there had been successful pictures that did not have these so-called important elements. *Crossfire*, which he had made, was one, and *All Quiet on the Western Front* was another. "Lew Ayres was the German equivalent of our boy," he said. "I'll almost bet you that Remarque knew *The Red Badge of Courage*. In the main, when you set out to make a picture, you say, 'I just have a hunch about this picture.' And that's what I felt about this one. Call it instinct if you will. I felt that this picture is liable to be a wonderful picture and a commercial success."

A man who had been standing at the bar picked up his martini and strolled over to a front booth near us. "I have a great story for you," he said to the group seated there. "This actor comes back from a funeral and he's bawling and carrying on, the tears streaming down his face. So his friend tells him he never saw anybody take a funeral so hard. The actor says, 'You should have seen me at the grave!'" The storyteller gave an explosive burst of self-appreciation. He took a sip of his martini and caressed the stem of the glass. "This old actor dies," he said, his eyes moving away from his audience as Walter Pidgeon entered with a large party and was seated in the front section. "Two other old actors come to see him laid out in the coffin. 'Joe looks terrific,' says one. 'Why not?' says the other one. 'He just got back from Palm Springs!'"

Schary began talking about L. B. Mayer. "I know Mayer," he said. "I know this man. I know Mayer because my father was like him. Powerful. Physically very strong. Strong-tempered and willful. Mayer literally *hits* people. But my father made this guy look like a May party." He gave me an easy grin.

Just then, a young man rushed over to the table, grabbed Schary's hand, and cried, "Dore! Wonderful to see you, Dore!" He held on to

Schary's hand, giving him an incredulous, admiring stare. "You look wonderful, Dore! You look wonderful!"

"Sweetie, how are ya?" Schary said amiably.

The young man continued to stare at Schary; he seemed to be waiting for confirmation of something. Then he said, "You remember me, Dore! Dave Miller!"

"Of course, doll," Schary said.

"RKO!" Miller announced, as though he were calling out a railroad stop, and in the same tone he announced that he was directing a picture at Columbia. Schary gave him a broad, understanding grin.

Miller shook his head unbelievingly several times and then, reluctantly, started to back away. "You're doing wonderful things now, Dore. Wonderful! The best of everything to you, Dore," he said. "The best."

The maze of paths followed by all the individuals at M-G-M who work together to make a motion picture led inexorably to the office of Louis B. Mayer, and I found him there one day, behind a series of doors, talking to Arthur Freed, a producer of musicals for the studio. Mayer's office was about half as large as the lounge of the Radio City Music Hall, and he sat behind a huge cream-colored desk overlooking a vast expanse of peach-colored carpet. The walls of the office were paneled in cream-colored leather, and there was a cream-colored bar, a cream-colored fireplace with cream-colored fire irons, cream-colored leather chairs and couches, and a cream-colored grand piano. Behind Mayer's desk stood an American flag and a marble statue of the M-G-M lion. The desk was covered with four cream-colored telephones, a prayer book, several photographs of lions, a tintype of Mayer's mother, and a statuette of the Republican Party's elephant. The big desk hid most of Mayer, but I could see his powerful shoulders, decked in navy blue, and a gay, polka-dot bow tie that almost touched his chin. His large head seems set upon the shoulders, without an intervening neck. His hair is thick and snow white, his face is ruddy, and his eyes, behind glasses with amber-colored frames, stared with a sort of fierce blankness at Freed, who was showing him a report on the box-office receipts of his latest musical, then playing at the Radio City Music Hall.

"Great! I saw it!" Mayer said, sweeping Freed back with his arm. "I said to you the picture would be a wonderful hit. In here!" he cried, poking his index finger at his chest. "It wins the audience in here!" He lifted his snowy head and looked at the cream-colored wall before him as though he were watching the Music Hall screen. "Entertainment!" he cried, transfixed by what he seemed to see on that screen, and he made the face of a man who was emotionally stirred by what he was watching. "It's good enough for you and I and the box office," he said, turning back to Freed. "Not for the smart alecks. It's not good enough anymore," he went on, whining coyly, in imitation of someone saying that winning the heart of the audience was not good enough. He pounded a commanding fist on his desk and looked at me. "Let me tell you something!" he said. "Prizes! Awards! Ribbons! We had two pictures here. An Andy Hardy picture, with little Mickey Rooney, and *Ninotchka*, with Greta Garbo. *Ninotchka* got the prizes. *Blue* ribbons! *Purple* ribbons! Nine bells and seven stars! Which picture made the money? *Andy Hardy* made the money. Why? Because it won praise from the heart. No ribbons!"

"Hah!" Mr. Freed said.

"Twenty-six years with the studio!" Mayer went on. "They used to listen to me. Never would Irving Thalberg make a picture I was opposed to. I had a worship for that boy. He worked. Now they want cocktail parties and their names in the papers. Irving listened to me. Never satisfied with his own work. That was Irving. Years later, after Irving passed away, they still listened. They make an Andy Hardy picture." He turned his powerful shoulders toward me. "Andy's mother is dying, and they make the picture showing Andy standing outside the door. *Standing*. I told them, 'Don't you know that an American boy like that will get down on his hands and knees and *pray*?' They listened. They brought Mickey Rooney down on his hands and knees." Mayer leaped from his chair and crouched on the peach-colored carpet and showed how Andy Hardy had prayed. "The biggest thing in the picture!" He got up and returned to his chair. "Not good enough," he said, whining coyly again. "Don't show the good, wholesome, American mother in the home. Kind. Sweet. Sacrifices. Love." Mayer paused and by his expression demonstrated, in turn, maternal kindness, sweetness, sacrifice, and love, and then glared at Freed and me. "No!" he cried. "Knock the mother on the jaw!" He gave himself an uppercut to the chin. "Throw the little old lady down the stairs!" He threw himself in the direction of the American flag. "Throw the mother's good, homemade chicken soup in the mother's face!" He threw an imaginary plate of soup in Freed's face. "*Step* on the mother! *Kick* her! That is *art*, they say. Art!" He raised and lowered his white eyebrows, wiggled his shoulders like a hula dancer, and moved his hands in a mysterious pattern in the air. "Art!" he repeated, and gave an angry growl.

"You said it," said Freed.

"*Andy Hardy*! I saw the picture and the tears were in my eyes," Mayer said. "I'm not ashamed. I'll see it again. Every time, I'll cry."

"In musicals, we don't have any of those phony artistic pretensions," Freed said.

Mayer gave no sign that he had heard Freed. "Between you and I and the lamppost," he said, straightening his bow tie, "the smart alecks around here don't know the difference between the heart and the gutter. They don't want to listen to you. Marie Dressler! Who thought you could take a fat old lady and make her a star? I did it. And Wally Beery. And Lionel Barrymore." He leaned back in his chair, one hand tucked into his shirt, his eyes squinting, his voice turning into the querulous rasp of Dr. Gillespie informing Dr. Kildare of his diagnosis of the disease. Then, resuming his natural manner, he said, "The audience knows. Look at the receipts. Give the audience what they want? No. Not *good* enough." He paused.

"Thoreau said most of us lead lives of quiet desperation," Freed said quickly. "Pictures should make you feel better, not worse."

Again Mayer did not seem to hear. "*The Red Badge of Courage*," he said. "A million and a half. Maybe more. What for? There's no story. I was against it. They wanted to make it. I don't say no. John Huston. He was going to do *Quo Vadis*. What he wanted to do to the picture! No heart. His idea was he'd throw the Christians to the lions. That's all. I begged him to change his ideas. I got down on my hands and knees to him. I showed him the meaning of heart. I crawled to him on hands and knees. 'Ma-a-ammy!' With tears. No! No heart! He *thanked* me for taking him off the picture. Now he wants *The Red Badge of Courage*. Dore Schary wants it. All right. I'll watch. I don't say no, but I wouldn't make that picture with Sam *Gold*wyn's money."

In the few days remaining before rehearsals started, Huston had to attend budget and production conferences, he had to examine, with his cameraman and technical crew, the exact spots on his San Fernando Valley ranch where the battle scenes for the picture would be shot, and he had to make a number of revisions in the screenplay, including some suggested by the Production Code Administrator of the Motion Picture Association of America, which had come to him in a copy of a letter addressed to Mayer:

> DEAR MR. MAYER:
>
> We have read the script for your proposed production THE RED BADGE OF COURAGE, and beg to report that the basic story seems to meet the requirements of the Production Code. Going through the script in detail, we call your attention to the following minor items.
>
> Page 1A: Here, and throughout the script, please make certain that the expression "dum" is pronounced clearly, and does not sound like the unacceptable expletive "damn."
>
> Page 21: The expression "damn" is unacceptable.
>
> Page 41: The same applies to the exclamation "Lord," the expression "I swear t' Gawd."
>
> Page 42: The same applies to "Lord knows" and the exclamation "Gawd."
>
> Page 44: The exclamation "Good Lord" is unacceptable.
>
> Page 65: The expression "hell to pay" is unacceptable.

Joseph I. Breen, the writer of the letter, stated that three other uses of the word *Lord* in the script were unacceptable, along with one *in God's name*, two *damn*s, and three *hell*s, and, before signing off—cordially—reminded Mr. Mayer that the final judgment of the Code Administrator would be based upon the finished picture.

Hedda Hopper, in the *Los Angeles Times*, headlined one of her daily columns with the news that Audie Murphy would star in *The Red Badge of Courage*. "The happiest and most appropriate casting of the year took place at M-G-M yesterday when Dore Schary gave Audie Murphy, the most decorated hero of World War II, the leading role in 'The Red Badge of Courage,' with John Huston directing," she wrote. "For a change, we'll have a real soldier playing a real soldier on the screen. It couldn't happen at a better time."

The administrative headquarters for the M-G-M studio is a U-shaped

white concrete building identified, in metal letters, as the Irving Thalberg Building. The steps leading to the Thalberg Building, between
broad, shrub-bordered lawns, are wide and smooth, and they shone
whitely under the midsummer sun, as cool and as stately as the steps
to the Capitol in Washington, as I headed for them one morning. A
taxi drew over to the curb and jerked to a halt. The door opened and
Huston leaped out. He plunged a hand into a trouser pocket, handed
the driver a wadded bill, and rushed toward the steps. He had stayed
in town the night before, he said, at one of his three places—a small
house in Beverly Hills he rented from Paulette Goddard—and he had
expected his secretary to telephone him and wake him up. She had
not telephoned, and he had overslept. He seemed angry and tense.
"Audie's waiting for me," he said irritably.

We went into a large reception room with gray-checkered linoleum
on the floor, and Huston strode across it, nodding to a young man
seated at a semicircular desk between two doors. "Good morning, Mr.
Huston," the young man said brightly. At once, the catches on both
doors started clicking, and Huston opened the one on the right. I
hurried after him, down a linoleum-floored corridor, whose cream-
colored walls were lined with cream-colored doors. On each door was
a slot holding a white card with a name printed on it. At the end of
the corridor, we turned to the right, down another corridor, and at the
end of *that* we came to a door with his name on it, engraved in black
letters on a brass plate. Huston opened it, and a young lady with curly
black hair, seated at a desk facing the door, looked up as we came in.
Huston turned immediately to a bench adjoining the entrance. Audie
Murphy was sitting on it. He stood up.

"Hello, Audie. How are you, Audie?" Huston said gently, as though
speaking to a frightened child. The two men shook hands. "Well, we
made it, kid," Huston said, and forced an outburst of ho-ho-hos.

Murphy gave him a wan smile and said nothing. A slight young
man with a small, freckled face, long, wavy reddish-brown hair, and
large, cool gray eyes, he was wearing tan twill frontier riding pants,
a matching shirt, open at the collar, and Western boots with pointed
toes and high heels.

"Come in, Audie," Huston said, opening the door to an inner office.

"Good morning," the secretary behind him said. "Publicity wants to
know what do you do when you hit a snag in writing a script?"

"Tell publicity I'm not here," Huston said in a tone of cold reproach. Then, his voice gentle again, he said, "Come in, Audie."

Huston's office had oak-paneled walls, a blue carpet, and three windows reaching from the ceiling to the floor. There was a long mahogany desk at one end of the room, and at the opposite end, facing it, was a blue leather couch. Several blue leather armchairs were scattered around the office.

"Sit down, guys," Huston said, and himself sat down behind the desk, in a swivel chair with a blue leather seat. "Well," he said, clenching his hands and resting his chin on them. He swung from side to side in his chair a few times, then leaned back and put his feet on the desk on top of a stack of papers.

Murphy sat down in an armchair facing one of the windows and ran a forefinger across his lower lip. "I've got a sore lip," he said. "'Bout six this morning, I went riding on my colt. I went riding without my hat, and the sun burned my lip all up." He spoke with a delicate plaintiveness, in the nasal, twangy drawl of a Texan.

"I've got the same thing, kid," Huston said, pursing his lips. "Tell you what, Audie. Bring your colt out to my ranch. You can have your colt right there with you, any time you want to ride while we're making the picture."

Murphy fingered his sore lip, as if trying to determine whether Huston's pleasant offer did anything for his affliction. Apparently it didn't, so he looked sadly out the window.

"We'll do a lot of riding together, kid," Huston said. "That's good riding country there in the hills, you know."

Murphy made a small, sighing noise of assent.

"I want you to hear this, Audie," Huston said, nervously unfolding a sheet of paper he had taken from his jacket. "Some new lines I just wrote for the script." He read several lines, then laughed appreciatively.

Murphy made another small noise of assent.

Huston continued to laugh, but his eyes, fastened on Murphy, were somber. He seemed baffled and worried by Murphy's unresponsiveness, because usually actors were quick to respond to him. He took his feet down from his desk and picked up a slip of blue paper one heel had been resting on. "'Inter-office Communication,'" he read aloud, and glanced quickly at Murphy to get his attention. "'To Messrs. Gottfried Reinhardt, John Huston . . . SUBJECT: Hair for RED BADGE

OF COURAGE Production. As per discussion this morning, we are pro-
ceeding with the manufacture of: 50 Hook-on Beards at $3.50 each,
100 Crepe wool Mustaches at 50¢ each, 100 Crepe wool Falls at $2.50
each—for Production No. 1512—RED BADGE OF COURAGE. These
will be manufactured in the Makeup Department.'"

Huston stopped reading, looked at Murphy, and saw that he had
already lost his attention. "Well, now," Huston said, "let's go get some
breakfast. I haven't had any breakfast yet."

The door opened, and a stoop-shouldered young man with enormous, eager-looking eyes came in. He was introduced as Albert Band,
Huston's assistant. Huston moved toward the door.

"Where you going?" Band asked, blinking his eyes. His eyelashes
descended over his eyes like two dust mops.

"Breakfast," said Huston.

Band said that he had had his breakfast, but he would come along
and watch Huston have his.

We went out a side door to the studio gates, where a policeman in
a stone hut looked carefully at each of us as we filed through. "Mr.
Huston," he said.

"Good morning," Huston said, giving full weight to each syllable.

We went down a narrow street between low, gray-painted buildings of wood or stucco, which had shingles identifying them as Men's
Wardrobe, International Department, Casting Office, Accounting
Department, and Danger 2300 Volts. Farther along the street were
the soundstages, gray, hangarlike buildings. We passed a number of
costumed actors and actresses, and people in casual summer dress
who exchanged nods with Huston and looked piercingly at Murphy,
Band, and me.

A portly gentleman in a gray pinstriped suit stopped Huston and
shook hands with him. "Congratulate me," he said. "My picture opens
next week in New York."

"Music Hall?" Huston asked.

"I have news for you," the man said in a dry tone. "Dore Schary
personally produces a picture, *it* gets into the Music Hall. *I* got Loew's
State."

The M-G-M commissary is a comfortable restaurant with soft lighting, cream-colored walls, an aquamarine ceiling, and modern furnish-
ings. When Huston, Murphy, Band, and I entered, about a third of the

tables were occupied, and most of the people sitting at them stared at our party without restraint. We took a table, and Huston ordered orange juice, a hard-boiled egg, bacon, and coffee. Murphy fingered his sore lip.

"How about some coffee, *amigo*?" Huston asked him.

Murphy nodded wistfully.

"Gottfried told me a great story yesterday," Band said, batting his enormous eyes at Huston. "Two producers come out of the projection room where one has just shown the other his picture, and he asks, 'Well, how did you like the picture?' 'Great,' the other producer says. 'What's the matter—you didn't *like* it?' the first producer asks. Isn't that a great story?" Band said with a short laugh.

"A *great* story, Albert," Huston said, putting a brown cigarette in one corner of his mouth.

"I've got another one," Band said. He took a kitchen match from his pocket, scraped the head of it with his thumbnail, and held the flame to Huston's cigarette. "This producer doesn't like the score that has been composed for his picture. 'The music isn't right,' he says. 'It's a picture about France,' he says, 'so I want a lot of French horns.'" Band laughed again.

"Got a newspaper, Albert?" Huston said. Band said no. "Get me a paper, Albert," said Huston. "I want to see the selections." He did not look up as Band went out. Drawing deeply on his cigarette, he looked down through the smoke at the table and brushed away some shreds of tobacco.

Murphy fixed his gaze on the windows along the far wall.

Huston looked at him. "Excited, kid?" he asked.

"Seems as though nothing can get me excited anymore—you know, enthused?" he said. "Before the war, I'd get excited and enthused about a lot of things, but not anymore."

"I feel the same way, kid," said Huston.

The waitress brought Huston's breakfast and Murphy's cup of coffee. Huston squinted at Murphy over his drooping cigarette and told him that his hair looked fine. "You might taper the sideburns a bit, kid," he said, taking the cigarette from his mouth and resting it on an ashtray. "That's all we need to do, kid." He took a few sips of orange juice and then pushed the glass aside, picked up the hard-boiled egg, and bit into it. "Audie, ever been in Chico, up north of San Francisco, near the Sacramento River?" he asked expansively. "Well, now, we'll be going up there on location to do the river-crossing scene and other stuff for the picture. And while we're there, we'll go fishing, kid."

Band returned and handed Huston a newspaper. Huston took a couple of quick swallows of coffee and pushed his breakfast aside. Opening the paper on the table, he said that his filly Tryst was running that day and that he wanted to know what the handicappers had to say about her. He picked up the paper and held it in front of his face. The headline facing us read, "Chinese Reported Aiding Foe."

Murphy stared vaguely at the paper. "I'd like to go fishing," he said.

From behind the newspaper, Huston grunted.

"You going *fishing*?" Band asked.

"When we get to Chico," said Murphy.

At an adjoining table, a young man was saying loudly, "He comes out here from Broadway and he thinks he's *acting* in movies. Today on the set, I'm doing a scene with him, and he says to me, 'I don't feel your presence.' 'So reach out and *touch* me,' I said."

"Look, I know you're busy, I don't wanna butt in, but this I gotta tell you," a roly-poly little man said, going up to the young man's table. "I'm at Sam Goldwyn's last night and he says he's got a new painting to show me. So he takes me over to the painting and points to it and says, 'My *Toujours* Lautrec!'"

Huston closed the newspaper and folded it under his arm. "Let's get back, guys," he said. He instructed Band to place a token bet on Tryst for him, and Band walked off.

Back in the Thalberg Building, Huston invited Murphy and me to see a number of test shots he had made on his ranch for *The Red Badge of Courage*. He had seen the tests and, with Reinhardt and Schary, had made the final decisions on the leading players in the cast. In addition to Audie Murphy as the Youth, there would be Bill Mauldin as the Loud Soldier, John Dierkes as the Tall Soldier, and Royal Dano as the Tattered Man. We trooped downstairs to a carpeted lounge in the basement and went into a projection room that contained two rows of heavy, deep leather armchairs. Beside the arm of one of the center chairs was a board holding a telephone and a mechanism called a "fader," which controls the volume of sound. The first shot showed the

Youth, who had returned to his regiment after running away from battle, having his head bandaged by his friend, the Loud Soldier. Mauldin,
dressed in Union blue, his ears protruding horizontally from under
a kepi, said as he bound a kerchief around Murphy's head, "Yeh look
like th' devil, but I bet yeh feel better."

In the audience, Murphy said in a loud whisper, "I was biting my
cheek so hard trying to keep from laughing."

"Yes, Audie," said Huston.

The next scene showed Murphy carrying a gun and urging some soldiers behind him to come on. "Let's show them Rebs what we're made
of!" Murphy called fiercely, on the screen. "Come on! All we got to do
is cross this here field! Who's with me? Come on! Come on!" Murphy
advanced, and Huston's voice came on the sound track, laughing and
saying, "Very good."

"I was biting my cheek so hard my whole cheek was sore," Murphy
said.

"Yes, Audie," Huston said.

Next there was a scene between Murphy and the Tall Soldier, played
by John Dierkes. The Tall Soldier died, his breath rasping and then
ceasing, and his hair blowing long and wild. The Youth wept.

The lights came on. "We're going to be just fine," Huston said.

Back in his office, where we found Band waiting for us, Huston,
taking another cigarette, said that Dierkes would be just wonderful in
the picture.

"Just great," said Band.

Murphy was back in his armchair, staring out the window as though
lost in a distant dream. Huston gave him a sharp glance, then sighed
and put his long legs up on the desk. "Well, now, Audie, we're going
to have such fun making this picture on my ranch!" he said. "Let me
tell you kids all about the ranch." There was a compelling promise in
his tone. He waited while Murphy shifted his gaze from the window
to him. Huston deliberately took his time. He drew on his cigarette
and blew the smoke away. He began by telling us that he had four
hundred and eighty acres—rolling fields, pasture, a brook, and hills
harboring mountain lions and jaguars. He had paddocks and stables
for his horses, a pen for eight Weimaraner puppies, doghouses for the
Weimaraner parents and three other dogs (including a white German
shepherd named Paulette, after Paulette Goddard), and a three-room

shack for himself, his adopted son Pablo, and a young man named Eduardo, who managed the ranch. Huston's wife, the former Ricki Soma, and their infant son lived at Malibu Beach, and Huston commuted between the two establishments. At the ranch, Huston had a cowboy named Dusty, and, with a good deal of laughter, he described Dusty's gaunt and leathery face and his big, black ten-gallon hat. "Oh, God!" he said, with a shake of his head. "Dusty wants to be in the picture." He coughed out a series of jovial ho-ho-hos. Murphy, who had given him a quiet smile, developed the smile into hollow-sounding laughter. Huston seemed satisfied that he had finally got a response out of Murphy.

The door opened and Reinhardt stood there, an expression of cynical bewilderment on his face, a large cigar between his lips.

"Come in, Gottfried," said Huston.

"Hello, Mr. Reinhardt," Murphy said, standing up.

Reinhardt took a few steps forward, bobbing his head paternally at everyone. "There's going to be trouble, John," he said, in a tone of dry, flat amiability. He chewed his cigar around to a corner of his mouth to let the words out. "The production office thought the river for the picture was a stream. In the script, it says, 'The regiment crosses a *stream.*' Now they want to know what you mean you need hundreds of men to cross the Sacramento *River?*" He bobbed his head again.

"Ho! Ho!" Huston said, crossing his legs on top of his desk. Murphy sat down again. Band paced the carpet in front of Huston's desk.

"Trouble!" Reinhardt said.

"Well, now, Gottfried, you and I are used to trouble on this picture," Huston said. He put a brown cigarette in his mouth. Band held a kitchen match to it. Huston cocked his head over the flame and gave Murphy a wry smile. "They're afraid the soldiers will get their little tootsies wet," he said, with a titter.

Murphy smiled sadly. Band laughed and batted his eyes first at Huston, then at Reinhardt.

"Now, *Albert* wouldn't be afraid to cross the river, would you, Albert?" Huston asked.

Murphy smiled.

"I have news for you," Band said. "I'm *going* to cross it. You promised me I could have a part in this picture."

Reinhardt laughed, the upper part of his body bouncing energetically. As Band continued pacing in front of Huston's desk, Reinhardt fell in ahead of him, and the two men paced together. Reinhardt's gold key chain looped into his trouser pocket flopped noisily as he paced. "Everybody in Hollywood wants to be something he is not," he said as Huston watched him over the tips of his shoes. "Albert is not satisfied to be your assistant. He wants to be an actor. The writers want to be directors. The producers want to be writers. The actors want to be producers. The wives want to be painters. Nobody is satisfied. Everybody is frustrated. Nobody is happy." He sighed, and sat down heavily in a chair facing Murphy. "I am a man who likes to see people happy," he muttered through his cigar.

The door opened, and John Dierkes entered. "Hi, John! Hi, everybody," he said cheerfully, in a rasping drawl. He had a thick shock of stringy orange hair. "Hi, sport!" he said to Murphy. "Hedda sure likes you, sport. Didja see what she said about you today?"

"Did you let your hair grow?" Reinhardt asked him.

"Sure did, Gottfried," said Dierkes. "It's been growin' and growin' for weeks." He sat down, clasped his hands between his knees, and beamed at Murphy. "You learnin' your lines, sport?" he asked.

Huston recrossed his legs impatiently and said that he had just seen Dierkes's screen test. "You look like an ugly bastard," Huston said. "You're the only man I know who is uglier than I am."

Dierkes dropped his long chin in an amiable smile. "That's what you said the first time we met, John," he said. "In London. I was in the Red Cross and you were sure spiffy in your major's uniform. Nineteen forty-three."

"I was on my way to Italy," Huston said. "That's when we made *The Battle of San Pietro.*"

Reinhardt turned to Murphy. "Did you ever see the picture *K-Rations and How to Chew Them?*" he asked in a loud voice. He tilted his cigar to a sharp angle and pointed a finger at himself. "Mine," he said.

"England was just wonderful in the war," Huston said. "You always wanted to stay up all night. You never wanted to go to sleep."

Reinhardt said, "I'll bet I'm the only producer who ever had Albert Einstein as an actor." Attention now focused on him. He said that he had been making an Army film called *Know Your Enemy—Germany*, the beginning of which showed some notable German refugees. "Anthony Veiller, a screenwriter who was my major, told me to tell Einstein to comb his hair before we photographed him. I said, 'Would *you* tell Einstein to comb his hair?' He said no. So we photographed Einstein with his hair not combed." Reinhardt bounced merrily in his chair and laughed.

"God, those English bootmakers!" Huston said. "The love and affection they lavish on their boots! Whenever I go to London, I head straight for Maxwell and order boots made."

Reinhardt got up and went to the door, saying that in the afternoon there was going to be a conference of the key members of the crew assigned to the picture. The cost of making a picture depended largely on the time it took, he observed. The director and his actors might work together only three hours of an eight-hour day; the balance of the time would be spent waiting for scenes to be prepared. Reinhardt wanted to discuss what he called the leapfrog method, which meant having an assistant director line up shots in advance, so that Huston could move from one scene to another without delay. "We bring this picture in early, we will be real heroes," Reinhardt said.

"Don't worry, Gottfried," Huston said.

"I will see you later?" Reinhardt asked.

"I'll be there, Gottfried. Don't worry," Huston said.

Huston gave me a copy of the script for *The Red Badge of Courage* and left me alone in his office to read it. The script was a mimeographed booklet in a yellow paper cover, which was stamped with the seal of M-G-M. Also on the cover were the words Production No. 1512 and the names of the film's producer, Gottfried Reinhardt, and its director, John Huston. A notation on the flyleaf stated that the number of pages was ninety-two. Each shot described in the script was numbered. I turned to page 92. The last shot was numbered 344, and its description read:

CLOSE TRUCKING SHOT—THE YOUTH
As he trudges from the place of blood and wrath, his spirit changes. He is rid of the sickness of battle. He lifts his head to the rain, breathes in the cool air, hears a sound above him.
CAMERA PANS UP to a tree and a bird is singing.
FADE OUT

I turned to page 73, one the Breen Office had found unacceptable expressions on:

> CLOSE SHOT—LIEUTENANT
>
> LIEUTENANT
>
> Come on, men! This is no time to stop! In God's
> name, don't just stand there! We'll all get killed.
> Come on! I never seed sech lunkheads! Get
> movin', damn yeh—Oh, yeh cowards.—Yeh rot-
> ten little cowards!

I turned back to the beginning and settled down to read:

> FADE IN
>
> MED. LONG SHOT—EMBANKMENT ACROSS A RIVER—NIGHT
>
> Low fires are seen in the distance, forming the enemy camp. Trees
> and bushes. A LOW WHISTLE IS HEARD from across the river.
>
> MED. SHOT—THE OTHER SIDE OF THE RIVER
>
> Moonlight reveals some bushes and trees, and a sentry walking
> into view. Crickets sing in the still night. The low whistle is repeated.
> The sentry puts his rifle to his shoulder, stands staring into the
> gloom.
>
> CLOSE SHOT—SENTRY—IT IS THE YOUTH
>
> THE YOUTH
>
> Who goes there?
>
> MED. LONG SHOT—ACROSS THE RIVER
>
> SOUTHERN VOICE
>
> Me, Yank—jest me. . . . Move back into the shad-
> ders, Yank, unless you want one of them little red
> badges. I couldn't miss yeh standin' there in the
> moonlight.

The script took me a couple of hours to read. It included several scenes written by Huston that did not appear in the novel, but for the most part the screenplay indicated that Huston intended to embody in his picture the Youth's impressions of war exactly as Crane had described them.

After finishing the script, I went into a sort of back room of Huston's office, used as a conference and poker room, where I found Mrs. Huston. Mrs. Huston had not seen her husband for several days. She is a striking girl with an oval face and long, dark hair drawn back tight from her face, parted in the middle, and done up in a bun in back. She was formerly a ballet dancer in New York, and is now an actress. She showed me around the room. There were a sofa and several chairs covered in brown leather. There were photographs of horses on the walls. There was a framed picture, clipped from a magazine, showing Huston with his father and captioned, "John Huston—for the last three years a major in the Army's Signal Corps—has produced an important and engrossing documentary film, *Let There Be Light*. His father, Walter Huston, does an equally fine narration for this picture on the crackup and treatment of neuropsychopathic soldiers." There were certificates of awards—the One World Flight Award for Motion Pictures, and the Screen Writers Guild Award to Huston for his *Treasure of the Sierra Madre*, which was described in the citation as "the best-written Western of 1948," and two Motion Picture Academy statuettes—one for the best screenplay of 1948, the other for the best-directed film that year. A silver tray on a corner table was inscribed "To John Huston, One Hell of a Guy. The Macadamized Award from all the Members of the Asphalt Jungle."

Albert Band came into the room. He said there ought to be a lot of fun with the new picture, especially when the company went on location at Chico.

Mrs. Huston said that she was going along to Chico, where she would do some fishing. "I just *love* fishing," she went on, as if trying to convince herself.

Huston entered, greeted his wife, and announced that everybody ought to have a drink. He called his secretary in and told her that the key to the liquor was under one of the Oscars.

"How's the young man?" Huston asked his wife.

The baby was fine, she said.

"Did you bring my car, honey?" he asked.

The car was outside.

"Tryst is running today, honey," Huston said tenderly.

"I have news for you," Band said. "Tryst ran out of the money."

Huston looked astonished and, after a moment, laughed in a strained way. "Albert," he said, "get over to Gottfried's office and find out when that goddamn meeting is supposed to start."

Since most of the film was to be shot about thirty miles from Hollywood, on Huston's ranch in the San Fernando Valley, Huston arranged to look over the terrain one day with Reinhardt and the production crew. I arrived at the ranch about eleven o'clock in the morning, and a few minutes later the crew drove up in a large black limousine. Huston came out of his ranchhouse to greet us, dressed in a red-and-green checked cap, a pink T-shirt, tan riding pants flapping out at the sides, tan leggings, tan suspenders, and heavy maroon shoes that reached to his ankles. Included in the crew were the cameraman, Harold Rosson, a short, stocky, gum-chewing, middle-aged man with a sharp face; the unit manager, Lee Katz, a heavyset man in his late thirties, with thin blond fuzz on his head, a brisk, officious manner, and a perpetual ingratiating smile; the leapfrog director, Andrew Marton, whom the others addressed as Bundy, a serious, pedantic Hungarian-American with a heavy accent and a nervous, solicitous manner, whose job it would be to arrange things so that Huston would not have to wait between scenes; the art director, Hans Peters, a stiff, formal German with cropped hair, who also had a heavy accent; another assistant director, Reggie Callow, a harassed-looking man with a large red face, a bowl-shaped midriff, and the gravelly voice of a buck sergeant; and the technical adviser, Colonel Paul Davidson, a retired Army officer with a mustache, dark glasses, and a soldierly bearing. All were carrying copies of the script.

Shortly after we arrived, Reinhardt and Band drove up in a gray Cadillac convertible with the top down. Reinhardt had a navy-blue beret on his head and a cigar in his mouth. He came over and pumped Huston's hand. "Happy birthday, John," he said.

"Oh, yes. I almost forgot," Huston said. "Well, gentlemen, let's get started."

Everybody was wearing rough clothes except Reinhardt, who wore neat gabardine slacks of bright blue and a soft shirt of lighter blue.

Band had on Russian Cossack boots, into which were tucked ragged cotton pants. Marton wore dungarees and a khaki bush jacket, which, he said, he had brought from Africa, where he had recently worked as co-director of *King Solomon's Mines*. Colonel Davidson wore Army fatigues.

Dusty, the Huston-ranch cowboy who wanted to play in the picture, stood around while the crew got organized. He went into the stables and returned leading a large black horse, saddled and bridled. Huston mounted it, and then Dusty brought out a white-and-brown cow pony.

"I'll ride Papoose, pal," Rosson said to Huston, and heaved himself aboard the cow pony.

"He was once married to Jean Harlow," Band said to Colonel Davidson, pointing to Rosson.

"Let's go, gentlemen!" Huston called, waving everybody on. He walked his horse slowly down the road.

"John can really set a saddle," Dusty said, watching him go.

Rosson started after Huston. Reinhardt and Band followed in the Cadillac. The rest of us, in the limousine, brought up the rear of the cavalcade.

Marton peered out the window at Rosson, rocking along on the cow pony. "He used to be married to Jean Harlow," he said thoughtfully. "Reggie, what do we do first?"

Callow said that they were going to stop at the location for the scene showing the Youth's regiment on the march, to determine how many men would be needed to give the effect of an army on the march. It was Scene 37. All the script had to say about it was "MEDIUM LONG SHOT—A ROAD—THE ARMY ON THE MARCH—DUSK."

"The mathematics of this discussion is important," Callow said.

Katz, whose primary job was to serve as a liaison man between the crew and the studio production office, was sitting up front. He turned around and said, smiling, "Mathematics means money."

"Everything is such a production," said Marton. "Why can't they just turn Johnny loose with the camera?"

Colonel Davidson, who was sitting in a jump seat next to Peters, cleared his throat.

"What, what?" Katz said to him.

"Warm today," the colonel said, clearing his throat again.

"Nothing," Marton said. "In Africa, we had a hundred and fifty degrees in the shade."

"That so?" said the colonel.

Katz turned around again. There were beads of perspiration on his forehead and in the fuzz on his head. "You boys are going to have a time climbing these hills today," he said cheerily. "Hot, hot."

Peters said, without moving his head, "Very warm."

"It's going to be a tough war," Callow said.

The road for the medium long shot was a dirt one curving around a hill and running through sunburned fields. A large oak tree at the foot of the hill cast a shadow over the road. Huston and Rosson sat on their horses near the top of the hill, waiting for the rest of the party to struggle up to them through dry, prickly grass. Reinhardt was carrying a sixteen-millimeter movie camera. A hawk flew overhead, and Reinhardt stopped, halfway up the hill, and trained his camera on it. "I like to take pictures of birds," he said. When everyone had reached Huston and was standing around him, Huston pointed to the bend in the road.

"The Army comes around there," he said commandingly. He paused and patted the neck of his horse. "Colonel," he said.

"Yes, sir!" Colonel Davison said, coming to attention.

"Colonel, how far apart will we put the fours?" Huston asked.

"About an arm's length, sir," said the colonel.

"Get away from my script!" Callow said to Huston's horse, who was attempting to eat it.

Huston gave Callow a reproachful look and patted the horse's neck. "Never mind, baby," he said.

"Gentlemen," Rosson said, "keep in mind we must not have these Western mountains in what was primarily an Eastern war." He dismounted and gave the reins of his pony to Band, who clambered clumsily into the saddle. The pony started turning in circles.

"It's only me, little baby," Band said to it.

"Albert!" Huston said. Band got off the pony, and it calmed down.

"Gentlemen," Huston said. "The range finder, please."

Marton handed him a cone-shaped tube with a rectangular window at the wide end. It would determine the kind of lens that would be needed for the shot. Huston looked at the road through the finder for a long time. "A slow, uneven march," he said dramatically. "The Union colonel and his aide are leading the march on horseback. Looks wonderful, just wonderful. Take a look, Hal." He handed the finder to Rosson, who looked at the road through it.

"Great, pal!" Rosson said, chewing his gum with quick, rabbitlike chomps.

"Doesn't it look like a Brady, kid?" Huston said to Rosson.

"Great, pal," said Rosson.

The two men discussed where the camera would be set up, how the shot of the column of soldiers would be composed, when the shot would be taken (in the early morning, when the light on the troops would be coming from the back). They also discussed the fact that the scene, like most of the others in the picture, would be photographed as if from the point of view of the Youth. Then they got to talking about how many men would be needed for the scene.

"How about four hundred and fifty?" said Katz.

"Eight hundred," Huston said immediately.

"Maybe we could do with six hundred and fifty," Reinhardt said, giving Huston a knowing glance.

Katz said that the column would be spaced out with horses and caissons, and that they could get away with less than six hundred and fifty infantrymen.

Huston gave Colonel Davidson a sly glance and winked.

The colonel quickly cleared his throat and said, "Sir, to be militarily correct we ought to have a thousand infantry."

"God!" Reinhardt said.

"Never, never," Katz said.

"Make the picture in Africa," Marton said. "Extras cost eighteen cents a day in Africa."

"That's exactly fifteen dollars and thirty-eight cents less than an extra costs here," Callow said. "We could change it to the Boer War."

"Is it to be six hundred and fifty, gentlemen?" Huston said impatiently.

"If that's the way you want it," Katz said. "Anything I can do you for."

We went from one site to another, trudging up and down hills and breaking paths through heavy underbrush. The afternoon sun was hot, and the faces of the crew were grimy and wet, and their clothes were dusty and sprinkled with burrs and prickly foxtails. Only Reinhardt seemed unaffected by his exertions. His blue slacks were still creased, and a fresh cigar was in his mouth as he stood beside Huston examining the site for a scene—to be shot some afternoon—that would show the Youth coming upon a line of wounded men, who would be moving down a path on a slope. Huston and Reinhardt looked at a grassy slope that led down to a road and a patch of trees. The distance from the top of the slope to the road was two hundred and seventy yards, Callow told Huston and Reinhardt. The three men estimated that they would need a hundred extras to make an impressive line of wounded men.

Huston looked through the finder at the slope. "The Youth sees a long line of wounded staggering down," he said, in a low voice.

"We've got to have something for these men to do in the *morning*," Katz said. "We can't have a hundred extras on the payroll and have them stand around with nothing to do for half a day."

Huston lowered the finder. "Let's just put the figures down as required for each shot, without reference to any other shot," he said coldly.

Katz smiled and threw up his hands.

"And if we find we need twenty-five more men—" Huston began.

"I will appeal to Mr. Reinhardt," Katz said.

"You have great powers of persuasion," said Huston.

Reinhardt bobbed his head and laughed, looking at his director with admiration.

Callow sat by the side of the path, laboriously pulling foxtails out of his socks. "I'm stabbed all over," he said. "I fought the Civil War once before, when I was assistant director on *Gone with the Wind*. It was never this rough, and *Wind* was the best Western ever made."

Reinhardt was aiming his camera at a small silver-and-red airplane flying low overhead.

"That's no bird; that's Clarence Brown," said Band.

"Clarence is up there looking for gold," Marton said.

"There is a great story about Clarence Brown," Reinhardt said. "A friend says to him, 'What do you want with all that money, Clarence? You can't take it with you.' 'You can't?' Clarence says. 'Then I'm not going.'" Band and Marton agreed that it was a great story, and Reinhardt looked pleased with himself.

Katz was saying that the first battle scene would have four hundred infantrymen, fifty cavalrymen, and four complete teams of artillerymen and horses, making a total of four hundred and seventy-four men and a hundred and six horses.

"More people than we ever had in *Wind*," Callow said.

Huston, now on his horse, leaned forward in the saddle and rested the side of his face against the neck of the horse.

"We accomplished a lot today," Reinhardt said.

Huston said, with great conviction, "It looks just swell, Gottfried, just wonderful."

"It must be a great picture," Reinhardt said.

"Great," Band said.

Huston wheeled his horse and started across the slope at a canter. He approached a log on top of a mound of earth, spurred his horse, and made a smooth jump. Reinhardt trained his camera on Huston until he disappeared around a wooded knoll.

That night, John Huston celebrated his forty-fourth birthday at a formal dinner party in Hollywood attended by a couple of dozen of his closest friends and associates. The party was given by Reinhardt, in the private dining room of Chasen's Restaurant. The host stood near the door. He looked cynical and scornful of everything about him as he pumped the hand of each arriving guest, but he managed, with a half-smoked cigar fixed firmly in a corner of his mouth, to beam with delight. The guests all exuded an atmosphere of exclusiveness and intimacy. It seemed to have nothing to do with Huston's birthday. The birthday, apparently, was merely the occasion, not the cause, of the guests' effusions. Good will was stamped on the faces of all, but there was no indication as to whom or what it was directed toward. As they entered, the guests exchanged quick glances, as though they were assuring each other and themselves that they were there.

At one end of the room, a couple of bartenders had set up a double file of champagne glasses on the bar. Waiters circulated with platters of canapés. Reinhardt's wife, a slender, attractive, sardonic-looking lady with large, brown, skeptical eyes and a vaguely Continental manner, moved with a sort of weary impishness among the guests. She was wearing a gossamer blue dinner gown embroidered with silver. The other ladies at the party—all wives of the friends and associates—were almost as festively adorned, but there was about many of them an air of defeat, as though they had given up a battle for some undefined goal. They stood around in groups, watching the groups of men. Mrs. Reinhardt, with the air of one who refuses to admit defeat, bore down on Edward G. Robinson, John Garfield, and Paul Kohner, who was Huston's agent. Robinson, who had recently returned from abroad, was talking about his collection of paintings. Garfield was acting exuberant. Kohner was a genial, tolerant onlooker. At Mrs. Reinhardt's approach, Robinson abandoned his paintings and, starting to hum, fixed on her a broad smile of welcome. "Silvia," he said, and continued to hum.

"There is a rumor making the rounds," she said, pronouncing each syllable slowly and emphatically. "The men are going to play poker after dinner, and the ladies will be given the brush. You know what I am talking about?"

Robinson smiled even more broadly.

Garfield said, "The girls can go to a movie or something. Eddie, you buy any paintings in Europe?"

"Julie, you are *not* playing poker," said Mrs. Reinhardt to Garfield.

"I have news for you," said Garfield, "I am. Eddie?"

"Not this trip," Robinson said, without ceasing to grin at Mrs. Reinhardt. "In New York, a Rouault. The time before in Europe, a Soutine."

"Last night, I met somebody owned a Degas," said a tall and glamorous-looking but nervous girl with red hair, who had detached herself from a group of ladies and was now at Robinson's elbow. Mrs. Reinhardt and the three men did not bother to acknowledge her remark. "This Degas," the red-haired girl said miserably, "it's getting *out* of the bathtub, for a change, not in."

"You are playing, too, Paul?" Mrs. Reinhardt asked Kohner as the red-haired girl, still ignored, moved back to her group.

"Maybe I'll go to Europe, Eddie," Garfield said. "I think I need Europe."

Mrs. Reinhardt joined her husband. "Gottfried! Did they make the crêpes Hélène, Gottfried?"

"Yes, darling. I personally showed them how," he said, giving his wife a pat on the head. "Mingle with the wives. You must mingle."

"I won't mingle," said Mrs. Reinhardt. "I have an odd interior climate." She wandered off.

Huston, very sunburned, arrived with his wife. In the lapel of his dinner jacket, he wore the ribbon of the Legion of Merit, awarded to him for his work on Army Signal Corps films in the war. "Well!" he said, looking oppressed and slightly alien to the overflowing intimacy that was advancing toward him.

"John!" Reinhardt said, as though it had been a couple of years instead of a couple of hours since they had last met. "Ricki!" he said, greeting Mrs. Huston with the same enthusiasm.

As Huston confronted the party about to envelop him, his face was contorted, like a baby about to explode into tears; then he relaxed into a slouch and went forward to meet his celebrators.

"Johnny!" someone said, and he quickly became the hub of a wheel of admirers. Mrs. Huston, looking tremulous and beautiful, started uncertainly after him but stopped behind the circle, which included a director, William Wyler; a writer, Robert Wyler; Huston's lawyer, Mark Cohen; and Paul Kohner. As Mrs. Huston joined a group of wives, there was a good deal of laughter in the circle around her husband. Cohen, a scholarly-looking gentleman with pince-nez, laughed good-naturedly at everything everybody said. Robert Wyler, William's elder brother and husband of an actress named Cathy O'Donnell, laughed at everything William said. Huston laughed without waiting for anything to be said.

"God love ya, Willie!" Huston said to William Wyler, putting a long arm all the way around his friend's shoulders and shaking him.

Wyler, a short, stocky, slow-speaking man with a self-absorbed expression, drew back and looked up at him. "Johnny, you're getting older," he said.

Laughter, led by Robert Wyler, thundered around the circle.

"Ho! Ho! Ho!" Huston said, forcing each laugh out with tremendous care. "I've had nine lives so far, and I regret every one of them."

At the door, Reinhardt greeted Sam Spiegel, Huston's partner in Horizon Pictures, and Spiegel's wife, Lynne Baggett, a tall, statuesque actress with fluffy blond curls piled up on top of her head.

"So, Gottfried, you start rehearsals next week," Spiegel said, his eyes flickering busily around at everybody except the man he was talking to. Spiegel, whose professional name is S. P. Eagle, is a stout, hawk-nosed man in his late forties with sad, moist eyes, an expression of harried innocence, and a habit of running his tongue swiftly along his upper lip. He was born in Austria, came to America in 1927, was working in Berlin for Universal Pictures when Hitler came to power, in 1933. He met

Huston later that year, when both were looking for work in the British motion-picture industry. In 1947, learning that Huston was looking for fifty thousand dollars, Spiegel got the money and gave it to him in exchange for a promise to found an independent motion-picture company—Horizon Pictures—and to put half the money into it. Spiegel had then promoted, from the Bankers Trust Company in New York, a loan of nine hundred thousand dollars for Horizon's first film. He had gone on to promote for himself an extensive knowledge of what all the other producers in Hollywood were up to, and a proprietorship over Huston that most of them were jealous of. Reinhardt beamed at him as warmly as he had at the other guests. Mrs. Reinhardt welcomed the Spiegels with an intensely playful air of surprise at their presence. Spiegel lingered at the door, stared at the admirers surrounding Huston, and told Reinhardt, without being asked, that he had just finished producing a Horizon film starring Evelyn Keyes, Huston's third wife (the present Mrs. Huston is his fourth), and that he planned to make two more pictures while he was waiting for Huston to complete his Metro assignment with Reinhardt. "Then John will make *The African Queen* with me," Spiegel said. "I get him next, Gottfried."

"Fine," Reinhardt said, bouncing up and down like an amiable bear.

"*The African Queen* can be a commercial success. It will be John's first commercial hit since *The Maltese Falcon*, which was made in 1941," Spiegel said blandly.

"Fine," Reinhardt said, ignoring the implication that *The Red Badge of Courage* would be a commercial failure.

"When do we start the poker game?" Spiegel asked.

"Fine," said Reinhardt, still bouncing.

"Gottfried," Spiegel said, "when is the poker?"

"Gottfried!" Mrs. Reinhardt said.

"Poker?" Reinhardt said. "After dinner."

Mrs. Spiegel spoke for the first time. "What do we do?" she asked.

"You go to a movie or something, baby," said Spiegel. "A nice double feature." He tapped her arm, and they moved on into the room.

Mrs. Reinhardt, watching them go, gave a cry of mock hysteria. "Gottfried, nobody ever listens to anybody else!" she said. "It's a condition of the world."

"Fine," Reinhardt said to her, and turned to greet a couple of latecomers. They were Band and his wife, a pert, slim girl, formerly a photographer's model, whose picture had appeared twice on the cover of a magazine called *Real Story*. The Bands were late because they had stopped to pick up a present for Huston. The present was a book of reproductions of French Impressionists.

"I believe in friendship," Band said to Reinhardt, then made his way to Huston and delivered the present.

Huston unwrapped his present. "This is just swell, *amigo*—just wonderful," he said to Band. He closed the book and took a cigarette box out of his pocket. It was empty. "Get me some cigarettes, will ya, kid?" he said.

Band rushed off for cigarettes.

Dave Chasen came into the room, sucking at a pipe, and asked Reinhardt if everything was all right.

"Fine," said Reinhardt.

"I'll stay a minute," Chasen said, and sighed. "What I have to listen to out there! And everybody wants to sit in the front. If I put everybody in the front, who will sit in the back?" He went over to Huston, saying "John!"

"Dave! God love ya, Dave!" Huston said, giving the restaurateur his long-armed embrace.

"Dave!" half a dozen voices called. "Dave! Dave!" Everybody seemed to make it a point to sound his name, but only Mrs. Reinhardt appeared to have anything to say to him. She told him that she was worried about her black French poodle. "Mocha is so neurotic, Dave, he refuses to eat. Dave, he wants lobster. Can I take home some lobster for Mocha, Dave?"

Chasen said all right, sighed again, and returned to his duties.

At dinner, the guests sat at circular tables seating six, and between courses they moved from table to table, discussing the party as compared to other parties. Everybody was talking about the decline of big parties. People were cutting down on the big parties, they said. When did Nunnally Johnson give that big tent party? Four years ago. The tent alone, put up over his tennis court, had cost seven hundred dollars. The tent was of Pliofilm, and you could look up and see stars in the sky through it. You hardly ever found a party anymore where the host rented a dance floor from that company that rented terrific dance floors. It was easier, and less expensive, to give a party at Chasen's.

"We entertain each other because we never know how to enjoy ourselves with other people," Reinhardt said to the guests at his table. "Hollywood people are afraid to leave Hollywood. Out in the world, they are frightened. They are unsure of themselves. They never enjoy themselves out of Hollywood. Sam Hoffenstein used to say we are the croupiers in a crooked gambling house. And it's true. Every one of us thinks, You know, I really don't deserve a swimming pool."

The guests did not seem to mind what he had said, but, on the other hand, there was no indication that anyone had listened to him.

(MAY 24, 1952)

Coco Chanel

We've met some formidable charmers in our time, but none to surpass the great couturière and perfumer Mlle. Gabrielle Chanel, who came out of retirement three years ago to present a collection of dress and suit designs that have begun to affect women's styles every bit as powerfully as her designs of thirty-odd years ago did. At seventy-four, Mlle. Chanel is sensationally good-looking, with dark-brown eyes, a brilliant smile, and the unquenchable vitality of a twenty-year-old, and when, giving us a firm handshake, she said, "I am *très, très fatiguée*," it was with the assurance of a woman who knows she can afford to say it. Since the Chanel look is causing such a stir these days, we took particular note of what its begetter was wearing: a natural-colored straw sailor hat; a natural-colored silk suit, with box jacket and straight skirt; a white silk blouse, with gold cuff links; low-heeled brown-and-white shoes; and plenty of jewelry—a pearl hatpin, pearls and diamonds in her ears, ropes of pearls about her neck, and, on her jacket, an enormous brooch of antique gold studded with rubies, emeralds, and diamonds.

"The brooch is of my design, and the dress is nothing, *très simple*," she said. "The cuff links were given to me by Stravinsky, thirty years ago. The occasion? Admiration, of course—the admiration I bore him!"

We lighted a cigarette for Mlle. Chanel and asked her how she had happened to be in retirement so long. Her brown eyes flashed. "Never was I really in retirement in my heart," she said. "Always I observed the new clothes. At last, quietly, calmly, with great determination, I began working on *une belle collection*. When I showed it in Paris, I had many critics. They said that I was old-fashioned, that I was no longer of the age. Always I was smiling inside my head, and I thought, I will show them. Now, in France, they are trying to adapt my ideas. So much the better! But when I see some things they call 'after la mode Chanel,' I protest vigorously. There are no potato sacks among my dresses!

"I must tell you something of significance. Fashion is always of the time in which you live. It is not something standing alone. The problem of fashion in 1925 was different. Women were just beginning to go to work in offices. I inspired the cutting of the hair short because it goes with the modern woman. To the woman going to work, I said to take off the bone corset, because women cannot work while they are imprisoned in a corset. I invented the tweed for sports and the loose-fitting sweater and blouse. I encouraged women to be well groomed and to like perfume—a woman who is badly perfumed is not a woman!"

Mlle. Chanel flicked the ash off the last inch of her cigarette, which she held pinched between the thumb and forefinger of her left hand. "Women have always been the strong ones of the world," she said. "The men are always seeking from women a little pillow to put their heads down on. They are always longing for the mother who held them as infants. It is just my opinion. I am not a professor. I am not a preacher. I speak my opinions gently. It is the truth for me. I am not young, but I feel young. The day I feel old, I will go to bed and stay there. *J'aime la vie!* I feel that to live is a wonderful thing."

(SEPTEMBER 27, 1957)

With Fellini

Federico Fellini, the one-of-a-kind moviemaker, came to New York the other day to be honored by the Film Society of Lincoln Center in its annual tribute to a film artist, and here with him for a few days was his one-of-a-kind gang: his wife, the actress Giulietta Masina (star of the Fellini movies *La Strada, Nights of Cabiria,* and *Giulietta of the Spirits*); Marcello Mastroianni (star of the Fellini movies *La Dolce Vita, 8½,* and *Ginger and Fred,* a still uncompleted one, in which he appears with Miss Masina); the actress Anouk Aimée (star of *La Dolce Vita* and *8½,* and also well known for her Claude Lelouch-directed movie *A Man and a Woman*); and various advisers, helpers, and experts on things American and many other things. We hadn't seen Fellini and the gang in several years, and so we were delighted when Fellini asked us to join them as they set out, the morning after their arrival, in a cavalcade of limos heading for Darien, Connecticut, and the country home of Dorothy Cullman, chairman of the F.S. of L.C., who had invited the whole gang, including us, for a typical Sunday-afternoon visit to her remodelled eighteenth-century colonial house with grounds and pool. The visit was scheduled to include the obligatory swim, the quintessential tour of what-was-there-before and what-is-there-now, and a good meal. Fellini, gray-haired, ageless as ever, and nattily decked out in as preppy an outfit—navy-blue blazer with gold buttons, gray slacks, black loafers, white shirt, red silk tie—as has ever appeared in Darien, directed us to sit in the limo with him, Miss Masina (she was up front with the driver), Miss Aimée, and Mastroianni. Northward we went, followed by the others, who included a full complement of tribute workers, an admirably efficient bunch: Joanna Ney, public relations; Vivian Treves, interpreter; and Wendy Keys, coproducer, with Joanne Koch, of the whole shebang, to be put on in Avery Fisher Hall the following night. There were lots of high-spirited "*Ciao!*"s and laughter and the Italian equivalents of "Get a horse!" from those in our limo to those in the one behind us, and then Fellini settled down. He called to his wife up front, asking whether she was tired, and she replied, keeping her eyes on the road ahead, that she was never tired when she was happy, and she was happy. Fellini gave affectionate pats to the rest of us.

"This is the first time we are all together in New York," he said. "And now we go to Conneckticut," he added, giving a phonetic rendition that was used comfortably by everybody thereafter.

"When we see each other, it is always the same," Miss Aimée said. More pats from Fellini, reciprocal pats from Miss Aimée, pats from Mastroianni to both of them. Mastroianni, who was wearing a cream-colored Panama hat, adjusted it to a more rakish angle. He was wearing an impeccable, creaseless cream-colored linen suit, a black-and-white striped shirt, and a black tie.

"Anouk is a good fellow," Fellini said, in his most playful manner. "She is a famous actress who makes Western pictures," he went on, to us.

"Is that Conneckticut?" Mastroianni asked, pointing out the window at New Jersey as we drove up the Henry Hudson Parkway.

Fellini pointed in the opposite direction, at Grant's Tomb, and we identified it for him.

"Cary?" Miss Aimée asked, looking stricken.

We explained Ulysses S., and everybody looked relieved.

"We go to swim, and we will have a big lunch," Fellini said. "Soon we will see Conneckticut."

We asked Mastroianni whether he had seen any of the rushes of *Ginger and Fred*, which is not about Rogers and Astaire but about two dancers who call themselves Ginger and Fred.

Mastroianni said he never goes to see rushes, because they are shown at night, after shooting, at the time he likes to go out to dinner. "Anyway, is *his* problem," he said, with a Mastroianni-charming smile-cum-shrug at Fellini.

"Is *my* problem," Fellini said. "I leave *Ginger and Fred* with four more days of shooting to shoot, and fly to New York, and is *my* problem to go back and finish *Ginger and Fred*. But is worth it to see Conneckticut."

There was a brief discussion about getting into bathing suits in Darien, and Mastroianni referred affectionately to the fact that Miss Aimée was still thin. More pats from Mastroianni for Miss Aimée, who laughed and tossed her hair back off her face.

"Do you remember, when we made *La Dolce Vita*, on location in that tough neighborhood, I didn't know Italian then, and I heard the young men hanging around and shouting at you?" Miss Aimée said to Mastroianni. "Then I learned later they were shouting, 'Be careful, Marcello! You will hurt yourself holding her! She has too many bones! Give her food, Marcello!"

"That place was full of thieves," Fellini said. "We had to pretend we were leaving, and we had to sneak back in the middle of the night, but the thieves all came back, too."

"Look at the trees!" Mastroianni called out, pointing at the countryside. "Look! There's Conneckticut!"

Not yet, we said.

Miss Aimée told us that she was going to work next making a sequel to *A Man and a Woman*, on its twentieth anniversary.

Mastroianni put on a mock-doleful expression. He told us that in the mid-sixties Miss Aimée had called him in Rome from Paris to say she was going to make *A Man and a Woman*, and had asked him to join her, playing the part later taken by Jean-Louis Trintignant. "She say to me a young director, unknown, no money; she plays a widow; I play a widower. I say no. I made a mistake."

"Two Academy Awards," Miss Aimée said, with a laugh. "Best Foreign Movie, Best Original Screenplay."

Connecticut! Everybody looked out at the colonial-style wooden houses, some painted yellow, most painted white. Mastroianni wanted to know why so many colonial houses were built of wood, unlike the old houses in Italy, which were built of stone.

Everybody looked bewildered.

"We go to the house of Dorothy Cullman, and we ask Dorothy Cullman why," Fellini said decisively, and everybody looked at ease again.

Destination reached: a light-beige-painted clapboard house with white trim, built around 1720, overlooking a slope of weedless, perfect lawn, as long as a city block, that was surrounded by weeping willow, apple, ash, dogwood, and Japanese white pine trees and led down to a waterfall and a huge, pondlike swimming pool with a Japanese-style boathouse in front of it. Here and there on the lawn were wooden sculptures, some of them abstract and some in the shape of people or birds. Up a white-and-tan pebbled walk Fellini and the gang strode— like characters in Fellini movies—toward the house, and we were all greeted on the walk by the hostess, an attractive woman with a very pale face. She wore an ample peach-and-white antique Japanese kimono over a white cotton jumpsuit, and she had on flat-heeled white sandals. On her wrists she wore handsome matching wide antique Indian bracelets of ivory and silver. She extended both hands to the guests.

"An apparition!" Fellini whispered in awe.

"Welcome, Mr. Fellini, I'm Dorothy Cullman," she said. "Lewis, my husband, has just taken our cook to the hospital, because our cook was suddenly taken ill. But I promise you there will be lunch."

Fellini kissed one of Mrs. Cullman's outstretched hands, Mastroianni kissed the other, everybody relaxed, and we were off on Sunday-in-the-country. In a glassed-in addition to the old house, with a complete view of the lawn, trees, sculptures, pool, and Japanese boathouse, we munched on crabmeat on apricot halves and pâté on toast, and chose drinks. Miss Aimée said that water would be fine, but Mrs. Cullman said, "No, no, no, you don't have to drink water—we have orange juice," so Miss Aimée took orange juice. Mrs. Cullman said that it seemed to be hot and the gentlemen might want to take off their coats, but Fellini and Mastroianni said they wanted to keep their coats on. Mrs. Cullman said that she had bought her peach-colored kimono and another one, just like it, to use as covers for her living-room cushions. Glass panels on three sides of the room were sliding doors; Mrs. Cullman slid them open, and everybody exclaimed over the view. Mr. Cullman appeared, wearing bluejeans and sneakers and an Italian striped cotton shirt, and reported that the cook was now healthy, so he had brought the cook back to the kitchen.

Mrs. Cullman sat down next to Fellini and said, "I have only two Italian words—*molto bene*."

Fellini smiled politely and lifted a crab-filled apricot half in a gesture of salute to her. "*Molto bene*," he said.

Mr. Cullman reappeared, now wearing a cream-colored Issey Miyake sweater shirt, cream-colored slacks, and white loafers, and led everybody on a tour of the old part of the house. "This is our pizza oven," he said, with an air of amusement, indicating a large fireplace. "This was the kitchen, and that other room was the parlor, where the minister came, and there are two bedrooms upstairs."

"Pizza oven," Fellini said, looking thoughtfully at Mastroianni, who gave his charming smile and shrug. Everybody regarded the fireplace with admiration.

Gang members from the other limos arrived and joined the tour, which wound quickly back to the room with the view.

"The rooms were small," Mr. Cullman said. "With low ceilings, to keep them warm on cold nights."

"Yes, very cold in Conneckticut," Fellini said sympathetically.

Mr. Cullman looked pleased. "The farmhouse, when it was first built, had only four rooms," he said. "Now we've got eleven."

"Very cold on a farm," Miss Aimée said.

Miss Masina said that the pâté on toast was very tasty, and she smiled gratefully at the host and hostess. Mr. Cullman invited Fellini to take off his coat, but Fellini graciously again said no. Mr. Cullman pointed up to the ceiling beams. "I got those beams from this guy who buys old farmhouses," he said to Fellini. "There's this guy Weiss, in Roxbury. Collects old barns, old timbers."

Fellini nodded respectfully.

"Why all the houses made of wood, not stone, in Conneckticut?" Mastroianni asked.

"Plenty of wood in this part of the country," Mr. Cullman said.

"I thought wood because the pioneers moved all the time—away from the Indians," Mastroianni said, acting the part of an Indian shooting an arrow at Mr. Cullman.

"Yeah," Mr. Cullman said.

Led by the host and hostess, the gang then trooped down the grassy slope to the boathouse, where Mr. Cullman pointed to a narrow wooden canoe hanging under the Japanese eaves. "It's a New Guinea canoe," Mr. Cullman said as the gang stared solemnly at the canoe. "Dorothy bought it there from a native for six dollars. It cost a hundred dollars to ship it home." He laughed heartily, and the gang cooperatively joined in with mild laughter.

On the boathouse deck, Miss Masina pushed some hanging Soleri bells, and they jangled, so she pushed them harder.

"The Whitney used to sell them," Mr. Cullman said. "Who's for a swim?"

Fellini looked at Mastroianni, who looked at Miss Aimée, who looked at Miss Masina, who turned from the bells, and all shook their heads. One gang member's son, age nineteen, said all right, he'd take a swim, and he did, while everybody else, still looking solemn, silently watched him. Mr. Cullman called to the young man, asking him what he thought the temperature of the water was. About sixty-eight degrees, the young man called back. Mr. Cullman said it should be at least seventy-two degrees, and called to the young man to get the pool thermometer and take the temperature of the water. The lone swimmer took the temperature and reported that it was sixty-eight degrees. The silent gang nodded with distress at this news. Mr. Cullman remarked that the pool held a million gallons of water. Everybody looked obligingly bowled over. Then everybody trooped up the green slope toward the house as Mr. Cullman briefed us on the sculptures. "Recognize the bird?" he said. "It's a Senufo piece, from Africa. Dorothy found it somewhere."

Back in the house, the gang again got to work on the crabmeat and the pâté. Mrs. Cullman sat with Fellini and discussed travel.

"You haven't spent much time here, Mr. Fellini," Mrs. Cullman said.

"In 1957, I came for some producers, as the guest of them," he said. "They gave me people to show to me anything I want to see, and they said, 'Do what you want.' What I want was to go back to Italy, so I left. In the plane, as we flew away from New York, I looked down, and I felt very moved, very guilty that I was leaving."

"Do you find when you travel that you're too close to it, and that later you feel differently about it?" Mrs. Cullman asked.

"Language is the medium for the relationship to reality," Fellini said, looking apologetic. "If I don't know the language, I feel lost."

"Would that be true in another European country?" Mrs. Cullman asked.

"Yes," said Fellini.

"Are you sure you won't take off your jacket?" Mr. Cullman asked.

We had a bite of crabmeat. Fellini came over. "Don't eat too much," he said. "These are only the hors d'oeuvres. There will be a lot of food."

He was right. He knew the script. The meal that followed was terrific: curried chicken, seafood pasta, steamed mussels, steamed clams, green salad, white wine, three kinds of cake, ice cream, candied-ginger sauce, fresh fruit, and espresso. Everybody ate for two hours. Then everybody hugged Mrs. Cullman and shook hands with Mr. Cullman and said very enthusiastically, "Thank you very much. Goodbye."

In the limo on the way back, Wendy Keys, the director and coproducer of the tribute, explained to Fellini how the program in Avery Fisher Hall would go—with projections of clips from his movies interspersed with three-minute speeches from Mastroianni, Miss Masina, Miss Aimée, Donald Sutherland, Martin Scorsese, and others.

"It will be pictures, people, pictures, people, et cetera, and, at the end, you," Miss Keys said.

"I want the Rockettes," Fellini said.

The next night was a black-tie occasion. Before the program started, Fellini ran into Mr. Cullman, whose bow tie, with his tuxedo, had spectacular blue polka dots the size of dimes on a bright-red background.

"It is the tie of a Conneckticut Yankee," Fellini said knowledgeably.

The tribute went off nicely. It was pictures, people, pictures, people, et cetera, and then Fellini, who read a short speech: "My dear American friends: You are truly a simpatico people, as I always suspected since I was a child. . . . In the small movie house of my village—with two hundred seats and five hundred standing room—I discovered through your films that there existed another way of life, that a country existed of wide-open spaces, of fantastic cities which were like a cross between Babylon and Mars. Perhaps, thinking about it now, the stories were simplistic. However, it was nice to think that despite the conflicts and the pitfalls there was always a happy ending. It was especially wonderful to know that a country existed where people were free, rich, and happy, dancing on the roofs of the skyscrapers, and where even a humble tramp could become president. Perhaps even then it wasn't really like this. However, I believe that I owe to those flickering shadows from America my decision to express myself through film. And so I, too, made some films and gave life to some flickering shadows, and through them I told the story of my country. And tonight I am extremely touched to find myself here, together with my beloved actors, and honored by the people who inspired me in those old years."

(JUNE 24, 1985)

Rag Trade
(Mario Testino)

Mario Testino, "the world's hottest fashion photographer," according to proclaimers at the opening, last week, of his Mary Boone gallery exhibition, was literally steaming under a barrage of warmer and moister-than-usual air kisses. The white-walled gallery looked cool and elegant, but it seemed to be getting warmer by the second as guests advanced on Testinos priced from twenty-five hundred to five thousand dollars a pop. The opening reception was packed with fashion editors, a few models, and a mixture of young, cute, eye-contact-making, spiky-haired boys and not-quite-mirror copies of Kate Moss. A vague eroticism floated unrestrained over the bodies in the room.

Testino is forty-four, a good-natured, fleshy, large-faced, loosely put together six-plus-two-inch footer, who was handsomely attired in a Bergère dark-green coat, a Charvet painterly-green shirt open at the collar, and black English brogues. He carried a couple of small Contax cameras and took photographs of his own photographs and of people looking at them. Sweating, and wiping his face with a damp handkerchief, he went from Testino to Testino offering comments. "I love being a voyeur," he said. "The whole life. The people. The clothes. The girls. The travel. I visit my mother at least twice a year in Peru. We are a close family. My brother is my business manager. I love my three sisters. I adore my mother.

"I am so lucky to do what I do," he went on, patting his face with the handkerchief and looking lovingly at a picture called *Roving Finger*, which showed a forefinger curled into a woman's cleavage. He spoke in a mysteriously pleasing and undefinable accent, derived over time from his Peruvian birthplace, American schools, and London waiter jobs. "As a boy in Lima, when we visited museums I was always told, 'Do not touch,' so I wanted to touch. Now I touch."

On to *Carolyn Murphy, Georgina Grenville, Kylie Bax and Carla Bruni at Dior*, all partly or completely nude in dressing quarters. Testino took a picture of his picture and said, "Very sexy, these girls. They are very young, about eighteen. I'm fascinated by youth. Young people have this big freedom with their bodies. I like to push them when they start. Then I drop them. There always have to be new ones. It's life. Life is about shedding certain things."

Sheet Marks. On a man's chest, sheet marks indeed. "I'm fascinated by sheet marks," Testino said, dabbing sweat from his face. "I'm often the first one awake in a house full of people, and I see the sheet marks. It's a part of life."

Extrovert, a shot, taken from behind, of a man in a Brazil hotel room exposing the better part of his buttocks. "Brazil is desperate for the perfect behind, perfect roundness—like sculpture," Testino explained, pinching and shaking the shoulders of his Bergère jacket for a breeze.

"He's the best, the sexiest of all the fashion photographers," one pretty young fashion editor said. "And he really loves his mother."

Another fashion editor, one with gray hair, and identified by Testino as "a legend," gave him a longer-than-usual air kiss and a big, knowing hug. "There's smoke coming out of the front door," she said to him with a loudly confident, born-to-the-old-New York guffaw. "You're so hot you're burning."

(NOVEMBER 16, 1998)

Wes Anderson
in Hamilton Heights

Last week, Wes Anderson, the director, was working up in Hamilton Heights, filming the final stretch of *The Royal Tenenbaums*, his third movie (this one budgeted at a "modest" twenty-five million dollars). He celebrated his thirty-second birthday on the set—over a peanut-butter-and-jelly sandwich, his daily staple meal—with his crew and with his actors, Gene Hackman, Anjelica Huston, Ben Stiller, Bill Murray, Danny Glover, and Owen Wilson, who appeared in Anderson's movie *Bottle Rocket* and who also co-wrote the *Tenenbaums* script. Everyone except Anderson ate a regular meal, and then they brought out a traditional cake, a Happy Birthday banner, and presents.

"He's the first director who doesn't scare me," Anjelica Huston said. "This is the first time a director asked me what I think of something. I suggested wearing my grandmother Rhea Gore's locket in the movie."

"Most directors only want it their way," said Bill Murray, who appeared in Anderson's last movie, *Rushmore*. "This guy wants it to be right."

The object of their ruminations may be the most waifish-looking film director since François Truffaut. He has, from the top, nondescript brown hair, sharp features, clear-frame glasses, shoulders permanently hunched in behind-the-camera position, and no noticeable hips. On the set, he was elegantly clothed in mauve corduroy pants, a maroon corduroy sports jacket, and red sneakers.

Bill Murray said, "This guy has his own tailor. It's so nice, for a change, to like a guy and not begrudge him anything."

"There aren't even restrictions in his clothes," Anjelica Huston said. "His pants are custom-made with the crotch coming down about four inches above his knees. He's so skinny, and he gets skinnier by the day. We all want to hold him and mother him. We're so proud of him."

The movie, Anderson said, "is about a family of talented people who peaked early and got short-circuited. They fell apart, and then they try to get together again in new ways. It's not about my own family, but I use tons of stuff about us. I'm the middle of three boys. My older brother, Mel, was a doctor in the Air Force. Eric, four years younger than me, is an artist, the concept illustrator of my movies. We're from Houston, Texas. My parents are divorced. My mom is an artist and an archaeologist, but now she works as a real-estate agent. My father was an amateur race-car driver, but now he's in public relations."

The main set for *The Royal Tenenbaums* is a nineteenth-century red-brick town house a few blocks from City College, near Alexander Hamilton's house. Last week, Anderson was directing a technically difficult forty-five-second outdoor shot at the house with a Panavision camera at the top of a huge crane on a dolly. Most of the key cast members participated, as did a wrecked white 1967 Austin-Healey convertible, a fire engine, firemen, a Dalmatian, and a number of cops. With all this going on, only one person raised his voice. It was the Dalmatian's handler: "On your feet! On your feet!" The dog complied. The shot was a success.

"Very brave shot," the producer, Barry Mendel, said.

"Wes can tell a personal story in a moving but still comic way," Bill Murray said. "Usually, these stories are sentimental or vicious. He makes me feel different, almost like I'm not obliged to be entertaining. I don't find myself pushing or selling my scenes. My own persona is greatly diminished."

"He's so stylized," Gene Hackman said. "This picture has a sense of fable."

An old Indian man named Kumar, who moved from Bombay to the United States as a juggler during the Second World War ("I can still juggle twelve or thirteen plates at a time"), is in the movie, too. He met Anderson in Dallas in the early nineties. "I ran the Cosmic Cup, a health-food restaurant and yoga center with jazz," Kumar said. "As a college student, Wes used to hang out at my Cosmic Cup with Owen

Wilson. Now he puts me in all his movies. I play Gene's buddy in this movie. Wes lifts me up. He has trust, an interesting mind, and humility. That's the beauty of him."

Anjelica Huston said, "I've started smoking again. When I stopped smoking, I was so depressed, I cried for months. Now I'm happy. This picture gives me license to be myself. I'm fatalistic."

(MAY 21, 2001)

Lunch with Agnes
(Agnes Martin)

Agnes Martin, the Saskatchewan-born Abstract Expressionist painter—a contemporary of Mark Rothko, Jackson Pollock, and Barnett Newman—whose tranquil paintings are in the Whitney, the Guggenheim, MoMA, and other museums, abandoned New York a good three decades ago to live spartanly and to work, somewhat reclusively, in New Mexico. Now residing in Taos at the age of ninety-one, she was due the other day to be called on at the small bungalow she lives in near the big Taos Mountain, by her friend and neighbor Tony Huston, in his white pickup truck. He is a master falconer and a screenwriter (of, among other movies, a film of James Joyce's "The Dead" made by his father, John Huston).

"Every now and then, I get to have lunch with Agnes," Huston said. "There's such solidity in her presence. She's not wobbly. She occupies all the space given to her. In 1997, she was awarded the Golden Lion at the Venice Biennale. The next year, President Clinton gave her the National Medal of Arts. Her paintings sell for millions, her dealer says. She spends a lot of time just sitting, painting in her head.

"She finds serenity and power in the Taos Mountain, as so many of us here do," he went on, driving bossily over a sun-blinding, narrow dirt road leading to Martin's home. "Either the mountain likes you or it doesn't, and I'm sure the mountain likes Agnes."

He turned off the dirt road into a circular enclave called Plaza de Retiro. A spotless white E320 Mercedes was parked in front of her place. "Her car's here," he said. He knocked on the door and peered into the window. "But she's not home. She probably got a ride to her studio."

Not long after, he found her, in her studio, in a three-hundred-year-old adobe cottage half a mile away. The studio has white walls, a skylight, and a small window with shutters, and inside it was arranged simply: a work table with paintbrushes and three rulers; a couple of chairs. Hanging on a wall was a painting in progress—a five-by-five-foot white canvas with one blue stripe at the top.

Agnes Martin has a full, strong, sun-browned face that looks as if it belonged on Mount Rushmore. She has gray hair, cut straight with bangs, in what used to be called a Buster Brown style, and she is muscular and full-bodied, with large, strong, thick-fingered hands. She was wearing black sneakers, blue jeans, and a blue tunic of thick Guatemalan cloth, with four engraved silver buttons going down from the neckline. "The silver buttons come from Tony Reyna's shop on the Pueblo reservation—no tax," she said. "I want to get more of these silver buttons. Tomorrow, I'll drive myself over here. I have twenty-twenty vision. A policeman just gave me the driver's test. He said I was a good driver."

Huston and Martin started talking about painting, and he asked whether she allows her dealer's opinions to influence her work.

"No, I paint to myself," she said. "It comes from outside. I don't believe in that inner stuff. You sit and wait. I'm always painting in my imagination. They go so quickly in your imagination. I only work three and a half hours a day. Painting is hard work. It's very hard to paint straight. You paint vertically, but the paintings hang horizontally—there are no drips that way."

The happiest part of making paintings, she continued, is "when they go out the door and into the world. They go straight to my dealer, Arne Glimcher, at Pace Wildenstein. It used to be simpler. They used to fly and get there in one day. Now they have to be in fancy crates, and they go by truck to New York. Takes five days."

It was well before noon. She had eaten breakfast, she said, at her routine time, 6:30 a.m., in the communal dining room at her enclave.

"I don't eat supper," she said. "And I never watch television. I have no television. I have no radio. For news, I read the headlines on the local papers. I listen to music. On CDs. Beethoven's *Ninth*. Beethoven is really about something. I go to bed at seven p.m. I go to sleep when it gets dark, get up when it's light. Like a chicken. Let's go to lunch."

At Huston's truck, she hoisted herself nimbly into the front seat for the drive to a restaurant, close to the Taos Mountain. It had grown cloudy. There was a distant rumble of thunder. At the restaurant, a waitress poured water. Martin drank almost a full glass. "This water is so good," she said. "I'll have the mushroom-filled ravioli. Yesterday, I had bratwurst and sauerkraut." Huston asked whether she ever missed New York.

Without skipping a beat, she said, "They tore down my wonderful studio there. They put a Chemical Bank in its place. I worked for thirteen years in that studio. A sailmaker's loft, on Coenties Slip. It was right on the East River, so close I could see the expressions on the faces of the sailors. That's when I was friends with Barney Newman. We'd talk about Picasso, who was a good painter because he worked hard. But he had a lot of goofy ideas. I liked Andy Warhol, but I was afraid to go visit him because of his friends. Barney would do wonderful talk with me. He'd say about painting, 'It's transcendent.' A lot of people didn't believe him. But I did. It has to be about life. Barney and the other Abstract Expressionists gave up defined space, and they gave up forms. They all liked my paintings. I feel as though I owe them a debt. Barney hung my shows. Too bad about Barney. The doctor told him to stop, to give it up. Because it's hard work. So he gave it up, but he started again, and he died of a heart attack." She drank another glass of water. "This water is so good," she said again.

(JULY 14, 2003)

Nothing Fancy
(Clint Eastwood)

Clint Eastwood recently began directing a new feature film, *Mystic River*, but, just days before starting, he embarked on making *Piano Blues*, one of seven parts of a documentary about the blues which Martin Scorsese is producing for public television. Eastwood was going to shoot *Mystic River* in Boston, but he got his blues film under way at the Mission Ranch, an inn that he owns in Carmel, on California's Monterey Peninsula, where he also owns a great deal of other property. Out there, he seemed to be oblivious to the frantic pressures that usually overwhelm key figures in an imminent big-time movie production, like the one awaiting him in Boston.

"Nobody pushes Clint," said Bruce Ricker, the producer of *Piano Blues* and one of Eastwood's battalion of longtime helpers. "Clint does what Clint decides to do in his own good time." Ricker is a bulky, fast-talking man who helped produce Eastwood's *Thelonius Monk: Straight, No Chaser*. As soon as Ricker arrived at the Mission Ranch—leading camera, sound, and lighting crews—he nervously scurried off to look for a baby grand piano that was to have been installed in the inn's former dairy barn, which is now used for weddings and parties.

Eastwood was already there, standing casually, six feet four inches tall, hands in his pockets, and watching a piano tuner plinking the keys. At seventy-two, he looks youthful, with bright-green eyes and high color in his cheeks. His hair is gray and white, full and uncombed, and that day he had on nondescript, loose-fitting gray pants, a tan cotton windbreaker, sneakers, and a blue-and-gray striped polo shirt, manufactured by his own clothing line, Tehama.

He had driven over from his home in nearby Pebble Beach, where he lives with his thirty-seven-year-old wife, Dina; their six-year-old daughter, Morgan; their year-old pink-and-black pig, Penelope; three chickens; a fat black-and-white rat named Whiskers, who has ten new babies and a much older mate, Norbert; and a caged twenty-something yellow-naped Amazon-green female parrot named Paco, who likes to say, among other things, "Happy birthday" and "I love you."

Eastwood greeted Ricker with a calm nod and a grin. "Piano sounds OK," he said.

Ricker looked somewhat reassured. "Everybody's here," he said quickly. "The crew is unloading the equipment and will be setting up. Pinetop Perkins and Jay McShann"—the Chicago bluesman and the Kansas City jazz player—"are both here. They made it."

Eastwood grinned again and gave the piano a pat.

"Pinetop looks good; he's eighty-nine, you know," Ricker said.

"Eighty-nine?" Eastwood said. "I wonder what he eats."

Ricker looked as though he'd just been paid a personal compliment. "And Jay is eighty-six," he said.

"We'll have some good Kansas City and Chicago stuff," Eastwood said. "We'll try to find out who influenced the great players—blues, boogie, and beyond."

"We're bringing Pinetop and Jay to meet each other for the first time," Ricker said eagerly. "They never played together before."

"I always felt that jazz is the only original art form we have," Eastwood said. "It was very influential in creating the blues, and even rock is a spinoff."

"The blues tempo is the connecting link," Ricker said. "It's what both Pinetop and Jay come out of. We can establish that in the film."

"I want to keep it pure," Eastwood said. "Let the music speak for itself. Nothing fancy."

Mission Ranch sits on twenty-two acres of meadowland overlooking the Pacific Ocean, at the mouth of the Carmel River. Half a dozen chubby sheep graze dreamily on the meadow. Eastwood bought the place in 1986; it was built in the eighteen fifties and has gone through various incarnations, including a dairy ranch and an officers' club during the Second World War. Eastwood rescued it from developers. The guest quarters are in small, renovated white clapboard cottages that resemble dollhouses, with paned windows, white lace curtains, flower boxes, and high-backed white rocking chairs on porches overlooking the sheep. Pinetop Perkins was accommodated in the Honeymoon Cottage.

Eastwood had crossed into the new century with some forty films on his résumé, several of them produced and directed by him, and some with music composed by him. On March 9, he received the Screen Actors Guild Life Achievement Award. He has come a long way from his *Dirty Harry* roles of the nineteen seventies. Among other things, he directed and played opposite Meryl Streep in *The Bridges of Madison County*. For that, he composed the theme "Doe Eyes," which became very popular, and which telephone callers to the Mission Ranch are obliged to listen to when they are put on hold.

Ricker told Eastwood that they could start filming late that afternoon, and then the two climbed into Eastwood's 1976 Mercedes sedan. "Let's go to my house," Eastwood said. "Mumsy will be there. She's ninety-four. Mumsy and I talk every night on the telephone. Last night, I took her to dinner at my golf club; it's called the Tehama, too, after an extinct tribe of California Indians. I built it three years ago because it was so difficult to get tee times at the Pebble Beach club."

On the way, Eastwood stopped at a wooden shack in Carmel Valley that looked like a leftover from one of his *Unforgiven* sets. A sign on the roof read Hacienda Hay and Feed. The proprietor, a spare fellow with spectacles, also looked left over from an Eastwood film set.

"Do you have one of those water bottles for animals?" Eastwood asked politely. "Where's George?" he said, looking around. "I don't see George."

"Dunno, haven't seen him," the proprietor said.

Eastwood walked over to a back door leading into a small yard. A goat munching on something lifted its head immediately and bounded over to him. Eastwood petted it, murmuring something friendly, then turned away. "Ah, there's George!" he said, raising his voice slightly for the first time that day. He bent down and picked up a spectacularly clean white rooster. "Glad to see you, George," he said, cradling the chicken against his chest. He set George down gently on the ground and went back inside to the proprietor, who handed him the bottle and said it cost three dollars and twenty-three cents. Eastwood counted out three dollar bills and a quarter, slowly picked up two pennies in change, and, clutching the bottle, headed back to his car.

The baby bottle, he said, was for Whiskers and her ten babies. "Dina is sort of an animal freak," he said. "Penelope, our pig, was the sick runt of a litter. Dina thought she was going to die, so she brought the pig into the house, and now Penelope is so strong and bold. When she was in the house, she would always be pushing our furniture around, out of place, from one room to the other." He looked very content, driving slowly. "Dina is everything I ever wanted and never found anywhere before," he said. "I'm very lucky. I've got a great girl. She's completely unselfish," he said, with a sudden passion. "It was a wonderful romance. We went together four or five months. Then I knew I could get married again. Instinctively, I knew she was the right person. I was never a guy on a white horse. She's a self-feeder."

The former Dina Ruiz is Eastwood's second wife. When they met, she was working as a news anchor at an NBC TV affiliate. His first wife was the former Maggie Johnson, whom he married in 1953, when he was twenty-one. They divorced thirty years later. They have two children—Kyle, now thirty-four, a jazz bassist, and Alison, thirty, an actress, who recently posed for *Playboy*. Eastwood has several other children: Kimber, thirty-eight, the daughter of Roxanne Tunis, is married and lives with her husband; Scott, seventeen, and Katie, fifteen, live with their mother, Jacelyn Reeves, in Hawaii; and Francesca, who is now nine, is the daughter he had with the actress Frances Fisher. "Dina has embraced everybody," Eastwood said. "She brought the whole family together, with no territorial demands, no big ego, none of that. Francesca and Morgan are great friends. The kiddies—and their mothers— visit each other regularly. I take some of the kids, and Mumsy, too, on our vacations, to Sun Valley or Hawaii, wherever. That's the way Dina feels it should be."

He headed for Pebble Beach, passing several thousand of his own acres here and there. "I never bought any real estate I didn't really like," he said. "I like land, the land out here. I first came here when I was twenty-one and stationed at Fort Ord. I liked it. When everybody was going crazy with stocks and investments not long ago, I stayed with the land. I like the tangible. I like to enjoy things, and I enjoy this land."

He ran for mayor of Carmel, and won, in 1986, he said, because he didn't like the way the city council was handling land, building, and water problems. He served for two years. "I enjoyed it," he said. "I enjoyed presiding over the council meetings, repairing the roads, deciding on water allotments. I liked doing things for people who can't stand up for themselves."

Eastwood's house—with eight rooms, two pianos, and a fully

equipped gym—is a one-story, seventy-five-year-old adobe-and-wood hacienda, with a courtyard that encircles a huge oak and a stand of eucalyptus and palm trees. He parked alongside a black GMC pickup truck, circa 1951, that was, he explained, the one he drove in *The Bridges of Madison County*. One of the doors still bore the name of the character he played: "Robert Kincaid—Photographer—Bellingham, Washington."

Eastwood's appearance in the kitchen, where Paco the parrot greeted him with repeated *I love you*s, didn't seem to slow down the lunch preparations that were under way. He introduced Dina, an ebullient, dark-haired woman. Morgan, a curly-haired miniature of her mother, was helping her make a huge salad. Dina's mother, a pretty, red-haired youngish woman, was cooking cheese quesadillas. Eastwood's sister, Jeanne, with her husband, was preparing a platter of rice and beans. His mother, Ruth, alert and trim in a gray warm-up suit, was smiling benevolently at everybody. Additional husbands, some wearing pastel-colored pants with conservative, long-sleeved shirts, materialized. The dishes were placed, buffet style, on available countertops.

Eastwood took his plate to a corner of the kitchen table, sat down, and pointed to the rats' cage nearby. "I put up the bottle," he said softly to his wife.

"Daddy gives the rats vegetables the way he does us," Morgan said.

"Clint believes in eating vegetables, fruits and vegetables," Dina said. "He's the first one up every morning. He makes fruit smoothies for himself and everybody else."

"He makes a waffle for me," Morgan said. "And a smoothie."

"Clint believes every animal should eat what we eat—the pig, the parrot, the rats," Dina said. "He believes a bug has as much right to be on this earth as anybody else."

Eastwood, chewing, looked thoughtful.

"He's been this way all his life," Ruth Eastwood said. "One time, he had thirteen snakes. When he was four, we discovered he was allergic to dogs and cats, so he collected snakes. I guess he's kind of a supernatural person."

"My grandmother had a small farm, where I stayed as a boy," Eastwood said. "Sometimes when you move a lot as a little kid, animals are your best friends. Animals just like you for you."

He looked at his wristwatch and, motioning to Bruce Ricker, said there was time, before the filming for *Piano Blues* started, to look in on the Forty-Fifth Annual Monterey Jazz Festival, which was taking place that weekend at the Monterey Fairgrounds, a short drive away. Ricker said that Marcia Ball, the blues pianist and vocalist, and the jazz pianist Dave Brubeck would be there, and they could try to find them and remind them to come over to the Mission Ranch for the filming. Neither Pinetop Perkins nor Jay McShann had ever met Dave Brubeck.

"If we get them playing together, it will also show the timelessness of the blues," Ricker said. "Maybe we'll even get some four-handed stuff!"

"That's the idea," Eastwood said.

Back at the Mission Ranch later that afternoon, Perkins and McShann were in the former milk barn, waiting near the piano. They were similarly attired, in white shirts and dark-blue suits. Perkins, dark-complexioned, with a white brush mustache and large round eyeglasses, was impish and restless, and had a black fedora perched on his head, along with a necktie decorated with a piano-key motif. McShann, who has light-brown skin, walked with the help of a cane. Both men watched alertly as the crew got lights, camera, and sound equipment ready.

Ricker told Eastwood that some of the other directors of Scorsese's blues series were shooting with handheld cameras, and using gels and smoke for atmosphere. Eastwood said he didn't want any gimmicks. "A good recording of the music is the most important thing," he said.

He pulled on a blue blazer over his sports shirt and walked over to the piano. Nodding a "Let's go!" to the crew, he sat down at the piano, beside Pinetop Perkins.

"Pinetop, you look fantastic!" he said. "You got a diet I should follow?"

"Heh-heh-heh!" Pinetop laughed, his face breaking up into dozens of creases. He pushed his fedora up on his head a bit, and fingered out a sharp, attention-getting "Shave and a haircut, two bits!" Eastwood laughed along with him and then began to ask deferential questions about the origin of the piano blues.

"We're trying to find out who the great influences were," he said.

Pinetop gave answers in words and in music. "My real name is Joe Willie Perkins," he said. "I used to listen to Pinetop Smith playin' his 'Boogie Woogie.' I tell ya, he was great, so when he died I took the name Pinetop."

"My idea of something to do when I was a kid was to put on Jay McShann playing 'Hot Biscuits,'" Eastwood said. "Didn't Tommy Dorsey take Pinetop Smith's 'Boogie Woogie'—sort of ripped it off, as I recall? Dorsey made a record of it, and it was a big hit."

"Yeh, heh-heh," Pinetop responded, and then he played some boogie and sang, "Come back, baby, please don't go . . ."

He stopped and said that he couldn't get the bass notes rolling with his left hand because, some years ago, a woman had stabbed him in that hand.

Eastwood said that he couldn't get the bass notes rolling in his left hand, either. "And I wasn't even stabbed," he said, laughing.

When Jay McShann sat down at the piano, he showed how he got a steady rhythm going with his left hand while improvising with his right.

McShann said that he was born in Muskogee, Oklahoma. He told Eastwood, "My dad worked in a furniture store, and he'd bring his truck home, and there'd be broken records in it. One day, I picked up the pieces of a broken record and stuck them together. That's how I heard Bessie Smith for the first time, singin' 'Backwater Blues.' That particular record, with her hollerin', 'I can't move no more. . . . There ain't no place for a poor old girl to go.' It got to me. It sure sounded good to me."

Eastwood said, "When I was a kid, my mother, when Fats Waller died, brought home his records and said, 'That's what I call real piano playing.' I listened to 'Your Feet's Too Big' and 'Ain't Misbehavin'' for the first time. I was always trying to save up money to go to Fifty-Second Street in New York, but I never could. Give us a taste, Jay. 'Hootie's Blues.'"

With a very light touch, in contrast to Pinetop's barrelhouse, McShann played and sang:

> She calls me her lover
> And I beg her to
> Ain't you sorry
> That little girl ain't you?

Then he played another version and sang, "She called me her lover; she called me her beggar, too . . ."

"I know those words," Eastwood said, laughing again. "I've used them. I've been in that position many times. You don't know how many lovely young ladies I've met by being able to copy your playing."

McShann started again, improvising.

"Beautiful," Eastwood said. He put his hand on McShann's upper back and rubbed it. "Would you describe yourself as happy, Jay?"

"Pretty much," McShann said. "But sometimes you can't see for lookin'."

They both went "Heh-heh-heh," and gave each other understanding looks.

Two weeks later, Eastwood was in Boston, directing *Mystic River*. He planned to pick up *Piano Blues* again in a few months, when he would be going to New Orleans. After that, Ricker said, they would film Ray Charles, in his studio in Los Angeles. In the meantime, ensconced in Boston's Ritz-Carlton hotel, Eastwood said that he could still hear the blues playing in the back of his head, as he contemplated what he might want to do with the score for *Mystic River*.

"I can do quite a bit simultaneously," he said. "As soon as I can get back to my piano at home, I may write some music of my own that will be suitable for this movie."

During the seven-week *Mystic River* shoot, Eastwood regularly spent an hour, after a day's filming, in the hotel's gym, where, among other routines, he bench-pressed two hundred pounds. As soon as he arrived in Boston, he went to a whole-foods market and stocked up on health foods. He installed a blender and a refrigerator in his hotel suite, and made smoothies every morning. When Dina and Morgan visited, a few weeks into the filming, he made smoothies for them, too.

Mystic River is a co-production of Warner Bros. and Eastwood's company, Malpaso, a Spanish word that means "bad step"; it was named after a creek in Carmel. His crew included many people who had worked with him during the past thirty years.

"They know the shorthand," he said.

Nobody ever broached the subject of Eastwood's retiring. He told me that he once discussed the topic with Jack Nicholson.

"About ten years ago. I was with Jack, driving out to the golf range," he said. "Jack said he was going to do just one more movie, *The Crossing Guard*, and that would be his last. I said I would do *In the Line of Fire* and

A *Perfect World*, and that would be it. Well, he went on to act in about ten more movies, and I went on to act in or direct six more." Then he grinned and added, "They keep saying yes to you, so you keep on going."

Mystic River centers on three working-class friends—Jimmy, played by Sean Penn; Dave, by Tim Robbins; and Sean, by Kevin Bacon—and how their lives have been haunted by an incident of sexual abuse in the past.

"These actors are so good and so enthusiastic, and they've all worked and prepared so hard, it's for me alone to screw up," he said. "There are so many characters, and the story weaves back and forth in time, so those are the only difficult aspects for me to deal with. I stay close to the impression of the story I got when I first read it. Sometimes embellishments just come. The actors bring them to me.

"I've even learned from my screenwriters. Seventeen years ago, when I produced, directed, and starred in *Heartbreak Ridge*, as Marine Gunnery Sergeant Tom Highway training a platoon of jarheads, I say, 'You improvise! You adapt! You overcome!' Helpful words to remember. I always equate a movie director with a platoon leader: he's only as good as the cast and crew behind him."

Someone on the set asked Eastwood how it felt to produce and direct the film but not to act in it.

"It feels great!" he said. "This is much more fun. As an actor, I'm constantly being fiddled with. I'm being told, 'You gotta do this, you gotta do that.' Somebody is always fussing over my hair, somebody else is tampering with my skin. I'm told to go to wardrobe and put on these clothes or those other clothes. Here, I come to the set in my T-shirt and jeans and sneakers, and nobody cares what I look like. I'm getting the scenes I want, and it makes me very happy. I'm free, free of extra pressure, the constant worry over how I'm doing and what I'm doing. As the director, I want to be watching my actors—it's fun to watch the emotions in my actors unfold. If it weren't fun, I wouldn't be doing it."

One day, while directing *Mystic River*, Eastwood watched Sean Penn do a scene in which Penn's character comes upon the body of his murdered teenage daughter. The members of the crew who were watching were visibly shaken by the performance. Someone asked Eastwood how he felt about the shot.

"It's important to follow what you have in mind," he said. "I try to get what I have in mind, but if an actor does what he has in his mind, and if it's anything like what I just saw here with Sean, I'm very grateful to take it. It's like going to a store and looking at all the suits on the rack and seeing one that makes you feel, 'That's exactly what I have in mind.' I never had to work with someone like a Marilyn Monroe, who, I've heard, made everybody wait three hours before showing up, that sort of thing—that would drive me fruitcake."

The actors seemed grateful, too. "He's the least disappointing icon in American film," Sean Penn said.

"The actors have never been on a set like this before," one of Eastwood's longtime assistants said. "Nobody's yelling. Nobody calls out, 'Lights! Camera! Action!' Once in a while Clint says, 'Actione,' perhaps as a tribute to his Sergio Leone days. Usually, he just kind of mutters, 'Go ahead.' He never shouts, or even says, 'Cut!' He just mutters, 'OK' or 'Stop.'"

When Eastwood is directing, instead of peering with the cinematographer through the lens, he uses a digital, battery-operated handheld monitor; it has a seven-inch screen, which is linked to the Steadicam lens. In Boston, he didn't follow the usual routine of watchting video playbacks on the set or having the actors watch or worry about their performances.

"It's like being on a Zen retreat," Marcia Gay Harden, who played Tim Robbins's (Dave's) wife, said. "Everything is so quiet and peaceful."

Buddy Van Horn, Eastwood's stunt coordinator, golfing partner, expert horseman, and second-unit director, started working with him in 1968, on the movie *Coogan's Bluff.* A former stuntman, Van Horn has the kind of weather-beaten, deeply lined face that moviegoers have spotted for ages wrecking wagons, fencing in *Zorro* pictures, starting bar scuffles, and finishing fights. He has also directed some of Eastwood's films, including *Pink Cadillac* and *Any Which Way You Can.* He was born on the back lot of Universal Studios, where his father worked as a veterinarian for the live animals until Buddy was two. He has seven grandchildren.

"Clint is really good with actors," Buddy says. "He knows actors' problems and lets them do their thing. If they need direction, he gives it to them."

Steve Hulsey, who has been Eastwood's driver since 1986, drove the director's nineteen-year-old motor home, a silver Prevost that he likes to use as a trailer on the set, from California to Boston, taking six days to make the trip. "It's got a queen-size bed, a kitchen, a dinette, a TV, and a VCR. We lent it to the Pope in 1984, when he visited Monterey," Hulsey said. "It's in mint condition, with only 62,768 miles on it." Everybody seemed to look upon the Prevost as a sacred family heirloom. (Alana, the twenty-three-year-old daughter of another driver, followed in Malpaso's fuel truck, a one-ton Chevy Crew Cab Dually.)

The movie's production designer, Henry Bumstead, who is eighty-eight and a winner of two Oscars—for *To Kill a Mockingbird* and *The Sting*—scouted locations for *Mystic River* last summer and built the sets for all the interiors. He is known as Bummy to the rest of the crew.

"I wouldn't be working for anyone else at my age," Bummy said. "Clint takes the BS out of making movies."

A common pastime on the set, during all the waiting that is an integral part of moviemaking, was swapping Clint lore: "For recreation, Clint reads medical journals." Or "When Clint first tried to get a job at Universal, in 1953, they told him he was too tall, that his Adam's apple was too obvious." Or "Clint flies his own helicopter. He's had it for twelve years." Or "He jumps out of a helicopter wearing his skis."

One evening after a day's work on the set, Eastwood was sitting in the hotel restaurant with some friends. He had completed his workout in the gym, had made a smoothie for himself in his room, and was nursing a single beer. Someone brought up Bummy and what he said about Eastwood taking the BS out of moviemaking.

"That's flattering, coming from him," Eastwood said. "I guess Bummy means all the moviemaking organization. Bummy knows his stuff. As a designer, he's still the best, still putting out, at his age. The actual ages of these people, the ones who can do what he does on that level, don't mean a thing. He knows how it was with some of the special people I worked with, too, in what might be called the great era of moviemaking. They were terrific people, like John Calley and Don Siegel. They read a lot. They knew a lot. If you asked one of them a question, you got an answer.

"Today, there are many differences. We have a lot more technology, a lot of toys to play with, but they don't necessarily do anything to make movies better. Unfortunately, today, when a movie is successful, they try to make twenty more like it," he went on. "Some people, for example, have wanted me to do *Dirty Harry* again. Harry or Josey Wales were just characters, and they came with a dramatic situation. They weren't like me, and the less they were like me, the more fun it was to do them. However, at some point in your life that kind of thing becomes less challenging. You have to start to grow within yourself, or else you'll start going backwards. I don't understand Sylvester Stallone. I hear he's going to do *Rocky* again. For me, it would look like you're doing it for a paycheck.

"I like to move on," he said. "I enjoyed making *The Bridges of Madison County*. I hadn't read the book. One day, the producer Lili Zanuck called me and told me to read it. She said, 'You're in it.' I hung up. The phone rang again. It was Terry Semel, who was then co-head of Warner Bros. He said, 'There's a lot of you in the character.' So I read the book and fought my way through the fancy, pretentious writing.

"I could see the story. In my mind, however, I saw it as the woman's story. So that's what it became as a movie. What often has set me off in making a movie is a song. I did it once before, in *Play Misty for Me*. In *Bridges*, for the love scene in the kitchen, where I—the photographer, Robert Kincaid—dance with Meryl Streep, I used the song 'I See Your Face Before Me,' by Johnny Hartman. Music often leads me into the sequence."

Eastwood gave no sign of being tired, even though other tables in the room had become deserted and he, like others in the crew, had an early-morning call. "Many people now making movies have been conditioned by television," he said. "I like using close-ups. I'm fond of them. But people today use all close-ups. A lot of them are claustrophobically hard to watch. They crank them in so tight I lose interest. Some of those old black-and-white movies have scope and size. My six-year-old daughter, Morgan, likes them. We were dialing around on television the other night, and we stopped on *Mildred Pierce*, with Joan Crawford. Morgan liked that movie, especially since it had a little girl her age in it. Dina and I took her with us the other night to see *Catch Me If You Can*. She sat there and sat there, expectantly, fifteen minutes into the movie, and then she asked, impatiently, 'When does the movie start?' She wanted some action, instead of close-ups of heads. The other night, we dialed to *In the Line of Fire* on television, and Morgan said, 'Hey! That's you!' But she didn't want to watch it."

The South Boston neighborhood people gathered in small, respectful huddles to watch *Mystic River* being filmed. They gave Eastwood dozens of T-shirts bearing the logos of local organizations—policemen, firefighters, Teamsters, Southies, Celtics, Red Sox—and he wore one to the set almost every day.

"You don't need to bring your own clothes when you work here!" Eastwood announced to his agent, Leonard Hirshan, during the latter's obligatory visit early in the filming. Hirshan regarded the T-shirts with detachment. He was neatly attired in the garb of agentry—blazer, gray flannel trousers, cashmere sweater, and well-worn white sneakers. He announced that he had given up agenting in favor of business managing, which he did exclusively for Eastwood. "In 1961, I became Clint's agent and Walter Matthau's agent, and now I'm wearing Walter's old Mephisto sneakers, which I inherited," he said. He stayed long enough to tell a number of people that the only independent moviemakers who have controlled their own pictures were Charlie Chaplin, Woody Allen, and Clint Eastwood. He reminded Sean Penn, "I used to get jobs for your father, Leo Penn." He pointed out that "Clint never says yes unless he intends to make the picture." He also stated, "I always say, 'Clint doesn't make deals, Clint makes movies.'" Then, looking around, he said, "Everything looks good here," and he left to return to Los Angeles.

Bruce Ricker, who lives in Cambridge, came to the set on every one of the production's thirty-nine days, to watch Eastwood direct and to eat lunch with the crew. (Eastwood has used the same set caterer, a Los Angeles outfit called Tony's, which leans toward steamed vegetables, for three decades.) As the filming neared the end, Ricker made a few musical suggestions for the score. Eastwood said he wanted to see what he might compose himself. "I want to write something that will be in tune with the feeling of the lives of these people," he said.

When *Mystic River* wrapped, Eastwood went home to Pebble Beach. In his office at the Mission Ranch, he worked with Joel Cox, digitally editing the footage from the movie. When they finished, Cox took it with him to Los Angeles, to have it put on film for additional editing.

One afternoon in his living room, Eastwood sat down on the bench of his Chickering baby grand and started working out possible melodies for the movie. "I was improvising one melody and fooling around with another," he said. "Then Dina came into the room to listen to what I was playing, and she said she liked the first one. So I got that one on the road. I put it in the picture. There's no jazz in it. And there's no blues. It's more on the classical side, to be played by a full orchestra, eventually—by the Boston Symphony Orchestra, as it turns out. If I had to describe it, I'd say it's something bittersweet. It's like life, where you're constantly adjusting to everything. It's all improvisation."

Money Honeys

L ast week, the big Republican donors who traveled to the Convention seemed determined to be themselves, starting curbside at the
entrance to the Ritz-Carlton, where many of the major Party benefac-
tors were holed up.

"We're called the Rangers, but I call us the Power Rangers," Bobby
Kotick, a cocksure young L.A.-based CEO (Activision computer games),
said as he greeted some fellow donors. "Hey," he said to a burly, tanned
fellow alighting from a gleaming black Mercedes Maybach. "That yours?"

"They just gave it to me," the man said. "Because my business is
connected."

"Rangers give the most money, so we have special exclusive parties,"
Kotick said, heading inside to the cocktail lounge, where the menu,
obligingly embossed with an elephant, offered a "G. W. Bellini—peach
vodka, peach schnapps, champagne" and a "Compassionate Conservative—Stoli Orange Vodka, passion-fruit purée, champagne." A basket
of red, white, and blue tortilla chips was sitting on the bar.

"I have thirty-three parties to go to," said a donor named Richard
Merkin (president and CEO of Heritage Provider Network—health
care for the major insurance companies). He had on a black suit like
an undertaker's. "I'm going to another Ranger party, at the home
of Steve Schwartzman, the investment banker, and I'm invited to a
'Friends and Family' of the Bushes party, and, of course, the party for
Ah-nold," he said. "I'm invited to all the parties."

"For the three hundred thousand dollars you gave them, you should
get more than one ticket to Ah-nold's party," Kotick said. "But I like
to play both sides of the street. I also give money to the Democrats; I
like to protect myself. I'm with them on pro-choice, and pro stem-cell
research, but not on fiscal. I just don't want to pay taxes."

In the lobby, Holly (for Holland) Coors, the thin, blond doyenne of the Colorado beer outfit, had just returned from Madison Square Garden, where her son Pete, the chairman and former CEO of Coors, who is running for the Senate from Colorado, had given a speech. Mrs. Coors, wearing a red St. John Knits suit and pink sneakers, stood in the center of a circle of Rangers. A rhinestone pin spelling out "Bush 2004" was fastened to one lapel and a matching pin spelling out "Coors 2004" was pinned on the opposite lapel.

"Pete's got it all," she said to her admirers. "Pete wants to love people. Of course, if he's elected, he'll quit his job. He's one of my five sons. We have five Adolph Coorses, named for our original founder. We have three Petes. The newest Pete is only a year old; he's Adolph's great-great-great-grandson. I've got twenty-seven grandchildren and eleven great-grandchildren. My grandson Jonathan Coors works for Governor Schwarzenegger. Coors does all kinds of things. There's Coorstek, for example, where we make those nice bulletproof vests for our soldiers in Iraq."

"You do wonderful work in the campaign," one of the admirers said.

"It's the money, honey," Mrs. Coors said, with a wink.

Mrs. Coors then greeted Dianne Ingels Moss, a handsomely made-up and elaborately coiffed friend from Dallas, whose husband is in the oil business. Mrs. Moss said that she was staying at the Union League Club and had been to a lunch given in honor of Laura Bush by Fedpac, a Republican political-action committee.

"They're grassroots women, from every state," Mrs. Moss said. "It's so interesting to meet interesting people." She, too, was wearing a rhinestone Bush pin.

"We both order them from Ann Hand, in Washington," Mrs. Coors said. "Ann is an Independent, and her husband's a Democrat, but he's a sweetheart," she added.

Mrs. Moss told Mrs. Coors about the interesting lunch. "Laura B. looks almost svelte," she said. "She's lost weight. Her hair was perfectly done, and she had perfect makeup. And Barbara was there. And Neil was there, with his new wife."

Mrs. Coors looked shocked. "A new wife?"

Mrs. Coors asked Mrs. Moss if she had visited Crawford. "Yes, but there's no place to stay over. Crawford isn't the prettiest place in Texas." She sighed. "But the president likes it there, and that's what matters," she said.

"I look at them as stars," Mrs. Coors said, with passion. "Stars! And this man has humor. He stopped me on the dance floor once, and he said, 'Where's the kid?' So now my son is known as Holly's kid. It shows the president's closeness to people. It shows his humor."

"The man has integrity," Mrs. Moss said. "His sense of right and wrong."

"This man has a vision," Mrs. Coors said.

"Vision," Mrs. Moss repeated.

"It's his faith," Mrs. Coors said. "It breaks my heart to hear him criticized. They hated our Lord, too."

(SEPTEMBER 13, 2004)

Acknowledgments

A writer is comforted and supported by many hidden friends and enablers. Here are the names of some of my treasured helpers along the way:

Peggy Wright Weidman, Richard Giovanni, I. F. Stone, Harold Ross, William Shawn, Tina Brown, Harry Evans, Sanderson Vanderbilt, Gardner Botsford, James Thurber, Wolcott Gibbs, John Hersey, John McCarten, Bill Steig, Peter Arno, Charles Addams, Scottie Fitzgerald Lanahan, Andy Logan, Helen Ross, Simeon Ross, S. N. Behrman, Philip Hamburger, Joseph Mitchell, A. J. Liebling, Geoffrey Hellman, David Kuhn, Lola Finkelstein, Jeffrey Frank, Gloria Yanardi, Olga Torres, Sam Gelfman, Jane Gelfman, Cathy Gleason, Norman Mailer, Frank Stanton, George Sheanshang, Wayne Warnken, Prue Harper, Ernest Hemingway, Mary Hemingway, Patrick Hemingway, Chiz Schultz, Marian White, Roz Lippel, Mace Neufeld, John Huston, Anjelica Huston, Tony Huston, Danny Huston, Allegra Huston, Gottfried Reinhardt, Silvia Reinhardt, L. B. Mayer, Dore Schary, Robin Williams, Marsha Williams, Laurie Williams, Chris Columbus, Bobby Kotik, Cathy Register, John Register, Clint Eastwood, Dina Eastwood, Ruth Eastwood, Bruce Ricker, Rebecca Spencer, Dan Spencer, Cyndi Margolis, Wendy Ingraham, Lorne Michaels, Susan Forristal, Cristina McGinniss, Bing Gordon, Debra Gordon, Henry Rosovsky, Nitza Rosovsky, Michael Rosovsky, Bill Alfred, Emma Allen, Bruce Diones, Stanley Chang, Janet Sparrow, Maria Jaramovic, Harvey Goldberg, Sam Rappaport, John Buchheit, Dick Bernard, Bernard Holand, Jonathan Schell, David Remnick, Hendrik Hertzberg, Virginia Cannon, Bob Mankoff, Francoise Mouly, Lizzie Widdicombe, Evan Osnos, Jeff Toobin, Brenda Phipps, Seth Berkman, Lisa Birnbach, Lauren Collins, Nick Paumgarten, Marshall Heyman, Pam McCarthy, Tom Mangan, Richard Brody, Hilton Als, and Peter Canby.

Special thanks to Susan Morrison and Erik Ross for their indispensable and undescribable efforts.

Photo Credits